INTRODUCTION TO
COMPUTING WITH FORTRAN

JOHN K. RICE / JOHN R. RICE

Purdue University

HOLT, RINEHART AND WINSTON, INC.

New York Chicago San Francisco Atlanta Dallas
Montreal Toronto London Sydney

Library of Congress Number: 73-2437
ISBN: 0-03-086217-5
Printed in the United States of America
3 4 5 6 7 071 9 8 7 6 5 4 3 2 1

PREFACE

This text is based on the assumption that computers and computing are tools for problem-solving. We use these tools by means of some programming language, and we could say this text is on "how to use Fortran to compute the solutions of problems." In order to be successful, the student must master the basic elements of three areas: the Fortran language, computers and computer systems, and the formulation of problems and methods so solutions can be obtained. These three areas are the basic topics of this book.

The Fortran language is presented in four separate chapters, and there is a break between the first one and the others. This break allows the early study of the relationship between Fortran and problem-solving. One can cover the material on Fortran sequentially and then turn to problem-solving or, perhaps best, present the material on problem-solving interspersed with additional Fortran features. The final Fortran chapter, Advanced Elements, contains topics that may be omitted safely in a first course on computing.

Problem-solving and computers are discussed in a general way in Chapter 2 and then specific points in program construction are illustrated in Chapter 3. Problem-solving is taken up at several points in the later chapters on Fortran and a large number of problems to test various levels of ability are given at the end of Chapter 5. The final five chapters of the book might be called application areas but they really deal with the solution of problems in several different areas. The problem areas (sorting, file management, mathematics, economics, simulation) illustrate the diversity in computer applications and are important topics in themselves.

Computers and computer systems are discussed in three chapters (7, 8, and 9) and form the "middle" of a course in computing. One always has the problem of whether to present programming (Fortran) or computer systems first and, of course, they both should come first. A few pages at the start are designed to give the student some vague notion about computer systems and their relations to programming. An instructor who wants to go further into computer systems at the start of a course can start with Chapters 7, 8, and 9 and then return to Chapter 1.

There is more material in this text than normally covered in a one-semester course. The core of a course consists of Chapters 1 to 5 and 7 to 9. (Chapter 7, history, could be covered by reading assignments.) A selection of material from Chapters 6 and 10 to 14 can be made and these chapters are designed to be somewhat independent of one another.

The goal of a course using this book is to provide a good introduction to computing and problem-solving for students who intend to make significant use of computers in later course work and then in their careers. The background assumed is that of the typical entering college student. A few sections in the application areas deal with problems that are a little more advanced (for example, mathematics), but even there the discussion is at a completely intuitive level.

This book is derived from our previous book, *Introduction to Computer Science* although only scattered specific resemblances remain. We are particularly indebted to Edouard Desautels as we have based our presentation of Fortran on his in the previous book. He also has made many suggestions on the presentation in this book. Carl de Boor read parts of this book and suggested several valuable improvements. Our thanks are also due to many people for the comments received from our previous book. We have tried to incorporate the pertinent ones into this book. Finally, we wish to thank Wanda Michalenko who quickly mastered our poor handwriting, deciphered the organization of the original manuscript, and typed the final manuscript.

John K. Rice
John R. Rice

CONTENTS

INTRODUCTION TO

COMPUTING WITH FORTRAN

1

Computers and Fortran

BASIC ELEMENTS

1—1 Introduction

This book is basically concerned with "How to solve problems using computers." There is almost as much emphasis on "How to solve problems" as there is on "using computers." The computer is one of the most versatile and powerful tools available for solving problems and processing information. Its use has revolutionized and will further revolutionize many aspects of business, science, and the life of the ordinary person.

The use of a computer to solve a problem involves four rather distinct steps and only one of these is unique to computing. The first step is to formulate the problem carefully and to determine exactly the objective to be reached. This step seems obvious and easy (sometimes it is), but usually it is more subtle and difficult than it first appears. Carelessness in this first step is one of the primary causes of the much publicized "computer goofs." Due to the lack of careful study and analysis, some circumstances or situations are not foreseen and provisions not made for them. Then when one of these situations occurs, the result is nonsense. The blame is, of course, placed on the computer rather than where it belongs—on the people who use the computer.

The second step is to find a method or procedure to solve the problem. In computing, these procedures are often called *algorithms.* These first two steps should be carried out whether or not one is using a computer.

The third step is to organize the information associated with the problem in a way suitable for processing. This step is often concurrent with the search for a method to process the information. There are many, many problems where the amount of information to be processed is small and this step is very straightforward. The majority of the problems and examples discussed in the first chapters of this book are of this type. However, there is an important class of problems where the amount and complexity of the information to be processed lead to considerable difficulty. Indeed in some problem areas (for example, airline reservation systems, library information systems, management information systems) the crucial step is the proper organization of the information. One of the later chapters is devoted entirely to this step in problem-solving with particular emphasis on *files* of information.

The final step, the one peculiar to computing, is to prepare instructions for a computer to carry out the method developed. This step is called computer *coding* or, sometimes, computer programming. The usual activities of a computer programmer include not only the coding but also a considerable amount of the work of finding the method and organizing the information. In fact, in many instances the computer programmer has responsibility for all four of these steps.

1—2 Programs and Computer Systems

1–2.1 The Computer Program

A computer program, or simply a program, is a list of statements in a computer-programming language. Most of the program statements specify actions to be taken by the computer. These are called *executable statements* and typically include actions such as:

"add X to Y and call the result R"
"subtract 2 from X, divide by Z, and call the result RES"
"if X is 0, then go on to statement 37"
"if NAME1 is JONES, then save NAME1, NAME2, and NAME3 in LIST4."

The other statements say what kind of variables or quantities appear in the executable statements. For example, X and Y might be decimal numbers (called "real" in Fortran) and R and RES might be integers. These others are called *declaration statements* and it is standard practice to place them in the program before the executable statements. Thus, the general organization of a simple program is as follows:

PROGRAM: Declaration statements
Executable statements

The ordering of the executable statements is essential as they are processed in the order they appear in the program.

There are generally two kinds of executable statements: those that do the calculations or make decisions and those that do the input and output of data and answers. The statements that do arithmetic are very close to mathematical equations in appearance. The ones that do input and output are of the type

> "Read a value for X, using the digits in columns 1, 2, and 3 of the next card on card reader 2."
>
> "Print the value of R, consider it to be an integer, and use 4 digit positions, suppress leading zeros and print the minus sign if the value is negative."

Much abbreviated forms of input-output statements are actually used in Fortran (and most other programming languages). We can now break the organizations of a simple program down more as follows:

	Declarations for variables Declarations for input and output	Declarations
PROGRAM:	Input statements Computations and processing Output statements	Executable statements

1–2.2 Programming Languages and Compilers

Each computer has its own private language, which is called its *machine language*. We can write programs in machine language but it is very tedious because:

1. Machine language programs are usually coded in numeric form.
2. The program statements (instructions) are usually so primitive that it takes many statements to get anything done.
3. A detailed knowledge of how the computer works is required.
4. The program can be run only on machines that use the same machine language.

It is possible to eliminate the first difficulty by writing programs in what is called an *"assembly language."* Such a language makes it possible to use a meaningful name, say ADD, instead of the code number for the addition operation. The "assembler" is a program that has the task of translating the assembly-language program into machine language. Most computing machines have their own assembly language and associated assembler program.

In an attempt to eliminate the remaining three limitations, languages referred to as high-level languages have been developed. Fortran, Algol, PL/1, and Cobol are the most important of these. Since a computer does not directly accept a high-level language, a program known as a *compiler* is used to read the high-level language program and translate it into machine language. The processing of a machine language and a higher level language program are illustrated in Figure 1–1.

A high-level language program must be translated at least once, and it may need more computer time for execution than a hand-coded machine- or assembly-language program. However, it normally takes a person much less time

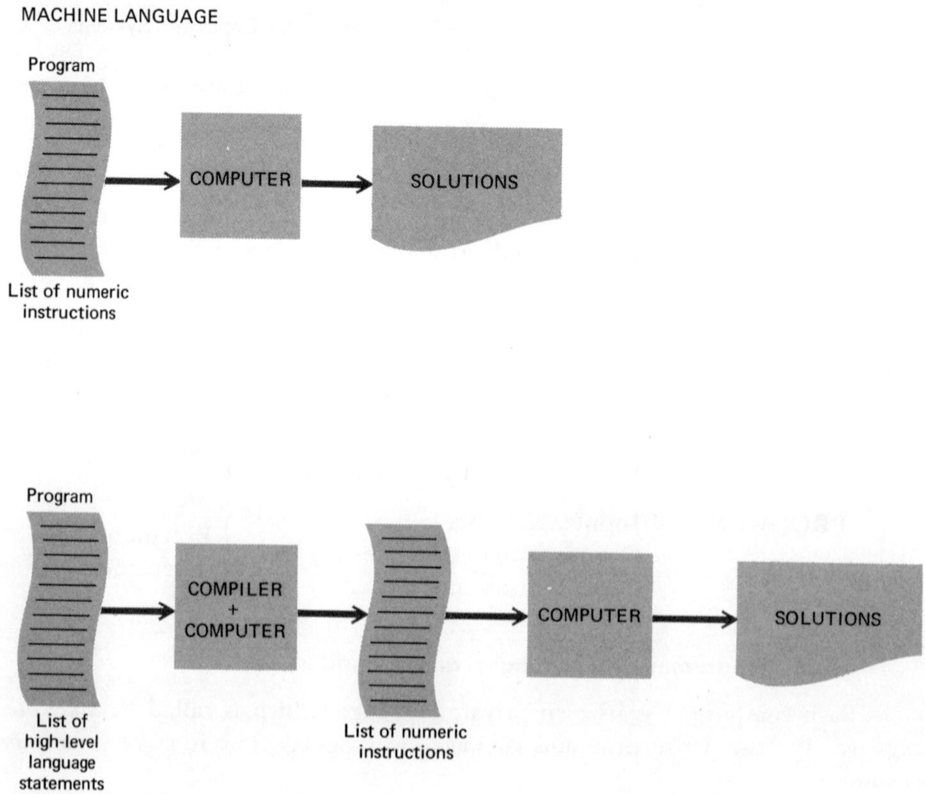

FIGURE 1–1. The processing of a machine language program and of a high-level language program.

to write a program in a high-level language and to make it operate correctly; the program may also be modified more easily in the future and may possibly be used on several different machines. A computer can help in the task of using a computer to solve problems, notably by spending computer time (in compiling) in order to reduce the total elapsed problem-solving time.

The solution of a problem using a high-level computer language usually involves four basic steps:

1. Analyzing the problem and developing a suitable method for its solution.
2. Translating (by hand) the method into the high-level language. The translation is then put in some machine-readable form (for example, punched cards), which is referred to as the *source program*.
3. Compiling the source program into a machine-language program (called the *object program*) by using a compiler; this happens at "compile" time.
4. Executing the compiled program; this happens at "execution" time.

There are well over 100 programming languages in use. The most widely used are Fortran and Cobol. Algol and PL/1 are also widely used. The following list includes a few pioneering languages and the date when they were first used.

Language	*Description*	
Fortran	Formula Translator	(1956)
Algol	Algorithmic language	(1959)
Cobol	Common Business-Oriented Language	(1960)
JOVIAL	for command and control systems	(1960)
LISP	a list processing language	(1960)
MAD	Michigan Algorithm Decoder	(1960)
NELIAC	for real-time control systems	(1959)
PL/1	Programming Language I	(1964)
SLIP	a list processing extension of Fortran	(1963)
SNOBOL	a string processing language	(1964)

1–2.3 Operating Systems and Control Statements

When a small computer is used to process Fortran (or some other high-level language) programs, it often happens that each person who wishes to run a program on that computer is expected to operate the computer directly. This means that the Fortran compiler must somehow be placed in the computer's memory, and it must be followed by the program that it is to compile. When larger and more expensive computers are used, they are usually run by full-time computer operators. In order to help the computer operator reduce computer time wasted in setting things up for the many different jobs to be run, an *operating system* (*executive system, monitor system*) is normally used. An operating system is a large and complex program (often involving some special pieces of equipment, too) to control the operation of a computer. Among many other things the operating system sees that:

1. The required compilers are loaded into the computer as needed.
2. Each user's output is properly identified.
3. The accounting is done for each user.
4. A user's job that seems to be taking an unreasonable amount of time is terminated, so that the computer can go on to the next user's job.

On his part, the programmer must provide special *control statements* for the operating system, usually immediately in front of the program that he wishes to run. The control statements specify things such as:

1. Which compiler to use
2. The programmer's name and identification of his input
3. The job code or account number
4. Estimates of the running time on the computer for the program, of the amount of printed output, and so on.

Such control statements, if they are required, must be provided with each program that is to be run, and they must be prepared according to the format specified at the local installation. The operating system control statements are completely independent of the Fortran language, but they must be used with each Fortran program.

The word "system" is used occasionally in a very broad sense: it encompasses the computer, the Fortran and other compilers, and the operating system, all specific to the same computer, perhaps even unique to one installation.

1–2.4 Program Debugging and Diagnostics

When a program has been written and prepared in machine-readable form (for example, on punched cards or punched paper tape) it becomes input to the compiler. If the compiler detects any errors in the course of compiling the program, it writes messages describing the errors. These messages are called *diagnostics.* Errors in a program are frequently called bugs. The process of submitting a program for compilation, examining the diagnostics, resubmitting the changed program, and repeating all of this as often as is necessary, is called *debugging* a program.

The debugging process does not necessarily end when the compiler issues no diagnostics, as this means only that the *syntax*, or grammatical structure, of the program is correct. That is to say, the compiler is able to translate each statement into machine language. The *semantics,* or meaning, of the program might be something other than originally planned. A diagnostic-free program may well produce "wrong" answers. The answers are wrong in that they are not the desired ones, but the fault is not in the computer or in the compiler. The fault is with the author of the program who either has a faulty method or has failed to correctly transform the method into a program, or has incorrect input, and so on.

The difficulty in going from a mathematical method to the corresponding program is often compounded by a poor understanding of the elements of the programming language used. The compiler itself can be a great help in learning a programming language. When there is any doubt about a statement or combination of statements in a language, a test case can be made up and compiled and the results studied to see if the compiler's interpretation is the same as the programmer's.

There are three main tools or techniques to use in debugging a program. They are intermediate output, test of simple cases, and hand calculations. The most important of these three is the first.

Intermediate Output A program is normally written to solve a problem and output the answer. If a program is producing incorrect answers, then the error in the method or algorithm must be located. Of course, the current program should be studied to verify that a blunder has not been made. In theory all errors can be located by reading the program and examining the input, but many errors are very difficult to locate this way.

A much more efficient way is to request intermediate (and temporary) output at several key points in the program. The variables printed should be such that the programmer has some idea of what their value should be. Then he can, hopefully, detect where the incorrect values first occur and narrow the search for the location of the bug or error. If this technique does not succeed at first, he should increase the number of places where variables are output. This approach is something like the game of 20 questions, the idea is to continually narrow down the location of the error. It is not unheard of in complicated programs to have 10 or 20 pages of intermediate and debugging output even though the final program has only a page of output. Fortunately, most bugs can usually be located with just a little intermediate output.

The usefulness and importance of this technique is illustrated by the fact that many instructors in computing courses refuse to examine a program until the student has inserted a reasonable amount of intermediate output. Furthermore, they often insist that the input data (if any) read in also be printed out. It is inadvisable merely to assume the data punched on cards are processed correctly unless verified by a printout.

Simple Cases The idea behind this technique is to choose special cases with one or more of the following properties:

1. A number of parts of the program are not used.
2. The programmer already knows what all of the intermediate results should be.
3. He knows the answer of the problem from an independent source.

Each of these properties can be an aid in detecting errors in a program. The third property merely allows the programmer to check for the existence of an error somewhere. The other two properties are helpful in isolating the location of the error, particularly if the programmer has some intermediate output.

Hand Calculation Hand calculation means that the programmer goes through the program step by step. At each step he performs the necessary calculations (a slide rule is usually accurate enough) and records the values of all of the pertinent variables. One might say that the programmer is to "play computer." The objective is not to check on the arithmetic of the computer, which is almost infallible, but to force the programmer to focus his attention on each detail of the program. A variation of this is to explain the program to a friend statement by statement. A secondary objective is to obtain a complete set of intermediate output.

Because this technique is time consuming and tedious, it is used only as a last resort. Nevertheless there are times when it is the proper thing to do. The usual result of such a calculation is that the programmer suddenly recognizes that the program says to do the wrong thing. The error frequently occurs in a statement that has been examined a number of times and verified as correct each time. After a statement has been accepted as correct once or twice, it seems that the mind is unable to examine it critically any longer.

The main sources of error in programs are listed below. The list begins with the most frequent and ends with the least frequent.

Blunders and keypunch errors

Faulty method

Solution of the wrong problem
Faulty use of programming language
Data incorrect or inconsistent with formats
Error in compiler
Error in executive system
Machine error.

Errors in compilers and executive systems are very infrequent in most computing centers, even though programmers have a natural tendency to blame their troubles on the computing center. Before jumping to conclusions, the programmer should pin down the supposed error with a special test program that clearly shows the presence of an error. Machine errors are extremely rare and can be checked by rerunning the identical program. Different results from run to run of exactly the *same* program are usually attributed to transient system or machine errors.

1—3 A Simple Fortran Program

1–3.1 The Development of Fortran

Fortran is the most widely used of all the current programming languages. As with any language in widespread use, there are local variations of Fortran, referred to as dialects. Although there are many dialects of Fortran, they may be grouped into three classes:

1. Fortran II
2. Basic Fortran
3. Fortran IV

Fortran was originally developed in 1956 for the IBM 704. The language evolved and was used with other computers and by 1958 it had evolved into Fortran II. Fortran II compilers were written for many computers. In 1962, a major reorganization of the language introduced many powerful features, and it became known as Fortran IV. Compilers of it are available for most medium- and large-scale computers. The Basic Fortran is a subset of Fortran IV adapted for use on the smaller computers.

This text deals only with Fortran IV and Basic Fortran. Only the core of the language is examined in detail, but the more advanced features of the language are presented in Chapter 6. No specific computer is associated with any of the language features or with any of the examples or exercises. The dialect that is discussed is the one defined in 1966 by the United States of America Standards Institute (USASI American Standard Fortran). Since Basic Fortran is a proper subset of Fortran IV, this text can also be used as an introduction to Basic Fortran, bearing in mind that not all the features of Fortran IV are available in Basic Fortran. Any Basic Fortran program is a Fortran IV program. Unfortunately Fortran II is not a subset or extension of Fortran IV although they have many characteristics in common.

1–3.2 Implementations of Fortran

A computer manufacturer or a compiler writer is not bound to adhere fully to the USASI standards in writing a Fortran compiler. Many Fortran compilers were in use before the standards were written, and more recent compilers have sometimes deviated from the standards with the intention of improving the language.

In using this text, each student is expected to determine to what extent the locally available Fortran deviates from the standard. Some of the problems and exercises in the text are designed to facilitate this, for the differences between the local and standard Fortran are given perhaps only implicitly in the reference manual for the local Fortran.

1–3.3 A Simple Fortran Program

The following three sets of statements, each set having one statement per line, form three complete Fortran programs. They are identical in structure and give exactly the same results. They differ only in the variable names used and perhaps also in that one form is more easily understood by the reader.

(i)

```
Column 567
      INTEGER A,B,C
      A = 150
      B = A*40
      C = B/5
      PRINT 1,B,C
    1 FORMAT(I5,I5)
      STOP
      END
```

(ii)

```
      INTEGER RATE,WEEK,DAY
      RATE = 150
      WEEK = RATE*40
      DAY = WEEK/5
      PRINT 1,WEEK,DAY
    1 FORMAT(I5,I5)
      STOP
      END
```

(iii)

```
      JRATE = 150
      KWEEK = JRATE*40
      KDAY = KWEEK/5
      PRINT 1,KWEEK,KDAY
    1 FORMAT(I5,I5)
      STOP
      END
```

The first statement of program (i) declares that the variables A, B, and C are integers (whole numbers). The statement A = 150 assigns to the variable A the integer value 150; B = A * 40 assigns to B the value 40 times the current value of A, that is, 6000. The statement C = B/5 assigns to C the current value of B divided by 5, that is, 1200.

The next two statements cause the current values of B and C to be printed according to the format labeled as format 1. Since this format describes two pieces of data, the first I5 applies to B and the second I5 to C. This causes one line to be printed; the first (leftmost) five characters are the value of B and the next five are the value of C. The line contains only these 10 characters (two of them are blanks), and it appears as

```
Column    5    10
       6000 1200
```

We have assumed that the *standard output* is used by the PRINT command. The standard output is usually a line printer, but it could be a teletype terminal or something else. In some computing centers this is not the case and the PRINT 1 command must be replaced by WRITE(6,1) where 6 refers to the number of the standard output unit. This alternative is discussed in some detail in Section 1–5.5.

After the PRINT statement has been executed, the STOP statement is executed. It is a signal to the system that the program is finished and the system should either go on to the next job or alert the computer operator.

The last statement is the END statement. Each program must finish with an END. It is not an executable statement.

All of the above comments also apply to program (ii), with the proper name substitutions made. The only effect of the name changes in program (ii) is to make the program more readable or understandable to human beings. Programs (i) and (ii) are completely equivalent as far as the system is concerned. The point is that convenient and meaningful variable names should be used, without expecting them to have any meaning whatsoever to the system.

Program (iii) is also equivalent to programs (i) and (ii). It has no statement INTEGER . . .; to compensate for this, all the variable names have been chosen in a particular way. A general rule in Fortran is: *a variable need not appear in an* INTEGER *statement if the first letter of the variable name is one of* I, J, K, L, M, or N. This rule, known as the "implicit type" rule, allows one to automatically specify that a quantity or variable is to be treated as an integer.

1–3.4 Preparing a Program in Machine-Readable Form

There are many forms in which a program may be presented to a computer. Among them are punched cards, punched paper tape, magnetic tape, on-line keyboard printer, cathode ray tube, keyboard, and mark sense cards.

We discuss the preparation of Fortran programs on 80-column punched cards as shown in Figure 1–2. The Fortran statements are punched in these cards between columns 7 and 72 inclusively, with the statement label (if present) punched between columns 1 and 5 inclusively. The punched cards for program (iii) are shown in Figure 1–3. This small program would be submitted to the computing center along with one or two system control cards and one would receive back a listing as shown along with the one line of output. There would probably also be other lines printed by the local computing system.

One card may contain only one statement. If a statement does not fit on a single card, it may be continued on the next card (again between columns 7 and 72) by having any nonblank and nonzero character punched in column 6. This can be done for up to 19 continuation cards. The example in Figure 1–4 shows three ways of punching the same statement. One may place anything in columns 1 to 5 in a statement continuation card.

Anything desired may be placed in columns 73 to 80. These columns are not read by the Fortran compiler. The intended use of these columns is for sequence numbers of the statements. Sequence numbers can be a great work-saver if a deck, especially a large one, is dropped.

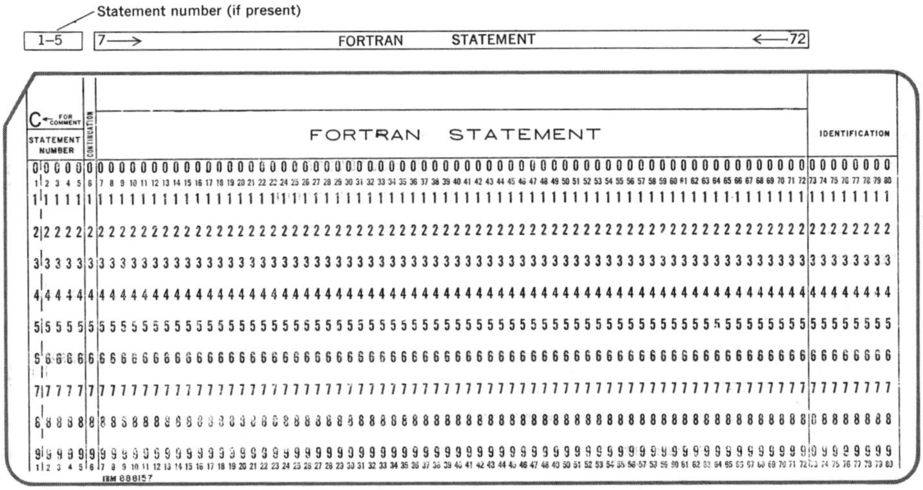

FIGURE 1–2. The standard 80-column Fortran card.

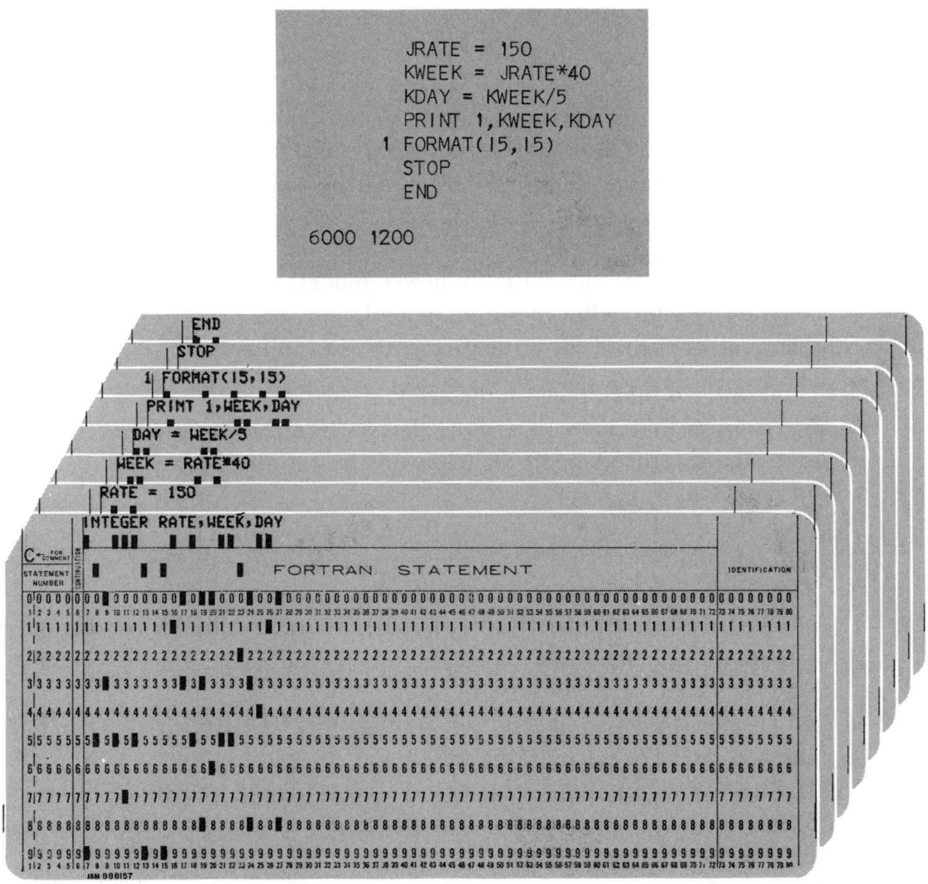

FIGURE 1–3. The punched cards for program (ii), the resulting listing, and the line of output produced.

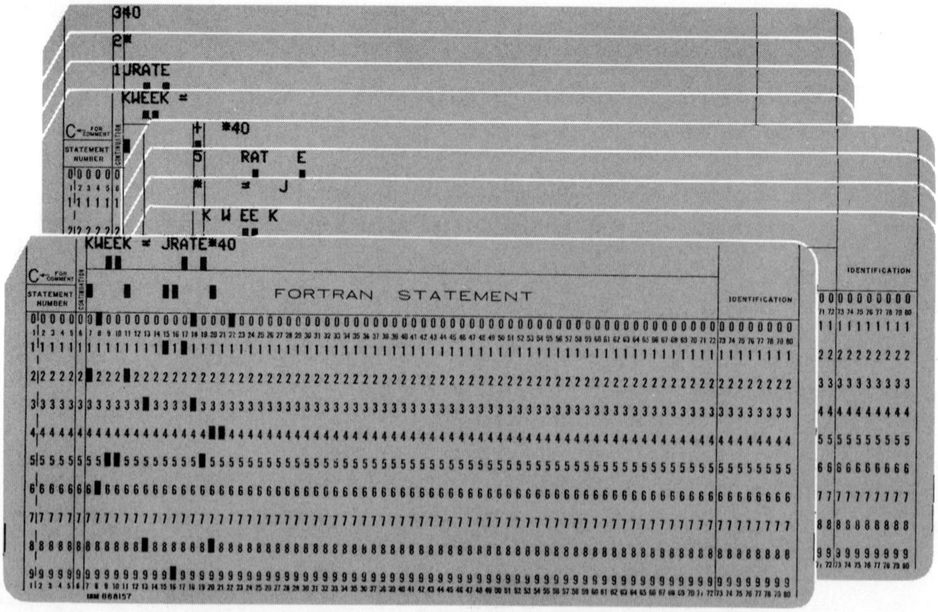

FIGURE 1–4. Three ways to punch the same Fortran statement.

Many computing centers supply special Fortran *coding sheets* as shown in Figure 1–5. Each line of the coding sheet corresponds to one punched card. The headings on the sheet show the layout of the Fortran statements.

The most common machine used in preparing punched cards is the IBM 026 keypunch shown in Figure 1–6. It has a keyboard similar to that of a typewriter and operates much in the same way except for additional mechanisms to control the movement of the cards. A newer model, the 029, has a keyboard with more characters and a slightly different design.

The normal procedure for punching cards is as follows:

1. Load cards in the hopper on the right.
2. Turn on power (there is a short delay while the machine warms up) and turn the three toggle switches on the top of the keyboard to the off position.
3. Push the FEED key to place a card in the right-hand position.
4. Push the REG key to align (or register) the card with the punches.
5. Type the statement that is to appear on the card. There is a small pointer in the window which indicates in which column one is about to punch a character. Note that the upper case "shift" key is the NUM key.
6. When the statement is finished, punch the REL (release) key. This moves the card to the middle position.
7. One continues in this way until all the cards are punched. In order to get the last cards out of the machine one must push the REL and REG keys twice.

It is very common to make mistakes in keypunching and there is a facility to aid in correcting cards. One places the card with the keypunch error in the

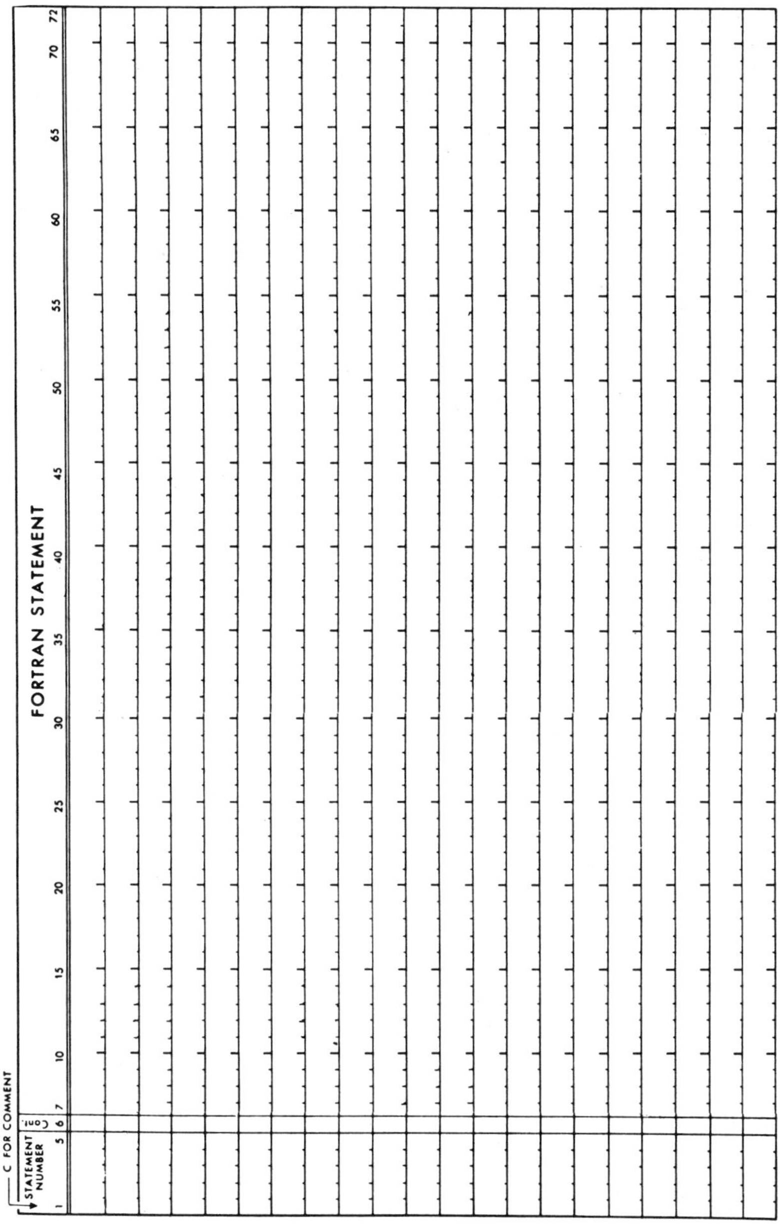

FIGURE 1–5. A typical Fortran coding sheet.

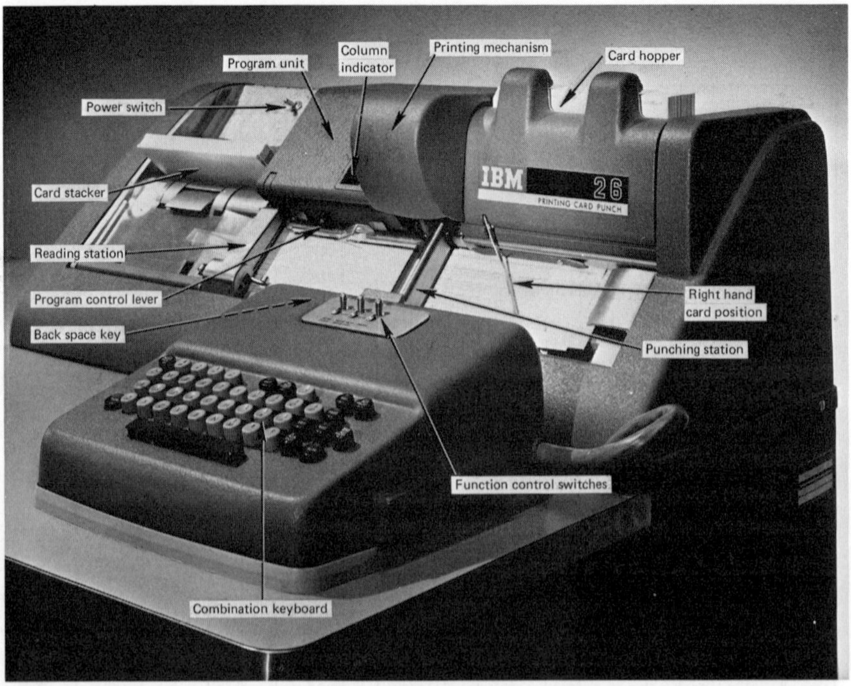

FIGURE 1–6. IBM 026 Keypunch.

middle position and a blank card on the right. Push the REG key, then the DUP (duplicate) key until the position of the error is reached. Then type the correct character and finish the card with the DUP key. This works only when one has to replace some bad characters by exactly the same number of correct characters. On most keypunch machines one can also insert or delete characters even though the machines are not designed to allow this. To insert a character, one duplicates up to the insertion point, then presses tightly against the top right card in the middle position while typing the character (or characters) to be inserted. The card in the middle must not move. The remainder of the card is then duplicated. One deletes characters in a similar way except the card in on the right is held and the space bar is pressed. We see in the next section that in Fortran programs one can safely replace unwanted characters by blanks in almost all circumstances.

Other useful features of the keypunch include a backspace button (also try this button when the keypunch seems to be locked up) and an automatic feed switch to feed in a new card whenever the REL key is pushed or when a card is completely full. There is a facility to "program" the keypunch which is useful if hundreds of identically laid out cards are to be punched. It is not so useful for Fortran cards and the "program" feature should be disengaged by pushing the program card switch down on the left.

Problems

1–3.1 Find out what operating system control statements are needed, if any, to run Fortran programs at your installation.

1–3.2 Submit one of the programs (i), (ii), or (iii) of this section and verify that it does indeed run on your computer. First find out which unit number refers to the system output unit or if you can use the simple PRINT statement.

1–3.3 Make up new variable names for the programs of this section and run the programs. Since the rules for making up names have not yet been discussed, you may get some diagnostics.

1–3.4 Modify the above programs by breaking up some of the statements using continuation cards.

1–3.5 (a) Vary the parameters in the FORMAT of the example programs and run them again. That is, instead of I5, try I3, or I7, and so on.
(b) Write the variables B and C out several times using several formats, such as I3 and I4.

1–3.6 Write a program that takes in three exam scores of 97, 86, and 57 and computes the average of these scores by giving a weight of 1 to the first two and a weight of 3 to the third. Write out the exam scores and the average.

1–3.7 Write a program that takes in three integers A, B, and C. Multiply A by 3, add 2 times B divided by 5, and subtract C. Write out A, B, C, and the result. Do this for two sets of A, B, C values: 12, 25, 16, and 4, 12, 10.

1–4 Characters, Integer Variables, and Constants

1–4.1 Characters and Symbolic Names

The Fortran character set contains the following 48 characters, which fall into four groups:

26 uppercase letters of the alphabet `A B C . . X Y Z`

10 digits `0 1 2 3 4 5 6 7 8 9`

11 special characters `= ≠ + - * / ( ) , . $`

1 blank or space character

The blank may be used freely at any point within any statement to improve its readability. With only one exception, which is discussed later, blanks are not considered significant in Fortran statements. Blanks are significant in input data.

The names of variables contain from 1 to 6 letters or digits. The first (leftmost) character must be a letter. The rule is quite simple: If a name must be made up for anything that appears in a Fortran program, it must use only letters and digits, no more than 6 of them, and the first character must be a letter.

A name that is "made up" as opposed to one that is already in the Fortran language (for example, INTEGER) is called a symbolic name.

Symbolic Names

One to six alphanumeric characters (letters or digits), the first one a letter. A symbolic name refers to the contents of some word or address in the computer memory and not to some actual value.

EXAMPLES

```
A       X23456     A2Z      K4444K
KYZ     X2Y3ZA     NAME     YOU2
```

A symbolic name is declared to be an integer variable by the word INTEGER followed by that symbolic name. Several declarations can be made at once. The following have the same effect:

```
INTEGER AZ2H4        INTEGER AZ2H4,B,ZEBRA        INTEGER ZEBRA
INTEGER B                                         INTEGER B,AZ2H4
INTEGER ZEBRA
```

These variables can assume only integer values. A variable is automatically assumed to be an integer if the first letter is I, J, K, L, M, or N and its name does not need to be placed in an INTEGER statement. This rule is called the *implicit type* rule (for integers).

An integer constant is any consecutive list or string of digits, up to some maximum length depending on the computer and compiler being used. A plus or minus sign may precede the constant, for example, 12345, −792, +35.

Integer Constant

One to 10 digits, with or without sign. The maximum number of digits depends on the local system.

EXAMPLES

```
12345   -8866   4   +163   1234567890
```

Common Errors

1. Names are too long. Often occurs because something (such as , * +) is left out between two names.
2. Wasting effort by placing names starting with I, J, K, L, M, N in INTEGER statements.
3. Placing a decimal point after an integer (such as 12. instead of 12).
4. Placement of a comma in a large integer (such as 12,000 instead of 12000).

Things You Can Do

1. Name variables with Fortran words (such as STOP, END, PRINT). It is poor practice, though.

1–4.2 Integer Arithmetic

Integer arithmetic may be performed by using the five following "arithmetic operations" or procedures: + addition, − subtraction, * multiplication, / division, ** exponentiation. A collection of variables, constants, arithmetic operations, and parentheses is called an *arithmetic expression*. It is a *legal expression* if it obeys the standard mathematical rules for arithmetic.

Expression

A collection of variables and constants with arithmetic operations indicated. A *variable* has a Fortran name such as RATE, I3, JWEEK and its value can change (or vary) as the program is executed. All the variables up to this point have numerical values, but in later chapters other kinds or *types* of variables are used.

EXAMPLES

```
3*X+BARB       4*Y**(8+3*X-Z/5)          ((K/5)+6/N)/K
A-B+C/D**E     (((A)))+((B)+(C+D))/E      515
```

Another special character is involved in arithmetic, the computational verb =; it is used to form *assignment statements.*

Assignment Statement

A statement with a variable on the left of an = sign and an expression on the right of it.

EXAMPLES

```
KBAR = I            B16 = (B+16)/(B-16)*16         N = N+1
J = K-31+4137       ZING= ZAP**(ZZ+3) - 4*ZING     K = 404
```

Consider the example:

```
ZEBRA = A/2 + B*3 - C**2
```

If the current values of A, B, and C are 3, 4, and 5, respectively, then the computations performed assign to ZEBRA the value 3/2 + 4 * 3 − 5 ** 2, or 1 + 12 − 25, or −12. Note that the arithmetic operations behave in the standard mathematical way. Since integer division is required to produce an integer result, *it will always truncate the result of the division,* leaving only the integer part of the quotient; for example, 3/2 has the value 1, and −7/3 has the value −2. A variety of arithmetic assignment statements is included in the following program and the values computed are shown printed out.

```
Column  5|6|7
            INTEGER A,BB,A3
            A = -16
            BB = 2*A-27
            N = 4
            N2H=10
            MBAD = (N/5)*N2H
            MBAR = (N*N2H)/5 - (N-1)*(N**3+BB)
            A3 = A**3
            JOLLY = MBAR**N -N**(4100-A3)
            PRINT 5, BB,MBAD,MBAR, A3, JOLLY
          5 FORMAT(I8,I8,I8,I8,I8)
            STOP
            END
```

OUTPUT

```
Column       8|      16|      24|      32|      40|
           -59|       0|      -7|   -4096|    2401|
```

Note again that integer division causes an unexpected result in the value of MBAD. We might think that

$$\text{MBAD} = \frac{\text{N * N2H}}{5} = \frac{4 * 10}{5} = 8,$$

but it is not. The division is done first and the value of 4/5 is zero. Note also that N/5 * N2H is *not* the same as N/(5 * N2H). Later in this chapter we see that Fortran has a second type of numbers called REAL where the arithmetic is more natural.

When exponentiation is used merely for squaring numbers, as in C ** 2, the equivalent expression C * C may require less computer time for its evaluation in some systems.

If an expression involves both multiplication and division, say A * B/C, there might appear to be some doubt about how it is evaluated. The evaluation in Fortran always proceeds from left to right, giving in this case (A * B)/C. Parentheses may be used freely in any arithmetic expression, provided of course that each left parenthesis has a matching right parenthesis (that is, parentheses must balance).

In evaluating an expression involving parentheses, the innermost subexpression is evaluated first. Thus, in the expression A * (B + (C − D/2)) the innermost subexpression C − D/2 is evaluated as C − (D/2). Its value is then added to the value of B and a final multiplication by the value of A takes place.

When in doubt about how an expression might be evaluated, parentheses should be inserted to remove that doubt.

Common Errors

1. Omitted parenthesis in fractions

$$\frac{K}{N+1} = K/(N + 1) \neq K/N + 1.$$

2. Dividing by zero. This results in different errors on different computers.
3. Unbalanced or incorrectly placed parentheses in long expressions. Check them if your program does not work.
4. Omitted * in multiplication, such as in 2 J, A (B + F), (K + 1)(JJ + 3 − K).
5. K**L**M is not allowed; one must use parentheses to indicate which ** is to be done first.
6. INTEGER placed after some executable statement (allowed on some systems).
7. Use of a variable that has not been set equal to something. On some systems the variable is zero, on others it is garbage.

Things You Can Do

1. Avoid the problem of obtaining zero as an intermediate result by placing all multiplies first; for example,

   5*8*14/35 = 16
   14/35*8*5 = 0 in Fortran.

2. Put the same variable on both sides of the = in an assignment as in

   N = N + 2.

   If N were 6 before this statement, it would be 8 after it.

Problems

Some or all the programs suggested below can be combined into a single program. However, it may happen that a particular system will not detect every error in a program that has many different kinds of errors.

1–4.1 Invalid names are usually detected by a compiler. Write a program with several arithmetic statements in it, each using some invalid variable name.

1–4.2 Some compilers require that all declarations be made at the beginning of the program. Write a program that uses the INTEGER statement, placing it toward the end of the program.

1–4.3 Determine experimentally the length of the largest positive integer by writing a program that involves constants of ever-increasing lengths. What does the compiler do with an integer constant that is too large?

1–4.4 Write and run a program that has expressions in which parentheses do not balance.

1–4.5 In a mathematical text, an expression such as a(B + c) has a meaning. What meaning does the expression A(B + C) have in Fortran? What general conclusion might be drawn from this observation?

1–4.6 In the following expressions, insert all of the parentheses that are implied by the arithmetic rules.

(a) A * B ** C + D/E (b) A – B + C * E * D/F ** G
(c) X * Y – Z ** A + 2 * N/K + 3 (d) X + ZBAR – KK/MBAR + 1

1–4.7 Delete all of the redundant or unnecessary parentheses in the following expressions:

(a) ((X + Y) – Z) * (X/Y) ** Z
(b) ((A) * (B ** C) ** D)/E
(c) (X + Z)/(Y – ((X + Y) – 2 * (Z/K)))
(d) ((((X + Y) ** (K + 1)) * HK) * 2 + 3)/(A – 4)

1–4.8 In integer division in Fortran, the remainder is always lost. How can it be calculated?

1–5 Reading and Writing Integers and Messages

1–5.1 PRINT and FORMAT Statements

Two statements are usually required in order to obtain output from a program. For instance,

```
Column 5|6|7
        |  |PRINT 1, A
       1|  |FORMAT(I4)
```

causes the value of A to be printed according to the integer format I4. If A is not an integer, then the output is not well defined, and almost anything might be written, perhaps accompanied by a diagnostic. If A is a positive integer of 3 or fewer significant digits or a negative integer of 2 or fewer integers, then it is printed correctly on a line of output.

PRINT Statement

The word PRINT followed by an integer referring to a FORMAT statement followed by a list of variables.

EXAMPLES

```
PRINT 1,A                        PRINT 12345,BBC,IBM,JACK
PRINT 303,B,C,K,LID              PRINT 4,B4,C8A,F909
```

The various possibilities are shown by the following simple PRINT statements.

```
  K = 123
  PRINT 1,K
1 FORMAT(I4)
  K = -67
  PRINT 1,K
  K = 10082
  PRINT 1,K
  K = -123
  PRINT 1,K
  X = 13.1
  PRINT 2,X
2 FORMAT(I6)
```

OUTPUT

```
Column  1|
         |123
         |-67
         |
         |082 <——— The left digits are lost here and
         |          cause a double space
         |
         |123 <——— The minus sign is lost and
         |          causes a double space
```

The result of the last PRINT is a garbage number ———> 19974

Note that the variable X in one program is not declared to be an integer, but rather it is a real (or decimal) variable and the PRINT statement produces garbage.

For all practical purposes, the final effect of a PRINT statement involving the system output unit is to cause printing to occur on a continuous length of paper. In some systems, the output first goes onto a magnetic tape or some other device, then to a printer.

Typically the output paper is 15 inches wide and is fan-folded as pages that are 11 inches deep. The maximum number of characters that may be printed on one line is determined by the printer in use. A maximum line length of 132 characters and page depth of 60 lines is common and is assumed here.

A single PRINT and its associated FORMAT cause one or more lines to be printed. The first (leftmost) character of each line is not printed, but is used to control the spacing of the paper. If the first character of a line is blank, 0, 1, or +, then the vertical spacing before printing that line is as follows:

blank	Space one line
0	space two lines
1	advance to first line of next page
+	no advance

Any other character used as the first character of a line may either have an unpredictable effect or have some function assigned to it by the local installation.

An output page is illustrated in Figure 1–7.

The PRINT statement normally contains a list of variables. Associated with each variable in the PRINT list is a field descriptor in the FORMAT. We have been using the integer field descriptor I (for example, I4). For instance,

```
      I = 123
      J = -789
      K = 57102

      PRINT 21, I,J,K
   21 FORMAT(I4,I5,I6)
```

The three variables in the PRINT list will be interpreted according to the field descriptors I4, I5, and I6. Assuming I, J, and K have values 123, −789, and 57102, respectively, the printed line is

```
Column     4|    9|    15|
         123| -789| 57102|
```

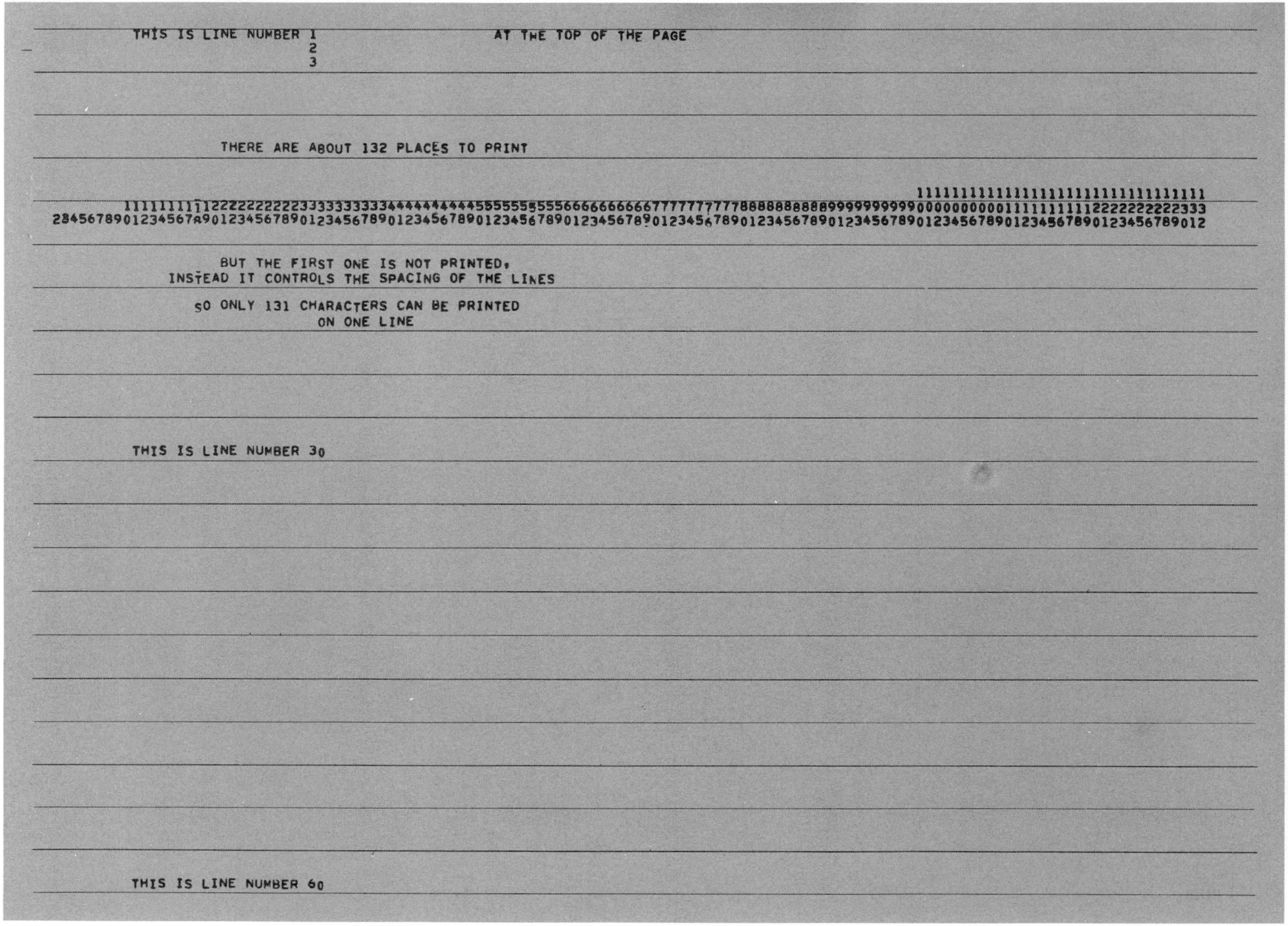

FIGURE 1–7. Typical computer output printed page specifications.

FORMAT Statement

An integer label (in columns 1 to 5) followed by the word FORMAT (in columns 7 to 72) and a list (in parentheses) of field descriptors.

EXAMPLES

```
    1 FORMAT(I6)                    12345 FORMAT(I8)
  303 FORMAT(I8,I9,I12,I8)              4 FORMAT(I12,I9)
```

The general form of the integer field descriptor is In. This specifies that the associated variable in the PRINT list is to be printed as an integer consisting of no more than n characters, including a minus sign if the integer has a negative value. All leading zeroes are replaced by blanks.

Common Errors

1. Number is too large for the space allowed and some digits on the left are lost or the minus sign is lost. Some systems print a special character as a warning.
2. Digits are to be printed in column 1 which are used for line and page control instead of printing.
3. Too many numbers asked to be put on one line.

Things You Can Do

1. Use the same FORMAT statement for any number of PRINT statements (and READ statements too).
2. Place the FORMAT statement away from the PRINT statement.
3. Print fewer values than given by the FORMAT (such as PRINT 2, K with 2 FORMAT(I6,I3,I8)).
4. Print more values than given by the FORMAT; it is reused as long as values are left to be printed (such as PRINT 7,I,J,K,L with 7 FORMAT (I4,I8)).

1–5.2 H Format for Messages and Slash / for New Lines

Messages may be written or printed by using the field descriptor H:

```
      PRINT 193
  193 FORMAT(17H1 THE SOLUTION IS )
```

The preceding statements cause the message

```
 THE SOLUTION IS        (at the top of a new page)
```

to be printed as the first line of a new page (the 1 following the H causes the new page).

Hollerith H Format

An integer, say N, followed by the letter H followed by N arbitrary Fortran characters. This is the one place in Fortran where blanks are significant and counted.

EXAMPLES

```
16HTHIS HAS SIXTEEN          14H**=/,+$I3,2H1X
10HPRINT 5, K                  5HX,Y =
```

When several field descriptors are to be included in one FORMAT, they should be separated by either of two things: comma or slash. The comma separation permits several items to be printed on a single line. The slash used as a separation indicates that a new line is to be started after each slash. The examples that follow show sets of statements and the printing they cause.

```
  PRINT 1, K,J            PRINT 2, K,J                 PRINT 3                  PRINT 4
1 FORMAT(I3,I5)         2 FORMAT(I3/I5)              3 FORMAT(2H X,2H Y)      4 FORMAT(2H X/2H Y)

     3|   8|                 3|          Column           2| 4|                    2|
    -2| 367|                -2|                           X| Y|                    X|
                            367                                                    Y|
```

Line and Page Control Formats Slash

The line and page control characters and their effects are:

blank	start a new line
0	skip one line and start a new line
+	continue printing on the same line
1	start a new page

Other characters in column 1 result in locally varying effects. The character slash / in a FORMAT list of descriptors causes a new line to be started when it is met.

EXAMPLES

```
FORMAT(14H1      NEW PAGE)       FORMAT(////7H SKIP 4)
FORMAT(1H0,I8/I10,I5//)          FORMAT(1H+,I8,9HOVERPRINT)
```

The different kinds of field descriptors can be used in conjunction with one another to enhance the readability of the output, as in

```
      K = -2
      L = 367

      PRINT 327, K,L
  327 FORMAT(19H1 THE SOLUTIONS ARE/ 4H0K =,I3 /4H B = I5
```

which gives the following output, starting on a new page:

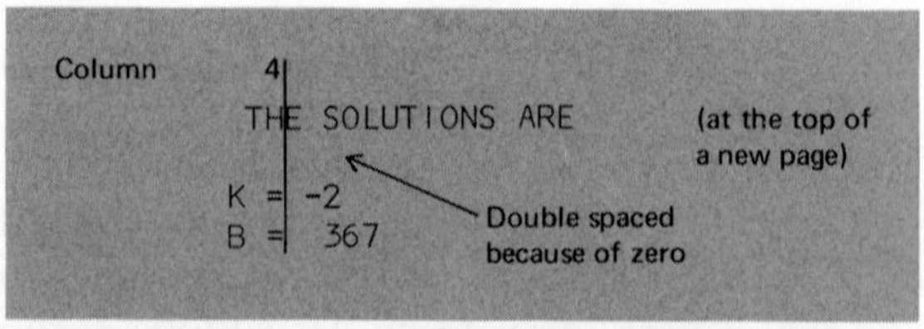

1–5.3 X Format for Spacing and Repeated Formats

We can control the spacing across a line by using the H field descriptor followed by the number of spaces desired. The same effect may be obtained with less human effort by using the X field descriptor. Its general form is nX, and it merely introduces n spaces or blanks into the output line. Thus, the following two formats are equivalent:

```
      PRINT 51,K,L
   51 FORMAT(8H       K=   ,I3/6H    L=,I4 )

      PRINT 52,K,L
   52 FORMAT(6X2HK=,I3/4X,2HL=I4)
```

Both would print the same way; the 1H _ or the 1X generate a space that is used for carriage control. The 2H __ or the 2X both generate two spaces, the first of which again is used for carriage control. Thus, if the values 17 and −6 were being printed using either of the above formats, we would obtain

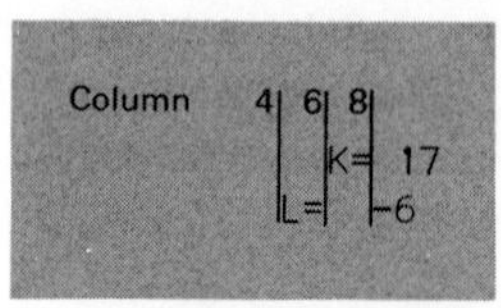

As a matter of convenience, when there are several consecutive I field descriptors with the same field width, then they may all be replaced by a single I field descriptor. The I is preceded by an integer specifying how often it is to be repeated. For instance, the following two pairs of formats are equivalent to one another.

```
FORMAT(1X,I2,I2,I3/I4,I4)              FORMAT(I8,I8,I8,I8,I8)
FORMAT(1X,2I2.I3/2I4)                  FORMAT(5I8)
```

I Format
X Format

I Format

An integer constant, say N, followed by the letter I followed by an integer constant, say M. M is the number of spaces used to print the integer (field-width) and N is the number of times to use this descriptor before continuing on in the FORMAT.

X Format

An integer constant, say N, followed by the letter X. N blank spaces are left on the line being printed when this descriptor is met.

EXAMPLES

```
FORMAT(6X,5I5/5X,I4)          FORMAT(2I8,40X,I18)
FORMAT(120I1)                 FORMAT(3I3,6X,8I5)
```

Common Errors

1. Incorrect H-format count. A count too low puts illegal items in the FORMAT, a count too high picks up part of the remaining FORMAT specifications.
2. A letter asked to be printed in column 1 does not print and may affect the line control.
3. A variable repetition factor or variable H-format count is not allowed (such as NI5 or KH***).
4. Too many numbers and messages asked to be printed on one line.
5. Trailing slashes or Hollerith as in PRINT 2,I,J

   2 FORMAT(I8/I9/5H_OOPS,I10)

   will print I on one line, J on the next and then start another line and print OOPS.
6. Broken Hollerith field at the end of a card without considering the blanks involved up to column 72.

Things You Can Do

1. Use multiple slashes (such as ////). Some systems allow numerical repetition (such as 5/ for /////).
2. Use numerical repetition of Hollerith formats (such as 5(2H+*) to obtain +*+*+*+*+*).
3. Omit the commas before and after slashes.
4. Omit the comma after a Hollerith field or X specification.
5. Place Hollerith fields in quotes (for example, "X IS") instead of using counts in H format (for example, 4HX IS), in some systems.

1–5.4 READ Statements and Input Data

Up to this point, the statements that have been discussed permit a program to communicate its results to the outside world. It frequently occurs that one has a program which solves a problem and then one wants to solve it again with different data or values of the variables. One way to do this is to change the Fortran statements that contain these variables. This is often inconvenient and sometimes almost impossible when there is a large amount of data involved or many different sets of data. Thus, it is necessary in these cases to communicate data to the program while it is in execution.

Input, or reading new values for variables in a program, is done with statements such as

```
Column 5|6|7
          READ 1,KEX
        1 FORMAT(I3)
```

CARD INPUT

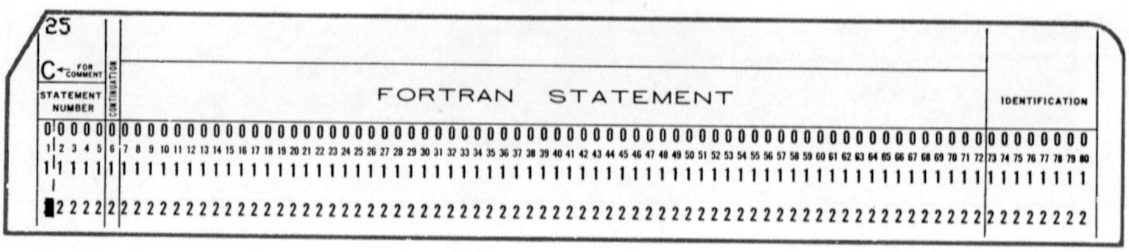

These statements cause digits to be read from a standard input unit, and the first 3 digits read from it will be the integer value assigned to KEX, provided of course, that KEX is declared to be an integer variable. The READ statement is just like the PRINT statement except for changing the word PRINT to READ.

How does the information get onto this unit? How is it prepared? We assume that the input medium consists of 80-column punched cards, and henceforth this is the standard system input unit. The following example shows how it is done. This program is to read one card that has four integers punched in it, compute their sum and product, and print the input and results. The actual deck is shown below and the program and output are shown below that.

CARD INPUT

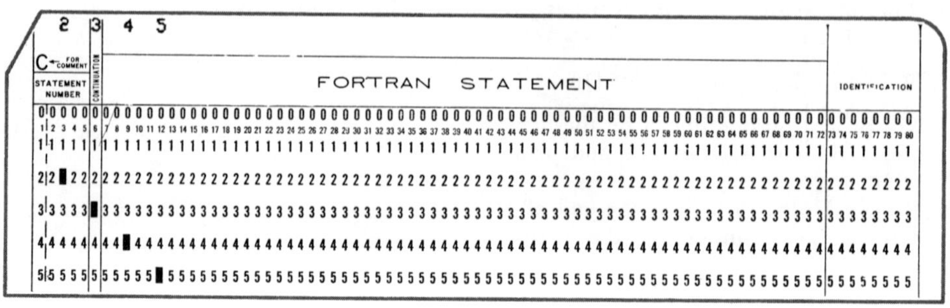

```
Column 567
        INTEGER SUM,PROD
        READ 5, I,J,K,L
        SUM =  I+J+K+L
        PROD=  I+J+K+L
        PRINT 10,I,J,K,L,SUM,PROD
      5 FORMAT(4I3)
     10 FORMAT(15H1  THE INPUT IS,4I4/13H   THE SUM IS,7X I5
       X/17H   THE PRODUCT IS 3X,I5 )
        STOP
        END
```

PRINTED OUTPUT – appears at the top of a new page

```
Column 3         13       21
  THE INPUT IS   2     3    4    5
  THE SUM IS            14
  THE PRODUCT IS       120
```

The Fortran program deck is separated from the input data card by a card which essentially says "input data follow." The specific form of this system control card must be determined locally. It informs the system that there is nothing left to compile and that input data follow immediately for the execution of the program.

The processing of this program goes as follows. First the Fortran deck is processed by the compiler which produces a machine-language program (the object program). The system control card (not shown) separates the Fortran program from the input data card. This input data card is then read and processed by the compiled program and the printed output is generated as shown.

The FORMAT is used with a READ in almost the same way it is used with a PRINT, except that the first character of a card plays no special role. All 80 columns of a card may be used, and the spacing of information over the card must, of course, agree exactly with the FORMAT being used.

Just as PRINT always prints one or more lines, READ always inputs one or more cards; as many cards as are required to satisfy both the READ list and the FORMAT field descriptors will be read.

Blank columns on an input card *are* significant. If they occur within a field expected to be an integer, each such space, or blank, is treated as a zero. For instance, the program shown here

```
  READ 3,I,J,K
3 FORMAT(I2,I3,I2)
  PRINT 3,I,J,K
```

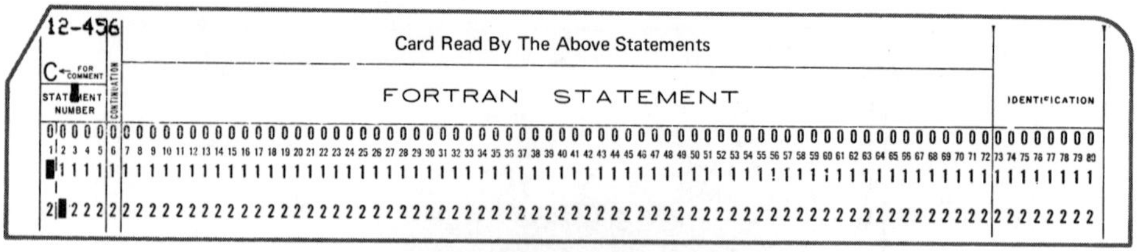

PRINTED OUTPUT

```
Column   1    6
         2-4560
```

reads a card that is punched starting in column 1 as 12-456 (as shown) then I, J, and K are given the values 12, −45, and 60, respectively. The output is also shown using the same FORMAT. Note that the leading 1 is missing in the printed output. It has caused the output to start at the top of a new page instead.

A single READ can cause several cards to be read, merely by using the slash between field specifications. If the X field descriptor occurs, it indicates that the corresponding number of columns of the card being read are to be skipped, or ignored. Thus the program shown here

```
      READ 18,I,J,K,L
   18 FORMAT(3X,I3,I4/I6,3X,I1)
      PRINT 18,I,J,K,L
```

CARD INPUT

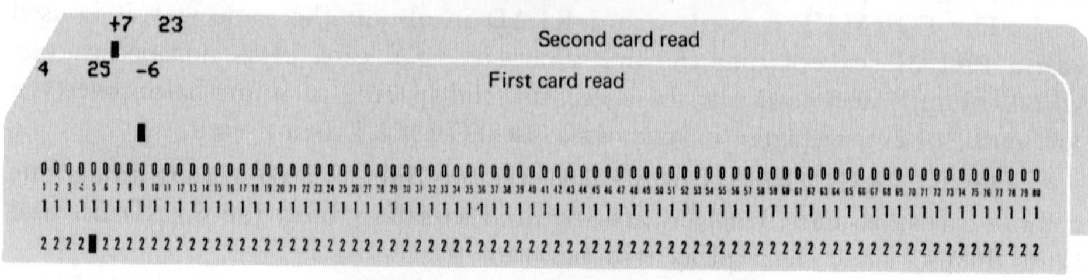

OUTPUT

```
Column   6   10
        25   -6
         7    3
```

would process the two cards shown and assign the values 25, −6, 7, and 3 to I, J, K, and L, respectively, skipping over the 4 in card 1 and over the 2 in card 2. The output is also shown using the same FORMAT statement.

If several consecutive input cards are to be read all in the same way, then the field descriptors appropriate for the first such card can be used over and over again, until each item in the READ list has been assigned a value. For example, the program shown below

```
      READ 71,I1,I2,J1,J2,KLUGE
   71 FORMAT(I4,6X,I5)
      PRINT 71,I1,J1,I2,J2,KLUGE
      STOP
      END
```

CARD INPUT

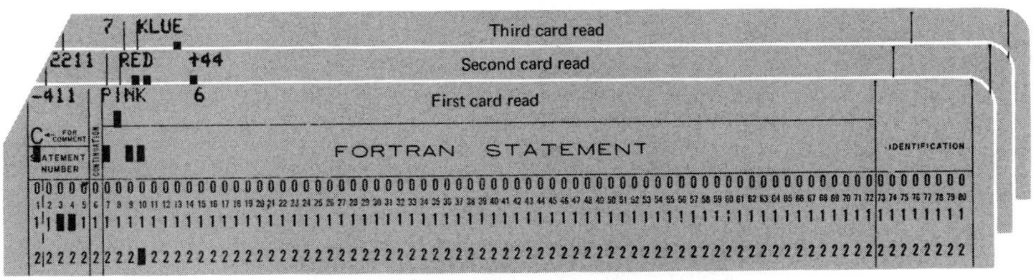


```
PRINTED OUTPUT

Column     4         15
         411       2211
           6         44
           7
```

causes a card to be read in order to assign values to I1 and I2. When the end of the format list is reached, then any items that remain in the READ list are processed using the entire FORMAT again. This causes a new card to be read. So, in this example, a second card is read, and J1 and J2 are assigned values. There is still a variable left in the READ list, so the FORMAT is used again and KLUGE is assigned a value. The output is shown using the same FORMAT statement, but with the variables in a different order. Note that minus sign on I1 is not printed because it falls in column one.

In using the PRINT statement, an output line may contain no more than some maximum number of characters. Similarly, in using READ to process a set of 80-column cards, the FORMAT field descriptors corresponding to each card must describe card "images" that do not exceed 80 columns each.

We might wonder what happens if the H field descriptor is used in reading cards. It has the rather unusual effect of changing the character string following the H in the FORMAT. Thus the program itself is changed, as if the FORMAT had been rewritten. In all other respects, the use of H may be regarded as a generalization of the use of X in reading. This feature is illustrated by the following program. Note, however, that there is another facility

```
      I = 1604
      IBM = 1403
      PRINT 7, I,IBM
    7 FORMAT(5X15HI AND IBM ARE =218 )
      READ 7,I,IBM
      PRINT 7, I,IBM
```

Card read with FORMAT 7

PRINTED OUTPUT — Before and after reading the card

```
Column              20|      28|      36|
       I AND IBM ARE =|    1604|    1403|
       DROP DEAD NOW  |11223344|55667788|
```

of Fortran (the A format, discussed in Chapter 4) which most people find more convenient and flexible for handling character strings.

1–5.5 READ and WRITE with Unit Numbers

Fortran has the ability to accept input from, and provide output to, a wide variety of devices in addition to cards and printed pages. Such devices include magnetic tapes, paper tapes, disk packs, and punched cards for output. These possibilities are discussed in more detail in Chapter 5, but we wish to note that the standard punched card input and printed page output may be included in this more general framework. The statements READ 100 and PRINT 200 are replaced by

```
READ(KIN,100)                        READ(5,100)
WRITE(KOUT,200)                      WRITE(6,200)
```

where KIN is the unit number for the standard (punched card) input and KOUT is the unit number for the standard (printed page) output. The unit numbers and the format label are included in the parentheses and separated by a comma. It is usual (but not required) that the standard input unit be 5 and the standard output unit be 6. The nonstandard input and output devices mentioned above would have different numbers and would be referred to by statements such as READ(3,2050), READ(1,310), WRITE(7,210).

Some Fortran systems reserve the simplified input and output statements (for example, READ 100 and PRINT 200) for the computer operator to use and require that a unit number be specified even for the standard card input and printed output. In any case, the card input and printed output do have a unit number and the statements READ 100, PRINT 200 are replaced by READ (5,100) and WRITE(6,200) assuming that 5 and 6 are the appropriate unit numbers.

Common Errors

1. Data punched in the wrong column.
2. Forgot that each READ statement starts reading a new card.
3. Asked to read more than 80 columns from a card.
4. Omitted leading blank in printing out input data from cards with something in column 1.
5. Forgot that trailing blanks are considered to be zeros (such as _4_ with I3 format is read as 40).

Things You Can Do

1. Use the same FORMAT for a READ and a PRINT.
2. Put in blanks in place of zeros.
3. Read many cards with one READ statement. A new card is read whenever a slash is met in the FORMAT or the FORMAT is restarted because the end is reached.

Problems

1–5.1 What is the maximum line length used at your installation? Will the compiler detect a format that specifies too long a line, or will this be detected only when the compiled program is executing?

1–5.2 Verify with a program that the four characters: blank, 0, 1, and + do indeed cause spacing to take place as described. Does your installation attach any special spacing functions to other characters?

1–5.3 Write a program that prints squares or triangles, such as

```
' ' '              +
'   '     or     +   +
' ' '            + + + + +
```

1–5.4 Obtain the following information, applicable to your installation:

(a) Which unit is the system input unit?

(b) What kind of operating system control statement, or control card, is needed to function as the statement ***INPUT DATA FOLLOW***?

(c) How is the end of input data indicated?

1–5.5 Write a program that reads in an integer N and computes the remainder upon division of N by 2, 8, and 15. Write the results out at the top of a new page in the form given in the example below. Double space all output.

```
NUMBER INPUT WAS 23
REMAINDER UPON DIVISION BY 2 IS 1
REMAINDER UPON DIVISION BY 8 IS 7
REMAINDER UPON DIVISION BY 15 IS 8
```

1–5.6 Write a program that prints a message with the H format followed by an I5,I6 specification. Rerun the program with the character count on the Hollerith field (message): (a) too low by 2 or 3, and (b) too high by 1. Note the effect of making the count too high so that the I5 is exactly included in the message.

1–5.7 Some compilers do not allow a program to be executed if any error is detected in any format statement. Others let the program go into execution, and terminate execution upon the first attempt to use an erroneous format. Why might a programmer be concerned about which approach is used?

1–5.8 Some nonstandard compilers may consider the blank or space a significant character. They may also consider the end of the statement field (beyond column 72) as a delimiter in the same sense. In such a case, how should the rules for preparing a machine-readable program be revised?

1–5.9 Write a program that should read five cards; use the format I3. Print each value read. What happens if the fifth data card is missing?

1–5.10 The compiler can detect, at compile time, some character strings that appear to be integer constants but that are not quite correct. See what the execution time diagnostics are when some character string that is not an integer constant is read using an I format.

1–5.11 Write a program that reads five integers punched right-adjusted in columns 1–5, 6–10, 11–16, 21–29, and 76–79. Write out the original numbers, the sum of their squares, and the product of their squares at the top of a new page with appropriate headings. After writing out the above, the program should read in seven more integers on data cards you have prepared so that the READ statement can use the format

```
511 FORMAT(25X,5I10//32X,I6/3X,I8)
```

Again, compute the sum of the squares and the product of the squares. Then write out these numbers, their sum, and their product at the top of a new page with appropriate headings.

1–6 Program Control

1–6.1 Labels

Thus far it has been possible to create only "straight-line" programs, where the executable statements are performed one after another until the STOP statement is reached. In order to specify a variety of paths through the program as it is being executed, some statements must be labeled. In Fortran, integer constants (unsigned) are used as labels, and any executable statement may be labeled by placing a label in columns 1 to 5 inclusive, as in

```
Column   2   567
             1 A = 17
          2    KBAR = 3*A -B
         4 12  PRINT 88, A,KBAR
            88 FORMAT(I6)
```

Here the labels 1, 2, 349, and 56 are used. Note that the label can "float" freely within the label field. It is preferable either to always begin the label in the same column or to always have the labels right-adjusted, so that they are aligned on column 5. This makes the labels easier for the programmer to read.

Fortran has several control verbs, or control statements, which are used to control the way in which the program is executed. Two of the simplest ones are discussed next.

1–6.2 Direct Transfer: GO TO

The simple direct transfer uses the control verb GO TO followed by a label. This label must be attached to an executable statement, and the effect of the GO TO is to transfer directly to that executable statement. Consider the following program.

```
      INTEGER HOURS,RATE,PAY
    1 READ 2,HOURS,RATE,PAY,ID
    2 FORMAT(1X,I2,I4,I5,I10)
      PAY = HOURS*RATE
      PRINT 2,HOURS,RATE,PAY,ID
         GO TO 1
      END
```

INPUT

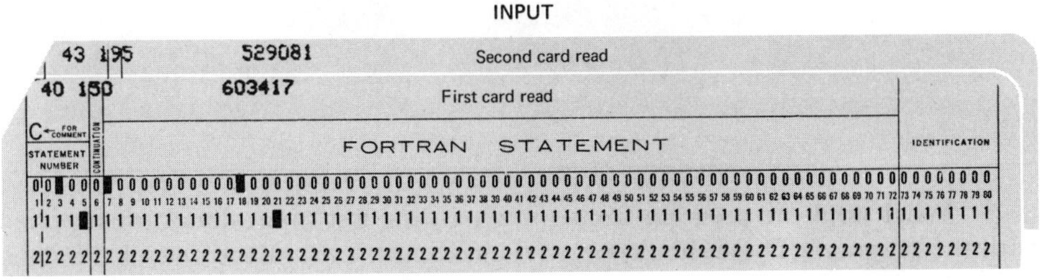

```
OUTPUT

40 150 6000    603417
43 195 8385    529081
```

It processes an indefinite number of cards, each containing a value for HOURS and RATE as well as an identification number in columns 13 to 22. For each such card it computes a value for PAY and prints it and the other information from the card. The input card should be punched as shown in the program. When the statement READ 2, HOURS, RATE, PAY, ID reads card 1, the 1X, I2 in the format causes 40 to be assigned to HOURS, the I4 causes 150 to be assigned to RATE, the I5 causes 0 to be assigned to PAY, and the I10 causes the employee identification number 603417 to be assigned to ID. When the statement PRINT 2, HOURS, RATE, PAY, ID is executed, we can expect the line

```
40 150 6000    603417
```

to be printed. The statement GO TO 1 then directs the computer to return to statement 1 (the READ statement) and to execute it again. Thus, the second card is read and the following line is printed:

```
43 195 8385    529081
```

This process is continued as long as there are any cards left to be read.

GO TO Statement

The word GO TO is followed by an integer constant which is the label of an executable statement. A direct, unconditional transfer is made to that statement and it is executed next.

EXAMPLES

```
  GO TO 1               GO TO607             GO TO 1492
  -----                 -----                -----
1 READ 5,X,ZIP       607 STOP           1492 BTOP = 16*BMID+31
```

What stops the program from going past the last input data card supplied with the program? There should be a system control card at the end of the data.

Just as a program must be preceded by another operating system control card, the last input data card must be followed by an operating system control card. With some systems, the last card is provided by the system itself.

In any event, if the READ statement attempts to read the operating system control card that signals the end of the input data, the operating system intervenes and regains control of the computer, terminating the execution of the program. Thus, when there are no more cards for a READ statement, the effect is the same as a STOP statement.

The GO TO's may be used wherever desired in a program, but some care must be taken to provide a path to all parts of the program. It makes very little sense to have an unlabeled executable statement following a GO TO.

Common Errors

1. Two statements with the same label.
2. Label missing for a GO TO.
3. Unlabeled STOP placed after a GO TO.
4. Skipped over part of program by mistake with a GO TO.
5. Generated infinite loop by a GO TO an earlier statement without any exit or STOP in between.
6. Use of a variable label (such as GO TO N).

Things You Can Do

1. Place the label in any of columns 1 through 5. Remember that a blank *between* two digits is taken as a zero, but blanks before or after all of the digits are not considered.
2. Have several STOP statements in one program.
3. GO TO any executable statement with a label.

1–6.3 Conditional Transfer: Arithmetic IF

The simplest conditional transfer in Fortran is called the arithmetic IF, to distinguish it from another type of conditional transfer to be discussed later, the logical IF.

IF Arithmetic

Its form is

IF (arithmetic expression) label −, label 0, label +

where label −, label 0, and label + are labels (integer constants) and the parentheses contain any legal arithmetic expression. If the value of that expression is negative, then a transfer is made to label −. If it is exactly zero, then a transfer is made to label 0 and if it is positive, a transfer is made to label +.

EXAMPLES

```
IF(K-4)5,10,15              IF(2*(K**2-4*L)+6*JL)1,8,400
IF(K+LAST-8)20,20,6         IF(16*KLOD +4*KUTE-5)800,12,73
```

This three-way branch can easily be thought of as follows: if the result is −, 0, or +, then transfer to the first, second, or third label, respectively. The labels need not be distinct, and in the special case when the three labels are identical, the IF can be replaced by a GO TO.

The following three examples provide the same conditional transfers:

```
A = B*B - 25          IF(B*B-25)10,32,6          IF(25-B*B)6,32,10
IF(A)10,32,6
```

They cause a transfer to statement 10 if B^2 is less than 25, to statement 32 if B^2 is 25, and to statement 6 if B^2 is greater than 25.

A complete description of the other conditional transfer known as the logical IF is given in Section 4–2.3. Because of its usefulness, a simplified description is given here. Whereas in the arithmetic IF, the value of the expression being tested must be positive, negative, or zero, in the logical IF it must be true or false. Then instead of selecting one of three labels as in the arithmetic IF, the logical IF causes the statement following the test to be executed if the test condition is true. Suppose we wish to transfer to statement 19 if variable A is greater than 13. Using the logical IF we can write IF(A.GT. 13) GO TO 19. The operator .GT. is an abbreviation for the relational operator "greater than." The complete set of relational operators is given in Section 4–2.3. To complete the discussion of this example, if A is not greater than 13, then the GO TO 19 is not executed; the next statement in the program is executed. Many statements other than GO TO's can be placed in the logical IF.

It is interesting to note that the Fortran statements that have been described allow us to program almost anything that can be programmed using all of the facilities of Fortran. Being able to read input data cards, perform arithmetic, print results, and effect conditional transfers, we have all that is really necessary. However, as we go on, it will be clear that ease of programming is also a very important consideration and that the rich set of control statements and other facilities in Fortran greatly facilitate writing programs to solve real problems.

In connection with ease of programming, it is possible to introduce comments in a program; any card with the letter C punched in column 1 is treated as a comment card. A comment card is printed along with the other statements of the Fortran program; it has no other function. Any number of comment cards can be used in a program; they must appear before the END statement. Consider the following program:

```
C           DECLARE INTEGERS
C       INTEGER A1,A2,A3
C           THIS PROGRAM READS THE COEFFICIENTS A1,A2,A3 OF THE
C           FORMULA         IBAR = A1+ A2*I + A3*I**2
        READ 1,A1,A2,A3
    1   FORMAT(3I6)
        PRINT 10,A1,A2,A3
   10   FORMAT(30H0 THE FORMULA COEFFICIENTS ARE 3I7)
C           THEN IT READS A VALUE FOR I
    2   READ 1,I
C           THEN IT EVALUATES THE FORMULA AND PRINTS THE RESULT
        IBAR = A1 + A2*I + A3*I**2
        PRINT 15,I,IBAR
   15   FORMAT(33H THE VALUE OF THE FORMULA FOR I =I4,3H IS I8)
C           NOW READ A NEW I AND REPEAT
        GO TO 2
        END
```

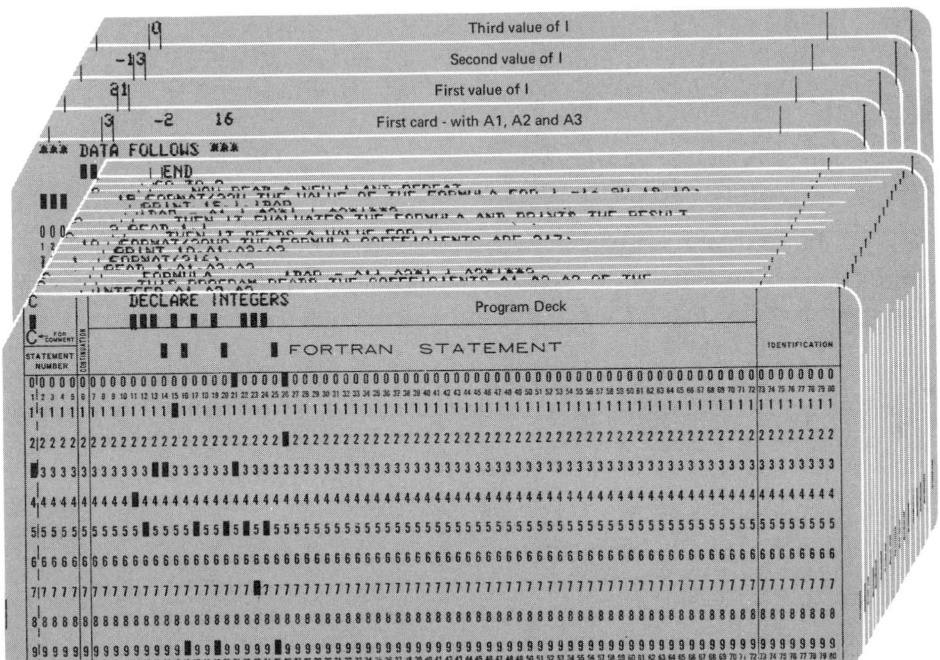


```
                        OUTPUT

 THE FORMULA COEFFICIENTS ARE      3      -2      16
THE VALUE OF THE FORMULA FOR I =  21 IS    7017
THE VALUE OF THE FORMULA FOR I = -13 IS    2733
THE VALUE OF THE FORMULA FOR I =   0 IS       3
```

Well-chosen variable names and appropriate comments can make a Fortran program much easier to understand.

Common Errors

1. Label missing that appears in the IF.
2. Comma placed before the first label.
3. Transfer to a GO TO statement from an IF. It is wasteful, not wrong.
4. Use of mixed arithmetic in the expression (such as IF(X-2)12,88,41).
5. Inefficient use of IF's as when K can be 1, 2, 3, 4, or 5, the following codes accomplish the same thing:

```
   IF(K-1)110,110,20          IF(K-2)110,120,40
20 IF(K-2)999,120,30       40 IF(K-4)130,140,150
30 IF(K-3)999,130,40
40 IF(K-4)999,140,50
50 IF(K-5)999,150,150
```

Things You Can Do

1. Use the same label more than once in the same IF.
2. Put the labels in any order you want (as long as it accomplishes what you want).
3. Place any expression in an IF.

Problems

In all future program assignments, introduce meaningful comments in the programs so that they may be used later for review purposes.

1–6.1 Write a program that reads exactly ten input cards and prints the first 40 columns of the first five cards and the last 40 columns of the remaining cards.

1–6.2 Write a program to obtain diagnostics for:
(a) Invalid labels
(b) Several statements having the same label
(c) Undefined label
(d) Unlabeled statement following a GO TO or arithmetic IF.

1–6.3 Write a program that reads an unspecified number of cards, each with four test grades on it. You are to compute and print with appropriate messages the average grade for each of the four grades on the card.

1–6.4 The last executable statement in a program must be a STOP or a transfer of some kind. Determine what happens if the STOP is left out.

1–6.5 Write a program that reads in an integer N from a data card and computes $N! = N\cdot(N-1)\cdot(N-2)\cdots 3\cdot 2\cdot 1$. Recall that $0! = 1$ by definition. If N is negtive or N! is too large to be represented in your computer, write out N and an error message that indicates why N! could not be computed. If N! can be computed, write out N and N!. In either case after writing one of these messages, your program should go back and read in a new value for N until all data cards have been processed. Use I fields for input and output and integer arithmetic to compute N!.

1–6.6 Write a program that reads in a card containing any two dates after the year 0 and computes the exact number of days between the given dates. Write out the dates and the number of days between them before reading in two more dates. Recall that 1900, and so on, are not leap years and ignore the days lost when the present calendar was adopted in the middle ages. The program is to read in the dates in the form year, month, day; both dates on one card (for example, 1617 11 28   1945 8 15). The result is to be printed with an appropriate message.

1–6.7 Write a program that accepts as input a punched card that gives the number of pins a bowler knocked down with each ball he threw during a game. There are 10 frames in a game. If it takes a bowler 2 balls to knock down 10 pins in a frame (a spare), his score for that frame is 10 plus the number of pins he knocks down on his next ball. If it takes him only 1 ball to knock down 10 pins a frame (a strike), his score is 10 plus the number of pins he knocks down on his next 2 balls. If he does not knock down all 10 pins in a frame (a miss), his score is the number of pins he did knock down in that frame. After reading the card, compute the bowler's score. Write out the card input, the computed score, the numbers of the frames in which he made spares, and the numbers of the frames in which he made strikes. Read in a new card and repeat until all data cards are read.

Example:

```
CARD INPUT
  9  1  0 10  10  10  6  2  7  3  8  2  10  9  0  9  1  7
SCORE    165
SPARES IN FRAME    1  2  6  7 10
STRIKES IN FRAME      3  4  8
```

1–7 Real Variables and Arithmetic

1–7.1 Real Variables and Real Constants

With integer arithmetic, it is sometimes necessary to perform some extra work to ensure that only "like" quantities are combined. Consider the following program.

```
C          MONTH IN CENTS, YEARTD IN DOLLARS
C      PROGRAM TO UPDATE YEARTD FROM MONTH
       INTEGER YEARTD
       READ 2, MONTH,YEARTD
       YEARTD = (MONTH + YEARTD*100)/100
       PRINT 2,MONTH,YEARTD
       STOP
     2 FORMAT(I7,I6)
       END
```

CARD INPUT

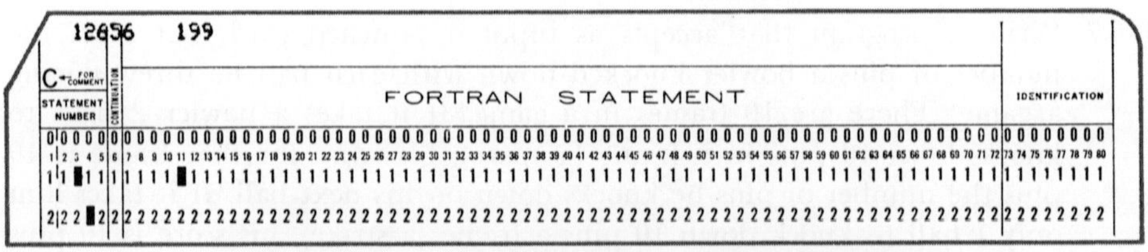

OUTPUT

```
Column       7|    13|
         12656|   325|
```

This program reads a card expecting a year-to-date total in dollars and a monthly total in cents. To correctly calculate the new year-to-date total to the nearest dollar, YEARTD is scaled up into cents by multiplying by 100. The sum is found in cents and then scaled back into dollars by dividing by 100. This type of scaling, or positioning of an imagined decimal point, can be taken care of by the computer when real variables and constants are used.

A real constant is a number with a decimal point. The maximum number of digits depends on the system. We assume a maximum of 8 digits. Thus 1., 1.0, +1.0, −1.00, .00123, and −1.2345678 are some real constants.

A real constant can also be written with an integer exponent; the integer exponent is written following the letter E. Just as the numbers 100, .0023, and −2,000,000. can be written as 1.0×10^2, $.23 \times 10^{-2}$, and $-.2 \times 10^7$ in standard mathematical notation, they can be punched as 1.0E2, .23E−2, and −.2E+7 in Fortran. Real constants written with an E are said to be in E format; without the E, they are in F format.

Real Constant
F Format
E Format

The F format form is a string of digits with exactly one decimal point in it, with or without a + or − sign. The E format is a string of digits with exactly one decimal point in it, followed by the letter E and followed by an integer exponent (which may also have a + or − sign). The number of digits allowed in either case depends on the local system.

EXAMPLES

```
 1.3       .0024    1900000.0     1.3E0      .24E-2      19.E+5
-16.74    18.       -199.88     -.1674E+2   1.8E+01   -.19988E3
```

A variable is defined to be real by placing its name in a REAL statement. Just as a variable may be defined to be an integer variable by having the first letter of its name chosen from among I, J, K, L, M, or N (recall the "implicit-type" rule mentioned in Section 1–4.1), a variable is defined to be real by default even if it does not appear in a REAL statement, provided that the first letter of its name does *not* begin with any of I, J, K, L, M, or N.

Arithmetic expressions involving only real constants and variables are formed in the same way as those involving only integer constants and variables. Using real numbers not only provides for automatic alignment of the decimal point but also greatly increases the range of numbers that can be handled. There is usually a loss of a few digits in precision, and real arithmetic may take longer to perform than integer arithmetic on some computers.

Standard Fortran has the popularly named "no-mixed-mode" rule that states that variables and constants of different types may not be mixed in the same expression. For instance, if N is an integer variable and X is a real variable, then X + 1, N * 2.5, and N − X would each violate the no-mixed-mode rule. Some systems have relaxed or eliminated this rule. In some cases, a more efficient (faster) program may result by abiding by the rule.

There are two pertinent questions here. First, why are there two kinds of numbers in Fortran and second, even if there are, why can't one mix them? There are several reasons why real numbers are needed, the most obvious is illustrated in the sample program above. In order to appreciate what is happening, one must consider how numbers are stored, or written down, in the computer. In almost all Fortran systems there is a fixed amount of storage, or size of space, for each number. For simplicity let us assume the computer uses paper and pencil and it has just enough room to write 10 decimal digits, plus a sign bit (or digit). Each space for a number looks like

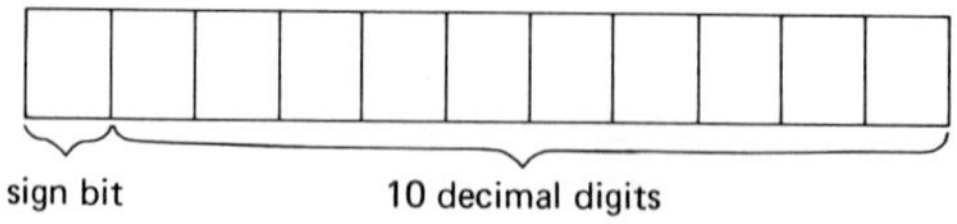

There is a very straightforward scheme to write down (or represent) integers.

Integer Number	Written Internally by the Computer										
16	0	0	0	0	0	0	0	0	0	1	6
+ 4187202	0	0	0	0	4	1	8	7	2	0	2
– 88866	1	0	0	0	0	0	8	8	8	6	6
– 123	1	0	0	0	0	0	0	0	1	2	3
	sign bit	10 decimal digits									

The numbers are written in the ordinary way except that a minus sign is a 1 in the sign bit and a plus sign is a 0. Real numbers are written differently and in a way that corresponds to the E format.

Real Number	Written Internally by the Computer										
.123E03	0	1	2	3	0	0	0	0	0	0	3
123.0	0	1	2	3	0	0	0	0	0	0	3
12.3E1	0	1	2	3	0	0	0	0	0	0	3
– 1666888.2	1	1	6	6	6	8	8	8	2	0	7
– 123.E-6	1	1	2	3	0	0	0	0	0	5	3
– 88.88E-24	1	8	8	8	8	0	0	0	0	7	2
	sign bit	8 decimal digits Fractional Part								2-digit exponent	

The main thing here is to realize that real numbers are represented completely differently in the computer than integer numbers. The computer must be told to treat a number as real or as an integer because a collection of digits could be either one. It is assumed in this particular machine that the exponent part is limited to ±49 so that we can represent a negative exponent by adding 50 to the magnitude. Thus −3 becomes 53, −22 becomes 72. Just how this is done is not important here, what is important is to note that you cannot blindly combine integer and real variables or constants. Thus, if we blindly took 123 − 123.0 and treated both numbers as integers, then we see the computer would have

	00000000123
minus	01230000003
equals	11229999880

which is −1,229,999,880 if interpreted as an integer number or −.12299998E−30 if interpreted as a real number. A more common name for this result is *garbage*, and this example is typical of what happens when one carelessly mixes real and integer numbers.

Compilers take a number of steps to help the programmer avoid this source of garbage. Thus, they will check the numbers in an expression and might convert all of them to real if there is a mixture. This is the friendly thing to do, but many compilers simply print a diagnostic message saying that a Fortran error is present.

Statements such as N = X and X = N + 1 do not violate the above rule since it applies only to expressions and not to statements. We can have the following combinations.

Left-Hand Side		*Right-Hand Side Expressions*	*Value of Result*
integer variable	=	integer-valued	integer
integer variable	=	real-valued	integer, truncated
real variable	=	integer-valued	real
real variable	=	real-valued	real

Thus, the sequence of statements

```
N = 5
X = 1.6
M = X + 1.1
Y = N - 1
```

leaves M with the value 2 (1.6 + 1.1, truncated) and Y with the value 4.0 (5 − 1).

We have seen the difficulties that occur in Fortran because it has two kinds of numbers, but we have not answered the question of why we need them. Some programming languages have only real numbers. The first computers could do only integer arithmetic and even now integer arithmetic is often faster than real arithmetic. One use for integers is that one sometimes cannot count exactly with real numbers. The reason for this is that real arithmetic is not performed exactly due to the limited length of the numbers. The following program illustrates this to a certain extent, another one is given in the next section when we see how to print real numbers.

```
Column   567
          THIRD = 1./3.
          TENTH = .1
      1   IONE  = THIRD + THIRD + THIRD
      2   ITWO  = 6.*THIRD
      3   ITHREE= 20.*TENTH + 3.*THIRD
      4   IFOUR = 35.*TENTH + 0.5
          PRINT 10,IONE,ITWO,ITHREE,IFOUR
     10   FORMAT (4I5)
          STOP
          END
```

OUTPUT – Would have expected 1 2 3 4 instead!

```
    0    1    2    3
```

In each of these calculations, the minute errors lead to values like 1.99999998 for the expression in statement 2. This value becomes 1 when set to an integer.

Common Errors

1. Mixed real and integer variables or constants in an expression like X + 1, (N + 1)*(XX – YY).
2. Omitted * in multiplication (such as in 2.73 X, X(Y + 1), (X + 1.)(X – 2.)).
3. Use of variable that has not been read in or assigned a value.
4. Negative number raised to a real power, even if the power is an integer as in (–2.1)**3.0. Most systems permit (–2.1)**3 and some permit (–2.1)**N.
5. Overflow (numbers too big) or underflow (numbers too small) generated in expression. Thus, for X = 10, Y = 21, and Z = 12 the expression

   (X**(Y + 2)*Z**(Y – 2))/8.1**Y

   has an intermediate value calculated of 3.2E + 43 even though the value of the expression is about 3.1E + 22. The first number is too big for many Fortran systems.
6. Assumption that real arithmetic is exact. Thus one is not sure that 10.*.1 = 1. or .2 + .2 + .1 = .5 with real arithmetic.
7. Decimal point omitted in E format (such as 1E + 5 instead of 1.E + 5 for 100000.).

Things You Can Do

1. Raise a real variable to an integer power as in

   X ** 3,   (Y + Z) ** (N + 1).

2. Set a real variable to an integer expression or variable or constant and vice versa.
3. Use the E format in an expression as in

   X = 2.E + 6 * (ZZ – 6.22E – 5).

1–7.2 Reading and Writing Real Variables

There are two field descriptors that can be used in a FORMAT statement for reading or writing real variables. They are designated by the letters E or F and correspond to the two ways to write real constants in a program. The letter E or F is followed by two integers w and d, as in Ew.d or Fw.d., where w specifies the total field width devoted to the real variable, and d specifies how many digits are to the right of the decimal point.

The F field descriptor is used with real constants that do not have an exponent for input, and for which no exponent is desired on output. Consider the example program shown below.

```
  READ 1,X,Y
1 FORMAT(F3.0,F5.2)
  PRINT 2,X,Y
2 FORMAT(3H X=,F5.1,3H Y=,F6.1)
  STOP
  END
```

INPUT

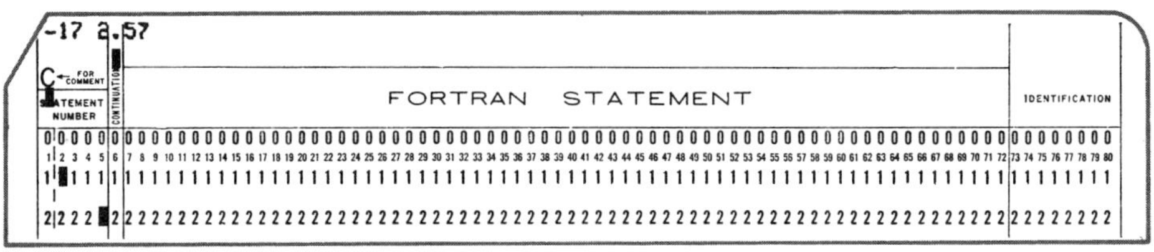

OUTPUT

```
Column   3    8 11     17
         X=-17.0 Y=    2.6
```

The output for this example is X = −17.0, Y = 2.6. This shows that the input data do not necessarily have decimal points for reading, and that the system may round real numbers while writing them out, if the fraction width specified is too small.

The E field description is especially useful when very large or very small numbers are involved. For instance, the numbers 3,146,000,000 and 0.000056 can be punched as 3146.E6 and 0.56E −4, respectively, then read using FORMAT (E7.0, E9.2). The punched card looks like

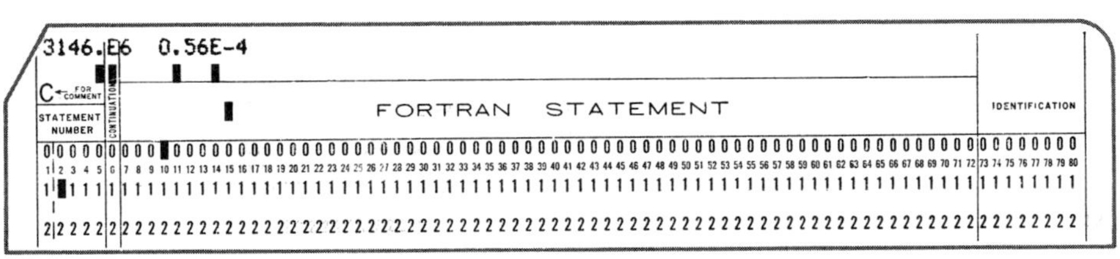

These formats are illustrated below when the number X = −123.409 is printed.

```
F8.2        F6.2        E9.1         E15.6
-123.41     123.41     -1.2E+01     -.123409E+03
                       -0.1E+02
```

Note that in printing with the E format, the system will consistently put the first digit on the left of the decimal point. Just how this is done depends on the system and two possibilities are shown for the E9.1 format. Note also that one can lose the minus sign, or even some digits, if the field width is too small.

Whenever input data are prepared for use with E and F formats, any blanks occurring within the specified field width w are treated as zeros. If the decimal point is punched so that the number of digits to the right of the decimal point (that is, the length of the fraction) differs from that specified by the d of the FORMAT, the position of the decimal point overrides the specification in the FORMAT. Thus, the statements

```
  READ 1,X,Y
1 FORMAT(2F5.2)
```

in processing a card

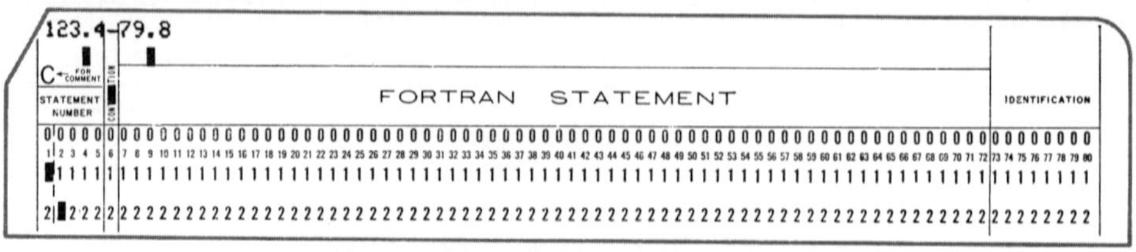

assigns the values 123.4 and −79.8 to X and Y, respectively.

Some systems require that the field width w exceed the fraction width d in the specifications Ew.d and Fw.d by some minimum amount. This must be determined locally.

The program given at the beginning of this section can now be rewritten as shown below.

```
  REAL MONTH
  READ 1,YEARTD,MONTH
1 FORMAT(2F6.0)
  MONTH = MONTH*.01
  YEARTD = MONTH + YEARTD
  PRINT 2,YEARTD,MONTH
2 FORMAT(15H YEAR TO DATE =,F7.0/8H MONTH =F8.2)
  STOP
  END
```

CARD INPUT

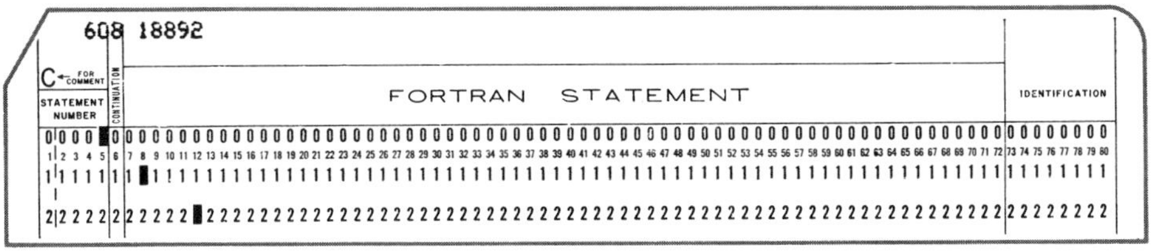

PRINTED OUTPUT

```
YEAR TO DATE = 796.
MONTH = 188.92
```

Notice how the calculation is somewhat simpler when real variables are used to provide automatic handling of the decimal point. However, the use of real numbers may introduce errors due to truncation if the real numbers involved cannot be represented exactly in the computer.

The following program is an extension of the one in Section 1–7.1 and illustrates more features and effects of real and integer arithmetic.

```
C           PROGRAM TO SHOW ERRORS IN REAL ARITHMETIC
C                AND SOME FORMAT ERRORS
      THIRD = 1./3.
      TENTH = .1
      ONE   = 0.1 + .9
      TWO   = 6./3.
      THREE = .5 + .5 + 2.0
      IFOUR = ONE + THREE
    2 PRINT 100,THIRD,TENTH,ONE,TWO,THREE,IFOUR
    5 PRINT 200,IFOUR,ONE,TENTH
  100 FORMAT(3F12.8/2F12.8,I12)
  200 FORMAT( F12.8, 2I14)
      STOP
      END
```

OUTPUT

```
0.33333333  0.09999999  0.99999999 } First PRINT
2.00000000  3.00000000           3 }
0.00000000   17314086911   16884590182 } Second PRINT
```

Statement 2 shows that the real arithmetic sometimes is exactly correct and sometimes makes very small errors. The size of the errors that it makes depends on how much space (or how many digits) the computer uses to record the numbers. Statement 5 prints out an integer and two real numbers with wrong formats and it is seen that the result is garbage.

Common Errors

1. Reversed field width and decimal digits in E or F format as in E6.15,F3.9 (wrong) instead of E15.6,F9.3.
2. Space for decimal point and minus sign not allowed for in the field width.
3. Field width too short for E format.
4. E format numbers on card input which are not justified to the right in the field.
5. Real numbers printed with I format or integers printed with E or F format.
6. Decimal digits not specified, as in E15 or F12.

Things You Can Do

1. Place an F format number anywhere in a field for card input. The position of the decimal point on the card overrides the F format specifications in the FORMAT statement.
2. Read an F format number on a card with an E format in the FORMAT statement.
3. Read an integer on a card with an F format such as F3.0,F6.0. The variable assigned the value read from the card must be real.
4. Omit punching the decimal point in an F input field (for example, F3.1 to read 155 as 15.5).

Problems

1–7.1 In most systems, real numbers are represented with fewer significant digits than integers are. Find out how many significant digits are carried in your system for real numbers.

1–7.2 Perform division of real constants, such as 1./2., 1./3., and so on, to see what error, if any, is involved in the machine representation of these fractions.

1–7.3 Find out what relation must hold between w and d in E w.d and F w.d for your system.

1–7.4 Depending on the system, the following program may execute the PRINT statement 9 or 10 times.

```
Column   5|6|7
           X = .1
           STEP = .1
        1  PRINT 2,X
        2  FORMAT(F8.2)
           X = X + STEP
           IF(X-1.0)1,3,3
        3  STOP
           END
```

If the computer internally uses a *decimal* representation for numbers, then it will execute it 9 times. Otherwise the internal representation of .1 may actually be a number slightly less than .1 and, in fact, this is the most common case. Run the above program as is, and then with different initial values for X and STEP, such as .1 and .2 or .5 and .5.

1–7.5 The following statements compute the sum

$$1 + \frac{1}{2} + \frac{1}{4} + \cdots + \frac{1}{2^n} + \cdots .$$

```
Column   5|6|7
           |SUM = 1.0
           |TERM= 1.0
         1 |TERM= TERM/2.
           |NUSUM = SUM + TERM
           |IF(NUSUM - SUM) 2,2,3
         2 |SUM = NUSUM
           |    GO TO 1
         3 |STOP
           |END
```

What happens when the IF statement is replaced by IF(TERM)3,3,2?

1–7.6 Write a program that computes daily and weekly pay as in the very first example program with the following modifications:

(a) All variables are real.

(b) The number of hours is a variable rather than a fixed constant 40.

(c) The rate of pay for each hour over 40 is 1½ times the normal rate.

(d) The rate of pay and number of hours are read from a card and the program is to be able to process an unlimited number of cards.

1–7.7 This is a continuation of Problem 1–7.6. Further modify the program so that the employee's Social Security number (of the form XXX-XX-XXXX) is read from the card and the output is of the form

EMPLOYEE XXX-XX-XXXX GETS $18.20 A DAY = $91.00 A WEEK.

1–7.8 Consider the following Fortran statement which generates a new value for R from an old one.

R = 77. * R – FLOAT(100 * IFIX(.77*R)).

Set up an iteration loop to compute 500 values for R-50. starting with R = 41. Count the number of times that these values are positive, zero, and negative and print out the counts in the following form:

```
NEGATIVE VALUES FOUND XXX TIMES
    ZERO VALUE   FOUND XXX TIMES
POSITIVE VALUES FOUND XXX TIMES.
```

1–7.9 Give three different Fortran representations for the number twelve hundred and forty two.

1–7.10 Write a program that converts a number of hours into weeks, days, and hours. Have the output in the form

3092 HOURS IS 18 WEEKS, 2 DAYS, AND 20 HOURS.

1–7.11 Write a program that reads a date punched like 06/05/70 or 12/25/75 and prints out lines like

```
06/05/70 IS        JUNE  5, 1970
12/25/75 IS DECEMBER 25, 1975.
```

1–8 Standard Fortran Functions

The computational power in Fortran so far has been limited to the four arithmetic operations +, −, *, / and exponentiation (or powers) **. The usefulness of Fortran is much enhanced by a number of other computational tools, the standard or built-in functions. A function has certain input quantities called *arguments* and it processes these to produce the function's value. This set of functions varies from system to system, the set described here includes the most useful ones. Some Fortran systems have two or three times as many standard functions as mentioned here. This set of functions is naturally divided into two groups, the basic arithmetic functions and the mathematical functions (or routines as they are often called).

A simple example of a useful function is the absolute value. One can obtain the absolute value as follows:

```
      IF(X)21,22,22                   IF(K) 41,42,42
   21 SIZEX = -X                   41 KSIZE = -K
      GO TO 23                        GO TO 43
   22 SIZEX = X                    42 KSIZE = K
   23  -----                       43  -----
```

The result of these four statements is that SIZEX is the absolute value (or size) of X and KSIZE is the absolute value of K. This is cumbersome if it has to be done frequently and the absolute value function replaces these four statements as follows:

```
      SIZEX = ABS(X)                  KSIZE = IABS(K)
```

Observe the following facts that one sees in Table 1–1. A built-in function that produces an integer number has a name which begins with I, J, K, L, M, or N. One has to have the argument of the correct type (integer or real) as well as choose the right resulting type. These possibilities lead to as many as four functions for the same operation; for instance, AMAX0, AMAX1, MAX0, and MAX1 for taking the maximum of a list of numbers. At times this also leads to considerable confusion and very elusive errors.

Functions

A function has a name followed by a left parenthesis followed by one or more arguments (depending on the function) and followed by a right parenthesis. The arguments may be any legal expression which produces a value of the correct type. There are separate functions for doing the same operations on real and on integer variables. A function produces a single numerical value which can, in turn, be used in an expression.

EXAMPLES
(detailed lists are given in Tables 1–1, 1–2)

```
ABS(X)          SIGN(X,Z)              IABS(KWAK)
ABS(X+3.1*Z)    SIGN(X**2-1.,Z+2.)     IABS(2+K*L-J)
```

TABLE 1–1
Some of the built-in functions

Function	*Mathematical Definition*	*No. of Arguments*	*Name*	*Type of Argument*	*Type of Result*
Absolute value	$\lvert a \rvert$	1	ABS	Real	Real
			IABS	Integer	Integer
Truncation	Sign of a times largest integer $\leqq \lvert a \rvert$	1	AINT	Real	Real
			INT	Real	Integer
Remainder	$a_1 - [a_1/a_2]a_2$	2	AMOD	Real	Real
			MOD	Integer	Integer
Choosing largest value	Max $(a_1,a_2,\ldots)$	$\geqq 2$	AMAX0*	Integer	Real
Choosing smallest value	Min $(a_1,a_2,\ldots)$		AMAX1	Real	Real
For minimum replace MAX by MIN			MAX0*	Integer	Integer
			MAX1	Real	Integer
Float	Conversion from integer to real	1	FLOAT	Integer	Real
Fix	Conversion from real to integer	1	IFIX	Real	Integer
Transfer of sign	Sign of a_2 times $\lvert a_1 \rvert$	2	SIGN	Real	Real
			ISIGN	Integer	Integer
Positive difference	$a_1 - \text{Min}(a_1, a_2)$	2	DIM	Real	Real
			IDIM	Integer	Integer

* Note that AMAX0 and MAX0 end with a zero.

The functions FLOAT and IFIX are particularly useful when one wants to mix real and integer variables in an expression. A calculation is shown below which illustrates the advantages and disadvantages.

```
  X = 7.0
  K = 4
  IX= X
  RK= K
1 JUNK = K+L-4*IX
2 ABC  = 3.17*X - RK/4.16
3 BLAH = ((X-RK)/(X+RK))/(RK**2-4.1)

  X = 7.0
  K = 4
1 JUNK = K+L-4*IFIX(X)
2 ABC  = 3.17*X - FLOAT(K)/4.16
3 BLAH = ((X-FLOAT(K))/(X+FLOAT(K))/(FLOAT(K)**2-4.1)
```

We see that using IFIX and FLOAT at the bottom has eliminated two statements. However, statement 3 is then much longer and more tedious to keypunch, write, or type. Table 1–1 gives a description of some of the built-in functions of the first group.

The argument of a function may be any expression having a value of the expected type. Thus X = ABS(ABS(Y) − Z) * Q shows a function used in a natural way, just as we naturally write $||y| - z|q$. Other examples of the use of functions in statements are

```
XBIG = AMAX1(X1,X2,X3)
YBIG = 4.1*AMAX1(Y1,Y2-Y3**2) + 4.2*AMIN1(Y3**2-Y1,6.07*Y2)
KZZ  = K**(IABS(J2-4*L))-MAX0(IABS(JJJ),20,K-L)
REALQ= AMAX0(IABS(K-7*L),IFIX(X**3.1-7.2),3*K+4*L-J**2)
```

Since a function returns a single value, it may be used in any statement in the same way as any other variable, except that it may never appear on the left-hand side of an equal side, or in an input-output list. A statement such as ABS(X) = Y has no meaning yet; a statement such as PRINT ABS(X) would be desirable, but it is not allowed.

Some functions have a variable number of arguments. Choosing the integer part of the largest value of a set of three or four real variables is done using MAX1, as in

```
IX = MAX1(A,A2,B,C)
IY = MAX1(Q,AI,3.0*D)
```

No declaration is made in a program in order to use a standard function. If a name appears in an expression and it is followed by a right parenthesis, then it can only be an array (these variables are discussed in Chapter 4) or a function. If it has not been declared as an array, then it is assumed to be a function. If the name happens to be that of a standard function, then that function is used.

The second group of standard functions can be used in the same manner as the above functions. They are called *mathematical subprograms,* or *library routines,* or *external functions.* They are more complicated and involve more machine-language code than can reasonably be included in a Fortran compiler, so they are stored as separate entities called subprograms in a library. When the system determines that a program needs a mathematical subprogram, it searches the library until it finds it. If the subprogram cannot be found, then the system usually does not permit the program to begin execution.

The arrangement, searching and storage of libraries is discussed later. Chapter 9 gives a presentation from the general point of view of the computer system. More specific details of searching and library files are presented in Chapters 10 and 11.

A list of some of the most frequently used mathematical functions is given in Table 1–2 along with their ordinary mathematical names and notation. The following program shows what is involved in obtaining the square root of a number, using the square root function whose name is SQRT.

```
C     COMPUTE THE HYPOTHENUSE
      READ 5,BASE,HEIGHT
      HYP = SQRT( BASE**2 + HEIGHT**2 )
```

TABLE 1–2
Basic mathematical functions

Function	Definition	No. of Arguments	Name	Type of Argument	Type of Result
Exponential	e^a	1	EXP	Real	Real
Natural logarithm	$\log_e(a)$	1	ALOG	Real	Real
Common logarithm	$\log_{10}(a)$	1	ALOG10	Real	Real
Trigonometric sine*	$\sin(a)$	1	SIN	Real	Real
Trigonometric cosine*	$\cos(a)$	1	COS	Real	Real
Square root	$(a)^{1/2}$ or $\sqrt{a}$	1	SQRT	Real	Real

* The arguments for sin and cos are given in radians, not degrees.

Any use of a mathematical routine must conform to its mathematical definition. For instance, since the square root of a negative number is not real but imaginary, SQRT can only be used if its argument has a positive or zero value. With a little practice, one can quickly translate an ordinary mathematical equation into Fortran using these functions. Note that a constraint on Fortran notation is that everything must be on one line (no superscripts, powers, or subscripts) and there are not as many symbols available as one might want (for example, $\sqrt{\ }$ is missing). Several mathematical equations and expressions are given below, then the equivalent Fortran statements and expressions are given.

$$X = \sqrt{3.2 * Y^2 + 4.7 * Z^3}$$
$$\cos(3X - 4)\sin(2X^3 - 4X) + \sqrt{1 + \log(4X + 1)}$$
$$Y = 4.752e^{(1+X^2+3.2\sqrt{X})/4} - \cos(\sqrt{X} + 1.3)$$
$$Z = e^{X+1}\cos(X - 2X^2) + 3$$

```
X  = SQRT(3.2*Y**2 + 4.7*Z**3)
COS(3.*X-4.)*SIN(2.*X**3-4.*X)+ SQRT(1.+ALOG(4.*X+1.))
Y =4.75*EXP((1.+X**2+3.2*SQRT(X))/4.)-COS(SQRT(X)+1.3)
Z = EXP(X+1.)*COS(X-2.*X**2) + 3.
```

Common Errors

1. Use of real functions for integer variables as in ABS(K) instead of IABS(K). The reverse of this.
2. The letter O at the end of AMAXO, MAXO, AMINO, MINO instead of zero.
3. Use of degrees in trigonometric functions SIN, COS, TAN instead of radians (1 radian = 57.29577 degrees).
4. Argument of SQRT is negative.
5. Argument of EXP is too large. The limit on many systems is about 80 to 90.
6. Confusion between logarithms to base e (use ALOG) and to base 10 (use ALOG10).

Things You Can Do

1. Use a variable in a function more than once and also reassign its value. Thus X = AMAX1(X, −X) replaces X by its absolute value.
2. Use any valid expression as an argument as long as it produces a value of the right type (that is, real or integer).
3. Compute cube roots, fourth roots, and so on, with the ** operation. Thus X = 2. ** .25, Y = 2. ** (1./3.) give the fourth and cube roots of 2.

Problems

1–8.1 Give the Fortran expressions for the following expressions given in ordinary mathematical notation.

(a) $X^{3/2}\sqrt{X^2 + Y^2}$
(b) $\sin(a + 2)$
(c) $\sin(b - 4)\cos(b + 4)$
(d) $2\log(X + 1)$
(e) $e^{\sqrt{X+2}}\cos(3X + 1)$
(f) $x\log_{10}(x^2 - a^2)$

1–8.2 Give the ordinary mathematical notation for the following Fortran expressions.

(a) X * (Y + 1.) ** (SQRT(X ** 2 + Y ** 2))
(b) EXP(R * COS(2. * R − 1.))

(c) (ALOG((X + 1.)/(X − 1.))) * (1. + EXP(X ** 2 − 1.)/ABS(X − 2.))
(d) 4.12 * ALOG10(X * SQRT(X ** (5./3.) + 1.))
(e) SIN(A + 90.) ** 2 + COS(B + 90.) ** 2 − 2. * COS(A + B)

1–8.3 Give the value of the following Fortran quantities.

(a) ABS(16.2 − 37.1)
(b) FLOAT(14)
(c) IFIX(14.1) − IFIX(−16.2)
(d) AMAX1(−13.1, −6.2, −27.3)
(e) AMAX0(13,27,−63)
(f) MOD(17,3)
(g) SIGN(−137.2,1.)
(h) SIGN(16.2 − 18.7, 4.5 − 9.2)
(i) IDIM(16,5) + IDIM(5,16)

1–8.4 Write a Fortran program that reads in a set of cards with 4 numbers per card in 4F10.3 format. The program is to compute the maximum of the four numbers and print it out with an appropriate message. Further, it is to find the maximum of all the numbers read in and print it out in the form: LARGEST OF ALL IS XXXXXX.XXX. The program is to recognize a blank card as the last card in the data set.

1–8.5 Write a program which evaluates the following four numbers and prints them out in the order smallest to largest.

$$A = \log_e\left(\frac{1}{\sqrt[3]{.00000000584}}\right) \qquad B = \sqrt[7]{24{,}502}$$

$$C = 6\cos(251.33) - .43\sin(2{,}260.3757)$$

$$D = \frac{479{,}058}{76{,}041} + \frac{211}{36{,}911}$$

The output should be in the following form (assuming that B < D < A < C which is not actually the case).

B = XXXX.XXXX
D = XXXX.XXXX
A = XXXX.XXXX
C = XXXX.XXXX

1–8.6 Write a program that reads in three numbers on a card which are supposed to be the lengths of the sides of a triangle. The program is to print these numbers back out along with a message indicating the type of triangle formed. One of the following four messages is to appear:

ACUTE TRIANGLE
RIGHT TRIANGLE
OBTUSE TRIANGLE
LINES DO NOT FORM A TRIANGLE

[*Hint:* One can test for the cases as follows: Let A, B, C be the lengths and let P be the maximum of A, B, and C. With Q and R denoting the other two lengths one has the following tests:

$P \geq Q + R$	no triangle formed
$P^2 > Q^2 + R^2$	obtuse triangle formed
$P^2 = Q^2 + R^2$	right triangle formed
$P^2 < Q^2 + R^2$	acute triangle formed

Your program should work for A = 3.0, B = 4.0, C = 5.0, but it might give the wrong answer for A = 3.002, B = 4.006002, C = 5.006002. Explain why. It might also give the wrong answer for A = .9, B = 1.2, and C = 1.5.]

1–8.7 Write a program that uses the functions SIN and COS to compute $\sin^2 x + \cos^2 x$ for $x = 0$ to 20 in increments of 0.1. By a well-known trigonometric identity, $\sin^2 x + \cos^2 x = 1$ for all x. In order to examine the accuracy of the Fortran functions, compute the percentage error for each computation $c = \sin^2 x + \cos^2 x$ using the formula

$$\text{p.e.} = 100 \times \frac{|1 - c|}{1} = 100|1 - c|.$$

Your output should begin at the top of a new page and be in the following form:

X	SIN(X) ** 2 + COS(X) ** 2	PERCENTAGE ERROR
0.00	1.0000000	0.0000000
0.10	1.0000000	0.0000000

and so on.

1–8.8 Write one Fortran program with each of the following errors in it.
(a) Undefined label
(b) Hollerith count too low in H format
(c) Variable name with eight letters
(d) INTEGER misspelled as INTERGER
(e) Mixed arithmetic as in 1.3 + 2 * 6
(f) No END card
(g) An illegal character (punch a 7 and a 9 in the same column)
(h) Two equal signs in one statement
(i) PRINT misspelled as PRINR
If the compiler does not detect all of these errors, can you rewrite the program so that it does? Why would the compiler fail to find all errors like these?

2

Problem-Solving and Computers

2—1 Introduction

There is a natural tendency, especially for beginners, to become very engrossed in the programming process and to overlook the other aspects of problem-solving. The aim of this chapter is to show how computers fit into the overall problem-solving process along with the other important parts. These parts are: precise formulation of the problem, construction of a mathematical model, and evaluation of this model. Each of the steps must be done well or the results are poor. Furthermore, one cannot compensate for an inadequate mathematical model by doing a superb programming job. Conversely, a superb mathematical model can be made useless if not adequately translated into a program.

One occasionally sees highly publicized, horrible examples of "goofs" by computers. In almost all cases, the mistakes are made by people, not by computers. It is, of course, much easier to blame the computers. In many instances the mistakes are not even in the "using the computer" phase of problem-solving. They occur, rather, in an incorrect formulation of the problem or in an incomplete mathematical model. The fact that these errors occur usually indicates that there has been inadequate testing and evaluation of the resulting programs. It is almost impossible to have 100 percent testing of a large and complex program, but in some instances the lack of testing is nearly complete. It is almost like building a car from scratch, then driving it around the block in low gear and reporting that it is all checked out and working perfectly.

2—2 Problems and Mathematical Models

Most problems go through four main stages. They are:

1. Precise formulation
2. Development of a mathematical model
3. Mathematical analysis
4. Computation of a solution

A more detailed breakdown is given at the end of Section 2–4. The first stage is rarely mentioned in formal education, particularly at the undergraduate level. The development of the mathematical model is a common part of the instructor's lectures. The usual education concentrates on the third and fourth points, which make up what we would call "problem-solving."

These stages occur in all problems, from scientific problems to common, everyday problems. In the first stage we recognize that something needs to be done, and we try to pin it down exactly. Then we bring into consideration some cause-and-effect assumptions; that is, we believe that "if I do this, then that will happen." These assumptions play the role of a mathematical model even though they may in fact be very unscientific rules of thumb, or wishful thinking. Nevertheless we begin to mull these things over in our mind and analyze the various possibilities. This analysis corresponds to a mathematical analysis even though we might actually be very illogical and unmathematical. The computational stage is much rarer in everyday problems because most people do not want to do any computation. However, we sometimes find (usually in financial problems) that we must do some calculation.

One of the greatest sources of difficulty is that the nature of the problem is not precisely known. We might expect this in some "nonscientific" areas such as personal relationships, juvenile delinquency, and poverty. However, it also occurs frequently in the supposedly well-determined, formalized scientific, and engineering areas. It is a common experience of consultants (supposedly hired to help solve problems) that people who bring them a problem actually do not know what the problem is. There is probably no systematic procedure for obtaining a precisely formulated problem from a vaguely formulated one, but it is important to be aware of this aspect of problem-solving. If one is experiencing difficulty in attacking a problem, he should first try to express in clear terms exactly what it is that he wants to do.

The development of the mathematical model involves two distinct parts. The first is the identification of the pertinent and important variables in the problem. The second is the identification of relationships between these variables and the solution of the problem. In many business applications, these relationships are the results of tax laws, accounting principles, company operating policies, and so on. The variables identified here are the basic pieces of data that go into the problem. These might be, for example, rates of pay, interest rates, equipment costs and depreciation rates, inventory levels, and so forth. In most scientific areas the relationships are the various physical, chemical, and so on, laws. In the "well-understood" areas of science, the identification of these variables and relationships is standard, and much of the early training of scientists consists in becoming familiar with standard identifications.

Problems tend to be one of two kinds. The first kind is where the important variables are known and the relationships clearly specified. That is, the mathematical model is well understood and the thing to do in the problem is to obtain the answers that are required. Typical examples of this kind of problem are:

1. Computations for the company's payroll checks
2. Preparation of invoices
3. Calculation of repayment schedules for loans
4. Calculation of tables of freight shipment rates
5. Calculation of the load a simple bridge of standard design will carry.

One might view these problems as completely solved except for organizing and carrying out the actual calculations.

The other kind of problem is where the important variables and relationships are not yet clearly identified and understood. This is by far the most common kind of problem, because these are the problems that are as yet unsolved and thus that require attention. The work at the frontiers of scientific study is primarily concerned with understanding these relationships. Thus the economist investigates, for example, the relationship between unemployment, interest rates, and inflation. The management scientist investigates, for example, the relationship between advertising strategy and sales. The agronomist investigates the relationship between various fertilizers and crop yields. The geologist studies the relationship between terrain features and mineral or petroleum deposits. It is easy to visualize these studies at the frontiers of research and knowledge, but not so easy to see that many common, ordinary problems are of this kind. Typical examples are:

1. How does one efficiently organize the data and computations for a company payroll?
2. How does one efficiently keep track of the accounts receivable and prepare the invoices?
3. How does a florist decide how much new capital is required for him to open up a branch florist shop?
4. How does one decide whether the extra speed of air freight delivery is worth the extra cost?
5. How does an engineer decide whether to use 2 large bolts or 3 smaller bolts at a particular place in a piece of machinery?

Problems like these are really tough and they occur over and over again in every kind of activity. It is important to realize that the most difficult part of these problems is the identification of important variables and relationships. Note that most of these problems are not "solved" in the ordinary sense and the successful person is the one who can consistently make good guesses at their solution.

Once the problem is precisely stated and reduced to a set of exact relationships and equations we have a mathematical model for the problem. Then we can do some mathematical analysis. That is, we can apply the various procedures and rules of logical reasoning in an effort to bring the problem (as represented by the mathematical model) into a more understandable form. The amount of analysis may vary from almost nothing to volumes.

There are two principal goals at this point. The first is to reduce the mathematical model until a form is reached from which the solution may be obtained. The second goal—often the more important—is to obtain a simple form of the problem so that the mind can grasp the mechanism by which the variables influence the solution.

Last, but not least, is the calculation of specific answers. Here, numerical, or actual, values (for example, 1.625) of the variables are used, whereas symbolic names (for example, X, Y) may have been used earlier. Computing machines have enormously increased the amount of computation that can reasonably be done, and this has made many problems solvable that previously could not be solved.

It is important to have a clear picture of the relationship between the real world and the mathematical models of it. This relationship is simply illustrated in the following diagram:

REAL WORLD PROBLEM → IDEALIZATIONS ← MATHEMATICAL MODEL

One of the effects of the high computational power of computers now available is that we can (and do) perform computations involving complex mathematical models. This activity is interesting and well defined; that is, we have a self-contained, complete, explicitly stated problem (to find answers from the mathematical model) and we can go to work on it. Sometimes we are so engrossed in this phase of problem-solving that we lose sight of the inaccuracy in the mathematical model. Thus, there is a real danger of expending considerable effort on obtaining the solution of the mathematical model to a much greater accuracy than the model represents the real world.

EXAMPLE 2–1

A MATHEMATICAL MODEL FOR MOTION

One of the most famous examples of a mathematical model is Newton's law of motion, which is often expressed as "force is equal to mass times acceleration." This law is expressed in mathematical terms by

$$f = ma.$$

We now know that this relation is only approximate, for the theory of relativity says that there are other factors that enter into the situation. And who is to say whether there are yet other effects that are not taken into account by the theory of relativity?

Newton's law is introduced in elementary physics courses, and one of the standard problems that students are asked to solve is the "rock-

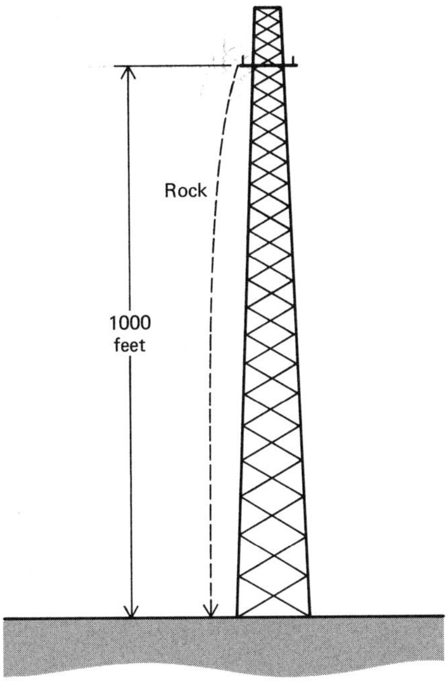

throwing" or "rock-falling" problem. This application involves further idealization about the real world. Consider the specific problem: A rock is released from a 1000-foot-high tower. How long does it take to fall to the ground? We find from Newton's law and experiment that the force of gravity per unit mass results in an acceleration of 32 feet per second. By a little bit of analysis we find that the distance d it travels in time t with constant acceleration a is given by

$$d = \frac{at^2}{2}.$$

In this problem we know that $d = 1000$ and $a = 32$. Thus we find that the time of fall t is

$$t = \left(\frac{2000}{32}\right)^{1/2} = 7.9 \text{ seconds.}$$

Now if we actually drop a rock from a 1000-foot tower and measure the time of fall, we find that it is not very close to 7.9 seconds. This is because our mathematical model does not include the effects of air. Thus, this idealized mathematical model is too crude to give accurate results of the real world problem.

EXAMPLE 2–2

A MATHEMATICAL MODEL FOR DEPRECIATION

A fact of life that one learns early is that automobiles are worth less as they become older, or they *depreciate*. A common rule of thumb for this depreciation is "their value decreases 30 percent a year." We can express this in mathematical terms by

$$V_n = V_{n-1} - .3V_{n-1} = .7V_{n-1},$$

where V_n is the value at the end of the nth year, V_{n-1} the value at the end of the $(n - 1)$st year. Thus, V_0 is the original value or cost and we see that

$$\begin{aligned} V_1 &= .7V_0, \\ V_2 &= (.7)^2V_0, \\ &\cdots \\ V_n &= (.7)^nV_0. \end{aligned}$$

This last equation is a mathematical model of depreciation.

Suppose then that one buys a car for \$3240 and keeps it for 5 years. This mathematical model says that the car's value V_5 is

$$V_5 = (.7)^5 * 3240 = .168*3240 = \$544.$$

Now if we actually try to sell this car, we may find that it is only worth \$475 or perhaps it is worth \$600. In any case, it is not likely to be worth exactly \$544 and the value predicted by this mathematical model is only approximate. This is because our model is only an idealization of how automobiles actually depreciate.

2–3 Computers in the Problem-Solving Process

It is easy to see how computers enter into the problem-solving process through the computations of answers. However, there are other ways that computers affect problem-solving and these actually have a much greater impact. First, beyond doing computations faster and more reliably, the power of the computer allows one to do less mathematical analysis. In the past much of the effort in mathematical analysis was aimed at obtaining a form of the mathematical model where the calculation of the answers would be simple. Now one does not have to spend so much effort on mathematical analysis simply to reduce the calculations. Note that there is another aim of mathematical analysis, namely to gain some insight and understanding that is not affected by this use of computers.

Much more significant is the fact that one can attack and handle more complex mathematical models. In the past one often had to make certain assumptions and idealizations simply because the model would be too hard to analyze and one would not be able to get any answers at all. Now people can and do attempt to obtain solutions from mathematical models that are very complex. Thus, a simple listing of the variables involved, the assumptions made, and the equations, relationships, and tables used might well be a report of 50 or more pages.

The idea of a mathematical model is not widespread and is probably unfamiliar to most readers of this text. Thus the current discussion seems vague and fuzzy. However, the idea of a mathematical model is so important in computing that it should be introduced early. As the reader studies computing further, he should keep these questions in his mind: What is the mathematical model here? *What assumptions have been made?* Note that in computing there will always be at least one form of the mathematical model: the computer program. The computer program contains all of the variables, the assumptions, and the relationships of the mathematical model. Programs are not so easy to read and a great deal of the difficulty in computing comes from small assumptions made in the computer program which are either incorrect or unknown to the users of the program. This is particularly apt to occur if no one has made a complete formulation of the mathematical model in a more readable form. Of course, one rarely makes a formal mathematical model for a short program, but many real-life programs (especially the more important ones) are long and complicated and one needs a formal listing of the variables, assumptions, and relationships in order to really understand what is going on.

Finally, there is yet another significant result of using computers. Even though we have just stressed the importance of making a mathematical model, it is frequently not done even in important projects. We can view the model as a complete description of what the computer program is to do and thus the absence of a model means that the person who writes the computer program will also make part of the model himself. These parts are usually small ones, but there have been occasions where important company policy decisions were made by a relatively junior person who happened to be writing the relevant computer program.

We consider two examples of applications of computers and what effects might result.

EXAMPLE 2–3

PUTTING THE COMPANY PAYROLL ON THE COMPUTER

The calculations for the company payroll are probably the most straightforward and well practiced in the whole company. After all, they have been getting the checks out every week or month for years. When management is considering changing to the computer, they are concerned with comparing the costs of doing it by hand and by computer. The analysis of these costs varies from company to company (one might even write a computer program to help in the analysis), but medium and large companies all seem to conclude that it is cheaper to do it on a computer. Once the decision is made, management tells the chief accountant to do it, the chief accountant tells the head payroll clerk to do it and assigns a programmer to help out. No one expects that company policy decisions need to be made or that explicit requirements for the payroll program need to be considered by management. They simply want the program to do the same thing that is being done by hand and they feel that is all that needs to be said.

They are correct for the 99 percent of the checks that are routine, but the other 1 percent lead to complications. These special cases are usually referred to someone in authority and some action is taken just to handle this case. This action can be very varied and involve modifying records, waiving requirements and rules, and so on. Many of these actions are much more difficult in the computer program. After all the rules and requirements are incorporated in the program and most programs have no provisions to "suspend" these rules. The result is that the person who writes the program makes critical decisions (often without realizing it) for the 1 percent or so of the cases that require special handling.

It is unlikely that anyone in management would authorize (or even allow) the company to withhold more Social Security taxes in a year than is required by law. Yet this happened to one of the authors of this book in the amount of 4¢. It turned out that this happened to about half of his fellow employees in amounts of 1¢ to 5¢ (the company never took out too little). This should, of course, never have occurred, but some programmer was not very careful in writing the part of the program that deducts these taxes. Moreover, a complaint to the payroll department had no effect because they had no provisions in their programs to correct such an error (which, of course, they never believed would happen). The payroll department's reply to the complaint is that one could get the 4¢ refunded from the government when one filed his income tax return. Most people have enough trouble with this return without trying to figure out how to get 4¢ back, so they just forget it. They will, however, always wonder who got their 4¢, the company or the government?

EXAMPLE 2–4

PUTTING INVENTORY CONTROL ON THE COMPUTER

Imagine a company warehouse that stocks several hundred different items. There is someone who is in charge and who, in particular, decides when to order new items when the stocks get low. Now this company has all its records about deliveries to and from the warehouse already in the computer. Thus one can write a program that figures out how much of each item is in the warehouse and which initiates a new purchase order when the stock of certain items gets low. Now consider what the computer programmer will do when he writes this program.

He needs to know at what level to reorder supplies and how long delivery takes. He gets this information from the man in charge of the warehouse and the scene is something like this:

"OK," says the programmer, "when do you reorder size #8 round head bolts?"

The warehouse manager thinks a moment, then replies, "When we have only 15 cases left." Actually, he reorders whenever that bin looks almost empty.

"How long does it take you to get the order?"

"Well, we get them in 6 or 7 days. Never more than 10 days. Why don't you put down 10 days to be safe?"

So the programmer incorporates in his program:

> reorder level—size 8 round head bolts = 15 cases;
> delivery time = 10 days.

Things go well until the company's main assembly line is shut down for 4 days because they ran out of #8 round head bolts, 1¼ inches long. The resulting investigation leads to transfers, demotions, and lots of loud talk, but not to the reason the shutdown occurred. In fact, the bins look empty to the warehouse manager when 18 or 20 cases are left, not 15 as he had guessed. Furthermore, because of August vacations and the Labor Day holiday, it took 13 days to get the new order of bolts. The manager always took this slow period into account in his reordering, but since it was January when he was talking to the programmer, it didn't come to his mind. The whole debacle is, of course, somehow blamed on the computer and the warehouse manager tells his wife, "I knew that #@!?# thing would foul it up sooner or later." It is interesting to note that this debacle will occur only when the time to reorder these bolts falls within a certain 3-day period in August. Since these bolts are only ordered about twice a year, the company could have, with a little luck, used this program for 30 or 40 years without any problem.

These two examples hopefully show that there is much more to putting things on a computer than just getting the arithmetic done faster. The implications are many and varied and often completely unforseen.

2–4 The Solution of a Real Problem

We now consider in some detail a real problem and go through its "solution." The problem chosen is a familiar, everyday one that many people attempt to solve. It is important to realize that the problems that we meet early in our education are *not* typical of real problems. These textbook problems have usually been carefully analyzed and have almost always been simplified, broken into small pieces, and put into a precise form. The real problem we consider now has no "standard" solution or "standard" techniques of analysis.

Original Problem Statement How do I minimize my automobile costs?

This problem is normally stated in this form. This form is not yet precise because it has some unstated assumptions. As the problem now stands, the solution is clearly not to own an automobile.

In order to obtain a precise formulation, we explicitly state some assumptions (different people use different assumptions here). First, we *assume* that we own an automobile at all times. Second, (for simplicity) we *assume* that we buy a new car, keep it until the "proper" time, and then buy another new car. Finally, we choose to measure most by the long-term average annual cost. With these assumptions, we can state the problem in a precise, if more complicated, form.

Precise Problem Statement How long should I keep a new car before trading it in on another new car so as to minimize my average annual cost?

We have identified the time, or a number of years, to keep the car as the unknown solution to the problem. The next stage is to identify the factors that affect the solution. The principal variable is the average annual cost. The variables that affect this cost are depreciation, operating costs (gas, oil, insurance, taxes, and so on), and repairs. Each of these costs depends on the age and the mileage of the car. We *assume* that the car is driven 12,000 miles a year. This assumption allows us to relate operating costs and repairs to time more easily. Denote the amount of these costs in the Ith year by DEP(I), OP(I), and REP(I), respectively, and the total cost in the Ith year by COST(I). Note that the notation COST(I) corresponds to the usual scientific notation of c_i. Here we replace the letter c by the word COST and the subscript i becomes I and is placed after COST in parentheses. This notation is standard in computing.

We now write the first part of the mathematical model of this situation:

$$\text{COST(I)} = \text{DEP(I)} + \text{OP(I)} + \text{REP(I)}.$$

The average annual cost AAC(K) for K years is then given by

$$\text{AAC(K)} = \frac{1}{\text{K}}\sum_{\text{I}=1}^{\text{K}} \text{COST(I)}.$$

The next step is to determine the dependence of these quantities on time. Those people who have studied this problem know that it is not possible to determine these costs exactly. Thus, we must assume some idealized situation in order to develop the mathematical model further. The following assumptions seem reasonable:

Depreciation We *assume* that the depreciation in the Ith year is 30 percent of the value of the car at the beginning of the year. We introduce VAL(I) as the value of the car at the end of the Ith year and we have

$$\text{DEP(I)} = .3\text{VAL(I} - 1).$$

Operating Cost We *assume* that

$$\begin{aligned} &\text{OP(I)} = 450 && \text{for I} = 1,2 \\ &\text{OP(I)} = 500 && \text{for I} > 2. \end{aligned}$$

Repair Cost We *assume* that

$$\begin{aligned} &\text{REP(I)} = 0 && \text{for I} = 1,2 \\ &\text{REP(I)} = 100 && \text{for I} = 3 \\ &\text{REP(I)} = 200 && \text{for I} = 4,5 \\ &\text{REP(I)} = 300 && \text{for I} \geq 6. \end{aligned}$$

Our mathematical model is now complete and it consists of the equations for COST(I) and AAC(K) and the three sets of assumptions for depreciation, operating cost, and repair cost. We need some analysis before we actually compute. Letting VAL(0) be the original cost of the car, we obtain the following expression for VAL(I):

$$\begin{aligned} \text{VAL}(1) &= \text{VAL}(0) - \text{DEP}(1) = .7\text{VAL}(0), \\ \text{VAL}(2) &= \text{VAL}(1) - \text{DEP}(2) = .7\text{VAL}(1) = (.7)^2\text{VAL}(0), \\ &\cdots \\ \text{VAL(I)} &= \text{VAL(I} - 1) - \text{DEP(I)} = .7\text{VAL(I} - 1) = (.7)^{\text{I}}\text{VAL}(0). \end{aligned}$$

The average annual cost is minimized by evaluating it for each possible number K of years to keep the car (up to some reasonable limit). We start computing with K = 1 and then successively increase K. We then examine the resulting values for the various K and select the K that gives the minimum average annual cost. We have made the analysis of this model and have given a method to compute the minimum cost and best value of K.

The only unspecified piece of data is the original value VAL(0). We assume it to be $3000 and obtain the following table of values for the average annual cost:

Year	1	2	3	4	5	6	7	8	9	10	20	100
AAC	1350	1215	1157	1120	1079	1058	1036	1016	998	982	895	819

We find that the mathematical model leads us to conclude that we should buy a car and keep it forever! This is unreasonable and indicates that some essential ingredient is missing from the mathematical model. In particular, now that we think of it, repair costs increase sharply at a certain point because of the unavailability of spare parts and the frequency of major repairs. We take this into account in our mathematical model by modifying our assumption about repair costs as follows:

Modified Repair Cost

$$\begin{aligned} \mathrm{REP(I)} &= 400 \quad \text{for } 11 \leq \mathrm{I} \leq 13 \\ \mathrm{REP(I)} &= 600 \quad \text{for } 14 \leq \mathrm{I} \leq 19 \\ \mathrm{REP(I)} &= 750 \quad \text{for } \mathrm{I} \geq 20. \end{aligned}$$

This reexamination leads to the modified table of costs:

Year	10	11	12	13	14	15	20	100
AAC	982	976	972	967	977	986	1022	1204

Now the mathematical model leads us to conclude that we should keep a car until it is about 13 years old. Since the model is admittedly rough, we should actually conclude that somewhere between 10 and 15 years is the "optimum" time.

Almost everyone wants to minimize his cost, yet few people keep their car this long. Thus we should examine the mathematical model once more. It seems reasonable that the important factor that has been omitted is the intangible value of having a car that is

1. flashy, 2. reliable, 3. clean, 4. worry-free, and so on.

In order to have a more realistic model, we must assign a monetary value to these intangibles. Since different people have different value systems, let us assume we have three types of individuals:

Big Shot
Average Joe
Penny Pincher.

We *assume* that these individuals are willing to pay a premium in order to have a newer car. We include this in our model by putting in an intangible cost INTAN(I) of owning a car that is in its Ith year.

Intangible Cost

	Big Shot	*Average Joe*	*Penny Pincher*
I = 1	0	0	0
I = 2	200	0	0
I = 3	400	100	10
I = 4	700	100	20
I = 5	1000	200	30
I = 6	1500	200	40
I > 6	1500	200	50

The average annual costs for this new mathematical model are given as follows:

	Year									
	1	*2*	*3*	*4*	*5*	*6*	*7*	*8*	*9*	*10*
Big Shot	1350	1315	1357	1445	1539					
Average Joe	1350	1215	1190	1170	1159	1158	1150	1141		
Penny Pincher	1350	1215	1160	1127	1091	1075	1058	1041	1025	1012

We would generally conclude from our mathematical model that a Big Shot should not keep a car more than 2 years, the Average Joe can trade in any time he feels like it after 3 years, and the Penny Pincher is still going to keep his car for about 12 years.

We now have a mathematical model that gives reasonable results. It is not sure that these are really accurate results, but this particular problem contains many unpredictable elements and it is probably not meaningful to talk about accurate results.

There is an interesting view of the process of adding the intangible cost to the model. This is not, of course, an actual expense in the same sense as gasoline. It is, however, an indication of how much it costs not to follow the least expensive course of action. Thus we can view this analysis not as a search for the cheapest strategy, but rather as a search for how much more expensive is the strategy already chosen than the least expensive strategy. This kind of analysis can sometimes give one really worthwhile insight into the consequences of one's decisions.

A Fortran program is given below which combines all three of the mathematical models developed for this example. There is a variable MODEL which runs from 1 to 3 and if this program is run, it produces the results of all three models. For the sake of simplicity only the intangible case of "Average Joe" is included. Note that this model, while certainly not super-simple, is much more

```
C     PROGRAM FOR THE SOLUTION OF THE AUTOMOBILE COST PROBLEM
C        MODEL INDICATES FIRST, SECOND OR THIRD MATH MODEL
      REAL INTAN
      MODEL = 1
    1 PRINT 2,MODEL
    2 FORMAT(1H120X22HRESULTS FOR MATH MODEL 12/9X4HYEAR,6X12HAVERAGE CO
     *ST )
      VALUE = 3000.
      KYEAR = 1
    5 YEAR = KYEAR
C            COMPUTE DEPRECIATION, REPAIR AND OPERATING COSTS
      DEP = .3*VALUE
      VALUE = VALUE - DEP
      IF(KYEAR-3)20,30,35
   20 OP  = 450.
      REP =   0.
                        GO TO 240
   30 OP  = 500.
      REP = 100.
                        GO TO 240
   35 OP  = 500.
      IF(KYEAR-6)40,60,60
   40 REP = 200.
                        GO TO 240
   60 REP = 300.
      IF(MODEL-1)240,240,100
  100 IF(KYEAR-10)240,240,110
  110 REP = 400.
      IF(KYEAR-14)240,140,140
  140 REP = 600.
      IF(KYEAR-20)240,200,200
  200 REP = 750.
C            HAVE FINISHED DEPRECIATION, REPAIR AND OPERATING COSTS
  240 INTAN = 0.
      IF(MODEL-3)300,250,250
C        PUT IN THE INTAGIBLE COST (FOR AVERAGE JOE)
  250 IF(KYEAR-2)300,300,251
  251 IF(KYEAR-4)270,270,280
  270 INTAN = 100.
                        GO TO 300
  280 INTAN = 200.
  300 COST = DEP + OP + REP + INTAN
      AAC = (COST + (YEAR -1.)*AAC)/YEAR
C        PRINT SELECTED VALUES OF AAC
  400 IF(KYEAR-20)410,410,401
  401 IF(KYEAR-40)500,410,402
  402 IF(KYEAR-100)500,410,500
  410 PRINT 420,KYEAR,AAC
  420 FORMAT(I12,F14.0)
C        GO ON TO THE NEXT YEAR UP TO 100 YEARS
  500 IF(KYEAR-100)510,600,600
  510 KYEAR = KYEAR + 1
                        GO TO 5
C        GO ON TO THE NEXT MODEL
  600 IF(MODEL-3)610,700,700
  610 MODEL = MODEL + 1
                        GO TO 1
  700 STOP
      END
```

compact and less ambiguous than the English description in the text. It is also easy (once one is familiar with the program) to modify the model in various ways.

If one visualizes how this program developed, one sees that the first program written did not have the statements 100 to 200 (they were added to make model #2) or statements 240 to 280 (they were added to model #2 to obtain model #3). Other statements were added or changed also to "support" these additions. Thus the statement REAL INTAN was added, the equation for COST (statement 300) was modified, and so forth.

This example illustrates the important steps in solving a problem from beginning to end. The steps are:

1. Recognize the problem.
2. Identify the important variables and introduce quantitative measures.
3. Formulate a precise problem.
4. Make idealizations and assumptions about the variables and their relationships. Other variables are often identified here.
5. Make a mathematical model.
6. Make an analysis of the model.
7. Compute some specific results.
8. Check these results for reasonableness. If they are unreasonable, reexamine steps 2, 3, and 4 (also 6 and 7).
9. Check these results for accuracy by comparing them with observations and measurements from the real world. If the accuracy is inadequate, reexamine steps 2, 3, and 4 (also 6 and 7).
10. Tentatively accept the mathematical model and the results it predicts about the real world, keeping in mind the assumptions and simplifications involved.

Once the problem is recognized, we begin to formulate it in precise terms. This means that we identify exactly what we want done and settle on a means of measuring the variables in the problem. From this process we can formulate a precise problem. We often introduce at this stage some assumptions or idealizations about the real problem in order to simplify things. Once we have a precise problem statement, we identify pertinent variables and relationships between them. Again, we often introduce assumptions at this point. For example, we may know that two variables are related (car-repair bills depend on the age of the car) but we might not know how they are related; thus, we assume a relationship that appears reasonable. From the mathematical model we can then do some analysis and computation and obtain a solution of the mathematical problem.

It is advisable (in fact, essential) in "vague" or "fuzzy" problems to check the solutions for reasonableness. If they appear reasonable, we may accept them. If they are unreasonable, then we must reexamine the whole process of problem formulation and solution. Thus it is particularly important to clearly display any assumptions or idealizations made. It is likely that one of the assumptions has led to the unreasonable answer. The process of making mathematical models, checking the results against reality, and refining the model can be never-ending.

Consider the example of Newton's laws of motion. For many, many years it was believed that they were exact models for motion in the physical world. Then people began to observe things that did not agree with the models. As more and more such observations were made, people began to look for a new model; Einstein's theory of relativity is the result of this research. People are still checking this new model for "reasonableness," and it is optimistic to think that relativity theory will pass all the tests put to it.

Most mathematical models stand on much less firm ground than the relativity theory, even in science. Thus, when difficulties begin to appear in correlating answers with observed results, we should not hesitate to question the validity of the mathematical model involved. In the less-understood areas, such as economics and social phenomena, we should be prepared to reexamine the mathematical model with considerable frequency.

It is interesting to note that the "word problems" that give students so much trouble are basically exercises in the construction of mathematical models. Such problems are given in a precise form and the required relationships are specified precisely in ordinary English statements. Thus, one simply must "translate" this statement of the relationships into a mathematical model; for example, a set of mathematical equations. There is no need for idealization in constructing the mathematical model. The steps taken in solving these problems are similar to the steps for solving problems in general. These steps are:

1. Recognize the problem.
2. Identify the important variables.
3. Identify the given relationships.
4. Make a mathematical model.
5. Make an analysis of the model.
6. Compute the solution.

We can take the view that the first four steps are, in fact, a language translation. The word problem is originally given in ordinary English, and at step 4, it is given in terms of mathematical symbols and variables. If the first four steps are done correctly, these two expressions of the problem are identical in content.

Problems

The following problems are "word problems" that are to be brought into mathematical form; that is, you are to introduce variables and derive a set of mathematical relations and equations that are equivalent to the word problem. Compute the solution of the problems from the mathematical model constructed.

2–4.1 A donkey and a mule are carrying some bags of wheat. The mule grumbles to the donkey: "If I had five more bags, I would be carrying twice as much as you." The donkey replies: "Yes, but if I had five more bags,

I would be carrying three times as much as you." How many bags is each carrying?

2–4.2 A man leaves \$32,000 to his three sons. The will states that the oldest son is to receive \$4000 more than the youngest and that the youngest is to receive \$2000 more than the third son. How much does each son receive?

2–4.3 A man leaves a certain sum of money to his children. He specifies the sum is to be divided as follows: The first gets \$1000 plus one tenth of the remainder of the sum. The second gets \$2000 plus one tenth of the remainder of the sum. The third gets \$3000 plus one tenth of the remainder of the sum. The fourth gets \$4000 plus one tenth of the remainder of the sum, and so on.

It is discovered that the sum is such that each child receives an equal share. How much was the sum and how many children did the man have?

2–4.4 Four persons are playing a game together. In the first game the first player loses, and each of the other players doubles his original sum. In the next game, the second player loses, and each of the other players doubles his money. In the next game, the third player loses half of his money, and the first player loses \$5.00 less than the second player lost in the second game. In this same game the second and fourth players win the same amount. Finally, in the last game, the fourth player loses twice as much as the third player lost in the preceding game, and the second player loses \$10. The first and third players share the winnings in the fourth game equally.

After playing, the players discover that they each have \$50. How much did each have before they started?

2–4.5 If 10 cows eat 10 acres of grass in 6 weeks and 8 cows eat 8 acres of grass in 3 weeks, how many cows can you put in a 20-acre pasture for 15 weeks without them going hungry? Note that the grass is growing while the cows are eating.

The following problems are given in a vaguely defined form. You are to take the incompletely defined problems and introduce various reasonable assumptions, idealizations, and so forth, to obtain a precisely defined problem. Once you have a precise statement, you are to identify the important variables and find, or assume, some specific relationships among them that lead to a mathematical model of the problem.

Note that some of the problems are actually immensely complex and you will probably need to make several idealizations in order to keep the size of the problem statement reasonable. You are not required to do any computing. You are, in effect, to do the first five steps of problem-solving.

2–4.6 Building costs are quite high, but rent is also very expensive. Construct a mathematical model to help decide which is more economical for you: to build or rent a house.

2–4.7 You are a girl's advisor in a college. A young lady comes to you for advice about the field in which she should major. Describe the important variables that enter into this decision and make a mathematical model that can be used to analyze the decision problem.

2–4.8 You are a sophomore majoring in math. You do not like it and want to change your major to business, with sales option, or engineering. How do you make your choice?

2–4.9 "Beware the Population Explosion!" This is a headline in nearly every publication today. Describe a mathematical model of the situation causing the population explosion. Define some precise indicators of the severity of this so-called "explosion," and show how you would evaluate the indicators. Some of the following variables and data might enter your considerations.

		U.S.A.	*Mexico*	*California*
Area, sq. mi.		3,625,000	758,000	156,000
Population	1950	151,000,000	25,700,000	10,500,000
	1960	179,000,000	38,000,000	15,000,000
Annual increase, %		1.4	3.4	3.7
Family size	1950	3.37	5.51	3.85
	1960	3.35	5.40	3.75
Births	1950	4,167,000	1,750,000	328,000
	1960	4,100,000	1,830,000	385,000
Deaths	1950	1,452,000	400,000	141,000
	1960	1,712,000	403,000	147,000
Pop./sq. mi.	1960	50.5	50.4	100.4
Births/1000 women	1960	2.5	6.3	3.8
Immigration	1950	104,000	52,000	375,000
	1960	265,000	68,000	694,000

2–4.10 A farmer has 640 acres producing wheat. He has a 10-year-old combine that is still good for several seasons' use even though it is rather slow and inefficient. A new machine is quite expensive but will cover his farm in about one half to two thirds the time required for the old one and will give about 5 percent more recovery of grain. What would you advise him to do: use the old one or buy the new one?

2–4.11 An instructor has grades at the end of the semester as given in the table below. He assigned regular homework plus two special, more difficult, problem sets and gave four pop quizzes. The two 1-hour exams seem quite satisfactory, but the midterm exam had several poorly stated questions on it which misled several students. The final exam was too difficult and all but the very best students made very low grades.

Present what you feel to be a reasonable method for grading the students, and apply it to the grades listed below. Do you find that your method results in a good ranking of the students?

	Stu. 1	*Stu. 2*	*Stu. 3*	*Stu. 4*	*Stu. 5*	*Stu. 6*
Regular homework (225 points)	182	212	64	168	71	219
Special homework (50 points)	31	45	28	33	13	49
Pop quizzes (40 points)	28	36	32	29	16	38
First hour exam (100 points)	68	57	91	62	37	88
Midterm exam (150 points)	112	98	103	91	60	61
Second hour exam (100 points)	59	55	87	61	32	88
Final exam (150 points)	16	11	89	19	6	57

3

Algorithms and Program Construction

3–1 Algorithmic Processes

The word "algorithm" is derived from the name of a ninth-century Arab mathematician, Al-Khuwarizmi. He was interested in solving certain problems in arithmetic, and he devised a number of methods for solving them. These methods were presented as a list of specific instructions (much like a recipe), and his name has become attached to such methods.

An algorithm is, intuitively speaking, a recipe, a set of instructions or the specifications of a process for doing something. That something is usually solving a problem of some sort. Thus, the term "algorithmic process" is slightly redundant, but there are extra connotations to the term. Thus, we expect an algorithm to have several properties. First an algorithm must be unambiguous; that is, we are operating in a certain framework or context, and in this framework each instruction in an algorithm must mean exactly one thing. The following examples illustrate this point.

Cooking Algorithm

BAD: Put some spice in the batter.
GOOD: Add 1 teaspoon of ginger to the batter.

Computing Algorithm

BAD: Take two numbers and add them.
GOOD: Take x, add 10 to it, square the result, and call it y.

Note how much neater the language of mathematics is for expressing this algorithm

$$y = (x + 10)^2.$$

The prime examples of algorithms are computer programs and it is because we want to construct such algorithms (or programs) that we are interested in discussing their properties.

It is surprisingly difficult to be unambiguous. Consider the number of times that we receive (or give) confusing instructions on how to do something. Instructions to a computer are rarely ambiguous, but this is because computers only accept certain simple instructions. However, we find, more often than we like, that the computer does something completely unexpected when we thought we had written an airtight, foolproof set of instructions.

In addition to being unambiguous, an algorithm must stop. That is, the process described must come to a conclusion. Furthermore, when it stops, it is somehow supposed to report whether or not it has achieved its objective. It is quite easy to write a set of instructions for a computer which does not include a termination.

Let us examine some problems and algorithms.

Problem Is 7319 a prime number?

Algorithm Divide 7319 by each of the numbers 2,3,4, . . ., 7317, 7318. If any division is exact, the answer is no; otherwise it is yes.

This is a sure-fire, unambiguous solution procedure for this problem. There are much more efficient algorithms for this problem, but this one does provide the solution to the problem.

Problem Make a million dollars.

Procedure Take ten million dimes and go to Las Vegas. Play the dime slot machines there until we have either (1) twenty million dimes or (2) no dimes at all.

Note that this procedure might not solve the problem and, in general, we do not require an algorithm to do so. Of course we are most interested in those that always do solve the problem. This procedure fails to be an algorithm because it might never terminate. We might play the slot machines forever without either losing or making a million dollars (the people in Las Vegas arrange things so that it is unlikely that this procedure continues too long).

Problem Fill up that ditch from that pile of sand.

Algorithm Take a shovel and start shoveling sand into the ditch. When the ditch is full, stop.

This algorithm is very simple and unambiguous. We are certain that it eventually stops even though we might have no idea of how long someone has to shovel.

We have seen a number of examples of algorithms and described them in general terms. One of the most satisfactory definitions of the word algorithm is based on the intuitive concept of a machine (or mechanical process). We envisage idealized machines, which might not exist as physical objects and which, indeed, might be impossible to construct. Nevertheless, these machines have a means to receive instructions, and they react to these instructions in a certain deterministic way. A simple model of how a machine receives instructions is to visualize that the machine has buttons on it. When a button is pushed, the machine responds. This model is a little too simple because we want the machine to be able to react in different ways according to the state that it is in. Thus, we want to give a machine an instruction such as: "Look at yourself. If you are in such and such a state (or condition), do thus and so. Otherwise, do this and that." This kind of instruction is compatible with the idea that the *machine is completely deterministic.* We emphasize that the machine operations involve no random or uncertain processes. Thus, a process whose actions depend on the outcome of flipping coins does not satisfy this condition.

We define an algorithm as a *list of instructions* for such a machine or mechanical process. When the operations are carried out as instructed, a termination point must be reached.

There are many real machines to which this definition applies directly, for example, a desk calculator (the operations involve arithmetic and entering numbers into the machine), a typewriter (the operations include hitting the keys, setting margins, shifting, and returning the carriage). These real machines are, of course, not infallible like the idealized machines used to define algorithms.

We are most interested in machines that perform mathematical and logical operations. The prime and most important example of a real machine to which this definition applies is the computer. Indeed, it is not too far wrong to say that computer science is the study of what can be done, and how to do it, with mathematical machines (either real or idealized). However, this view of computer science is perhaps too narrow, for present computers can already perform a variety of "nonmathematical" operations (for example, draw pictures, turn off ovens, open doors, and order spare parts). It is clear that future computers will be able to take a very broad range of action.

3–2 Flowcharts

We have reached the point where we need a better way to describe algorithms. So far we have described them in one of two ways. The first is to use a combination of natural English and mathematical notation. There are several drawbacks to this method:

1. The description is usually not concise.
2. The English language is ambiguous.
3. These descriptions do not reveal the basic structure of the algorithms. They are hard to grasp.

The second way is by a Fortran program. There are also several drawbacks to this method:

1. The description is usually not concise.
2. These descriptions do not reveal the basic structure of the algorithms. They are hard to grasp.
3. Many people do not understand Fortran and it takes considerable study to learn it.

We introduce here another "language" for describing and expressing algorithms. We use the word language to indicate a means of expressing information for communication. The language we are about to use does not resemble English, or most artificial languages, but it is effective for communication.

Flowchart Language A flowchart consists basically of a diagram of lines connecting boxes that contain some statements (often abbreviated) in natural language or jargon. The boxes represent groups of elementary steps of the algorithm, and the lines indicate the relationships among the groups. The statements in the boxes are simply the instructions in the algorithm. They are to be performed in *top-to-bottom* order. The lines have arrows on them which indicate the order in which the various boxes are executed. Thus, we can follow the lines and see the "flow" of the algorithm. This is where the name flowchart originates.

One feature of a flowchart is that a question may be put into one of the boxes. Then various lines leaving that box are labeled (often by yes or no), and the line is followed that corresponds to the answer to the question. We distinguish the boxes where decisions are made by rounding their corners.

Consider the example of an algorithm for fixing a flat tire (see Figure 3-1). We can follow through the algorithm quickly and see its general structure in a few moments. A description of the algorithm in ordinary English is considerably longer, and the relationship of the various parts of the algorithm is not nearly so apparent.

One of the essential distinctions between flowcharts and natural language occurs at the branches of an algorithm. Natural language (and a programming language like Fortran) is serial in nature. Thus, when a branch is to be made, one branch must be followed first, then the other. In a flowchart, the branch is represented naturally in a graphical manner and the two (or more) branches are presented simultaneously. (Examples are seen in Figure 3–1 at the boxes which contain: Front tire?, Is it flat?, Ruined?.) This fact is often described by saying that flowcharts allow a two-dimensional expression of algorithms, whereas

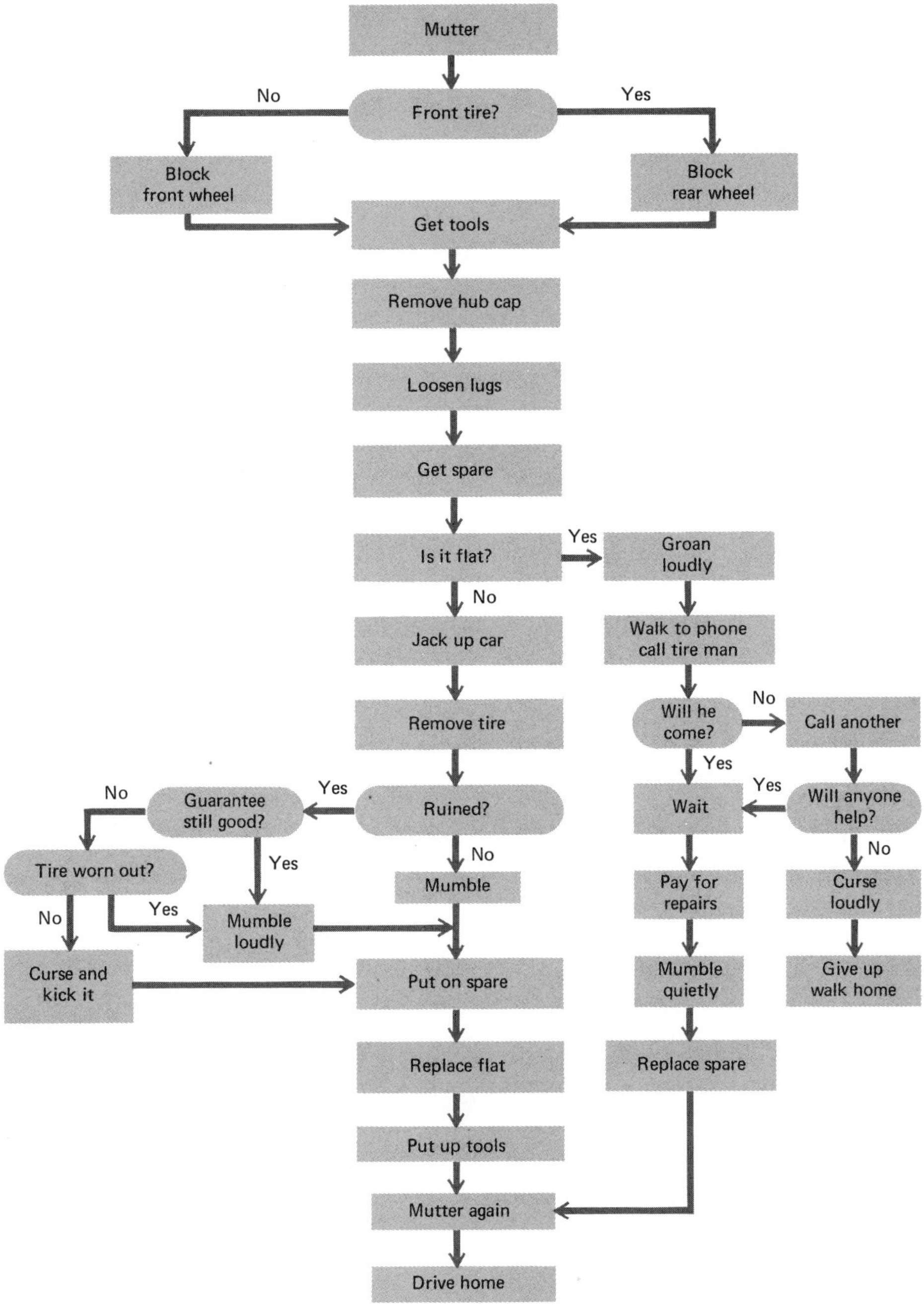

FIGURE 3–1. Flowchart of an algorithm for fixing flat tires.

natural language (and most other languages) give a sequential, linear, or one-dimensional expression of the algorithm.

Since branching occurs on the basis of various tests or questions, the location and relationship of the branches indicate the logical structure of the algorithm. The primary use of flowcharts is to express the logical structure in a form that is readily grasped by the mind.

The systematic use of flowcharts spread with the beginning of automatic computation in the late 1940s. For a period it was thought that a flowchart should be made for every program to be executed by a computer. Keep in mind that instructing computers (that is, writing programs) was much more complicated then than now. There arose a much more formal flowchart language than that presented here. It included many shapes of boxes to indicate the various types of elementary steps in the algorithm, and many elaborate flowcharts were made. However, experience soon showed that all the detail was not required, and many people wrote computer programs without making flowcharts. Thus the role of flowcharts in algorithm expression (particularly for computers) is much smaller than had been anticipated some years ago.

The main use of flowcharts now lies in two areas:

1. The communication and analysis of the logical structure of algorithms by people.
2. The documentation of complicated programs. This latter use is actually a special case of the first.

The first use is particularly important during the construction of programs. At that time we often do not know what a program is doing—or should be doing—and it is very useful to draw rough flowcharts to visualize the structure of the program and the flow of the process.

Flowcharts are used frequently in the remainder of this chapter and later chapters in order to describe programs. Most people find flowcharts the easiest way to describe and understand programs and algorithms, particularly complicated ones. One might make an analogy between a flowchart for a program and an outline for a theme or term paper.

Problems

Describe an algorithm and make a flowchart of it for each of the first five problems.

3–2.1 Getting to class.

3–2.2 Adding two 5-digit numbers.

3–2.3 Enrolling for classes.

3–2.4 Making coffee.

3–2.5 Solving a problem in physics or economics or balancing a checking account.

3–2.6 Translate the following flowchart into a Fortran program and run it with some data.

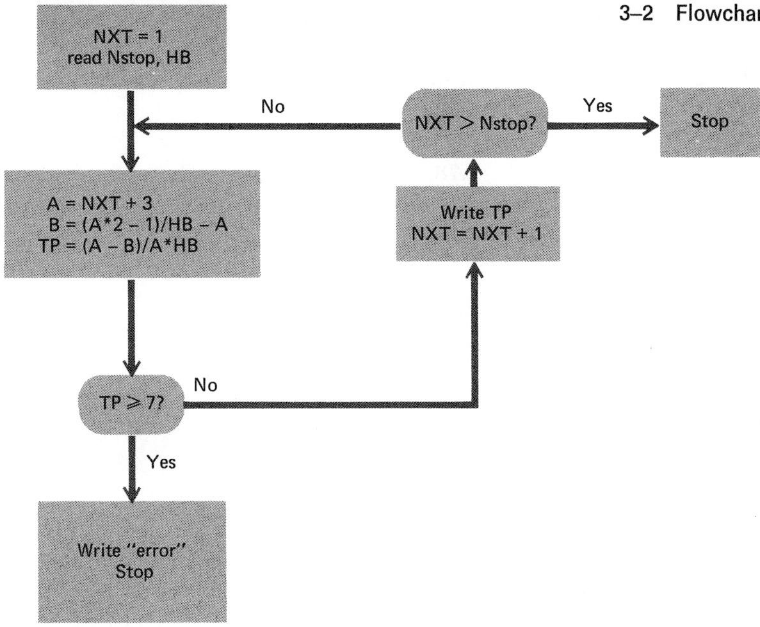

3–2.7 Translate the following flowchart into a Fortran program. Run it for NX = 20 and some set of X values. It is to compute the largest value of the average of two successive pairs of X values and print out this value and an indicator of where it occurred.

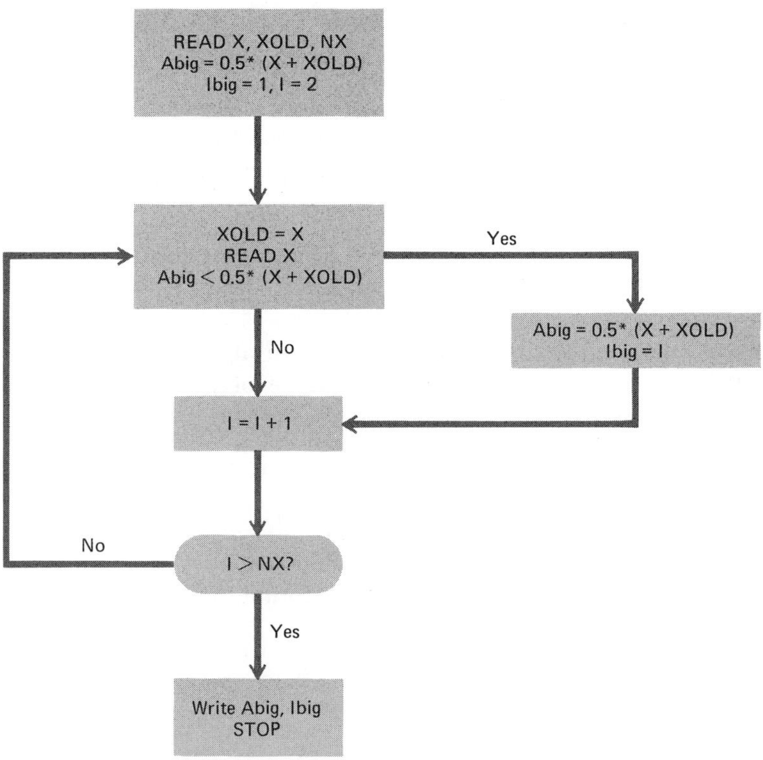

3–2.8 Translate the following flowchart into a Fortran program and run it for several values of data; for example,

.78,	3,	12.1,	1
16.1,	2,	3.7,	1
14.2,	2,	1.32,	3

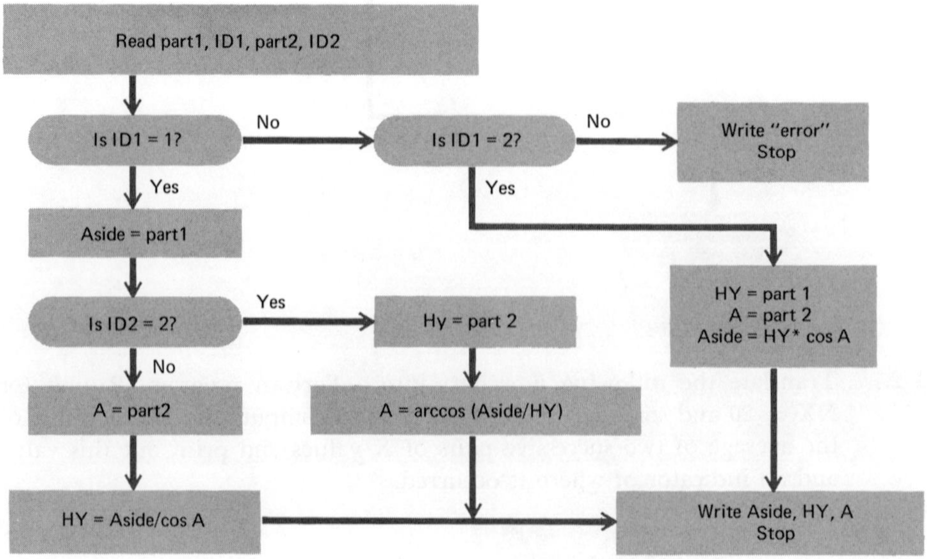

This program is to "solve" right triangles. The parts read in are two of the three quantities: one side (ID = 1), the hypotenuse (ID = 2), one angle (ID = 3, value in radians). The output of the program is all three of these values (Aside, HY, and A).

3–2.9 Suppose the solution of a problem is given in the form

$$x = \cot(25 + t),$$

where t (in degrees) is known. Describe an algorithm that uses trigonometric tables to obtain a numerical value of the solution. Verify that it works correctly for $t = 945°$ and $t = -630°$.

3–2.10 Suppose the solution of a problem is given in the form

$$x = \log(4t + 1),$$

where t is known. Describe an algorithm that uses a table of logarithms to obtain a numerical value of the solution. Verify that it works correctly for $t = 89$ and $t = -.1$.

3–2.11 Modify the algorithm of Problem 3–2.9 to use a slide rule instead of trigonometric tables.

3–3 Basic Components of Programs

Four different examples are considered in this section and programs are developed to solve the problems in them. Each of these problems is of some interest in itself and the programs obtained might well be what someone wants. However, the main motivation for considering these examples is that they involve techniques that occur over and over again in programming. They seem always to be modified in some slight detail in each application, but they are among the basic building blocks of programs.

EXAMPLE 3–1

SUMS AND AVERAGES

The simplest situation arises when we have a known number of items and want to find their sum and average. Thus, if we have five quantities A1, A2, A3, A4, and A5, we can use

```
SUM = A1+A2+A3+A4+A5
AVER= SUM/5.
```

and the calculation is done.

Frequently this approach is not feasible because either there are too many terms in the sum to write down or we do not know how many terms there are when the program is written. Thus an instructor may want one program to compute his average grades for each term. His number of students varies and he decides to punch their grades on cards and then read them into his program to compute the average.

In order to do this he must know when his last grade card is read, otherwise his Fortran program stops when it runs out of cards. One can indicate this by putting an extra nonsense card at the end of the deck and then check each card to see if it is this nonsense card. Let us assume that he places a grade of −99 behind his deck of grade cards.

His strategy is now shown in the flowchart in Figure 3–2. We see that he introduces two crucial variables, SUM and KOUNT. SUM is the total of the grades read in so far and KOUNT is the number of grades. Each of the variables are set equal to zero before any grades are read. The algorithm given in this flowchart can be written in Fortran as shown.

```
Column          5|6|7
         C           INITIALIZE VARIABLES
                    KOUNT = 0
                    SUM   = 0
         C           READ A GRADE
                2   READ 5,GRADE
                5   FORMAT(10X,F4.0)
         C           TEST FOR THE END
                    IF(GRADE+99.) 10,50,10
```

```
   10 KOUNT = KOUNT + 1
      SUM   = SUM + GRADE
          GO TO 2
C         FIND AVERAGE, PRINT RESULTS
   50 AVER = SUM/FLOAT(KOUNT)
      PRINT 52,KOUNT,SUM,AVER
   52 FORMAT(5X 9HTHERE ARE I4,7H GRADES /
     *5X10HWITH SUM =F6.0, 12H AND AVERAGE F5.1)
      STOP
      END
```

OUTPUT

```
Column   5
         THERE ARE 22 GRADES
         WITH SUM 1642. AND AVERAGE 74.7
```

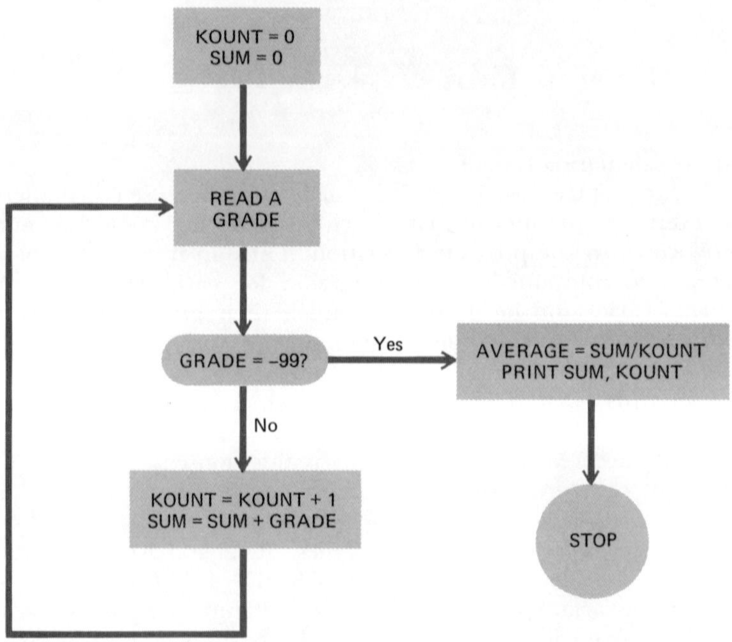

FIGURE 3–2. Flowchart of a program to compute the average grade.

EXAMPLE 3–2

MAXIMUM AND LOCATION OF THE MAXIMUM

This example is a slightly more complicated variation of the previous one. Now we want to find the largest number in a list of numbers and where it occurs (that is, is it the first, the second, or ?). With a short list of known length one can directly use the built-in Fortran function AMAX1 as follows.

```
ABIG = AMAX1(A1,A2,A3,A4,A5)
```

However, this does not tell us which one is the largest and there is no simple, one line Fortran statement to obtain it. The following Fortran code does obtain the position POSBIG, but it is not so simple. One cannot do much better with the basic Fortran statements we have available at this point.

```
     IF( ABIG-A1) 1,10,1
   1 IF( ABIG-A2) 2,20,2
   2 IF( ABIG-A3) 3,30,3
   3 IF( ABIG-A4)50,40,50
  10 POSBIG = 1.
        GOTO 60
  20 POSBIG = 2.
        GOTO 60
  30 POSBIG = 3.
        GOTO 60
  40 POSBIG = 4.
        GOTO 60
  50 POSBIG = 5.
  60    -----
```

This looks very cumbersome indeed. The next chapter presents Fortran statements that accomplish this a little neater, but not much.

Let us reconsider the situation in Example 3–1 again and assume that the instructor wants not only the average grade, but also the highest grade and who made it. The flowchart of Figure 3–2 still indicates the general strategy; we need merely to put more in the box where the SUM is computed. Assume that the card contains not only the grade, but also a student ID number in columns 1 to 10 (we skipped these in the program for Example 3–1). We now introduce two more variables, HIGH, the highest grade found so far and IHIGH, the ID of the highest grade found so far. The key box in Figure 3–2 is then enlarged to be as shown in Figure 3–3. We see that the highest grade is no longer computed using AMAX1 and the determination of HIGH and IHIGH is made on the basis of one comparison (which used to be incorporated in AMAX1). The reason for the simplification is that the flowchart already contains the machinery to go through the grades, whereas in the earlier Fortran segment we had to go through them completely just to find the position of the largest element.

One question still remains, namely, what are the proper initial values for HIGH and IHIGH? We see that IHIGH does not have to be initialized at all since it does not depend on previous ID's. We want HIGH to start out so that the largest of HIGH and the first value of GRADE is always GRADE. This would happen if HIGH starts out as minus infinity, but most Fortran systems do not have such a number. We can set its initial value to anything that we are certain will be smaller

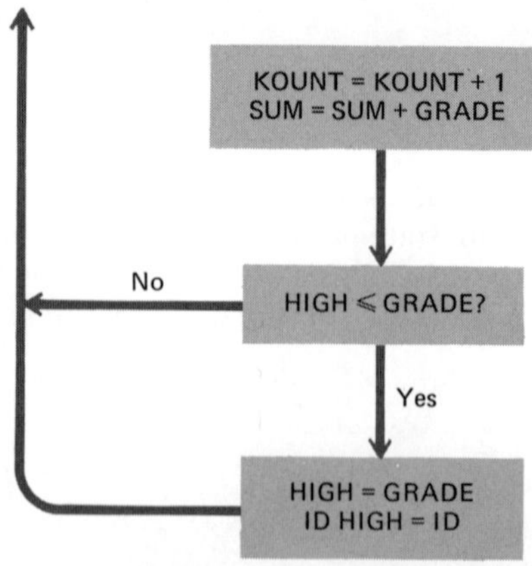

FIGURE 3–3. Replacement for the lower box of Figure 3–2.

than any possible grade. Let us assume that the lowest possible grade is zero, so an initial value of −1 is small enough for HIGH.

A complete Fortran program for Example 3–1 and Example 3–2 is given below.

```
C          INITIALIZE VARIABLES
      KOUNT = 0
      SUM   = 0
      HIGH  = -1.
C          READ GRADE, ID NUMBER
    2 READ 5,ID,GRADE
    5 FORMAT(I10,F4.0)
C          TEST FOR THE END
      IF(GRADE+99.) 10,50,10
   10 KOUNT = KOUNT + 1
      SUM   = SUM + GRADE
      IF(HIGH-GRADE) 2,15,2
   15 IHIGH = ID
      HIGH = GRADE
          GO TO 2
C          FINAL RESULTS AND OUTPUT
   50 AVER = SUM/FLOAT(KOUNT)
      PRINT 52,KOUNT,SUM,AVER,HIGH,IHIGH
   52 FORMAT(5X 9HTHERE ARE I4,7H GRADES /
     15X,10HWITH SUM = F6.0,12H AND AVERAGE F5.1/
     25X,16HHIGHEST GRADE IS F4.0,3H BY I10)
      STOP
      END
```

OUTPUT

```
THERE ARE 22 GRADES
WITH SUM = 1642. AND AVERAGE 74.6
HIGHEST GRADE IS 96. BY    136048
```

Note that if there is a tie for the highest grade, this program prints the last one of these that tied.

EXAMPLE 3–3

TABLE LOOKUP

It is common to have some information given in the form of tables. In the previous chapter we saw several small tables associated with the automobile cost problem. There are a variety of ways to look things up in a table and we discuss a few of the basic ones here. Assume that one has a table of life expectancy versus age as in Table 3–1. Consider a computation involving insurance in a particular company where it is necessary to estimate the life expectancy for retired employees.

TABLE 3–1

Life expectancy table (U.S. white males) giving expected number of years remaining

Age	*40*	*45*	*50*	*55*	*60*	*65*	*70*	*75*	*80*	*85*
Life Expectancy	31.6	27.2	23.0	19.3	15.8	12.8	10.2	7.9	5.8	4.2

Given a person's age, call it AGE, the simplest thing to do is to find the closest age entry in the table and then use the corresponding life expectancy estimate. There is no ordinary mathematical formula for the multiple of 5 closest to a given AGE (which is what we need). There are, however, ways to obtain this in Fortran. The first way shown below uses the peculiar nature of integer arithmetic in Fortran and the other two use built-in functions (we assume AGE is real).

```
ANEAR = (IFIX(AGE+2.5)/5)*5
ANEAR = 5*INT((AGE+2.5)/5.0)
ANEAR = AGE - AMOD((AGE+2.5),5.0)
```

Assume that we know that ANEAR, the nearest entry in the table to AGE, always comes out to be between 40 and 85. We could set ANEAR = AMIN1 (85.,ANEAR) just to make sure that we do not get a value larger than 85.

The natural way to find the match of ANEAR with a table entry is to start at 40 and check each entry until a match is made. The resulting code in Fortran appears as follows:

```
Column    5|6|7
              IF( ANEAR-45. ) 40,45,1
            1 IF( ANEAR-55. ) 50,55,2
            2 IF( ANEAR-65. ) 60,65,3
            3 IF( ANEAR-75. ) 70,75,4
            4 IF( ANEAR-85. ) 80,85,85
           40 EXPECT = 31.6
                 GO TO 100
           45 EXPECT = 27.2
                 GO TO 100
C             -----
C             STATEMENT 50 TO 80 SET EXPECT FOR 50 TO 80
C             -----
           85 EXPECT =  4.2
          100 -----
```

Note that only half as many IF's are required as table entries. There are complaints one can make about this method. First, it takes a lot of programming. We will later see ways to do the same searching with many fewer Fortran statements (about 5 will do it instead of 24). This fact illustrates the point that even though the Fortran given in Chapter 1 allows one to do everything, the remaining Fortran statements can simplify things very much.

More critical is the fact that this scheme probably does much more computation than really required. Most retired employees have ANEAR equal to 65, 70, or 75. For these people we have to always go through the first two IF's and usually the third one. Each IF statement involves three comparisons which means that most of the time one makes 6 or 8 unnecessary operations. One can greatly increase the average efficiency by simply reordering the table and the corresponding program (one really does not reorder the table but just visualizes it as reordered). The new table is shown in Table 3–2 and the corresponding IF statements below that.

TABLE 3–2
The life expectancy table rearranged

Age	*65*	*70*	*75*	*80*	*85*	*60*	*55*	*50*	*45*	*40*
Life expectancy	12.8	10.2	7.9	5.8	4.2	15.8	19.3	23.0	27.2	31.6

```
  IF( ANEAR-65. )  3,65,1
1 IF( ANEAR-75. ) 70,75,2
2 IF( ANEAR-85. ) 80,85,85
3 IF( ANEAR-55. )  4,55,60
4 IF( ANEAR-45. ) 40,45,50
```

This table lookup scheme requires the same amount of Fortran code, but it finds the most frequent cases first and thus is more efficient on the average. A little study shows that we did more than just reorder the table. We split it into three parts with the first IF statement (the age 60 and younger part, the age 65 part, and the age 70 and older part) and then did a systematic search in each of the parts. Further, we went from old to young in one of the parts because we thought there would be more older cases for that part of the table.

The net result of this scheme is more than just reordering and doing a usual table lookup. Note, for instance, that some cases (ANEAR = 80 and 85) go through all five IF's in the first scheme, but none of them go through more than three IF's in the second one. The two schemes are compared graphically in Figure 3–4.

The idea used in the second scheme is called *binary search.* The word binary refers to breaking the search into two parts. This is not quite correct for the arithmetic IF as it allows one to break the table into two "big" parts plus one exact entry. The efficiency of the binary search approach is illustrated in Figure 3–5 where a table lookup for ages 30 to 100 is illustrated. Note that even with this larger table, no case ever goes through more than three IF statements and only 7 are used in the program. The first scheme proposed would require 14 IF statements in this situation.

Table 3–1 is rather coarse and a big change takes place in ANEAR between ages 57 years 3 months and 57 years 7 months. The expectancy changes from 19.3 years to 15.8 years which is clearly excessive. One way to

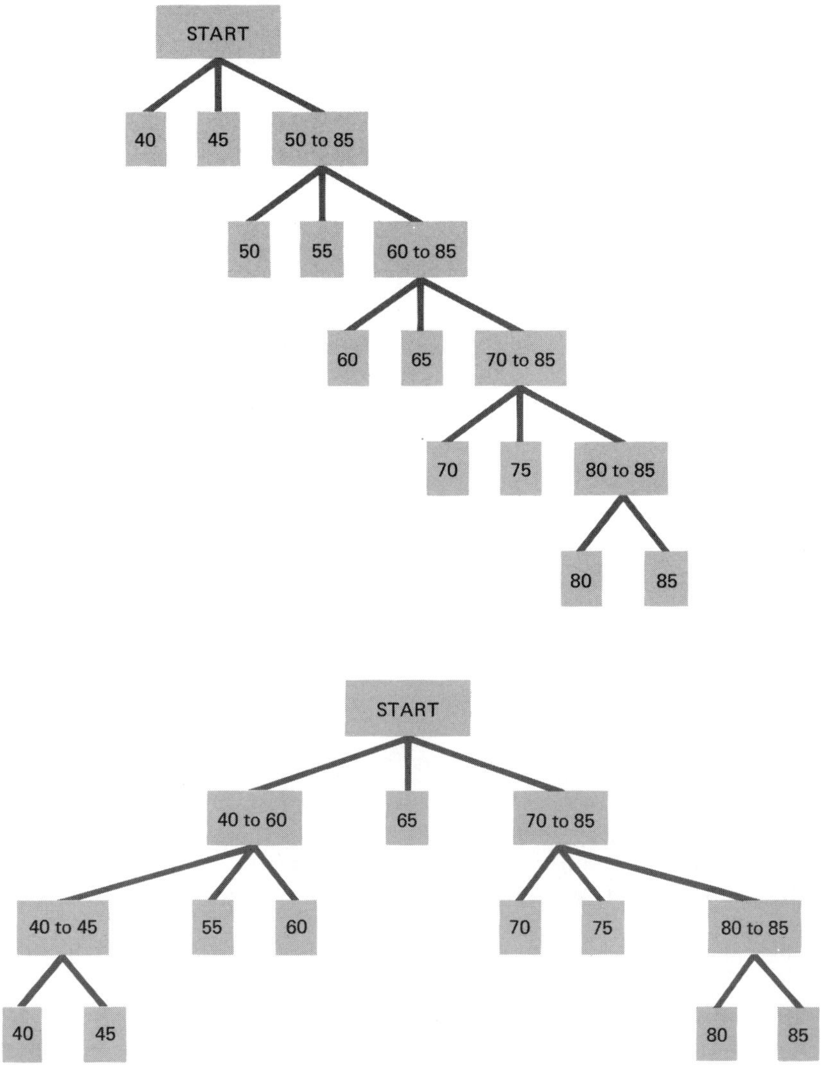

FIGURE 3–4. Graphical display of the table look up tests and branches made for the first scheme (top) and the second scheme (bottom).

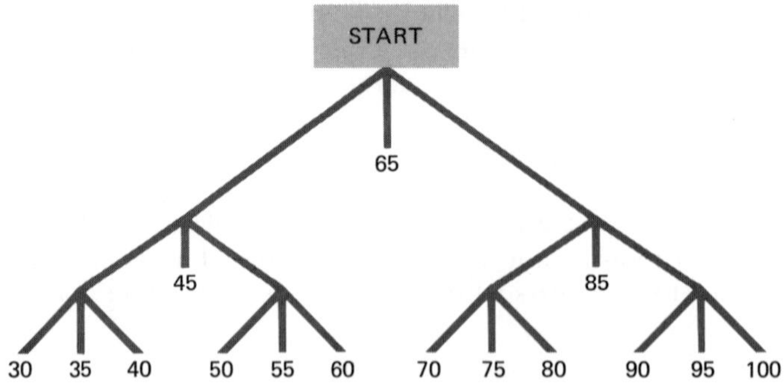

FIGURE 3–5. Table look up using binary search (with arithmetic IF's) for a table with ages from 30 to 100 (15 entries).

avoid this sudden, discontinuous change is to use *linear interpolation.* To do this one must find the table entries just above and just below the age at hand. Then one takes a weighted average of the table values with the weights chosen to emphasize the closest entry. Let AHIGH and ALOW be the table entries just above and below AGE. They may be calculated in Fortran by

```
ALOW = 5*(IFIX(AGE)/5)
AHIGH= ALOW + 5
```

Suppose that a table lookup is made to locate the corresponding life expectancy values EXLOW and EXHIGH. The weighted average to use then is

```
Column  5|6|7
         | |EXPECT = EXLOW*(AHIGH-AGE)/(AHIGH-ALOW)
         |+|           +EXHIGH*(AGE-ALOW)/(AHIGH-ALOW)
```

which can be expressed more simply (since AHIGH − ALOW is always 5) by

```
EXPECT = .2*(EXLOW*(AHIGH-AGE)+EXHIGH*(AGE-ALOW))
```

The use of this linear interpolation makes the values used from the table vary nicely as the ages vary.

There is another approach to table lookup which is frequently possible and very efficient. We have not seen the Fortran statements required to do it well (see Example 4–1 of Chapter 4), so we only describe the general idea here. The first thing to do is to *calculate* where the table entry is located rather than search for it. Note that this requires a very systematic table and thus is not always possible. For Table 3–1 we can calculate the table position index by the formula

```
INTRY = IFIX(AGE+2.5)/5 - 7
```

for the nearest entry and the low and high table indexes are just INTRY and INTRY+1. What we need (and what is missing at this point) is a way to go directly to this position and obtain the required value. Thus if INTRY turns out to be 5 (as it would for AGE = 60), we want to obtain the fifth life expectancy entry of Table 3–1. In Chapter 4 we will see how to do this directly in Fortran.

One of the main points of this example is that there are several ways to do table lookup and some are much more efficient than others. Most important, however, is the idea that one should think about the frequency one uses the various entries and proceed accordingly. Thus in Chapter 2 there is a small table of repair costs versus years for 1 to 100 years. In that problem each entry is to be used once. The last 80 entries are the same and thus we can do the table lookup with one IF test for 80 percent of the cases if we first test whether the year is larger than 20 or not. The simple linear search (from high to low) is not quite the most efficient scheme for the remaining 20 percent of the cases, but it is close. The conclusion is that even though a binary search is usually much more efficient than a linear one, one must verify that for each table lookup problem in order to be sure.

A much more detailed discussion of searching is given in Chapter 10. In many real computer applications, the success or failure of the project depends on finding an efficient searching method.

EXAMPLE 3–4

INFORMATION EXTRACTION FROM A CARD FILE

Consider an insurance company that wishes to study the occurrences of single car accidents and, in particular, to study their relationship to horsepower and to characteristics of male drivers. This company has a file of thousands of cards where it keeps its accident records. There are three cards for each accident and they contain the following information in the columns indicated:

Card 1:

Manufacturer 1–15	Model 17–35	Horsepower 40–43
Manufacturer code 16	Model code 36–38	Weight 44–48

Card 2:

Accident type 1–15	Damage—Car 1: 18–23	Other Damage 30–34
Accident code 16–17	Damage—Car 2: 24–29	Persons Injured 35–36

Card 3:

Driver's Name 1–24	Age 31–33	Arrests 40–42
Policy number 25–30	Sex 34–35	Accidents 43–45
	Area Rate Code 36–39	

The cards for two accidents are shown in Figure 3–6.

On the basis of the loosely stated requirements and knowledge of the information available, a programmer is instructed to extract a set of information which sheds some light on the situation and which is of interest to management. The programmer decides that the following information is needed:

1. The total number of single car accidents
2. The number involving high horsepower cars
3. The number involving male drivers
4. The number involving male drivers under 30 and high horsepower
5. The number involving male drivers under 30 with a total of traffic arrests and accidents of 2 or more.

In addition, for each accident in groups 2, 4, and 5 a line is to be printed as follows:

Policy Number, Horsepower, Damage, Sex, Age, Record

(where record is the number of traffic arrests and accidents).

In order to process the cards, we must know the following code numbers:

Single car accident: code = 6,
Male driver: code = 1.

The basic strategy of the program is to read three cards (extracting the proper information) then check to see which, if any, group the accident falls into. If it is an accident of one of these groups, the appropriate totals are increased and, in groups 2, 4, and 5, a line printed out. The variables

T1, T2, T3, T4, T5

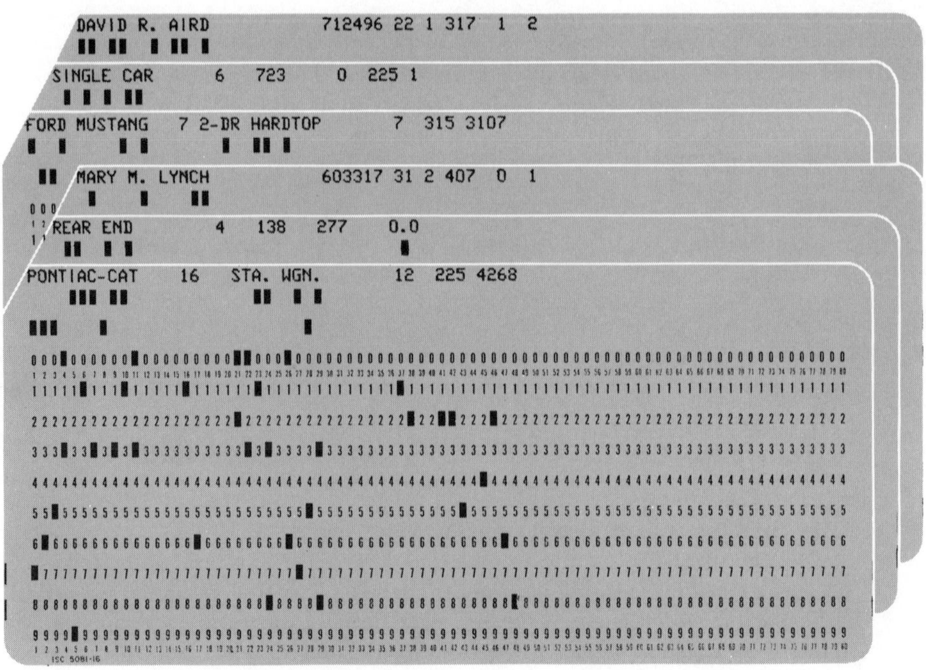

FIGURE 3–6. The card information for two accidents.

are introduced as the totals for groups 1 to 5. At the end of the card file their totals are printed out as a summary. The end of the card file is signaled by three blank cards. Thus, accident type, horsepower, and policy number are all zero, and the program goes into the final summary in this case. Note that it is not safe to check on just one of these numbers as such files often have incomplete information which is just left blank.

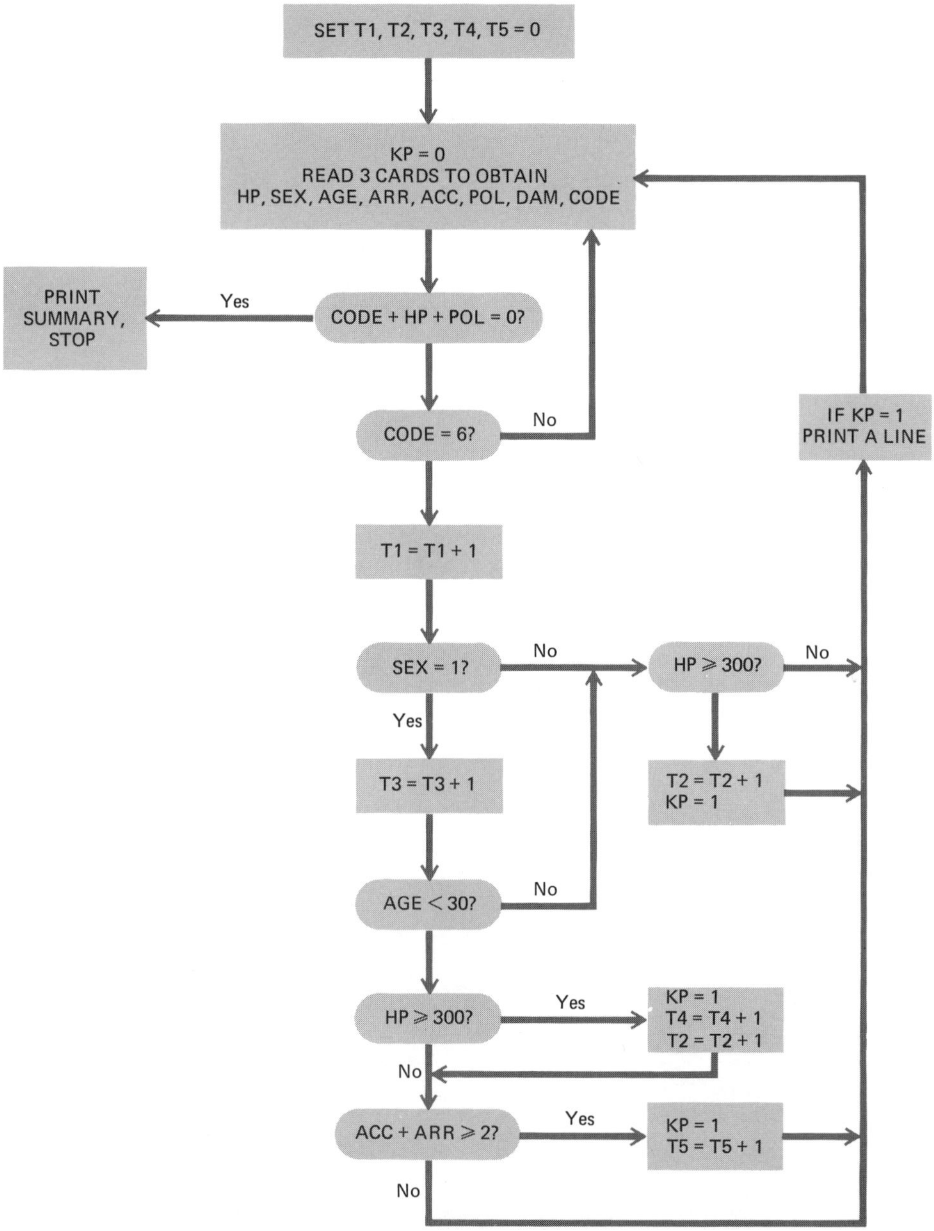

FIGURE 3–7. Flowchart of processing the insurance company files to extract information on single car accidents.

The algorithm is given in some detail in the flowchart of Figure 3–7. The variables appearing there are, in addition to T1, . . ., T5,

HP = horsepower
SEX = driver's sex
AGE = driver's age
ARR = number of traffic arrests in records
ACC = number of traffic accidents in records
POL = policy number
DAM = damage to car #1
CODE = code for accident type
KPRINT = switch set = 1 when a line is to be printed.

A Fortran program to carry out this study is given also.

```
C          INITIALIZE COUNTERS
      T1 = 0
      T2 = 0
      T3 = 0
      T4 = 0
      T5 = 0
C          PRINT HEADING
      PRINT 1
    1 FORMAT(1H120X16HSINGLE CAR CASES /
     * 8X,6HPOLICY,7X,2HHP,6X,6HDAMAGE,4X3HSEX,4X3HAGE,4X6HRECORD)
    2 KPRINT = 0
      READ 10, HP,CODE,DAM,POL,AGE,SEX,ARR,ACC
   10 FORMAT(39X,F4.0 /
     *         15X,F2.0,F6.0 /
     *         24X,F6.0,F3.0,F2.0,2F3.0 )
C          TEST FOR END OF CARD FILE
      IF(CODE+HP+POL) 200,200,15
   15 IF(CODE-6.)  2,20,2
C          HAVE A SINGLE CAR ACCIDENT
   20 T1 = T1+1.
C          CHECK SEX
      IF(SEX-1.) 50,25,50
   25 T3 = T3 + 1.
C          CHECK AGE
      IF(AGE-30.) 30,50,50
C          HAVE MALE UNDER 30
   30 IF(HP-300.)40,35,35
   35 T4 = T4 + 1.
      T2 = T2 +1.
      KPRINT = 1
   40 IF(ACC+ARR-2.)60,45,45
   45 T5 = T5 + 1.
      KPRINT = 1
           GO TO        100
C          CHECK HP FOR FEMALES, OLDER MALES
   50 IF(HP-300.) 2,55,55
   55 T2 = T2 +1.
      KPRINT = 1
   60 IF(KPRINT-1) 2,100,2
C          PRINT A LINE FOR GROUPS 2,4,5
```

```
  100 REC = ARR + ACC
      PRINT 105, POL,HP,DAM,SEX,AGE,REC
  105 FORMAT(5X3F10.0,3F7.0)
          GO TO 2
C         FILE IS FINISHED
  200 PRINT 205, T1,T2,T3,T4,T5
  205 FORMAT( 1H1,20X32HSUMMARY FOR SINGLE CAR ACCIDENTS //
     1 F9.0,21H SINGLE CAR ACCIDENTS  /
     2 F9.0,22H HIGH HORSEPOWER CASES /
     3 F9.0,18H MALE DRIVER CASES     /
     4 F9.0,41H YOUNG MALE DRIVERS WITH HIGH HORSE POWER /
     5 F9.0,44H YOUNG MALE DRIVERS WITH RECORD OF 2 OR MORE )
      STOP
      END
```

Output – starts with list of all single car accidents

```
POLICY      HP       DAMAGE       SEX       AGE       RECORD
409706.     300.      1804.        1.       18.        2.
643811.     301.       602.        1.       29.        2.
707892.     330.      1607.        1.       24.        4.
864202      400.       704.        2.       19.        1.
```

– – – CONTINUES – – –

```
                  SUMMARY FOR SINGLE CAR ACCIDENTS
```

(New page started here)

```
407. SINGLE CAR ACCIDENTS
267. HIGH HORSEPOWER CASES
326. MALE DRIVER CASES
173. YOUNG MALE DRIVERS WITH HIGH HORSEPOWER
142. YOUNG MALE DRIVERS WITH RECORD OF 2 OR MORE
```

There are three interesting points in the flowchart and program. First we have set up and used a switch (the variable KPRINT) to control the printing of the single output line. One might be tempted to print this line at each point where KPRINT is set to 1, but there are two drawbacks to this. It would require three PRINT statements rather than one and there would be two identical lines of output if the accident involved a male driver under age 30 with both a high horsepower car and a record of 2 or more arrests and accidents.

Next, note that all three data cards for an accident are read in the Fortran program with one READ statement and the items to be ignored on the cards are skipped using the X format.

Finally observe that a heading is printed for the lines of output of individual accidents. In order to have the headings line up with the numerical output, one must coordinate the format statements involved (here the ones involved are formats 1 and 105). In order to get really attractive output, one usually must make several tries.

Problems

3–3.1 *(Simplified Income Tax)* The tax is based on the adjusted income. The rates are given by the following table:

Tax rate on adjusted income

	Adjusted Income	*Tax Rate*
between	\$0 and \$2,000	15%
	\$2,000 and \$5,000	\$300 + 20% of excess over \$2,000
	\$5,000 and \$10,000	\$900 + 25% of excess over \$5,000
	\$10,000 and \$15,000	\$2,150 + 30% of excess over \$10,000
	\$15,000 and \$25,000	\$3,650 + 40% of excess over \$15,000
	over \$25,000	\$7,650 + 50% of excess over \$25,000

The adjusted income is obtained by subtracting the following deductions from the actual income:

Personal deduction

Taxpayer	\$0
Wife	\$5,000
First child	\$2,000
Second child	\$1,000
Third child	−\$2,000 (i.e., add \$2,000 to income)
Fourth child	−\$2,000 (i.e., add \$2,000 to income)
Each additional child	−\$1,000 (i.e., add \$1,000 to income)

Other deductions to be subtracted from actual income are:

1. All gifts to charity
2. All state and local taxes
3. Medical expenses in excess of 5 percent of actual income.

Write a program that reads in the following information:

actual income
number of personal deductions (the taxpayer counts as 1)
amount of gifts to charity
total of all state and local taxes
total medical expenses.

This information should be placed on one card and printed out with appropriate messages as soon as it is read in. The income tax due is to be computed and printed out as follows:

INCOME TAX DUE IS XXXXX.XX DOLLARS

3–3.2 You are married and have two children. Suppose you expect to make about \$10,000 per year for the next 20 years. How much more tax would you have to pay if you have a third child? Use the tax rules of Problem 3–3.1. Estimate your gifts, taxes, and medical expenses.

3–3.3 The most common conditional transfers are on a true or false basis and hence they result in 2-way branches. However, general n-way branches are useful in many situations.

(a) Show how any n-way branch can be constructed from a set of 2-way branches.

(b) Give an example where it is natural to use a 10-way branch.

(c) Show how a 10-way branch can be constructed from nine 2-way branches so that any path through the branch process actually hits at most four 2-way branches.

(d) What is the largest value of n for an n-way branch that can be constructed from 2-way branches so that at most four 2-way branches are hit on any path through the branch process?

3–3.4 *(Table of the Present Value of Money)* A dollar to be received next year is not worth as much as a dollar to be received today. Likewise, a bill of \$10 to be paid 5 years from now is less than a bill of \$10 to be paid now. One can put a lesser amount in savings and the interest earned can be applied to the bill as well as the original amount. The present value of money to be paid or received in the future depends on two things: the interest rate and the length of time involved. If the interest rate is R percent and the number of years is Y, then the present value of X dollars (to be received Y years from now) is

$$X/(1. + .01 * R)^{Y}.$$

Write a program that computes and prints out a table of the present value of \$1000.00 for four rates of interest, 2, 4, 6, and 8 percent and for periods of 1 to 40 years. The table is to start on a new page with appropriate headings for each of the five columns required. These are the number of years (on the left) and the present values for each interest rate.

3–3.5 *(Table of the Present Value of Regular Payments)* If one is to receive or make regular monthly (not yearly) payments for a long period of time, then these payments have a present value. This is the sum of the present value of each payment as described in the preceding problem.

Write a program that computes and prints out a table of the present value of \$100.00 a month payments for four interest rates, 2, 4, 6, and 8 percent and for periods of 1 to 30 years. Even though the payments are every month, print values only for every year (that is, after 12, 24, 36, . . . payments). Appropriate headings are required as in Problem 3–3.4.

3–3.6 *(Table of the Future Value of Regular Payments)* If one makes regular payments (say into a savings account) over a long period of time, then the amount at the end is larger due to the interest earned. If the interest rate is R percent, then the future value of a payment of X dollars after M months is

$$X * (1. + .01 * R/12.)^{M}.$$

Write a program that computes and prints out a table of the future value of regular monthly payments of $100.00 for four interest rates, 2, 4, 6, and 8 percent and for periods of 1 to 30 years. Even though the payments are every month, print values only for every year (that is, after 12, 24, 36, . . . payments). Appropriate headings are required as in Problem 3–3.4.

3–3.7 It is a common practice for savings institutions to credit the interest earned only a few times a year even though monthly payments are made. Write a program to recompute the quantities in Problem 3–3.6 for 6 percent interest where the interest is added only once every 3, 6, or 12 months. The formula involved changes to

$$3. * X * (1. + .01 * R/4.)^{Q}$$

for the 3-month case where Q is the number of quarters (3-month periods) and the formula gives the future value for all three monthly payments made in the quarter. You are to find similar formulas for the 6- and 12-month cases. Put appropriate headings on the printed output.

3–4 Iteration

A basic component of algorithms is iteration. This word is synonymous with controlled repetition, which indicates exactly what an iteration is: the repeated execution of some of the steps of an algorithm or program. Let us recall some of the algorithms we have seen so far that involve iteration: In the algorithm for determining whether 7319 is prime (in Section 3–1) there is one basic step, division and testing for exactness, that was repeated 7317 times! We would, in practice, of course, stop as soon as K is larger than $86 = \sqrt{7396}$.

Another example is the filling of the ditch with sand. There the basic step is to put one shovelful of sand into the ditch. The step is repeated until the ditch is full.

Each of Examples 3–1 and 3–3 involves an iteration of the reading of cards and processing the information on them. There is an important difference between these iterations, the first one repeats a definite known number of times, the others repeat a definite, but unknown, number of times. Thus, there is more to iteration than a set of operations to be repeated—there must also be a mechanism for stopping the iteration. We illustrate this mechanism in flowchart form in Figure 3–8.

In the above examples, the tests are, respectively, "Have we done this 7317 times?," "Is the ditch full?," and "Have we read all the cards?" Figure 3–8 suggests the common terminology of *iteration loop*.

This diagram is oversimplified, and a little reflection shows that it does not actually apply to the algorithm for the prime-number problem. Recall that

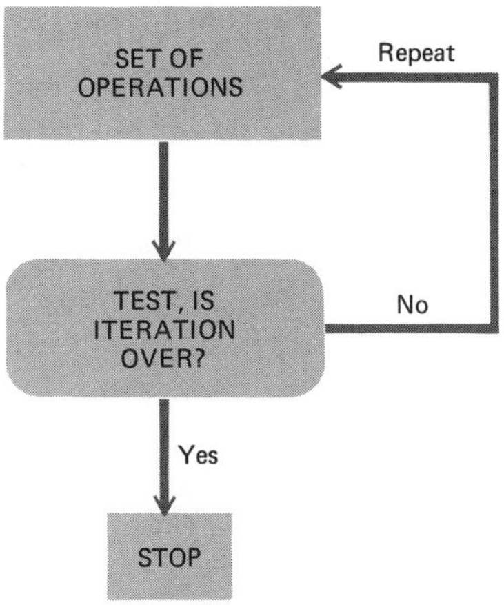

FIGURE 3–8. Flowchart of a rudimentary iterative process.

the first thing we do in that problem is divide 7319 by 2. We certainly do not want to repeat that. What we actually want is to modify the operations slightly before repeating them. A more exact description of the algorithm is presented in Figure 3–9.

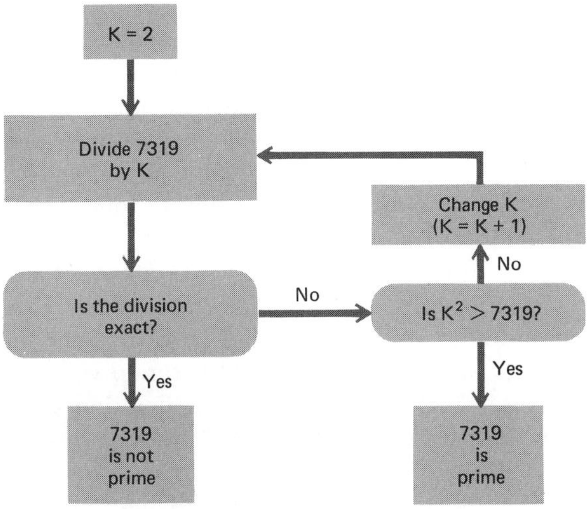

FIGURE 3–9. Flowchart of a simple-minded algorithm for testing whether 7319 is prime.

Now we see clearly the modification required in the iteration. We have to change one of the variables, K, before repeating the basic operations in the loop.

We are still not quite finished, because the flowchart must contain instructions on where and how to start. We must, in order to faithfully represent the algorithm, note that we start off with $K = 2$. This step is called the *initialization* of the iteration and is required in most iterations.

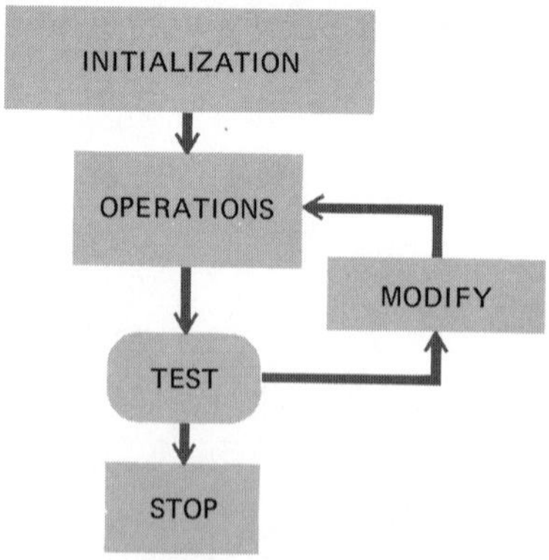

FIGURE 3–10. Flowchart of a simple iteration.

We now have all of the major parts of a simple iteration in an algorithm or program. They are:

1. Initialization
2. The set of operations to be executed
3. Test (for termination)
4. Modification (for next repetition).

These parts are shown in Figure 3–10.

We see later that there are more complicated algorithms involving iteration in which it is not so simple to identify the parts of the iteration.

It is appropriate to ask the question: Why do we bother to introduce the concept of iteration? Certainly for the algorithms considered above, we did not require it in order to make the statement of the methods unambiguous, or simple, or readily understood. In fact, it seems as if we have needlessly complicated very simple and straightforward situations.

There is one obvious reason to justify this approach. It is a fact of life that present computers require rather detailed instructions on what they are to do. Thus, we must break programs down into rather small steps in order for present computers to proceed. If we want something done 7317 times, we must tell the computer to do it each of these 7317 times. The use of iteration statements allows us to do this without actually writing down 7317 lines of instructions for the computer.

This obvious reason obscures the important reason for studying iteration. The concept of iteration is required for clarity of thought in programming. Iteration is a fundamental procedure and we must be able to think in terms of iteration loops in order to be adept at constructing algorithms. When writing programs that involve some repetitious calculations one must have a clear idea of what is happening (and when) and at times one must stop and lay out the iteration involved. Large programs tend to have many iteration loops in them with various interconnections that can lead to considerable confusion if one does not take care. Flowcharts are very helpful in the design of such programs and aid in the analysis of the logical structure during the programming.

Problems

Describe an algorithm and make a flowchart of it for each of the following problems. Write a program which computes the solution. In those problems where some data are unspecified, make provisions in the program to read the appropriate data from cards.

3–4.1 You are a clerk in a store and a man hands you a \$20 bill to pay for a purchase of x dollars. Determine what bills and coins you give him as change. You are to print out two lines of output as follows:

RECEIVED: \$20 COST = \$11.47
CHANGE: 0 \$10 BILLS, 1 \$5 BILLS, 3 \$1 BILLS,
2 QUARTERS, 0 DIMES, 0 NICKELS, AND
3 PENNIES.

You are also to check to see if you received enough money.

3–4.2 Given $0 < X < 1$, find the integer $I \geqq 0$ such that $0 < I * X < 30$ but such that $I * X$ is as close to 30 as possible.

3–4.3 Compute the maximum number in a list of numbers.

3–4.4 Find all the prime numbers less than 1000.

3–4.5 Find the sum of all the odd integers from 1 to 1001.

3–4.6 A man wishes to retire in 10 years and deposits \$25,000.00 at 4½ percent interest compounded quarterly. At retirement, he finds inflation has deflated the buying power of his money until the purchasing power is no more than his original deposit. What was the average annual percentage of inflation?

3–4.7 Find the sum of the first 30, 50, and 100 terms in the infinite series $s = 1 - 1/2 + 1/4 - 1/6 + 1/8 - 1/10 \cdots$.

3–4.8 Modify the algorithm in Problem 3–4.7 for the series $s = 1/2^2 + 1/4^2 - 1/6^2 + 1/8^2 + 1/10^2 - 1/12^2 + 1/14^2 \cdots$.

3–4.9 Find the sum of the first 10 numbers in the sequence 1, 4, 9, 16, 25, $\ldots, n^2$.

3–4.10 *(Random number generation)* Consider the numbers between 1 and 100,000. A number is said to be chosen randomly from this set of numbers if any of the numbers are equally likely to be chosen. A number of important computer applications require choosing many random numbers from a specified set of numbers. Such algorithms are called random number generators. One of the simplest schemes to generate a sequence, or set, of random numbers is as follows. Call the random numbers R_i, $i = 1, 2, \ldots,$ and set

$$R_1 = A,$$
$$R_{i+1} = C * R_i \bmod(B).$$

Recall from algebra that $x \bmod(B)$ is the remainder when the largest integer multiple of B that is less than x is subtracted from x. Examples are 431 mod(100) = 31, 7 mod(3) = 1, 19 mod(5) = 4. The algorithm depends on the three constants A, B, and C. The choices,

$$A = 61, \qquad B = 100{,}000, \qquad C = 91,$$

are suitable to generate a few thousand random numbers between 0 and 100,000.

(a) The procedure x mod(B) is not an elementary arithmetic operation. Give a method to compute x mod(B) in Fortran.

(b) Use the algorithm of part (a) to construct an algorithm to generate a set of K random numbers.

(c) Given an algorithm to generate random numbers between 0 and 100,000, show how it can be modified to generate random numbers between any two given numbers XLO and XHI.

3–4.11 *(Testing random numbers)* The algorithm given in the preceding problem is useful for generating only a certain number of random numbers. There are a number of tests that can be applied to a set of random numbers to see if they exhibit a systematic, nonrandom behavior. To fix the discussion, assume the numbers are between 0 and XHI and we have generated K random numbers R_i. Some of the more common tests are:

Test 1: The average value of the R_i should be about XHI/2.

Test 2: The number of the R_i divisible by 3 should be about XHI/3.

Test 3: The number of the R_i between (L/10) * XHI and [(L + 1)/10] * XHI should be about K/10 for each L = 0, 1, 2, . . ., 9.

Test 4: The number of times that a particular value x appears in the random set should be about K/XHI.

(a) Construct a program to apply the four tests to a set of random numbers. Note that Test 3 involves 10 separate tests and Test 4 involves XHI separate tests, so that some variables must be introduced in a way to make it convenient to express the tests. Present a flowchart of the algorithm you use.

(b) Apply the test program to the sequences of random number generated by the following choices for the algorithm of the preceding problem.

1.	$A = 7$	$B = 10$	$C = 3$	$K = 30$
2.	$A = 2$	$B = 10$	$C = 4$	$K = 30$
3.	$A = 3$	$B = 10$	$C = 7$	$K = 100$
4.	$A = 41$	$B = 100$	$C = 77$	$K = 100, 500$
5.	$A = 41$	$B = 100$	$C = 85$	$K = 100, 500$
6.	$A = 77$	$B = 1000$	$C = 72$	$K = 100, 500.$

Discuss the conclusions that can be made from an examination of the results from the test program.

3–4.12 Roofing tiles cost \$0.20 each and an additional \$15.00 per 100 square feet for installation. One tile covers an area of 1 square foot. Sheet copper roofing costs \$0.20 per pound and 1 pound covers 1 square foot with installation costing $20.00 per 100 pounds. The life expectancy of tile is 20 years whereas the copper should last 30 years. Insurance on the copper roof costs $30.00 more per year per 1000 square feet than on the tile roof. Which is the more economical over a period of 120 years?

3–5 The Organization of Components Into Complete Programs

Three general aspects of programming are discussed in this section. First we consider the objectives that one has in writing a program and present situations where various ones of these are critical. Then we discuss general strategies to meet these objectives. As one might expect, the possible objectives are not completely compatible and one must make compromises. Finally, a few observations are made about common weaknesses in the "style" of programming, particularly those found in beginner's programs.

It may surprise readers at this point that there are any objectives in programming besides getting the programs to work. Certainly that is the ultimate objective in beginning programming assignments and one's grade normally depends entirely on whether the program works or not. However, after some experience in programming one sees that there are many programs that work for the same problem and one realizes that some of these are much better than others.

One might make an analogy (slightly far-fetched) with golf. There the objective is to hit the ball into each of the holes on the course. Even the most novice golfer can achieve this objective if he is patient and tries long enough. However, there is still a big step between this and being a good golfer. The knowledge and skill required to write programs that work (even bad ones) is much more than required for golf, but, as in golf, meeting this first objective still leaves one with a big step to take.

There are two important general requirements for a good program: efficiency and understandability. It is not so easy to precisely measure either one of these. One commonly measures efficiency by the amount of computer time required to solve the problem. At one time this was a very reasonable measure, but the situation is more complex now. This is primarily because computer systems have become much more complex and simple running time does not accurately reflect the cost of the resources used. However efficiency is measured, it is a primary criterion for judging the value of a program.

The second requirement, understandability, for a good program is not as widely recognized and is much harder to measure. Experience has shown, however, that this can be just as important as efficiency. The ultimate objective is, of course, to have a program that works efficiently, is easy to understand, and works in a straightforward, natural way. The relationships of these objectives are illustrated in Figure 3–11.

We now consider some common situations and the resulting values of these objectives. One of the most common is the *short, one-shot program.* Such a program is not a big calculation and once the answers are obtained the pro-

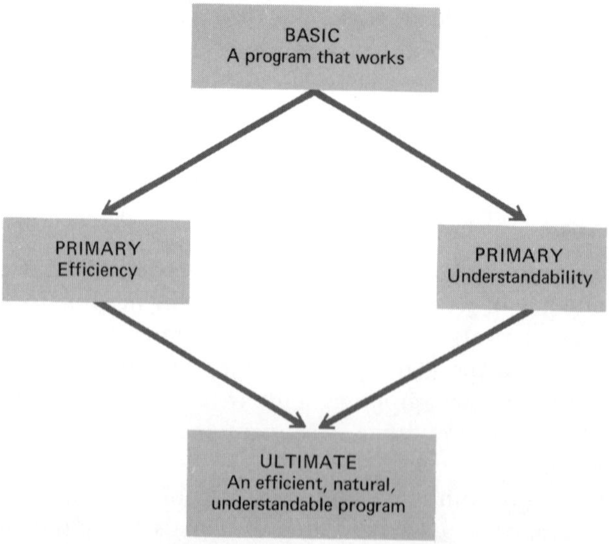

FIGURE 3–11. The objectives in the construction of programs.

gram is not likely to be run again. This situation includes the typical homework programming assignments in an introduction to computing course. In this situation only the basic objective is really of value. There is not much point in spending time and effort on efficiency and clarity in a program that is a short computation to be run only once. Of course, an instructor in a course might well ask for efficiency and clarity in homework assignments.

There is another quite different situation where efficiency and clarity assume secondary importance. This is for programs that solve an important problem for the first time. This occurs often at the frontiers of knowledge and naturally the first and foremost requirement is to be able to obtain the solution somehow. Even here clarity plays a role as such programs are sometimes rewritten several times and by several people. If one attempt at the program is unintelligible, this may prevent a necessary improvement from being recognized and made.

Efficiency becomes the most important objective when extensive production is made with a program. Typical examples of such programs are Fortran compilers, payroll and accounting programs, programs that handle requests in an airline reservations system or a stock market price quotation system, programs that perform basic design computations for a company's products, programs that do very long and complicated scientific computations, and programs that control the processes in an oil refinery. In these and similar situations there is a definite payoff for effort spent in increasing the efficiency of the programs involved. In fact, in some of these cases, efficiency may be the only difference between a program that "works" and one that does not. Thus, an airline reservation system cannot allow 10- or 15-minute delays in responding to requests. Nor is it worthwhile to have a weather prediction program that takes 36 hours of computer time to make a 24-hour forecast. Weather prediction computations are very long and this possibility is not exaggerated (in fact, it has really happened).

Understandability is very important for a program which has a relatively long life span during which it undergoes gradual modification. Machine independence is also significant for such programs. A typical example is the payroll accounting program for a company. Such a program has an indefinite life span, yet it probably must be changed every time the state or federal government changes the tax laws, every time a new union contract is negotiated, every time a new pension or insurance plan is adopted, and so forth. Often the changes required are quite minor, only a few lines. But it may be very difficult to locate the right lines in a program that is many pages long, without comment cards, and generally incomprehensible. Many organizations have had the bitter experience of being forced to completely rewrite a program from scratch because they could not make a required minor change in an old program. In fact, there are many stories around about a job security strategy that involves this situation. One somehow gets assigned to write a program which is vital to the company's (or organization's) operation. One then writes it without comment cards, with all the variables named QAI2Z, QB13Y, Q1A2Z, QB12Z, and so on, and, at every opportunity, one does things in a peculiar way. It also helps to sprinkle in complicated statements that are not used at all. After the program is working well and everyone realizes that the company cannot live without it, one becomes much too busy to ever write a report about how the program works or how to modify it. This way one becomes an irreplaceable, indispensable key employee (hopefully, also unfirable).

Another situation where clarity is important is in the construction of complicated mathematical models. Imagine, for example, an economist who is constructing a mathematical model for the economic behavior of a small town. His program must, of course, represent all the important economic features of a small town. This economic behavior is quite complex and the economist will probably have to modify his model many times before he is satisfied. It is clearly to his advantage to make his program clear and understandable as he will have to read and reread it during the modifications. Most inexperienced programmers fail to do this even though it reduces their work in the long run. Everyone clings to the hope that there is just one more bug in the program before it is finished, and thus it is not worthwhile to put in a comment card explaining what these ad hoc three lines of code do.

Even if the economist is able to learn to live with his program, the day will come, he hopes, when he will tell the world about his new and extraordinary model. The world, of course, will want to examine it closely and will rightfully be unimpressed by an unintelligible program.

It is the task of the programmer to judge his particular situation and to place correct emphasis on efficiency and clarity. Experience in programming allows each programmer to develop his own "style." His programs will incorporate his favorite little constructions and idiosyncrasies. Hopefully, he will develop the ability to write good code unconsciously, just as a good writer writes good prose unconsciously. The development of this ability requires practice (and usually a lot of it), but practice alone is not enough. The programmer must continually examine his programs critically if he is to improve.

It is not possible to give a few paragraphs that say how to write good programs any more than it is possible to say how to write good short stories in a few paragraphs. However, the key requirement is to be able to visualize the *entire* computation in one's mind. It is frequently helpful to make one or two rough flowcharts of the program in order to get a better view of what is to be done. If the programmer does not have a good view of the whole program, then the program will be a set of disconnected pieces that are unlikely to fit together smoothly or efficiently.

The maximum in efficiency usually requires that the computations and processing be carefully integrated and coordinated with one another. Thus if a quantity is needed both for the fourth and seventh steps of a computation, it should be computed at the fourth step, then the result saved until the seventh. Further, if most of the ingredients of a part of the computations required in the seventh step are available at the third step, one should finish that part in the third step and save the result. It is easy to believe that the objective of efficiency works against the objective of clarity and simplicity.

It is interesting that these two objectives also work together. It frequently occurs that the most efficient code is simple. That is, it is a simple set of Fortran statements that might very well be hard to understand.

The maximum in understandability usually requires that the program be very modular. That is, the program is broken down into a number of modules (pieces of code) each of which has a readily understandable purpose. This organization is almost essential if the program is to be modified from time to time. While modularity does tend to be slightly inefficient, it rarely is necessary to make great sacrifices in efficiency in order to achieve modularity. Nevertheless, the desire for modularity often leads to inefficient programs because the programmer chooses a set of modules that are inappropriate for the computation to be made. In other words, if one does not have a good visualization of the computation, one may well break it up into pieces or modules that make efficiency impossible.

A frequent fault with beginning programmers is to identify the main steps in the computations with the things to be computed. This leads to a program organization as shown in Figure 3–12. Visualize the effect of this organization for Example 3–4 where information is to be extracted from a car insurance company's card file. The result might be a program organized as shown in Figure 3–13. One might feel this example is far-fetched, but in fact it is common among inexperienced programmers. In this case the difficulty is that the programmer has failed to realize that the crux in this program is processing the information on the cards. If this is seen as the main feature, then the organization appears as in Figure 3–14. A more detailed flowchart would, of course, show that the box "Find what information . . ." breaks up into a number of boxes with decisions. Efficiency is to be gained at this point by choosing to make the decisions in the right sequence.

Another frequent fault in beginners' programs is confusion in the logical statements. A symptom of this is the excessive use of IF's and GO TO's. Excessive, of course, is to be judged in view of the task at hand. Note that the nature of Fortran is such that one uses GO TO's with considerable frequency. As an

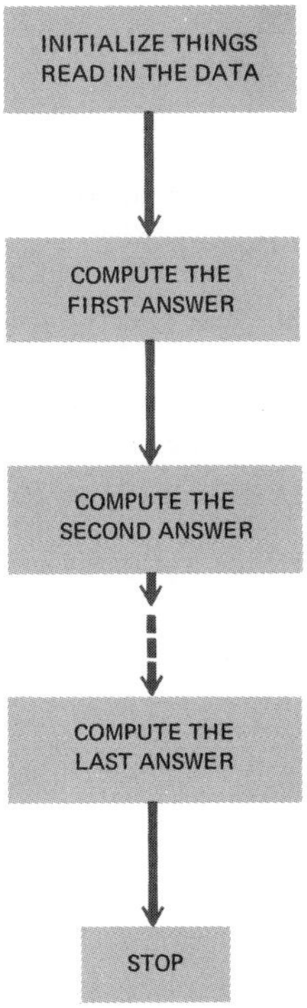

FIGURE 3–12. The straight-forward, one answer at a time organization of a program.

example of how bad things can be (and often are), consider a computation where Z = 4 * X + Y, but Y is to be increased by 1 if X is zero or positive. Two pieces of code are shown for this, the one on the left is clearly poorly constructed.

```
      IF(X) 20,30,40
   20 Z = 4.*X + Y
         GO TO 50
   30 GO TO 40
   40 Y = Y+1.
      Z = 4.*X + Y
   50    ....
```

```
      IF(X) 30,20,20
   20 Y = Y+1.
   30 Z = 4.*X + Y
   50    ....
```

The short, efficient way

Constructions such as those on the left above result in programs that are hard to understand. Any confusion in the logic will, of course, have this effect. Other direct causes of unintelligibility are: random numbering of statements, no comment cards, and irrelevant names of variables. Last, but not least, of the sources of lack of clarity are programming tricks (intentional or otherwise). Consider the effect of the following statement:

```
AB99 = .5*(G+3.*AB99+ABS(G-AB99))-AB99
```

It takes a fair amount of puzzling to see that this statement results in AB99 being the larger of G and AB99. The statement

```
GBIG = AMAX1(G,GBIG)
```

has the same effect (AB99 has been changed to GBIG), is more efficient, and is much more intelligible.

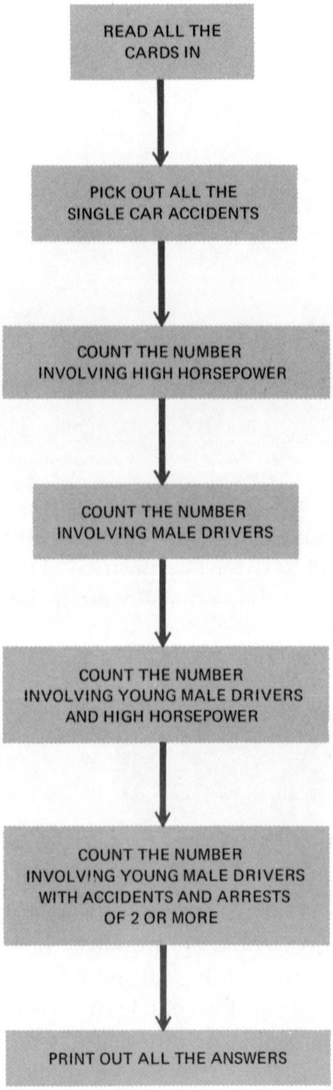

FIGURE 3–13. The result of using the "one answer at a time" organization for Example 3–3.

Problems

3–5.1 Consider a set of punched cards with the following information on each card:

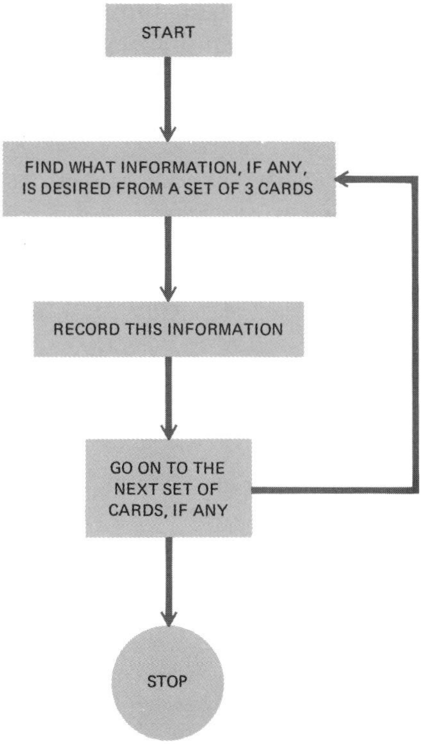

FIGURE 3–14. An alternate organization of the processing for Example 3–3.

(1) Five test scores
(2) A student ID number.

Write a program which does the following:

(1) Prints out the information on the cards plus the average test score for each card
(2) After all cards are read it prints out the average for each of the five tests plus the average of the students average.

Assume that there are NSCORE (also read in) cards and supply appropriate headings and messages in the printed output.

3–5.2 A department store keeps its records of sales made in each department on punched cards. Each card contains the following information:

(1) Department code (3 digits)
(2) Date (in the form 2-16-72 for February 16, 1972)
(3) Sales for the date (that is, dollars and cents).

Write a program that processes these cards and produces the following information:

(1) Total in monthly sales for each department
(2) Daily total sales for the store. Arrange the cards in the input so that all cards of the same date are together
(3) Total monthly sales for the department store
(4) Sales tax to be paid to the state (3 percent of sales)
(5) Sales tax to be paid to the city ($\frac{1}{2}$ percent of sales).

Each of these items is to be printed on one line with an appropriate identifying message. For one test run assume there are only 3 departments (codes 1–3) and 20 days of selling. For a second test run assume that there are 31 departments and 2 days of selling. You are to invent appropriate data for the program to process.

3–5.3 Assume that you are the registrar of a small college. For each student enrolled you have a deck of cards of the following type:

Card 1: Name (columns 1–24)
ID number (columns 25–30)
Class (columns 31–40)
Major (columns 41–50)

Card 2: (one card for each course)
Department name (columns 1–10)
Department code (columns 11–12)
Course number (columns 13–17)
Credits hours (columns 18–20)

The last card is identified by a student number of –1.

You want a program that computes the tuition for each student, the total tuition to be collected, and the number of regular students. The tuition is \$60.00 per credit hour up to 11 hours. The tuition for 12 or more hours is \$720.00 and a student is called a regular student if he pays this full tuition. Write a program that processes these cards and produces the desired information. Give appropriate headings and messages for the printed output. Make a test run for 10 students who are enrolled in 1 to 5 courses with total credits hours ranging from 3 to 18.

3–5.4 Write a program that processes the same cards as in Problem 3–5.3 but which produces a list of enrollments in the courses in the college. Assume, for a test run, that there are 4 different departments which each give 4 different courses.

3–5.5 The results of a 20-question true-false test have been punched on cards (in columns 1 to 20) along with each student's ID number (in columns 21 to 25). The answers are encoded with 1 for a true and 0 for a false. The first card in the deck has the correct answers, the last card has a 2 in column 1.

Write a program that reads this deck of cards and produces the following output:

(1) The number of correct responses for each student (along with his ID number)

(2) The percentage of people who answered each question correctly.

The output should have appropriate headings and messages.

4

Fortran–
ARRAYS AND PROGRAM CONTROL

The additional features of Fortran presented in this chapter and the next complete a subset of Fortran appropriate for the bulk of the programs one writes. The features remaining (in Chapter 6) are extremely useful from time to time, even sometimes essential. However, one might program for years without using some of them. It depends on the area of application and type of programs with which one is involved.

4—1 Arrays

4–1.1 Array Declaration and Use

One of the most important and useful features of Fortran is the ability to handle arrays. The most common arrays are one-dimensional such as

$$A(1), A(2), A(3), \ldots, A(17), \ldots, A(40).$$

A one-dimensional array is also called a list (and it also corresponds to a vector or sequence in mathematical terminology). An array has a name (the one above is called A) and the elements in the array are indexed by a counter.

A one-dimensional array is ordered from beginning to end and the position of a particular element is indicated by its index. Thus, A(1) is the first element, A(10) is the 10th, and so on. The usual mathematical notation for arrays is to place the index as a subscript, that is, $A(1) \sim A_1$, $A(10) \sim A_{10}$, $A(i) \sim A_i$.

Two-dimensional arrays (often called matrices or tables) are also important and are allowed in Fortran. They have two indices, for example:

A(1,1)	A(1,2)	...	A(1,17)	...	A(1,40)
A(2,1)	A(2,2)	...	A(2,17)	...	A(2,40)
...	...	...	...	...	...
A(7,1)	A(7,2)	...	A(7,17)	...	A(7,40)
...	...	...	...	...	...
A(20,1)	A(20,2)	...	A(20,17)	...	A(20,40)

This is a two-dimensional array with 20 rows and 40 columns. Typical examples of one-dimensional arrays are:

1. List of the amount of rainfall for each day in the year
2. List of the grades on the final exam in a course
3. The job vacancies in the state highway department
4. The district warehouses of a company
5. The dates of the season's horse races.

   0401, 0402, 0403, 0407, 0408, 0409, 0410, 0412,
   0414, 0415, 0416, 0923, 0924, 0925, 0929, 0930,
   1001, 1002, 1004, 1006, 1007.

The first two digits are the month and the second two the day, so the season starts on April 1 and stops on October 7. Typical examples of two-dimensional arrays are:

1. List of the amount of rainfall for each day in the year at each weather station in a state
2. Elevation above sea level at 1-mile intervals in a 100-square-mile region
3. The multiplication table for the numbers less than 10:

1	2	3	4	5	6	7	8	9
2	4	6	8	10	12	14	16	18
3	6	9	12	15	18	21	24	27
4	8	12	16	20	24	28	32	36
5	10	15	20	25	30	35	40	45
6	12	18	24	30	36	42	48	54
7	14	21	28	35	42	49	56	63
8	16	24	32	40	48	56	64	72
9	18	27	36	45	54	63	72	81

   Call this array MTABLE and we see that MTABLE (J,K) is simply J times K.

Three-dimensional arrays are also allowed and some systems allow even more than three dimensions (such as up to 7).

It is important to appreciate the advantages of using indexed arrays.

These advantages include:

1. The ability to systematically process the array or list in iteration loops (one uses the index as the counter in the iteration).
2. The ability to make statements about members of the list which are valid even if the list is changed in length or content. Thus, the statement

```
PAY(I) = HOURS(I)*RATE(I)-DEDUCT(I)
```

gives the pay of the Ith employee no matter how many there are.
3. One can add items to the list by changing the variable that indicates the list's length and by placing the new items on the end. In general we can change or shuffle the items in the list without changing the statements that manipulate the list.
4. There is a name for the list which can be referred to simply.

If a name is to be that of an array, this fact must be declared in the Fortran program. A typical declaration is as follows:

```
DIMENSION A(5),D(2,6),K(3,2,5)
```

This statement declares that A is a list with up to 5 elements, D is a two-dimensional array (matrix) with up to 12 elements (12 = 2 * 6, 2 rows and 6 columns), and K is a three-dimensional 3 × 2 × 5 array of 30 elements.

DIMENSION

The word DIMENSION followed by a list separated by commas. Each item in the list is a name followed by 1 or more integer constants separated by commas and all enclosed in one set of parentheses. The number of integer constants indicates the number of dimensions (usually up to 3) and the value of the integer constants indicates the maximum value of the corresponding index of the array.

EXAMPLES

```
DIMENSION A(10),BX(10),KAT(3,2),JACK(25)
DIMENSION ZEG(4,4,16),BB(8),XLOW(3,75)
```

An element of an array is referred to by its name with the proper number of indexes or subscripts. Each index or subscript must have an integer value between 1 and the maximum index value specified in the DIMENSION statement for that index position. For the array ZEG declared above, the first index can take on the values 1, 2, 3, or 4, the second index can take on the same values, and the third index can take on the values 1 through 16.

When an array is used in an arithmetic expression, it is referred to as a *subscripted variable.* Thus, the statements

```
A(I) = B(2,I)*C(J,I,K)
XX   = A(I+1)*6.5/B(3,I)
ALOW = AMIN1( A(I),A(I+1),XX )
B(4,I) = B(2,I)+B(3,I-1)
```

involve three subscripted variables, and the computation takes place as expected provided that the integer variables I, J, and K lie within their appropriate ranges of values.

Some simple expressions may be used as subscripts. Besides using an integer constant or variable as a subscript, expressions of the following form may be used:

```
VAR + KON                    I+3        JACK+4
VAR - KON                    J-7        KK-16
KON * VAR                    3*I        16*KK
KON * VAR + KON2             3*I+2      16*KK+4
KON * VAR - KON2             3*I-2      7*KUG-17
```

where KON and KON2 are integer constants and VAR is an integer variable. Even minor variations are illegal in many systems, including the forms

```
KON + VAR                    3+I        4+JACK
KON - VAR                    3-I        16-KK
VAR * KON + KON2             I*3        KK*16+4
VAR * KON - KON2             I*3-2      KUG*7-4
```

This strange restriction has its origin in the Fortran originally developed for the IBM 704; special high-speed registers (index registers) can be used for stepping through arrays, provided that the subscripts have a simple form. These illogical restrictions are gradually being loosened and one must check the local Fortran systems to find out just what kinds of expressions may be used for indexes.

An array may have real-valued or integer-valued elements, but not both. The type of element in an array is indicated by placing the array name in a declaration statement, as in

```
DIMENSION A(10),B(3,5)
REAL A
INTEGER B
```

The declaration statements REAL and INTEGER can function as a DIMENSION statement, so that the following two statements are equivalent to the above three statements:

```
REAL A(10)
INTEGER B(3,5)
```

The type (real or integer) of an array is determined by the first letter in its name unless it is explicitly declared otherwise in a REAL or INTEGER statement.

How many arrays can be used in a program? How large can they be? These questions can be answered only with reference to a specific system. In general, we can say that if a computer has a memory or storage capacity of MEM words, then each variable in a program is associated with one of these words. If an array has N elements or components, then it will be associated with N consecutive words. Of the MEM words available in the computer memory, perhaps one tenth are set aside for the operating system. The compiled program itself will need some part of the remaining .9 * MEM words. What is left over can be used for variables and arrays.

Since the number of words needed for the machine-language program generated by the compiler cannot easily be predicted in advance, more than one attempt at compilation may be necessary before the maximum number of words available for variables and arrays can be determined. See the diagram in Figure 4–1.

EXAMPLE 4–1

TABLE LOOKUP RECONSIDERED

Arrays are naturally applicable to computations involving tables and table lookup. Consider the table of life expectancies of Example 3–3. We can make this table available in a Fortran program by using 10 assignment statements and a declaration as follows:

```
DIMENSION TABEXP(10)
TABEXP(1) = 31.6
TABEXP(2) = 27.2
TABEXP(3) = 23.0
TABEXP(4) = 19.3
TABEXP(5) = 15.8
TABEXP(6) = 12.8
TABEXP(7) = 10.2
TABEXP(8) =  7.9
TABEXP(9) =  5.8
TABEXP(10)=  4.2
```

The simple-minded linear search method of table lookup can now be placed in an iteration loop as follows. Recall that AGE is given, we find the nearest value ANEAR to AGE that is a multiple of 5, then we look up the corresponding table entry and assign its value to EXPECT.

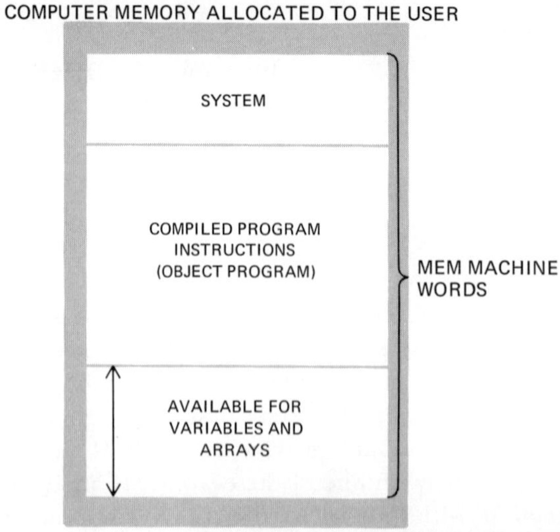

***FIGURE 4–1.* Rough illustration of the use of the words in a computer's memory.**

```
      ANEAR = (IFIX(AGE+2.5)/5)*5
      ITAB  = 1
    5 IF( ANEAR - (5.*FLOAT(ITAB)+35.) ) 10,20,10
   10 ITAB  = ITAB + 1
          GO TO 5
   20 EXPECT = TABEXP(ITAB)
```

This program is much shorter than that shown previously and, furthermore, it is valid whether the table has 10 or 110 entries. However, it is also less efficient because one IF is used for every table entry even though they are not individually written down. The program can be improved by noting that one IF can be used to test for two table entries and by redoing the calculations of the age entries. The result is

```
      ANEAR = (IFIX(AGE+2.5)/5)+5
      TABAGE= 45.
    5 IF( ANEAR - TABAGE)20,30,10
   10 TABAGE= TABAGE + 10.
          GO TO 5
   20 TABAGE= TABAGE - 5.
   30 ITAB  = TABAGE/5. - 7.
      EXPECT= TABEXP(ITAB)
```

This program is two statements longer but it runs about three times as fast. Both of these codes are, in fact, terribly inefficient and we were led into this inefficiency by simply imitating what we had done before in table lookup. We can find the desired value directly by

```
      ANEAR = (IFIX(AGE+2.5)/5)*5
      ITAB  = ANEAR/5. - 7.
      EXPECT= TABEXP(ITAB)
```

This simple, efficient approach is possible because the age entries in the table are systematically spaced at 5-year intervals. If they were randomly spaced, then one would have to rely on a table lookup scheme to find the right values.

One can do the linear interpolation discussed in Example 3–3 just as directly as follows:

```
Column  5|6|7
        | | ALOW = 5*(IFIX(AGE)/5)
        | | ILOW = ALOW/5. - 7.
        | | EXPECT= .2*(TABEXP(ILOW)*(ALOW+5.-AGE)
        | *         +TABEXP(ILOW+1)*(AGE-ALOW))
```

Common Errors	*Things You Can Do*
1. Illegal index expression. 2. Index is negative, zero, or too large. 3. Dimensions of arrays are set so large that all computer memory space is used up, but most of the space is not used. 4. Arrays are used but not dimensioned. The compiler acts as though some function or subprogram is involved. 5. Dimension of arrays involves a variable as in REAL XXX(N).	1. Use array elements any place an ordinary variable can be used, except as subscripts. 2. Replace DIMENSION statements with REAL or INTEGER as in REAL XX(100) or INTEGER IJ(25).

4–1.2 Reading and Writing Arrays

An array can be read or printed by naming each of its elements in the READ or PRINT statement, as in the following program.

```
      INTEGER A(5)
      READ 1,A(1),A(2),A(3),A(4),A(5)
    1 FORMAT(5I8)
      PRINT 1,A(1),A(2),A(3),A(4),A(5)
      STOP
      END
```

CARD INPUT

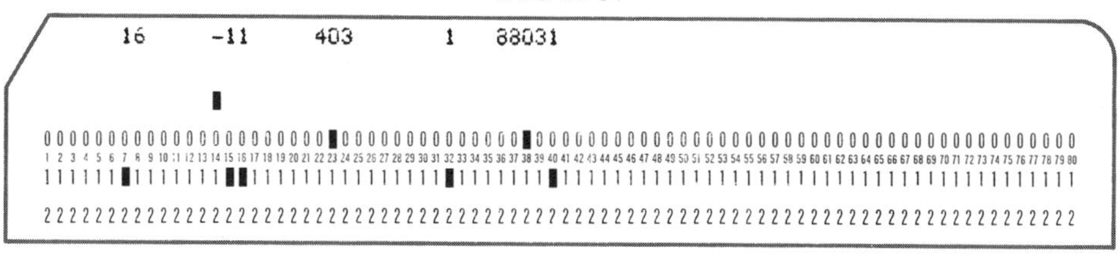

OUTPUT

```
Column         8|      16|      24|      32|      40|
              16|     -11|     403|       1|   88031|
```

When an entire array is to be read or written, as is the case in the above program, then it is sufficient merely to name the array. Thus the following program is identical in operation to the preceding one.

```
      INTEGER A(5)
      READ 1,A
    1 FORMAT(5I8)
      PRINT1,A
      STOP
      END
```

There may be a problem with this abbreviated method on two counts. First, it requires one to read (or print) *all* the elements. Thus, the two program segments on the left below are identical, but the ones on the right are quite different.

```
      REAL TAB(3)                              REAL TAB(10)
      READ 1,TAB(1),TAB(2),TAB(3)              READ 1,TAB(1),TAB(2),TAB(3)
    1 FORMAT(3I8)                            1 FORMAT(3I8)

      REAL TAB(3)                              REAL TAB(10)
      READ 1,TAB                               READ 1,TAB
    1 FORMAT(3I8)                            1 FORMAT(3I8)
```

Second, there are certain standard conventions for arrays that are more than one-dimensional. The following program

```
      REAL B(2,2)
      READ 7,B(1,1),B(1,2),B(2,1),B(2,2)
    7 FORMAT(4F6.1)
```

expects the elements of the 2 × 2 array B $= \begin{bmatrix} 1. & -2. \\ 3. & -4. \end{bmatrix}$ to appear on a card with the four elements in order by row; the elements are punched as $+1.0 - 2.0 + 3.0 - 4.0$. If the above READ is replaced by READ 7,B, then B is assigned the value $\begin{bmatrix} 1. & 3. \\ -2. & -4. \end{bmatrix}$. Two-dimensional arrays are handled column by column when they are referenced only by the array name. In terms of subscripts, the use of an array name is equivalent to using a list of the array elements with the leftmost subscript varying more rapidly. Thus, READ 7,B is equivalent to READ 7,B(1,1), B(2,1),B(1,2),B(2,2). Similarly, a three-dimensional array D as declared in INTEGER D(2,2,2) can be referenced as D or as the list

D(1,1,1),D(2,1,1) ·D(1,2,1),D(2,2,1) D(1,1,2),D(2,1,2) D(1,2,2),D(2,2,2)

In reading or writing all or part of an array, there is a very compact notation that can be used if the variation in the subscripts follows a simple pattern. As an illustration of its use consider

```
      READ 12,(A(I),I=1,5)
```

The parenthesized list (A(I), I = 1,5) represents in a shorthand notation the list A(1), A(2), A(3), A(4), A(5). The programmer (and the system) interprets the shorthand READ 12, (A(I), I = 1,5) as "read in A(I) for I taking on the values from 1 to 5 and use format number 12."

Any integer variable can be used in place of the variable I which appears in the above example. This variable is called the control, or dummy, variable. The general form of the list for reading or writing a one-dimensional array is

array name (subscript expression), **control variable** = initial value, terminal value, increment

Any subscript expression of the form c * v ± k may be used where v is the control variable and c and k are integer constants. The initial value, terminal value, and increment may be integer constants or variables (they may not be any other type of expression). They determine the range of the control variable as follows: Suppose we have (X(K),K = L,M,N). Then the control variable K takes on the j + 1 values L, L + N, . . ., L + jN where j is the largest integer such that $L + jN \leq M$ [that is, $L + (j + 1)N > M$]. The j + 1 values are the range of K. The initial, terminal and increment values must be nonzero and positive. If an increment is not specified, it is assumed to be the constant 1. Thus, (Y(A),A =1,15,1) and (Y(A),A = 1,15) are equivalent. The rules involving the reading and writing of arrays in this way are the same as those for the Fortran DO statement (discussed in the next section) and these parts of the READ and PRINT lists are often called *implied DO loops*.

Several examples of PRINT statements are given below along with the number of values printed.

```
PRINT 10,(A(J),J=5,8)                4 VALUES
PRINT 10,(A(J),J=1,16)              16 VALUES

K = 5*7
J = 6
PRINT 10,(A(M),M=J,K)               30 VALUES
PRINT 10,(A(M),M=1,6,2)              3 VALUES M=1,3,5
PRINT 10,(A(M),M=5,K,5)              7 VALUES M=5,10,...,35

J = 3
K = 2*J+1
PRINT 10,(A(M+2),M=1,K)              7 VALUES A(3),A(4),...,A(9)
PRINT 10,(A(M),  M=3,K+2)              ILLEGAL
PRINT 10,(A(M),  M=2,10,J)           3 VALUES M=2,5,8
```

Several different arrays, as well as simple variables, may be involved in a single statement; for example,

```
      INTEGER A(20),B(20,40)
C             B(K,L) IS READ IN AS  100*K + L
C             40 CARDS WITH 20 VALUES ON EACH
      READ 5,B
    5 FORMAT( 20I4)
      I = 0
   10 I = I+1
      A(I) = I
      IF( I-20) 10,12,12
```

```
12 X = 17.77
   N = 8
   PRINT 15,(I,X,A(2*I-1),A(2*I),B(I,N),I=1,N)
15 FORMAT(I4,F8.2,2I5,I8)
   PRINT 20, (K,B(K,K+4),A(K-10),K=11,16)
20 FORMAT(23H K,B(K,K+4),A(K-10) ARE 3I8 )
   STOP
   END
```

Card input described in comment statements is not shown

The specified format prints a single line for each new value of I; then N lines are printed, each line numbered on the left, from 1 to N as shown below.

OUTPUT

```
              A-array
  I      X     odd  even    B(I, 8)

  1  17.77       1     2     108
  2  17.77       3     4     208
  3  17.77       5     6     308
  4  17.77       7     8     408
  5  17.77       9    10     508
  6  17.77      11    12     608
  7  17.77      13    14     708
  8  17.77      15    16     808
 K,B(K,K+4),A(K-10) ARE       11    1115     1
 K,B(K,K+4),A(K-10) ARE       12    1216     2
 K,B(K,K+4),A(K-10) ARE       13    1317     3
 K,B(K,K+4),A(K-10) ARE       14    1418     4
 K,B(K,K+4),A(K-10) ARE       15    1519     5
 K,B(K,K+4),A(K-10) ARE       16    1620     6
```

Output from the second PRINT statement

Higher-dimensional arrays are handled in much the same way as the one-dimensional arrays. A new control variable may be associated with each subscript position, but fewer control variables may be used if desired. For each control variable, a range must be specified. The order in which the control variable ranges are specified determines the order in which the subscripts vary. For instance,

```
PRINT 5,  ((D(I,J),I=1,IM),J=1,JM)
```

Inner loop

Outer loop

is underlined to show the scope of each control variable. The shorter line indicates the scope of the control variable I; the longer that of J. Interpreting the list from the outside in, J assumes the initial value 1 and then I runs through its range. Then J assumes the value 2 (unless 2 > JM) and once again I runs through its range. This process continues until J equals JM. Thus, the above statement reads the array of values as specified by the list.

```
D(1,1)    D(2,1)    D(3,1)    ...   D(IM,1)
D(1,2)    D(2,2)    D(3,2)    ...   D(IM,2)
D(1,3)    D(2,3)    D(3,3)    ...   D(IM,3)

......    ......    ......    ...   .......

D(1,JM)   D(2,JM)   D(3,JM)   ...   D(IM,JM)
```

Punctuation in these statements must be handled with care. Each comma and parenthesis is significant. The ordering of the control variables is significant; their ranges must be planned carefully. Consider what a difference the substitution of D(J,I) for D(I,J) makes in the above example.

Common Errors

1. Parentheses left off of implied DO loops as in READ 1, A(J), J = 1,8.
2. Confusion about placement of values on cards when reading more than one array. A new READ statement starts a new card, but two arrays in a statement as in

   READ 5, (X(J), J = 1,9), (Y(J), J = 1,9)

   do not start a new card when the first array is finished unless the FORMAT statement says to do so.
3. Confusion about the order of the indices in two- or three-dimensional arrays. One must be consistent.

Things You Can Do

1. Read or print an entire array as in READ 1, ARRAY or PRINT 2, LIST.
2. Use a short FORMAT specification (such as 5F10.2) for an array no matter how long it is.
3. Read or print several array elements and the index with one implied DO loop as in PRINT 8, (X(J),J,Z(J), J = 1,N).
4. Read the values for a DO loop control in the same READ statement as the DO loop; for example, READ 8,L,K,(X(J), J = L,K).

4–1.3 The "Index-Out-of-Range" Problem

We have stressed that the index used in an array must be within the range declared in the DIMENSION statement. However, in most Fortran systems there is no check made to enforce this rule. The reason for this is that it increases the execution time too much. Consider the two programs below.

```
                            DIMENSION IB(30)
                            REAL A(20),IB
Illegal index  ——————————   A(27) = 13.1
(obvious)                   KB = 2.1*A(27) + 5.1
Illegal index  ——————————   IB(KB) = A(KB-12)
(not obvious)               PRINT 10,KB,IB(KB),A(27)
                         10 FORMAT(I12,2F12.4)
                            STOP
                            END
```

```
                           REAL A(20)
                           KA = 1
                           XJ = 17.1**2 - 62.3*SQRT(5.1)
                           YJ = XJ**3 - SQRT(3.1*XJ)*XJ**2
                           ZIP= 48912.*XJ/(XJ+8.7)
                         2 XJ = YJ - ZIP*FLOAT(KA)
                           IF(SQRT(8.8)/YJ-1./XJ) 10,10,5
                         5 KA = KA+1
                             GO TO 2
Illegal index ---------- 10 A(KA) = XJ
(very hard to know)        PRINT 15,KA,A(KA)
                        15 FORMAT(I12,F12.4)
                           STOP
                           END
```

It is obvious that an error occurs on the left with A(27). It is not so obvious that a similar error occurs with IB but a little calculation shows that KB = 32. It is virtually impossible to guess what the value of KA is when statement 10 is reached in the right-hand program (it is 43). This means that the legality of an index value cannot be checked during the compilation. It can be checked during execution, but at the price of making two (at least) tests every time an array element is used. One test is to see that the index is greater than 1, the other to check that the index is less than the maximum permitted value. A few Fortran systems do this checking, and it means a substantial increase in the cost of using arrays, except on those computers with special hardware devices for this purpose.

When an array is used with an illegal index, the results can be disastrous. It can cause strange and mysterious errors to occur at places completely unre-

word	0001		Machine language instructions (the compiled program)
word	0002		
.			
.			
.			
word	0105		
word	0106		
word	0107	13.1	Program constants
word	0108	2.1	
word	0109	5.1	
word	0110	27	
word	0111	12	
word	0112	KB	Program variable
word	0113	A(1)	Array A
word	0114	A(2)	
.			
.			
.			
word	0132	A(20)	
word	0133	IB(1)	Array IB
word	0134	IB(2)	
.			
.			
.			
word	0162	IB(30)	

***FIGURE 4–2.** Typical memory allocation for a program with arrays.*

lated to where the actual use of the illegal index is made. In order to see how this can happen, we must expand a little on Figure 4–1 and discuss in more detail how the program appears at execution time. We consider the concrete case of the program above on the left. The allocation of the words in the computer's memory is illustrated in Figure 4–2. A Fortran system processes arrays by keeping track of the location of the first element (A(1) is in location 0113) and then finding the other elements by adding the index less 1 to this location. Thus, A(10) is at address 0122 = 0113 + 10 − 1. Actually, the system keeps track of where A(0) would be if it were allowed. For the array A this location is 0112 and A(10) is then at location 0122 = 0112 + 10. This arrangement allows the system to locate A(10) or A(8) directly without any table lookup, and so on.

We can now see where A(27) is located, namely at 0112 + 27 = 0139. This happens to be the location of IB(7) because 0139 = 0132 + 7. Thus the first statement of this program changes IB(7) to 13.1. Likewise, in the second statement when A(27) is used in the expression, the value written at 0139 [which is IB(7)] is used. Finally, at the third statement a value is placed in IB(32) which is location 0132 + 32 = 0164. This location is not used by this program. It might be completely unused or it might be used by the system. In the second case, completely unpredictable results can occur.

Suppose that the first statement is changed to

```
A(27) = -16.4
```

Then the value of KB becomes −29 and IB(−29) is at location 0132 − 29 = 0103. This location is in the actual program to be executed and it means that one of the machine-language instructions is changed to nonsense and the program will behave unpredictably when it comes to this instruction. Even stranger things can occur. Suppose that the first instruction is replaced by

```
KA = -4
A(KA) = 13.1
```

The second of these statements causes 13.1 to be written at location 0112 + KA = 0112 − 4 = 0108 which is the location of the constant 2.1. It is then changed to be 13.1 and the statement

```
KB = 2.1*A(KA)+5.1
```

becomes, at execution time,

$$KB = 13.1 * 13.1 + 5.1$$

which sets KB equal to 176. This in turn causes the next statement IB(KB) = A(KB − 12) to set the value at location 0132 + 176 = 0308 equal to the value of A(KB − 12) which is at 0112 + 176 − 12 = 0276. No one knows what the eventual effect of these actions will be. However, it can be very difficult to locate errors of this type because the effect is so unrelated to the cause.

Note that the positioning of the arrays in memory is not a part of the Fortran language and thus it varies from system to system. This means that a program with a subtle index-out-of-range problem is likely to behave very differently with different systems.

Problems

4–1.1 Read a 10-element list in F format, write it in E format, and compute the average of the elements of the list. Also write the list out in reverse order.

4–1.2 Read a set of 16 real numbers, order them (sort) by finding the smallest and printing it, then find the next smallest and print it, and so on.

4–1.3 What diagnostics does your compiler issue when it processes statements such as

(a) A = 2 * A + 1.5
(b) A = C(C(1))
(c) A = C(1.0)
(d) A = C(2 + 1)
(e) C = C(I2).

4–1.4 Consider the following sets of printed output and PRINT statements. Indicate which of the PRINT statements produces the output shown using the given FORMAT.

(A)

```
Column      6| 8|     15|
        17.3| 1| 7.301|
        18.8| 2| 7.321|
         6.4| 3| 4.404|          10 FORMAT( F6.1,I2,F7.3 )

        A.   PRINT 10,X(1),1,Q(1),X(2),2,Q(2),X(3),3,Q(3)
        B.   PRINT 10,(X(J),J,Q(J),J=1,3)
        C.   PRINT 10,(A,J,B,C,J,D,E,J,F),J=1,3
        D.   PRINT 10,(X(J),J=1,3),(J,J=1,3),(Q(J),J=1,3)
```

(B)

```
Column      6|     12| 15|   20|
       6.072| 4.123|  3|  7.2|
       0.101| 5.724| 12| -4.1|
       1.707|                     20 FORMAT( 2F6.3,I3,F5.1 )

        A.   PRINT 20,R1,R2,(K,X(L),L=1,3),(J,Y(J),J=1,2 )
        B.   PRINT 20,A,B,3,R,S,T,(K,Y(J),J=1,2)
        C.   PRINT 20,A,B,K,(X(L),L=1,3),INX,P,Q
        D.   PRINT 20,R1,R2,KEX,XEX,(X(1,L),X(2,L),L,L=1,2)
```

4–1.5 Give a FORMAT statement which can be used to read the cards below using the READ statement shown.

(A)

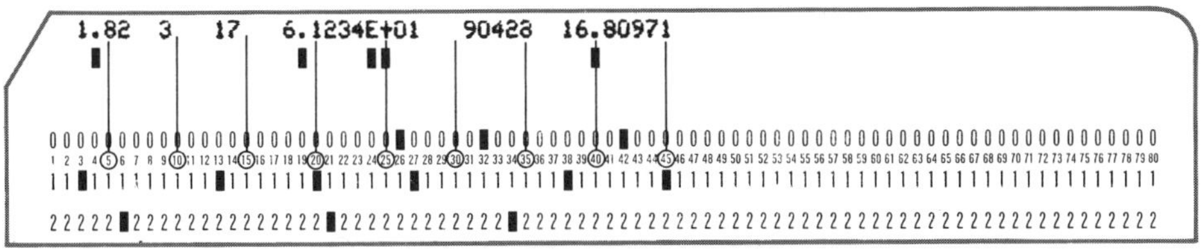


```
  READ 5,A,I,J,B,K,C
5 FORMAT
```

(B)

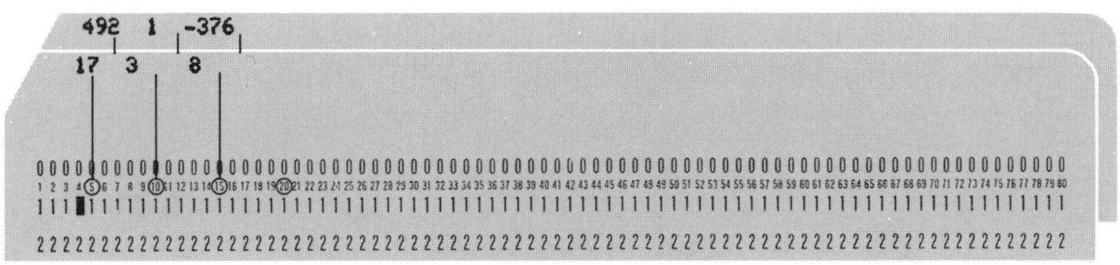


```
  READ 6,I,J,(INT(M),M=1,4)
6 FORMAT
```

(C)

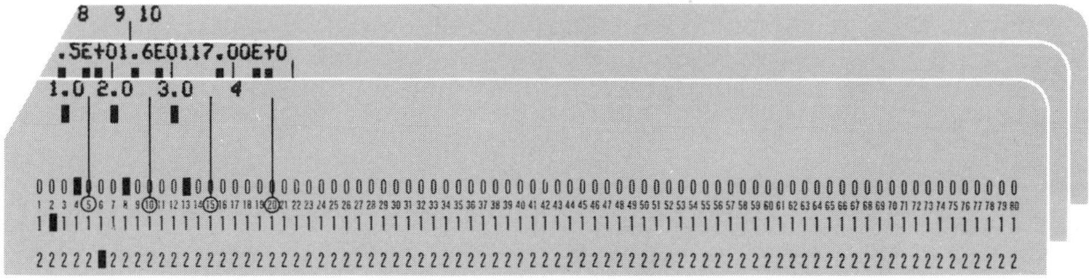


```
READ 7,(X(J),J=1,3),K,Z1,Z2,Z3,(IBN(J),J=1,3)
```

(D)

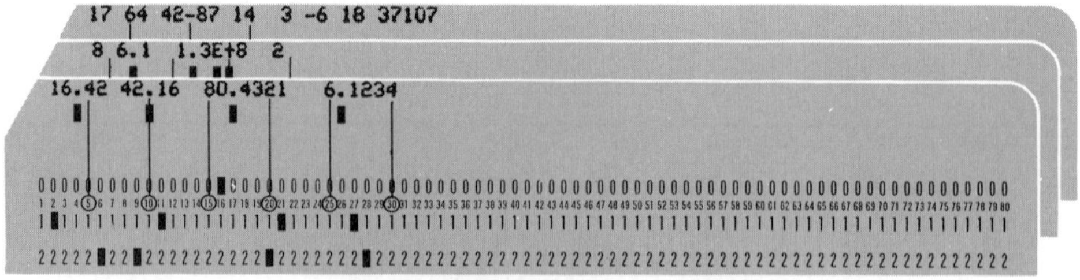


```
   REAL S(2),T(2)
   INTEGER INT(10)
   READ 8,S,T,KK,XX,EE,JJ,INT
 8 FORMAT
```

4–1.6 You have 3 cards which contain the values of variables NYEAR, NMONTH, NDAY, GROSS, ADJ, KLAZ(K), K = 1 to 3, TAX(K), K = 1 to 3 and DEDUCT(K), K = 1 to 4. The values are on these cards in the order listed above

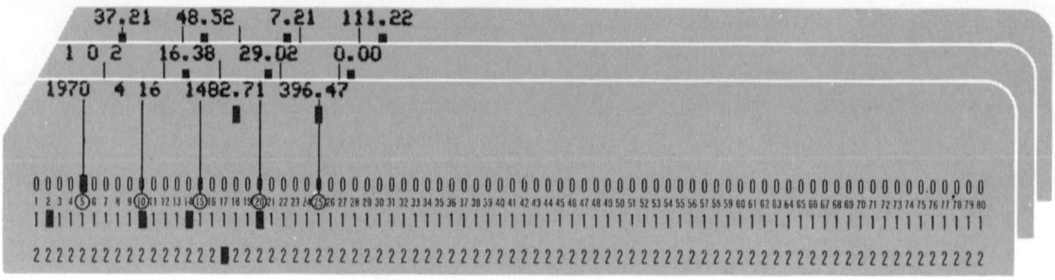

Give one READ statement and associated FORMAT statement that correctly reads these cards and assigns the values.

4–1.7 Consider the following Fortran program:

```
   REAL X(50),Y(50),A(50),B(50)
   INTEGER T,U
   READ 5, (X(T),Y(T),T=1,25),A(1),B(1)
 5 FORMAT(10F6.3)
   T=1.
10 DIST = SQRT((X(T)-A(T))**2 + (Y(T)-B(T))**2)
   A(T+1) = A(T) + 2.*(X(T)-A(T))/DIST
   B(T+1) = B(T) + 2.*(Y(T)-B(T))/DIST
   T = T+1
   IF( DIST-1. ) 15,15,10
15 PRINT 20,(U,A(U),B(U),U=1,T)
20 FORMAT( I10,2F14.3)
   STOP
   END
```

(a) How many cards are read in?
(b) How many (in terms of the value of T) numbers are printed out?
(c) How many (in terms of the value of T) lines of printed output are there?
(d) Identify the iteration loops in the program and give the names of their parts and the corresponding Fortran statements.

4–1.8 Find the number of lines (or cards) and the number of values printed out (or read in) by each of the pieces of Fortran programs given.

(A)

```
      REAL X(100),Y(100)
      J = 1
   10 PRINT 30,X(J),X(J+1),X(J+2)
   30 FORMAT( 5X,2E12.3 )
      PRINT 40,A,(Y(K),K=1,20),Z
   40 FORMAT( 3X6F10.2)
      J = J+1
      IF( J-8 ) 10,10,50
   50 STOP
      END
```

(B)

```
      INTEGER ATOP(100),ABOT(100),NAME(15)
      READ 5,NAME
    5 FORMAT(6(3X,I5))
      NA = 47
      READ 10,(ATOP(K),K=1,NA),(ABOT(K),K=1,NA)
   10 FORMAT(8(2XI8))
```

4–1.9 An array in which most of the elements are zero is said to be sparse. Write a program in which you define a 3 × 3 array, set its elements equal to zero, and then read in the values, along with the subscripts, that constitute the nonzero elements of the array. Write out the data and resulting array.

4–1.10 Using one PRINT statement, write out the diagonal elements of a square array. Show how either the upper or lower triangular parts of a square array can be written using only one PRINT statement.

4–1.11 Read in the size of a one-dimensional array and each one of its elements, then write it out in reverse order. Use just one READ statement and one

PRINT statement. Try it again, reading one number at a time and using arithmetic IF statements to control the reading and writing.

4–1.12 For some program that you have already written, determine exactly how many machine words are available for use as arrays. Try rerunning the program with an array that is somewhat too large.

4–1.13 Write a program that reads in two integers N and M and then reads in an N × M matrix row by row using the format FORMAT(2I5/16(16I5/)). Note that N and M are at most 16. Write out the original matrix, its transpose, and maximum row sum norm, the maximum column sum norm, the smallest element of the matrix, and the largest element of the matrix. Let $A = (\alpha_{ij})$ be any $N \times M$ matrix, then the maximum row sum norm =

$$\max \left\{ \sum_{i=1}^{M} |\alpha_{1i}|, \sum_{i=1}^{M} |\alpha_{2i}|, \ldots, \sum_{i=1}^{M} |\alpha_{Ni}| \right\}.$$

and the maximum column sum norm =

$$\max \left\{ \sum_{j=1}^{N} |\alpha_{j1}|, \sum_{j=1}^{N} |\alpha_{j2}|, \ldots, \sum_{j=1}^{N} |\alpha_{jM}| \right\}.$$

4–1.14 Write a program that reads in a one-dimensional array of up to 99 integer elements punched 10 per card and evenly spaced in columns 1 through 80 [use FORMAT(10I8)]. First, write out the array, then search the array for its greatest and least elements. Write out the greatest and least elements along with their positions in the array as described below.

If, for example, ARRAY(31) was the largest, and ARRAY(62) was the least, your output should contain these lines.

```
ARRAY(31) =  62047 IS LARGEST
ARRAY(62) =   -493 IS SMALLEST
```

4–1.15 A flowchart is given to add two integers of arbitrary length. The digits of the first number are in the array TOP and those of the second number are in the array BOT. There are K digits in each array and TOP(K), BOT(K) are on the left and TOP(1), BOT(1) are on the right. The digits of the sum of these two numbers are in the array ANS.

(a) Write a Fortran program based on this flowchart that adds integers of length up to 1000.

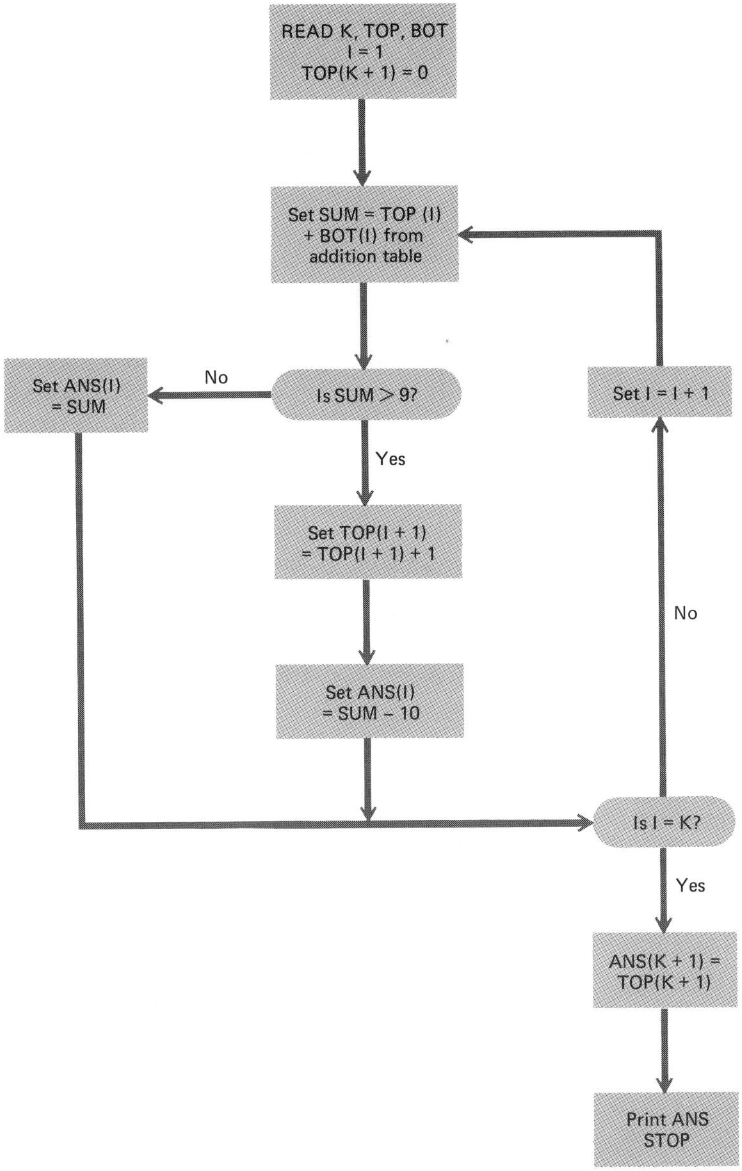

(b) Modify the program (if need be) so that the printed output is of the form

$$\begin{array}{r} 12341234555666 \\ +\quad 770000111888 \\ \hline =13111234667554 \end{array}$$

Allow only integers of up to 100 digits.

4–1.16 Write a Fortran program to subtract one integer from another where each number has up to 100 digits. If the result is negative, place a minus sign at the proper place, otherwise use the format specified in Problem 4–1.15, part (b).

4–1.17 Write a Fortran program to do integer multiplication with up to 20 digits in each factor.

4—2 Program Control

4–2.1 DO Statement

The control statement DO allows us to set up a simple iteration loop in one statement. This can materially shorten a program that handles loops using arithmetic IF's. For instance, three of the four statements used to set an array A to zero on the left below can be replaced by a single DO statement, as shown on the right.

```
      J = 1                        DO 1 J = 1,N
    1 A(J) = 0                   1 A(J) = 0
      J = J+1                        ...
      IF(J-N) 1,1,2
    2 ...
```

In the execution of a DO statement, all the statements in the range of the DO are executed in sequence, with the counter or control variable assuming a new value on each pass through these statements. The DO loop is terminated when the counter (or control variable) reaches a value larger than the terminal value. Then the statement following the terminal statement is executed. Consider the following statements; they set the array B equal to the array A and also find the sum of the elements of A:

```
                      INTEGER SIZEA
                      SUM = 0
                 ┌─── DO (22) J = 1,SIZEA
   Range of DO   │    B(J) =A(J)
                 └(22) SUM = A(J) + SUM
                      PRINT 25, SUM
```

The range of this DO loop includes the statements B(J) = A(J) and the one following it. Only after these two statements have been executed SIZEA times is the PRINT executed.

There are a few things we might be tempted to do within a DO loop which are not allowed:

1. Changing the value of the control variable
2. Changing the value of the terminal variable
3. Changing the value of the increment.

DO

> The word DO followed by an integer constant (label) followed by an integer variable separated by an = sign from three integer constants or variables (these are separated by commas). The general form appears as
>
> DO label counter = initial value, terminal value, increment.
>
> The initial value, terminal value, and increment are specified just as they are in the implicit DO for input-output statements; that is, they must be integer constants or variables (they must have nonzero, nonnegative values). If the increment is not specified, it is assumed to be the integer constant 1. The label following the DO must be the statement number of a statement that comes after the DO statement, and it marks the end of the range of the DO loop (this statement is called the terminal statement). The counter, also referred to as the control variable, must be a simple (nonsubscripted) integer variable.
>
> EXAMPLES
>
> ```
> DO 5   M   = 1,11,2      DO 707 KOUNT  = INITAL,LAST ,INCRE
> DO 55  MM  = 1,11        DO 888 K888   = K1    ,KLAST
> DO 617 M55 = 1,MB        DO 9   IJKLMN = I1    ,I2   ,K3
> ```

With these restrictions in mind, it is possible to place any Fortran statements within a DO loop. For instance,

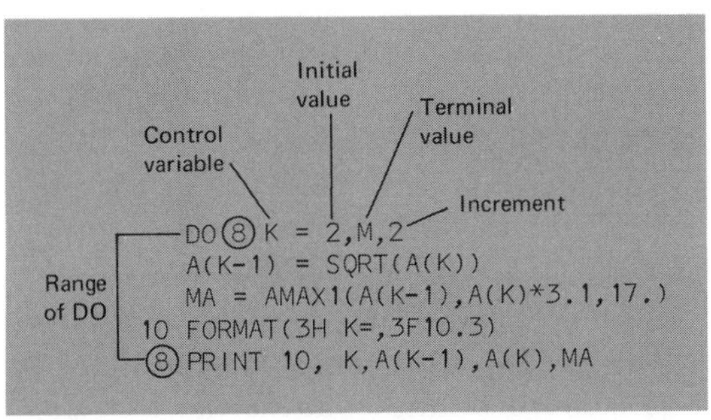

The counter never exceeds the terminal value except in one special situation. Thus, in the program

```
   J=3
   K=8
   DO 10 LL=J,K,J
10 ABC(LL) = LL**2 - K/J
```

the counter LL takes on the values 3 and 6 and the DO loop is not executed for LL = 9. The special situation occurs because the DO loop is always executed once, no matter what the initial and terminal values might be. For example,

```
      J=3                                  DO – loop executed
      K=1                                  once even though
      DO 10 II=J,K,J                       K<J
   10 ABC(II) = II**2 - K/J
```

is executed one time and results in ABC(3) set equal to 9 because LL does start at the initial value. The exact action of the DO statement is shown in the flowchart of Figure 4–3. Note that the counter is undefined after the DO loop is finished. Every variable in Fortran does have a value, but one does not necessarily know what it is at this point. Some Fortran compilers leave the counter at the terminal value (this is the most logical thing to do), others leave it at the terminal value plus 1, and still others leave it with a completely garbage value.

It is possible to transfer to any executable statement that has a label. However we should not transfer to a statement within the range of a DO from outside the range and expect it to work. The only way to enter a DO loop is at the DO statement. This is reasonable since the DO loop is only set up by the DO statement and an entry into the range of the DO statement results in unpredictable actions.

```
         GO TO (10)                          GO TO (15)
         ....                                ....
Range ┌10 DO (20) L = 1,N           Range ┌  DO (25) J = J1,K
      │  ....                             │  ....
      └(20) X = A(L)                      │15 A(J) =A(J)**2 -1
                                          │  ....
                                          └(25) P = SQRT(FLOAT(J)+A(J))
```

Legal Illegal

Leaving a DO loop is subject to only one restriction; if the departure is from the terminal statement of the DO, then the control variable may not be used again until it is assigned a value. Any departure from within the DO loop allows the control variable to be used outside the DO loop with the value it had at the time of departure.

```
┌ DO (8) K = 1,N                  ┌ DO (8) K = 1,N
└(8) A(K) = 0                     │ IF(Q(K)) 8,12,8
     B(K) = 0                     └(8) Q(K) = Q(K) - 7.5     Jump out of DO – loop
                                       K = N+1               K is well defined
K no longer defined here          12   K = K-1               at statement 12
```

Illegal Legal

The last statement in the range of a DO may not be any of the following types of executable statements: GO TO, arithmetic IF, another DO, or RETURN

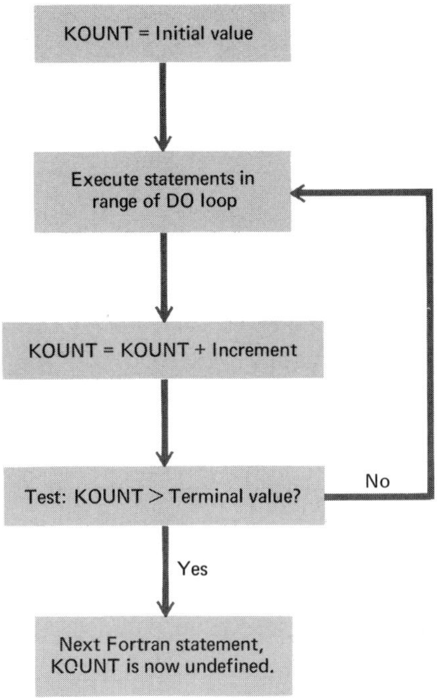

FIGURE 4–3. The operation of the* DO *statement in Fortran.

(this latter statement is discussed later). Of course, a DO loop cannot end with an unexecutable statement such as a FORMAT, INTEGER, and so on. As it is sometimes convenient to use an IF at the end of a DO, this can be accomplished by use of the CONTINUE statement, whose sole function is to permit a label to be defined. Thus the statements on the left are not valid, but the desired effect can be obtained as on the right.

```
      DO 7 M = 1,J                     DO 7 M = 1,J
    7 IF(A(M)) 7,7,9                   IF(A(M)) 7,7,9
                                     7 CONTINUE
      Illegal transfer                 Legal transfer
```

Several DO loops may be contained one within another, provided that their ranges are properly nested; that is, the range of the "shortest" DO is fully contained within the range of the next "shortest" DO, and so on. This is illustrated below.

```
      DO 1 J = 1,NROWS    ------------------
      DO 2 K = 1,NCOLS    --  Range of     |  Range of
    2 A(J,K) = 0          --  DO 2         |  DO 1
    1 CONTINUE            ------------------
```

The control variable J for the outermost DO is set; then the innermost DO is executed. When it is done, or "satisfied," J is incremented and the process repeats, until finally we have set A(1,1), . . ., A(NROWS,NCOLS) equal to zero. It is possible for one statement to be the terminal statement for several DO loops. Thus the following three statements are equivalent to the above four.

```
      DO 1 J = 1,NROWS
      DO 1 K = 1,NCOLS
    1 A(J,K) = 0
```

Range of DO 1 Range of DO 1

The slightest punctuation error in a DO statement can lead to amusing (disastrous) consequences. For example, if the only comma in DO 2 K = 1,10 is left out, we get DO 2 K = 1 10 or, ignoring all the blanks DO2K = 110 which says "set DO2K to 110."

The use of the DO statement is illustrated by a program for an example considered earlier in Section 3–4. The problem is to determine if 7319 is a prime number and a simple-minded iterative algorithm is shown in the flowchart of Figure 3–9. The program given below is based on this flowchart except that K is incremented by 2 rather than 1. To test for the exactness of the division, we compute the integer part IPART of 7319/K and then see if K * IPART is 7319. It will be if K is a factor of 7319. We also make the program slightly more general by using NPRIME for 7319.

```
      NPRIME = 7319
      K = 2
      IF( 2*(NPRIME/2)-NPRIME) 5,20,5
    5 LASTK = SQRT(FLOAT(NPRIME))
      DO 10 K = 3,LASTK,2
      IPART = NPRIME/K
      IF( K*IPART - NPRIME ) 10,20,10
   10 CONTINUE
      PRINT 15,NPRIME
   15 FORMAT(I15, 9H IS PRIME)
      STOP
   20 PRINT 25,NPRIME,K
   25 FORMAT(I15,13H HAS A FACTOR I8)
      STOP
      END
```

Jump out here if K is a factor of NPRIME

Points of note in this program include the following:

1. We test for NPRIME even (K = 2) first, then let the DO loop test the odd numbers.
2. We have to "float" the integer NPRIME before taking its square root.
3. A CONTINUE is used at the end of the DO loop because we would really like to have an IF there.
4. If a factor is found, we jump out of the DO loop and its value K is printed out.
5. There are two different places the program can stop.

Common Errors

1. Incorrect punctuation.
2. Use of an expression for the initial, terminal, or increment value of a DO loop.
3. Transfer into DO loop from outside.
4. Use of the same control variable for an implied DO loop (in READ or PRINT) and in a DO loop containing this statement.
5. Use of the same counter (control variable) for two nested DO loops.
6. Use of a negative increment for the DO loop. They do not "run backward."
7. Use of the DO loop counter after a normal termination of the DO loop.

Things You Can Do

1. Use the control variable of a DO loop after one jumps out of the "middle" of the loop.
2. Jump out of and return to a DO loop and continue the iteration *provided* that one does not change the DO loop variables and that the Fortran system allows it.
3. Make a DO loop "run backward" by introducing a pseudo control variable as in DO8 J = J1,J2,INC followed by JB = J2 + J1 − J. Then JB goes from J2 to J1 in steps of −INC.

4–2.2 Computed GO TO

The unconditional transfer of the form "GO TO label" is somewhat inflexible. The more flexible computed GO TO offers some choice in the selection of a destination. For instance,

GO TO(1,2),K

causes a transfer to the statement labeled 1 if K has the value 1, or to the statement labeled 2 if K has the value 2.

Computed GO TO

The word GO TO followed by a list of labels (separated by commas) in parentheses followed by a comma and ending with an integer variable. A direct transfer is made to the label in the list as indicated by the value of the trailing integer variable. Thus, transfer to the first label if the value is 1, to the second label if the value is 2, to the third label if the value is 3, and so forth.

EXAMPLES

```
GO TO(275,25,36),K            GO TO(88,17,403,1),KX
GO TO(5,4,8,96),ISWTCH        GO TO(9,8,10,25),MUM
```

Thus GO TO(5,4,8,96), ISWTCH causes a transfer to one of the statements labeled 5, 4, 8, 96 accordingly as the value of ISWTCH is 1, 2, 3, or 4. IF ISWTCH is not 1, 2, 3, or 4, then the computed GO TO is not defined and the results are unpredictable.

The variable that selects the label must be an integer variable. It is assigned values in the usual way. Consider the following examples:

```
  K = A(I)
  GO TO(2,17,3),K

  J = MAX1(B(1),RQ)
  IF(J-4) 1,1,22
1 GO TO(17,12,8,97),J
```

```
   DO 3 K = 1,4
      ...
      GO TO(1,2,3,3),K
      ...
1     X = A(K)
      ...
2     X = A(K) + 3.5
      ...
3  CONTINUE
```

Possible transfers

In the first example K is assigned a value that must be 1, 2, or 3. In the second example J is assigned a value assumed to be greater than zero. Then it is tested; if J is less than or equal to 4, the GO TO is executed. In the program on the right, the computed GO TO transfers appropriately as K takes on the values 1, 2, 3, and 4.

A situation where it is natural to use the computed GO TO is illustrated in Figure 4–4. We have a program with several different cases. The first part of the program separates the cases (among other things); then all cases are processed by the same code for a while. At the end it is necessary to separate the different cases out again. The way to do this is to "remember" which case was found earlier instead of retesting for the cases. To "remember" something in a program, one has to create a variable and assign it a value at the appropriate time. In this program the variable KASE is used and when the second separation is made the computed GO TO is used directly with KASE.

Common Errors	*Things You Can Do*
1. Omission of the comma just before the variable that controls the transfer. 2. The control variable is negative or larger than the number of labels present. This usually results in an infinite loop or garbage or a very elusive bug.	1. Use as many labels as you like, in any order, and with repetitions.

4–2.3 Logical IF

Recall that the arithmetic IF has the general form

IF (arithmetic expression) label 1, label 2, label 3

The specification of three labels permits a three-way branch to be specified. It is a rather clumsy statement to use when less than a three-way branch is required. The logical IF has a more natural form suitable for two-way branches, corresponding to the natural expression "if such and such is true, perform the indicated operation; otherwise go on to the next statement." As an illustration, suppose A is to be set to 1 if X is equal to 17; otherwise A is to be set to 2. This may be done with an arithmetic IF or a logical IF as follows:

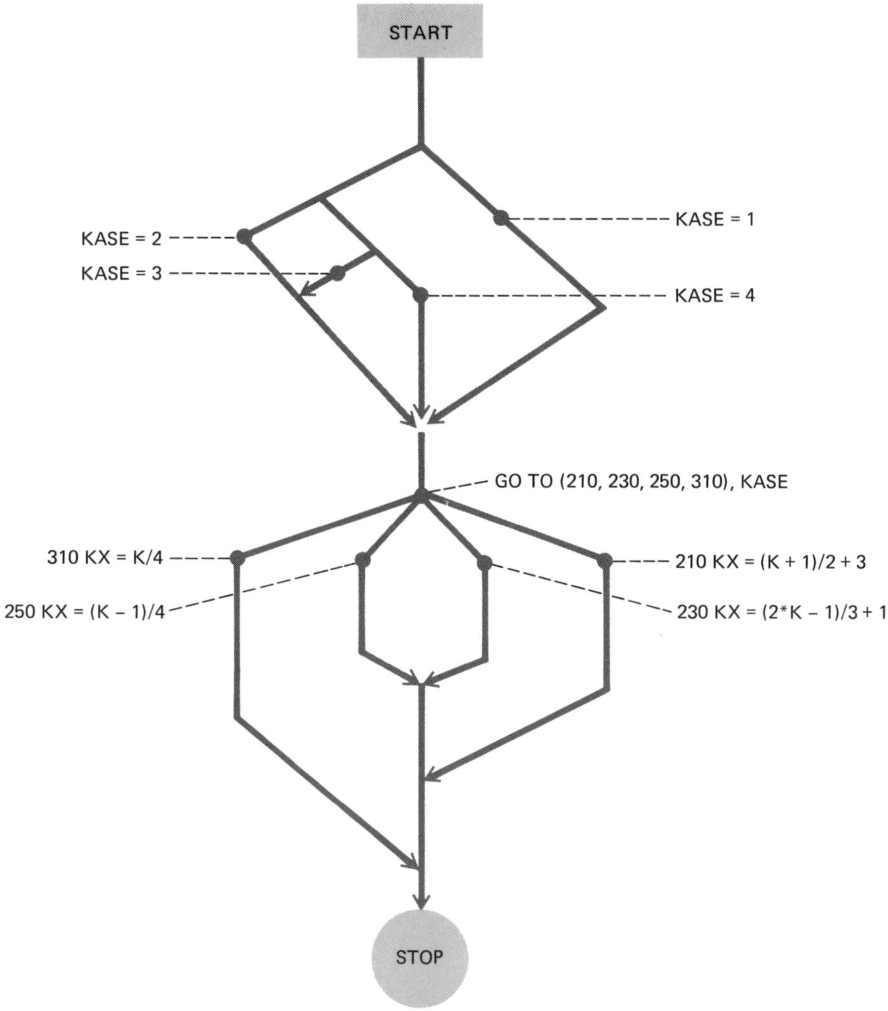

FIGURE 4–4. The variable* KASE *is used to "remember" the case determined early in the program, then the computed* GO TO *is used with* KASE *later to separate the computation into the four cases.

```
   A = 2                              A = 2
   IF( X-17. ) 1,2,1                  IF( X.EQ.17. ) A= 1
 1 A = 1
2    ...
```

Note that on the right labels 1 and 2 are not needed and the assignment statement A = 1 is included with the IF; notice also the use of .EQ. . The statement IF(X .EQ. 17) A = 1 is read as "if X equals 17, then set A to 1; otherwise go on to the next statement."

IF Logical

The form is

IF (logical expression) executable statement.

The simpler types of logical expressions are presented below. More complex ones involving logical variables are discussed in the next chapter. A logical expression has a value of either "true" or "false." If the expression is true, then the executable statement is done; otherwise, the program passes to the statement following the IF. If the executable statement does not transfer control (that is, as a GO TO would), then the program passes on to the following statement after the executable statement is done. The only executable statements not allowed are another logical IF and a DO.

EXAMPLES

```
IF(X.EQ.17.) Z=SQRT(X+Y)          IF(J.EQ.-1) STOP
IF(K.EQ.4)   PRINT 22,K,A(K)      IF(J.EQ.100) GO TO(1,2),K
IF(K.EQ.7)   GO TO 88             IF(Z(4).EQ.17.68) PRINT 8,Z(5),B
```

An expression is a logical expression if it is either true or false. A logical expression arises quite naturally when comparisons are made; for example, is $A > B$?; is $\sin(x) + \text{sqrt}(y) < \log(z)$? These are questions that may be answered with true or false. This type of logical expression is called a *relational expression*. In general, a relational expression consists of two arithmetic expressions, both real or both integer, separated by a relational operator. The relational operators are the six mathematical comparisons denoted by $=$, $\neq$, $>$, $<$, $\geq$, $\leq$. Since not all of these symbols are part of the Fortran character set, special names are set aside for them (even for $=$).

Relational Operator	*Fortran Name*	*Meaning*
$=$	.EQ.	Equal to
$\neq$	.NE.	Not equal to
$<$	.LT.	Less than
$\leq$	.LE.	Less than or equal to
$>$	.GT.	Greater than
$\geq$	.GE.	Greater than or equal to

More involved logical expressions can be built by combining logical expressions using the standard logical operators for disjunction, conjunction, and negation. Their Fortran designations are .OR., .AND., and .NOT. . They are defined as follows (given two logical expressions x and y):

Conjunction: x .AND. y is false unless both x and y are true
Disjunction: x .OR. y is true unless both x and y are false
Negation: .NOT. x is false if x is true, and vice versa.

A variable which is either true or false is called a *logical variable* or a *Boolean variable.* This type of variable is discussed in more detail in Chapter 6. The *value* of a logical expression is a logical variable (true or false) and not a number.

In order to compare how these statements may be used, suppose we want to set R to R1 only if S is 3 and T is 4. Here are three ways of doing it.

```
  IF(S-3) 1,2,1                    IF( S.NE.3 ) GO TO 1
2 IF(T-4) 1,3,1                    IF( T.EQ.4 ) R = R1
3 R = R1                         1 ...

      IF( S.EQ.3 .AND. T.EQ.4 ) R = R1
```

Three labels are needed in the left-hand program which uses the arithmetic IF. The arithmetic IF is replaced by the logical IF in the right-hand program and they involve relational expressions and need only one label. In the bottom program the relational expressions of the right-hand program are joined by the logical operator .AND. and the desired action takes place in one statement without introducing any labels.

Care must be taken in correctly constructing logical expressions. A spoken statement such as "if A is greater than P or Q, then go to . . ." is sometimes incorrectly written as

```
IF( A.GT.P.OR.Q ) GO TO 88
```

The statement should be

```
IF( A.GT.P .OR. A.GT.Q ) GO TO 88
```

or, even better,

```
IF( A.GT. AMIN1(P,Q) ) GO TO 88
```

All of the desired comparisons have to be specified; in this case, we want "$A > P$ or $A > Q$" not "$A > P$ or Q."

Parentheses may be used to group various parts of logical expressions to remove any possible ambiguity or confusion. For instance,

```
IF( A.GT.B+C.AND..NOT.X.LT.Y)Q=1
```

can be written in the more readable form:

```
IF( (A.GT.(B+C)) .AND. (.NOT.( X.LT.Y ))) Q=1
```

Common Errors

1. Use of equal sign = instead of .EQ..
2. Mixture of real and integer variables (such as XX .EQ. 4 or AB .LT. 10).
3. Testing for equality with real variables (such as XX .EQ. 1.5 or AB .EQ. 12.0). Round-off normally prevents equality from occurring.
4. Translating ordinary English (such as "if x is less than −2 or greater than +3") into Fortran [such as IF(X .LT. −2. .OR. .GT. +3.)]. Fortran does not use .AND. and .OR. in the same way as English uses "and" or "or".

Things You Can Do

1. Place the following Fortran statements with an IF.

CALL	PRINT	RETURN
GO TO	READ	STOP
		WRITE

   and any assignment statement.
2. Place a logical IF at the end of a DO loop. This includes a logical IF which has a GO TO with it.

4–2.4 The Automobile Cost Program

In Chapter 2 a program was given for the mathematical model developed to analyze automobile costs. Another program for this model is presented below. The programs produce identical results except that the program here has one more PRINT statement. The point of presenting another program is to show the difference in programming between using the basic elements of Fortran (as presented in Chapter 1) and using features of this chapter.

Recall at the end of Chapter 1 we stated that the features presented there are enough to do almost anything possible in Fortran. The merit of the features in this chapter and the next one is that things can be done more naturally and efficiently. The amount of computation for the two programs is about the same. However, the one here has only 33 statements (excluding comments) and 6 labels, while the one in Chapter 3 has 50 statements (excluding comments) and 28 labels. This program is "cleaner" and easier to read (and understand).

```
C       PROGRAM FOR THE SOLUTION OF THE AUTOMOBILE COST PROBLEM - NO. 2
C          MODEL INDICATES FIRST, SECOND OR THIRD MATH MODEL
C
        REAL INTAN
        DO 400 MODEL = 1,3
C                      PRINT HEADING
        PRINT 2,MODEL
      2 FORMAT(1H1,20X,22HRESULTS FOR MATH MODEL I2/  9X4HYEAR,6X,12HAVERA
       *GE COST )
        IF( MODEL .EQ. 3 )  PRINT 3
      3 FORMAT(15X20H CASE OF  AVER. JOE )
        VALUE = 3000.
        DO 400 KYEAR = 1,100
```

```
C           COMPUTE DEPRECIATION, REPAIR AND OPERATING COSTS
      DEP = .3*VALUE
      VALUE = VALUE - DEP
      OP = 450.
      IF( KYEAR .GE. 3 )  OP = 500.
      REP = 0.0
      IF( KYEAR .GE. 3 ) REP =  100.
      IF( KYEAR .GE. 4 ) REP =  200.
      IF( KYEAR .GE. 6 ) REP =  300.
      IF( MODEL .EQ. 1 )  GO TO 240
      IF( KYEAR .GE.11 ) REP =  400.
      IF( KYEAR .GE.14 ) REP =  600.
      IF( KYEAR .GE.20 ) REP =  750.
C           HAVE FINISHED DEPRECIATION, REPAIR AND OPERATING COSTS
  240 INTAN = 0.
      IF( MODEL .LT. 3 )  GO TO 300
C         PUT IN THE INTAGIBLE COST (FOR AVERAGE JOE)
      IF( KYEAR .GE. 3 )  INTAN = 100.
      IF( KYEAR .GE. 5 )  INTAN = 200.
  300 COST = DEP + OP + REP + INTAN
      YEAR = KYEAR
      AAC  = (COST +(YEAR -1.)*AAC)/YEAR
C         PRINT SELECTED VALUES OF AVERAGE AAC
      IF( KYEAR .LE. 20 )  PRINT 420,KYEAR,AAC
  400 IF( KYEAR.EQ.40 .OR. KYEAR.EQ.100) PRINT 420,KYEAR,AAC
  420 FORMAT( I12,F14.0 )
      STOP
      END
```

Problems

4–2.1 A program involving DO loops can sometimes be made to execute much more rapidly if there are computations within a DO loop that can be done outside. Determine how much faster the following statements run if such changes are made.

```
      DO 2 I=1,N
      DO 2 J=1,M
    2 A(I,J) = SIN(X)*COS(FLOAT(I))*Y +FLOAT(J)
```

4–2.2 Write a program that reads a set of integer scores all lying in the range from 0 to 100, and have it calculate the frequencies for each score from 0 to 100.

4–2.3 Outline a program that prints a histogram, or bar graph. Apply it to generate graphical output for the frequency counts of Problem 4–2.2.

4–2.4 Write a program, similar to that of Problem 4–2.2, that reads a set of real numbers, counts them, finds the largest and the smallest, then scales them into the interval, 0 to 1, and does a frequency count in steps of 1/10.

4–2.5 Using real arithmetic, compute the number S from the formula

$$S^2 = \frac{1}{n} \sum_{i=1}^{n} (x_i - \overline{x})^2,$$

where x is an array with n integer elements $x_1, \ldots, x_n$ and $\overline{x}$ is the average value of the x_i's. The number S is called the standard deviation.

4–2.6 Convert the following DO loop into an equivalent set of Fortran statements that do *not* include a DO statement:

```
      DO 22 KK= 3,LAST,JUMP
      KBAR(KK) = KBAR(KK+3) + 1
   22 CONTINUE
```

4–2.7 In recording experimental data, it often happens that the recorded information is to be transformed prior to being used in *standard formulas.* Suppose five kinds of data are measured. Assign to each a one-digit code. The transformations to be applied are:

type 1, square root; type 2, add $\pi/2$; type 3, log;
type 4, take inverse; type 5, cube root.

Write a program that reads the data and data types and then applies the appropriate transformation.

4–2.8 Write a program that reads in three integers M, N, and L. Then read in an M $\times$ N matrix called A and an N $\times$ L matrix called B. Print out the original matrices and the matrix product A * B. The matrix product has the I,Kth element defined by

$$\sum_{J=1}^{N} A(I,J) * B(J,K)$$

and it is an M $\times$ L matrix.

4–2.9 Write a program that reads in a list of numbers between 0 and 1000 and find the median of this list. The median is the number that is in the middle of the list after it is sorted and arranged from smallest to largest. Write the program so that the list may have at most 1000 elements. Write out the list and the median and average of the list.

4–2.10 We define a magic square as an $n \times n$ square array or matrix where each of the integers $1, 2, 3, \ldots, n^2$ appears exactly once and all column sums, row sums, and diagonal sums are equal. We give the following algorithm for constructing an $n \times n$ magic square for any odd n. The digits $1, 2, 3, \ldots, n^2$ are written in order according to the following rules:

(a) Write 1 in the middle of the top row.

(b) Move up one row and to the right one column to place the next integer $(k + 1)$, unless one of the four special cases below occurs:

1. If a move takes you above the top row in the jth column, move to the bottom of the jth column and place the integer there.

2. If a move takes you outside to the right of the square in the jth row, place the integer in the jth row at the extreme left.
3. If a move takes you to a square that is already filled, place $k + 1$ immediately below k.
4. If you move out of the square at the upper right-hand corner (off of the diagonal), place $k + 1$ immediately below k.

8	1	6
3	5	7
4	9	2

17	24	1	8	15
23	5	7	14	16
4	6	13	20	22
10	12	19	21	3
11	18	25	2	9

Write a program that creates magic squares for $n = 1, 3, 5, 7, \ldots, 21$. For each n write out the $n \times n$ magic square, the n column sums, the n row sums, and both diagonal sums.

4–2.11 *Radix sorting* is the method of sorting punched cards on a mechanical sorter. The problem here is to order a list of decimal numbers simulating the method used on a sorting machine. Since the numbers are decimal, we need 10 pockets into which we place numbers. These pockets are labeled 0, 1, 2, . . ., 9. The algorithm proceeds as follows:

(a) Examine the right-most digit of each list element and place it in the pocket corresponding to the digit.

(b) After (a) has been carried out for all elements of the list, create a new list by placing the contents of the 0's pocket at the top, the contents of the 1's pocket next, . . ., the contents of the 9's pocket last.

(c) Repeat steps (a) and (b) for the digit immediately to the left of the digit just examined.

(d) Keep repeating (c) until all the digits of the largest element have been examined. The last list formed should be ordered.

Example:

Original list 171,805,624,562,476,409,624,437,248,003,669,552,437,743,797, 020,109,217,317,816.

After pass 1

Pocket	0	1	2	3	4	5	6	7	8	9
	020	171	562	003	624	805	476	437	248	409
			552	743	624		816	437		669
								797		109
								217		
								317		

List after pass 1 020,171,562,552,003,743,624,624,805,476,816,437,437,797, 217,317,248,409,669,109.

After pass 2

Pocket	0	1	2	3	4	5	6	7	8	9
	003	816	020	437	743	552	562	171		797
	805	217	624	437	248		669	476		
	409	317	624							
	109									

List after pass 2 003,805,409,109,816,217,317,020,624,624,437,437,743,248, 552,562,669,171,476,797.

After pass 3

Pocket	0	1	2	3	4	5	6	7	8	9
	003	109	217	317	409	552	624	743	805	
	020	171	248		437	562	624	797	816	
					437		669			
					476					

Sorted list 003,020,109,171,217,248,317,409,437,437,476,552,562,624,624, 669,743,797,805,816.

Write a program that accepts as input an unordered list of positive integers and sort them using the above algorithm. To demonstrate that the above algorithm was used, pattern your output after the example given above showing the contents of the pockets and list after each pass.

4–2.12 Write a program to compute Pascal's triangle of binomial coefficients. The first part appears as

```
        1
      1   1
    1   2   1
  1   3   3   1
1   4   6   4   1
```

and later rows are generated by noting that each element is the sum of the two elements just above it.

(a) Give the printed output in the form

$N = 0$ 1
$N = 1$ 1 1
$N = 2$ 1 2 1
$N = 3$ 1 3 3 1

and so on, and use only one PRINT statement for the entire array with 20 rows ($N = 19$).

(b) Give the printed output in the triangle shape illustrated above. Note that it is not easy to do this and requires a rather long program just using the Fortran features discussed so far. With some of the features later in this chapter and in the next one, it can be done with 10 statements.

4–2.13 Translate the following flowchart into a Fortran program. The resulting program is a crude mathematical model for computing the motion of N bodies (say stars) with masses $M(K)$, $K = 1$ to N placed initially at positions $x(K,0)$, $y(K,0)$ relative to some two-dimensional coordinate system. Time is broken into discrete steps of TS and the successive positions of the bodies are in the x,y arrays. The variables with F,A, and V as first letters are forces, accelerations, and velocities, respectively.

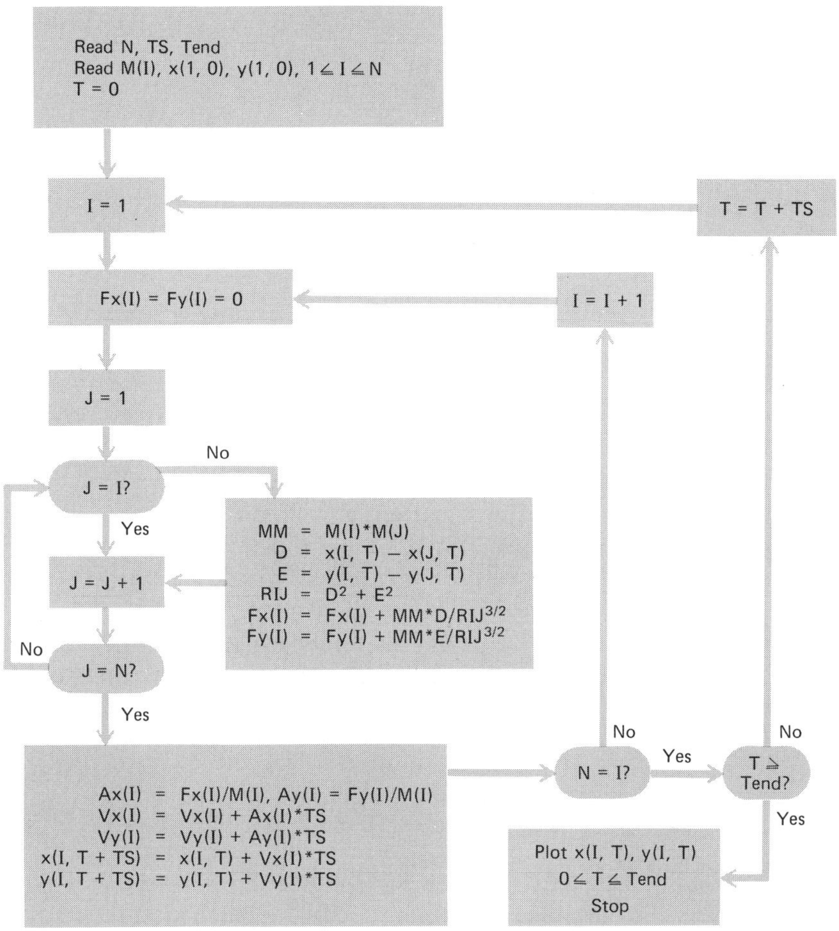

4–2.14 An executive tells his secretary, "Please ask Tom and Dick or Harry to come to a 3 o'clock meeting with me." Why should a bright secretary ask for clarification?

5

Fortran

INTERMEDIATE ELEMENTS

5—1 Functions and Subprograms

5–1.1 Arithmetic Statement Functions

The built-in functions provided by Fortran include only a small number of the functions that can be useful in writing a program. There are several ways in which we can define and use in a program any function that can be described in Fortran. The simplest way is to use functions that can be defined by a single statement. For instance, a polynomial $ax^2 + bx + c$ can be described in Fortran by the expression A * X * * 2 + B * X + C, or better, (A * X + B) * X + C. It becomes an arithmetic statement function simply by giving it a name and a list of arguments. Thus,

```
P(X) = A*X**2 + B*X + C
```

defines the arithmetic statement function P(X). It can then be used in a program in the same way as the built-in functions are used. The same kind of rules apply; the arithmetic statement function must be used with the proper number and type of arguments, and its value must be used within an expression without violating the no-mixed-mode rule. The expression defining the arithmetic statement function may contain the arguments and any other variables in the program. The variables (not arguments) that appear in the expression must be assigned values before the function is used. The arguments are assigned values when the

Arithmetic Statement Function

The general form is as follows:

name(arguments) = expression

where "name" is the Fortran name of the function, the arguments are the input variables to the function (there may be any number of them), and the expression is any legal Fortran expression. The statement defining the arithmetic statement function must come *after* all declaration statements and *before* all executable statements. Once the function is defined it is used as any built-in function is used. The types (real or integer) of the arguments, the variables in the expression, and the name must be compatible.

EXAMPLES

```
P(X) = A*X**2+B*X+C                    P(Z) = A*Z**2+B*Z+C
POLY(X,A) = A*X**2+B*X+C               JUNK(ZAP) = JZZ+IFIX(ZAP**2)
ROOT(A,B,C) = (-B+SQRT(B**2-4.*A*C))/(2.*A)
GUNK(X,I,T) = X*FLOAT(I) + COS(X+T*Y)


VALUE = P(7.1)
VAL2 = POLY(7.1,QA) + P(QA-7.2)
INDEX(4) = JUNK(14.1+XBAR) - 7
GGG = POLY(VALUE,XBAR)*ROOT(VAL2,P(XBAR),XBAR)
SIMP = P(X+1.)?P(x-1.)
```

function is used and the values are simply substituted into the expression in place of arguments. The arguments in the function definition are dummy variables (or placeholders) and it does not matter what they are named. Thus the two definitions of P(X) above are exactly equivalent. When P(X) [or P(Z)] is used, as in P(17.1), the value calculated is

```
A * 17.1**2 + B*17.1 + C
```

which does not depend on whether the function is defined as P(X) or P(Z) or P(GARBAG).

The type of the arithmetic statement function is defined either implicitly by its name or by including its name in a declaration statement. Its arguments, the dummy arguments, must also be typed in the same way. For example, we can have either of the following:

(i)	(ii)
`REAL LOX,MX`	`INTEGER P,A,B,C`
`LOX(X) = MX+A*X+B*X**3`	`P(IX) = A*IX**2 + B*IX + C`

Care must be taken in placing the definition of the arithmetic statement function after all the program's declarations, but in front of the first executable statement.

The usefulness of the arithmetic statement function comes into play only if it is used at several different points in the program. If it is used only once (or even twice if it is short), it is simpler to put the required expression at the place it is used than to define an arithmetic statement function. Consider the difference in readability (and keypunching!) for the two equivalent programs below which use the formula for the roots of a quadratic polynomial ($ax^2 + bx + c$).

```
      REAL MB
    2 READ 5,A,MB,C
      PRINT5,A,MB,C
    5 FORMAT(3F10.2)
      DISC = MB**2-4.*A*C
      IF(DISC .LT. 0.)  GO TO 20
      RPLUS = (-MB+SQRT(DISC))/(2.*A)
      RMINUS= (-MB-SQRT(DISC))/(2.*A)
      DIS2 = (MB+A)**2 -4.*(A-MB)*(C-MB)
      IF(DIS2 .LT. 0.)  GO TO 20
      SPLUS = (-MB-A+SQRT(DIS2))/(2.*(A-MB))
      SMINUS= (-MB-A-SQRT(DIS2))/(2.*(A-MB))
      RESULT= RPLUS*SPLUS-RMINUS*SMINUS
      PRINT 10,RESULT
   10 FORMAT( F18.4)
          GO TO 2
   20 PRINT 25
   25 FORMAT(10X20HSQRT OF NEGATIVE NO.)
          GO TO 2
      END
```

20 statements
386 characters to keypunch

```
      REAL MB
      DIS(A,B,C) = B**2-4.*A*C                  ]
      RT(A,B,D,S) =(-B+S*SQRT(D))/(2.*A)        ] Functions
    2 READ 5,A,MB,C
      PRINT5,A,MB,C
    5 FORMAT(3F10.2)
      D = DIS(A,MB,C)
      E = DIS(A-MB,MB+A,C-MB)
      IF( AMINI(D,E) .LT. 0. )  GO TO 20
      RESULT = RT(A,MB,D, 1.)*RT(A-MB,MB+A,E, 1.)
     *         -RT(A,MB,D,-1.)*RT(A-MB,MB+A,E,-1.)
      PRINT 10,RESULT
   10 FORMAT( F18.4)
          GO TO 2
   20 PRINT 25
   25 FORMAT(10X20HSQRT OF NEGATIVE NO.)
          GO TO 2
      END
```

18 statements
324 characters to keypunch

The dummy arguments can be only simple (nonarray) variables. The definition itself may be any valid Fortran expression, involving variables, constants, built-in functions, and any previously defined arithmetic statement functions. This is illustrated by the program below.

```
Declaration ——— REAL MEAN
Arithmetic statement {   P(X) = A+X*(B+C*X)
functions            {   MEAN(Y)= (ABS(P(Y))+ABS(P(Y+DELTA)))/2.
                     { 2 READ 1,A,B,C,X,DELTA
                     { 1 FORMAT(3F15.5)
Executable           {   HEIGHT = MEAN(X)
statements           {   WEIGHT =  HEIGHT*P(X)*DELTA*MEAN(DELTA)
                     {   PRINT 1,A,B,C,X,DELTA,HEIGHT,WEIGHT
                     {      GO TO 2
                         END
```

The arithmetic statement function MEAN(Y) is defined in terms of the arithmetic statement function P(X). The variables involved in the definition, aside from the dummy arguments, are referred to as *parameters*. The parameter values must be set before using the arithmetic statement function; they may be reset as desired. Note that the dummy variables may be used elsewhere in a program just as any other simple variables. There is also really no need for using the different dummy arguments X in P(X) and Y in P(Y). The same dummy arguments can be used in as many definitions as desired, provided that they are the proper type.

It is worth pointing out that the equal sign now has two interpretations in Fortran. The most common is: Set the variable on the left side of the equal sign equal to the value of the expression on the right side. The other interpretation is: The function named on the left side is defined as the expression on the right side. A statement isolated from a program can be either an assignment statement or an arithmetic statement function definition; for instance,

```
A(N) = N**2 + 2*N + 3
```

can be either. If A has been declared as an array, then it must be an assignment statement. Otherwise it must be an arithmetic statement function definition. This is an important point to look for when examining a program that seems to be generating unusual results.

5–1.2 Function Subprograms

If a mathematical function can be described with a single statement, then it can be defined as an arithmetic statement function. If several statements are required, then it can be defined as a function subprogram.

Consider the following example of a function that computes the average of a set of 100 numbers contained in a specified array.

```
  FUNCTION AVER(LIST)
  REAL LIST(100)
  SUM = 0.
  DO 5 I=1,100
5 SUM = SUM + LIST(I)
  AVER = SUM/100.
  RETURN
  END
```

The first line states that a function is to be defined, that its name is AVER, and that its argument is LIST. The argument is a dummy variable (or placeholder) just as in the arithmetic statement function. Observe that the function name AVER appears on the left side of the equal sign in an assignment statement. Notice also the appearance of the new control statement RETURN. It indicates the end of the calculation of the function value. A function subprogram may have several RETURN statements if there are alternative ways to compute the function value.

FUNCTION Subprogram

The general form of a function subprogram is

FUNCTION name (arguments)

.
.
.

Fortran statements that compute the value of the "name," assign that value, and RETURN.

.
.
.

END

The name can be any Fortran name and the arguments are dummy variables separated by commas. The arguments may be arrays, if so they must be dimensioned in the subprogram. The type of the function is specified by its name as usual or by placing the word REAL or INTEGER in front of the word FUNCTION.

EXAMPLES

```
FUNCTION BEST(X,YX,IJK)            FUNCTION X(T)
INTEGER FUNCTION BESTJ(IB,J)       FUNCTION XXXX(II)
REAL FUNCTION LOWVAL(X,XBAR)       FUNCTION A2Z(A,B,C,Z)
```

How is a function subprogram used? An example illustrates the use of the function AVER given above.

```
      REAL A(100),B(100)
      READ 8,A,B
    8 FORMAT(10F8.5)
      AVA = AVER(A)  } References to AVER cause that
      AVB = AVER(B)  } function subprogram to be executed
      PROD= AVA*AVB
      PRINT 8,AVA,AVB,PROD
      STOP
      END
```

Physically the card decks are placed as follows:

```
               { REAL A(100),B(100)
Main program   {    ...
               {    ...
               { END
               { FUNCTION AVER(LIST)
Function       {    ...
subprogram     {    ...
               { END
```

Some systems may require control cards in front of the main program and in front of each subprogram. There may be any number of subprograms, and a function subprogram can use any Fortran statement that is valid. However it may not refer to itself except that the function name appears on the left side of an equal sign in one or more assignment statements.

An executable program consists of a main program (the kind of program we have been writing all along) and any number of subprograms, maybe none. An executable program plus its data and system control cards is called a *job*. When the main program goes into execution, at some time it may use a subprogram. At that time, we say the subprogram assumes control, until sooner or later a RETURN is encountered. Then the subprogram releases control (returns) to the main program. Of course a subprogram can make use of another subprogram, and so on. Consider the example at the top of the following page. The main program passes the constant 1 to function F. Function F assigns the value 1 to its dummy argument J and calls on G so that it may compute G(J + 1) + 1. When the function G is entered, its dummy variable K has the value 2, which is printed, then G returns the value 1. So G(J + 1) + 1 has the value 2 and F returns the value 2, giving the nondummy variable I in the main program the value 1. The dummy variables J and K can be replaced by the dummy variable I and the program operates in exactly the same way.

Besides returning a value, a function subprogram can also change the

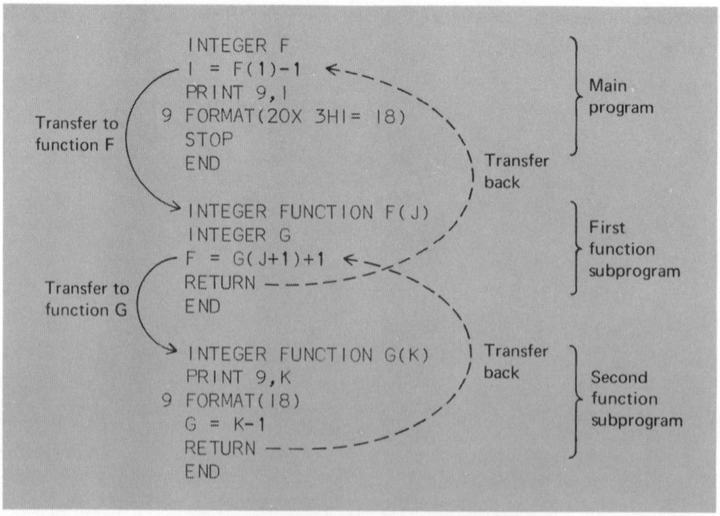

value of its arguments. This can sometimes lead to errors; consider the function subprogram

```
      FUNCTION ROOT(X,TEST)
      INTEGER TEST
      TEST = 3
      IF( X ) 1,2,3
    1 X = -X
      TEST= 1
    3 ROOT = SQRT(X)
      RETURN
    2 ROOT= 0.
      TEST=  2
      RETURN
      END
```

This function computes $\sqrt{|X|}$ and sets TEST to 1, 2, 3 depending on whether X is negative, zero, or positive. Using it in a statement such as A = ROOT(B * C,W) is fine, but an apparently well-formed expression such as D = W * ROOT(E,W) has no well-defined value because ROOT may change the value of W. Anything that a function subprogram does in addition to returning a value is called a side *effect*; side effects can be useful, but they must be handled with care.

An example of these possible effects is shown below.

```
      X = -9.0
      Y = ROOT(X,5)
      Z = X + 3.
      DO 5 J=1,5
    5 Y = Y - 2.
      PRINT 10,X,Y,Z
   10 FORMAT(3F10.2)
      STOP
      END
```

If one reads through this program casually, one expects the output to be

```
-9.00    -7.00    -6.00
```

The values that seem to be assigned to X, Y, Z in the first three statements are −9, 3, and −6. Then the DO loop subtracts 2 from Y five times to produce −7. The actual output is

```
9.00    1.00    12.00
```

The function ROOT changed the value of X from −9 to +9 and this in turn results in Z being assigned the value 12 rather than −6. The value of Y should not be (and is not) affected by this change in X. Why, then, is its value 1 rather than −7? The cause of this is that ROOT also changes its other argument TEST. The second argument sent to ROOT is the integer constant 5. Note in Figure 4–2 that constants, like variables, are written down in the computer memory and the computer does not know which locations are to be constant and which are variable. Thus it changes the location of "5" in the statement TEST = 1 in the function ROOT. Later, in the DO loop, the constant 5 appears, but its value has been changed to 1! So the DO loop is only executed one time and Y turns out to be 1, not −7, as one would expect. The effect illustrated here is, fortunately, not a common error, but when it occurs it can be very difficult to locate. When one understands clearly the way function subprograms can affect arguments, one is able to avoid this pitfall. The fact that a subprogram can change its arguments is extremely useful and valuable and, in fact, the subroutine subprograms introduced in the next section are designed to accomplish this (and perhaps other "side effects") solely.

EXAMPLE 5–1

PROCESSING DATA FROM REMOTE MONITORING OF BULK MATERIAL SUPPLIES

Consider a company that dispenses a bulk material (for example, flour, wheat, sand, iron ore) from containers as shown in Figure 5–1.

Under one leg of the container is a pressure sensitive scale that can be read by remote recording equipment. The company has hundreds of these containers and has decided to replace visual daily inspection by remote sensing and data processing. One key factor is the depth of the material remaining and, for simplicity's sake, we only consider processing the data to obtain this information. Assume the scale measures weight WT in 100-pound units. We must find relationships to relate this to the desired information, depth or DEPTH. Such relationships are

$$\begin{aligned} \text{volume (in cubic feet)} &= 50 * \text{triangle area} \\ &= 50. * \text{DEPTH} * \text{DEPTH}/2. \\ \text{WT} &= .046 * \text{volume}/4. \end{aligned}$$

where .046 is the weight (in hundreds of pounds) of 1 cubic foot of the

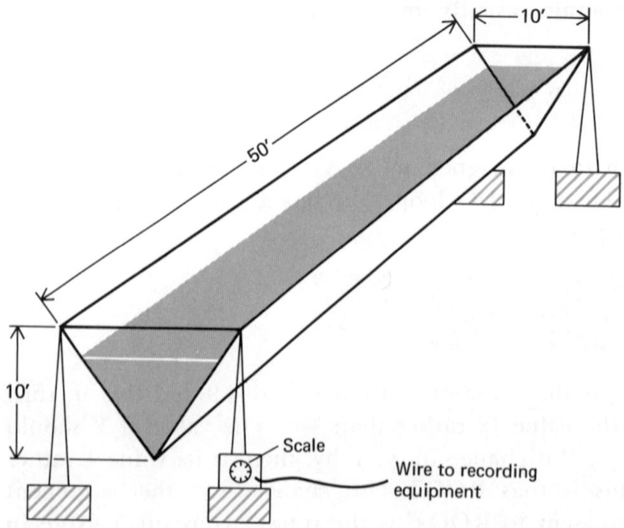

FIGURE 5–1. The container, dispenser of the bulk material.

material. We divide by 4, because the container has four legs. We can combine these equations to obtain

$$\text{DEPTH} = \frac{\sqrt{\text{WT} * 4.}}{\sqrt{25. * .046}} = \sqrt{\text{WT}} * 1.865.$$

The original idea was to have the recording equipment prepare data every day which were then processed to give a listing of the depth in each of the containers. The average depth is also needed to gauge the average level of bulk material in the company. Certain difficulties arose when these listings were first used. First, many containers are out of use at any given moment due to repairs, changes in production, and so on. These were included in the averages, though, and this gave a misleading indication of the supply status in the company. Second, some weights turned out to be negative. This resulted in two things: one was that nasty messages appeared in the middle of the listings which were hard to explain to management. After all, whoever heard of negative weights? The other was that the averages were even more misleading. An investigation showed that these negative weights are caused by a variety of malfunctions in the recording equipment and the scales. Since these malfunctions are expected to be present for a number of months, the program that processes the data is required to check for and eliminate these readings.

The program finally developed is given below. It has the readings in the array DATA (with up to 800 containers allowed). The function ROOT discussed earlier is used to take the square roots and to avoid any illegal square roots of negative numbers. The result of ROOT is checked to see if DATA(I) are valid and, if not, this value is ignored and an appropriate error message printed. The original data (WT) are replaced by the desired information (DEPTH) in the array DATA and the result listed on a new page with a summary heading.

```
      REAL DATA(800)
      READ 5,N,(DATA(I),I=1,N)          } Data Input
    5 FORMAT(I10/80(10F8.2/))
      KGOOD = 0
      AVAL  = 0
      DO 50 I= 1,N
      DATA(I) = ROOT(DATA(I),KASE)/2.147
      GO TO( 10,20,30 ), KASE
   10 PRINT 15,I,DATA(I)
   15 FORMAT(20X4HCASEI4,7H IS BAD,F10.2)
          GO TO 50                        Main loop
   20 PRINT 25,I
   25 FORMAT(20X4HCASEI4,11H IS MISSING )
          GO TO 50
   30 KGOOD = KGOOD+1
      AVAL = AVAL + DATA(I)
   50 CONTINUE
      AVAL = AVAL/FLOAT(KGOOD)
      PRINT 55,KGOOD,N,AVAL                                               Summary
   55 FORMAT(1H1,I8,9H CASES OFI5,19H ARE GOOD, AVERAGE= F10.2///)        and
   60 FORMAT(10(I4,F7.2))                                                 Output
      PRINT 60,(I,DATA(I),I=1,N)
      STOP
      END
```

The items of interest in this program include:

1. Formats 5 and 60. The first reads in one integer on one card and then up to 80 cards with 10 reals on each card. The second prints an unlimited number of lines with 10 pairs of integers and reals. In the next chapter (under format groupings) it is noted and explained how format 5 would read an unlimited number of cards with 10 reals on each card if the "80" were simply omitted.

2. The computed GO TO is used very naturally in conjunction with the variable KASE returned by the function subprogram ROOT.

3. A CONTINUE statement is required with this particular program organization with the DO loop. The iteration could be done without a DO and CONTINUE statement, but it would not be as simple nor more efficient.

4. The fact that we want the entire list of the array DATA separate from the list of bad or missing items of data leads to reading in all of the data first, then processing it second. It is possible to read and process the data simultaneously and still obtain these two lists separately. However, this would require a slightly more complicated (and considerably less natural) program than the one presented here.

Common Errors

1. Assumption that variables in the main program are automatically known in a function subprogram and vice versa.
2. Omission of the dimension statements for arrays in function subprograms.
3. Confusion about real and integer types of arguments, particularly the use of 1 or 4 instead of 1. or 4. for real arguments.
4. The unintentional or unplanned-for change of an argument by a subprogram.

Things You Can Do

1. Redefine the standard mathematical functions by putting in a function subprogram with the same name. This does not happen for some simple functions such as ABS, SIGN, IFIX, and so on.
2. Place as many RETURN, STOP, READ, PRINT, and so on statements in a subprogram as one desires.
3. Place the function subprogram decks in any order you like, but not inside the main program.

5–1.3 Subroutine Subprograms

A subroutine subprogram is similar to a function subprogram, except that no value is associated with the subroutine's name. Consequently the results of the subroutine are passed via the arguments.

The following subroutine generates the element-by-element sum and products of two lists A and B and it leaves the results in the appropriately named arrays.

```
                 Input                    Output
                 arguments                arguments
      SUBROUTINE SUMPRD(A,B,SUM,PRD)
      REAL A(20),B(20),SUM(20),PRD(20)
      DO 10 J = 1,20
      SUM(J) = A(J) + B(J)
   10 PRD(J) = A(J) * B(J)
      RETURN
      END
```

A subroutine is used by "calling" it with a CALL statement, as in

```
      REAL ARRAY1(20),ARRAY2(20),P(20),S(20)
      READ 88,ARRAY1,ARRAY2
   88 FORMAT( 5F10.4 )
      CALL SUMPRD(ARRAY1,ARRAY2,S,P)
      PRINT 88,S,P
      STOP
      END
```

Note that ARRAY1, ARRAY2, S, and P are declared to be real arrays in this program as well as in the subroutine programs SUMPRD. The dimensions here may be larger than those in SUMPRD, but if they are smaller the results are likely to be garbage or an error is likely to be made.

SUBROUTINE Subprogram

The general form is

```
SUBROUTINE name (arguments)
        .
        .
        .
    Fortran statements including one or more RETURN's
        .
        .
        .
END
```

The conventions on the name and the arguments are the same as for a function subprogram. The name, however, is not assigned a value and does not have a type of real or integer. The arguments serve as the inputs to subprogram and results are returned via the arguments.

EXAMPLES

```
SUBROUTINE BEST(X,YX,IJK)           SUBROUTINE ERRORA
SUBROUTINE SWITCH(A,B)              SUBROUTINE HELP(ME,PLEASE)
```

A subroutine might have no dummy arguments, as in

```
  SUBROUTINE ERRORA
  PRINT 5
5 FORMAT(2X8(1H*),16HERROR A OCCURRED)
  RETURN
  END
```

This is a very convenient way of producing messages that can arise at several points in a large program. One need only have CALL ERRORA in order to obtain the desired message.

Common Errors

1. Placement of the arguments in the wrong order when a subroutine is called.
2. Omission of one or more arguments in a subroutine call. Most Fortran systems do not detect this error.
3. The use of an argument to dimension an array can be done only in special circumstances (as explained in Chapter 6).
4. Too many arguments which cause the wrong ones to be used.

Things You Can Do

1. Define a subroutine with no arguments at all.
2. Rewrite any subroutine to be a function and use it as such. This sometimes makes a "more elegant" program to read and sometimes gives a convenient way to return one of the values.
3. Break a computation into as many subprograms as you like.
4. Dimension all one-dimensional arrays with dimension 1, for example, REAL X(1),BB(1) in a subprogram. The actual dimensions are then controlled by the main program. This does not apply to COMMON variables discussed in the next section or to systems which check subscripts of arrays.

What are the advantages of using function and subroutine subprograms? Certainly they correspond more or less to the way in which we think of solving problems—by breaking them down into well-defined subproblems and solving these in turn. Subprograms facilitate the task of solving "large" problems, particularly when several programmers are involved. Each programmer can freely use variable names in his subprograms without regard to which variable names or labels are being used in the other programmers' subprograms. Provided that there is a clear understanding of the inputs to, outputs from, and side effects, if any, of each subprogram, each programmer can do his part with relative freedom of action.

There is another significant advantage: one or more subprograms can be submitted to be run without a main program for diagnostic purposes. When a subprogram no longer has diagnostics, then it can be tested with a main program written merely for the purpose of checking the subprogram's behavior. When the tests are successful, then the full-blown main program and all the subprograms can be run together for final checks and production runs. This "modular testing" approach can significantly reduce the time and cost of program development.

Finally we can take advantage of the many Fortran subprograms that are not part of the mathematical library, but that have been written and used by individuals and then contributed to computing center program libraries. In some installations, these subprograms are already part of the mathematical library. In others, the source deck must be obtained. In any case, a description, or write-up, of each subprogram is available and must be read to determine what the subprogram does, how it does it, and how it should be used. Many computing centers have hundreds of subprograms with complete instructions on how they are to be used.

5–1.4 Program Control: Switches versus Subprograms

Consider a program that has a piece of code that is used at several points with different inputs. This might occur, for example, with codes that compute averages, maxima, minima, and other quantities associated with a list of numbers. If the program is merely to apply this code for different input, then it can be arranged in a more or less standard iteration loop as shown in Figure 5–2. Even this scheme might not be as simple to program as it appears on the surface. For example, it could be that there are data to be read from cards that are punched in different formats. This means that the setup of the next input requires using different READ and FORMAT statements. Since there is not an easy way to modify such statements (in fact, it is often impossible to do the natural thing with modifying input/output statements) one is tempted to organize the program as shown in Figure 5–3.

The situation illustrated in Figure 5–3 is simple compared to what commonly occurs in large programs. There one finds that a great deal of different processing is taking place, yet at various locations one wants to do basically the same kind of analysis or calculation. In fact, one sees that the same Fortran code does the job with only different input. One might visualize the situation as in Figure 5–4. Most of the boxes in this flowchart have been suppressed.

It is almost never efficient nor convenient programming to copy the same piece of Fortran programming several places in the same program. It can, however, result in more efficient execution, especially on some computers. We now examine how to avoid this copying by two different means: switches and subprograms. The idea behind switches is to set a *switch* variable at each point where the Fortran code is needed. One then jumps to the Fortran code and

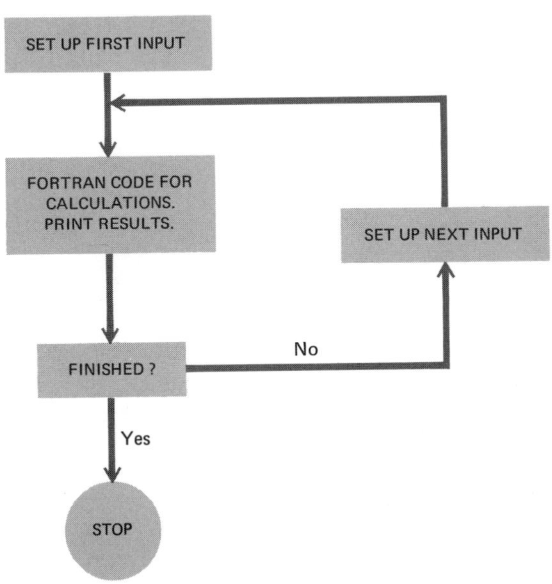

FIGURE 5–2. A simple iteration loop to reuse a piece of Fortran programming.

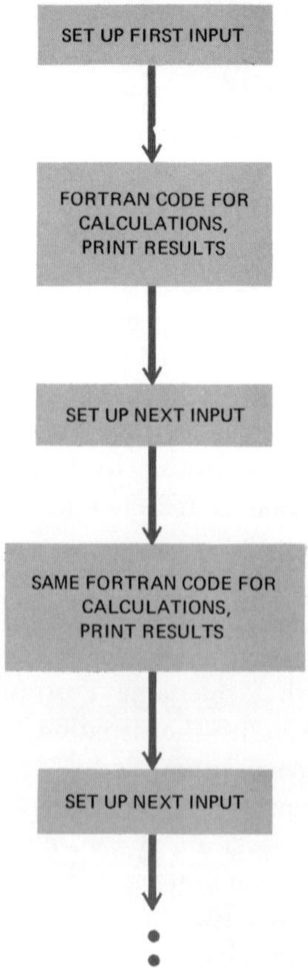

FIGURE 5–3. A sequential organization which uses multiple copies of the same piece of Fortran programming.

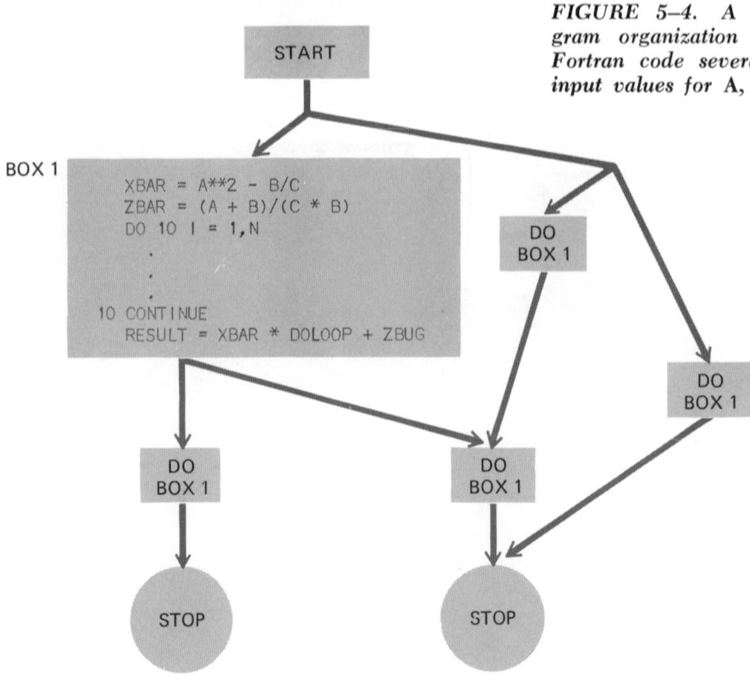

FIGURE 5–4. A more complicated program organization which uses the same Fortran code several times with different input values for **A, B, C, N,** *and so forth.*

executes it. Then one examines the switch to see where one came from and proceeds to return to that point. The idea behind a subprogram is to make the Fortran code a function subprogram or subroutine (as appropriate) and then simply use it at the spots where it is needed.

Two alternative ways to use switches are illustrated in the programs below. One uses logical IF's, the other computed GO TO's. It is assumed in these programs that one has to prepare two lists, X(I) and Y(I), and set the value of N.

```
Column 5|6|7
      ISWIT = 1
      DO 10 J = 1,100
      X(I) = ...
   10 Y(I) = ...
      N = 100
         GO TO 900
   15 IF(ISWIT.GT.1) GOTO 25
      N = 367
      ISWIT = 2
      DO 20 I = 1,N
      X(I) = ...
   20 Y(I) = ...
         GO TO 900
   25 IF(ISWIT.GT.2) GOTO 35
      READ 26,N
      READ 27,(X(I),Y(I),I=1,N)
      ISWIT = 3
         GO TO 900

  . . . . MORE CASES SET UP HERE . . . .

C     COMPUTE RESULT HERE
  900 N2 = N + 2
        ...FORTRAN CODE...
      PRINT 990,RESULT,ISWIT
         GO TO 15

      END
```

```
Column 5|6|7
      JUMP = 1
      DO 10 I=1,100
      X(I) = ...
   10 Y(I) = ...
      N = 100
         GO TO 900

   15 N = 367
      JUMP = 2
      DO 20 I = 1,N
      X(I) = ...
   20 Y(I) = ...
         GO TO 900

   25 READ 26,N
      READ 27,(X(I),Y(I),I=1,N)
      JUMP = 3
         GO TO 900

C     COMPUTE RESULT HERE
  900 N2 = N + 2
        ...FORTRAN CODE...
      PRINT 990,RESULT,JUMP
      GO TO(15,25,35,45,55,65),JUMP
   65 STOP
      END
```

The actions of these two organizations are slightly different. The logical IF construction always goes back to the "top" of the program and then filters down through the various cases until it locates the one to be set up next. The computed GO TO construction returns directly to the first statement following the GO TO 900. The computed GO TO alternative is preferable in most cases as it is more efficient and more readable.

The result of putting the Fortran code into a subroutine called FCODE is shown below.

Main program

```
      DO 10 I = 1,100
      X(I) = ...
   10 Y(I) = ...
      CALL FCODE(X,Y,100)
      DO 20 I = 1,367
      X(I) = ...
   20 Y(I) = ...
      CALL FCODE(X,Y,367)
      READ 26,N
      READ 27,(X(I),Y(I),I=1,N)
      CALL FCODE(X,Y,N)

      ....MORE CASES SET UP HERE...

      END
```

Subroutine FCODE

```
      SUBROUTINE FCODE(A,B,N)
      REAL A(500),B(500)
      N2 = N + 2
        ...FORTRAN CODE...
      PRINT 990,RESULT
      RETURN
      END
```

This organization is superior in several ways. First, it is shorter and more natural. That makes it easier to understand. Second, it is more flexible. When (and if) one wants to change the program, one does not need to worry about just how the switches (ISWIT or JUMP) are set or how the labels 15, 25, . . ., 65 are organized.

Note that the RETURN statement in the subroutine acts very much like the computed GO TO in sending control back to the "calling" point. The Fortran system has, in fact, set up a switch and can jump back automatically to the statement following the CALL. This is another example of where a Fortran feature makes it easier to do something that can also be done without it.

Problems

5–1.1 Use the built-in function MAX1 to find the minimum of a set of 6 numbers. Define this to be the arithmetic statement function MIN6 and write a short Fortran program that shows how it works.

5–1.2 Obtain diagnostics for the following situations (if possible):
- (a) An array left undimensioned
- (b) An arithmetic statement function definition appearing after its use
- (c) An arithmetic statement function and a function subprogram with the same name
- (d) A main program calling a subroutine that does not exist
- (e) Two or more references to a subprogram, first as a function, then as a subroutine (or vice versa)
- (f) A function or subroutine that calls itself.

5–1.3 Write a new function subprogram named SQRT which computes the square root of its first argument and returns the error $x - \sqrt{x^2}$ as its second argument. Write a program that shows that it works correctly.

5–1.4 Suppose an executable program has the following main program:

```
CALL READ
CALL CALC
CALL RESULT
STOP
END
```

Let READ be the subprogram that obtains the input data, CALC the subprogram that performs the calculations, and RESULT the one that prints the results. The program is to compute the average and standard deviation of an integer array as indicated in Problem 4–2.5. Without changing the main program, how can an indefinite number of input data sets be processed?

5–1.5 (a) Explain why it is not possible to turn an array, or list around in itself. That is, you are given LIST(K), K = 1 to 10, and you want to get the values of LIST(10), LIST(9), . . ., LIST(1) in the list instead of LIST(1), LIST(2), . . ., LIST(10). Explain how this can be done using just *one* extra variable (word); call it TEMP.

(b) Write a subroutine that has a one-dimensional array as its argument and which turns the array around (end for end). Call it SWITCH and thus when one has CALL SWITCH(LIST) the array LIST is reversed. Assume that LIST has 100 elements.

(c) Expand the subroutine SWITCH so it has two arguments, LIST and NLIST, which is the length of LIST. Now SWITCH is to reverse any length of LIST up to 100.

5–1.6 Write a subroutine which accepts a two-dimensional real array as an argument and which rearranges the rows so that the column KOLUM is in descending order. One also has as arguments the number NROW of rows of the array and the number NCOL of columns. Thus, if A is the array

6.2	3.4	25.1	−7.2
14.8	−4.1	16.7	18.2
.7	33.3	1.2	−1.8

then the statement CALL SORTER(A,2,3,4) (that is, KOLUM = 2, NROW = 3, NCOL = 4) results in A becoming

.7	33.3	1.2	−1.8
6.2	3.4	25.1	−7.2
14.8	−4.1	16.7	18.2

Write a main program that generates several arrays of different sizes and prints them out before and after they have been sorted on various columns.

5–1.7 Write a function subroutine which has 3 arguments: first is an array X of dimension ≤500, second is an array Y of dimension ≤500, and third is the number NFULL of elements in X and Y to be considered. The subroutine is to compute the maximum value of X(J) times Y(J) for J between 1 and NFULL and return this as its value. Write a main program that generates several arrays X and Y and run it to show that the function subprogram works.

5–1.8 Write a program that computes sin(x) for $x = 0, 1, 2, \ldots, 15$ using the infinite series

$$\sin(x) = \sum_{n=0}^{\infty} (-1)^n \frac{x^{2n+1}}{(2n+1)!} = x - \frac{x^3}{3!} + \frac{x^5}{5!} - \cdots.$$

Obviously we cannot carry out this sum to its upper limit; therefore, we place the condition on the algorithm that when

$$\left| (-1)^j \cdot \frac{x^{2j+1}}{(2j+1)!} + (-1)^{j+1} \cdot \frac{x^{2(j+1)+1}}{(2(j+1)+1)!} \right| < 10^{-5}$$

the $(j+1)$st term and all terms after it are not added in.

Write a real function called FACT(N) which computes N!. The FACT function should have some way of communicating with the main program when N! becomes too large to be computed. Use an arithmetic statement function called TERM(X,N) to compute the Nth term of the series. Note that TERM(X,N) will be written in terms of the FACT function. As you compute sin(x), keep a count of the number of terms needed to compute sin(x). Your output should appear in table form listing x, sin(x), and the count of terms—all with appropriate headings.

5–1.9 Suppose you are going to Las Vegas to gamble. You expect to lose about 10 percent of your money each day you gamble. On your last day you set aside enough money for the fare home and play roulette at high stakes for 1 hour, then quit. The fare home is $275 and your expenses are about $30 per day.

(a) You want to determine the amount of money you should take with you for a 10-day visit so that you can expect to have $500 left to play roulette with on the last day.

(b) Suppose you take your spouse with you. Your expenses become $50 per day and the fare home is $500. Each day you let your spouse gamble with half the money you have over $1200. You expect your spouse to lose 25 percent of this money each day. You want to determine the amount of money you should take for the visit of part (a).

In the process of solving this problem you are to write a function subprogram REMAIN with argument TAKE whose value is the amount that remains at the end of the last day if the amount of money you take is TAKE. Write such a subprogram for each case and run it with a main program that shows that it works.

Once this subprogram is done, use it with a trial and error method to determine values of TAKE that give the two required values for REMAIN.

5—2 Internal Communication

5–2.1 Subprogram Arguments

We have seen arguments used as the way to communicate the values of variables from one part of a program to another. We have also seen some unexpected consequences of the use of arguments. In this section we consider this communication in more detail and, in the second part, introduce another means of internal communication in a Fortran program.

For small programs, the problem of communication between parts in the program is solved by making the value of every variable available throughout the entire program. Thus, if the number X or the array A is used anywhere, the algorithm refers to its list of variables for the value of X or A. When programs become more complicated, there are some advantages to modifying this arrangement. The advantages stem from the desirability to make various parts of the program partially independent of one another. This independence is desirable, for example, when:

1. Different parts of the program are constructed by different people.
2. Different parts of the program are constructed at different times.
3. Different parts of the program are translated into another language (usually a computer's machine language) at different times.

In each of the situations, the value of essential variables must be communicated to other parts of the program. However, those variables that enter the program only in one part need not be made available everywhere. This helps prevent confusion from arising because of two different auxiliary variables having the same name. This confusion can easily occur when several people are working on one large program, as people tend to give variables simple, mnemonic names such as I, A, IMAX, XMAX, and so on. Furthermore, when such confusion in names does occur, it is often difficult to discover that this is the reason that the program does not work. This point applies to the first two possibilities above.

If parts of the program are to be compiled into machine language at different times, then it is essential that definite provisions be made for communication between the various parts of the program; that is, all those variables whose values are required elsewhere must be so identified.

There is a certain expense in translating a program from Fortran into a machine language. Thus, in a large program with many parts, it is uneconomical to recompile every part whenever a change is made in only one or two parts. Note that it normally requires many trial runs to perfect a complicated algorithm. As a result, once a particular part of the algorithm is satisfactory, it is translated into machine language and used in that form while the other parts are being checked out.

What we wish to accomplish is illustrated by Figure 5–5. It is clear that arrangements for these pipelines of communication must be made in each of the subprograms. The variables made available through these pipelines are the arguments of the subprograms.

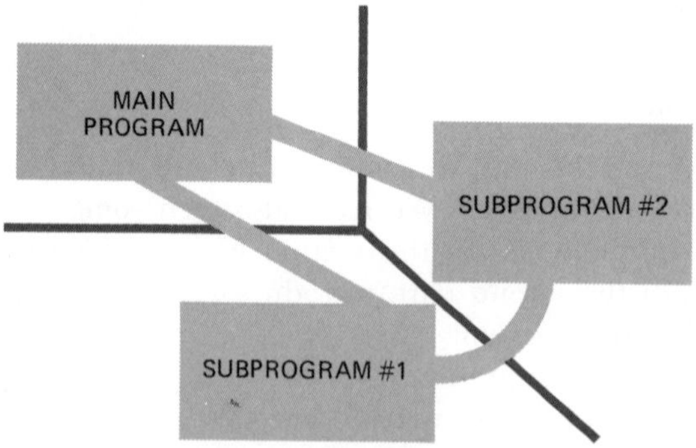

FIGURE 5–5. The three programs are completely insulated from one another except for the "pipelines" through which only specifically designated variables, the arguments, are passed.

The lines of communication are established in Fortran by listing the arguments when a subprogram is used, for example,

```
CALL PROCES(X,ZED,KONTRL,ANS1,ARRAY2)          Z = FUNK(A,B)
CALL PROCES(Y**2-7.1,2.,3,ANS1,ARRAY2)         Z = FUNK(17.3,8.8)
```

and by listing the arguments to be received in the heading or declaration statement of the subprogram, for example,

```
SUBROUTINE PROCES(XX,ZZ,KONT,ANS,ARRAY2)
FUNCTION FUNK(ARG1,ARG2)
```

Let us assume that we have a specific subroutine called PROCES. We want to call PROCES and have three things happen:

1. The required values of the arguments are transmitted to PROCES.
2. The statements that constitute PROCES are executed.
3. The values of the variables that result are transmitted back to the rest of the program (the calling program) through the arguments.

When a function or subroutine subprogram is used, some of the "actual" arguments (the arguments in the function or subroutine reference) may be expressions. How are they handled? Consider a specific case:

```
 ....
CALL LOWSUM(A*A,B)          } Main
 ....                       } program
END
SUBROUTINE LOWSUM(X,Y)      }
Y = AMIN1(X,Y,X+Y)          } Subroutine
RETURN                      }
END
```

In executing the statement CALL LOWSUM(A * A,B), the expression A * A is evaluated and the value is assigned to a temporary variable not accessible to the programmer; call it TEMP. The second argument is a simple variable, and effectively its name is made available to the subroutine LOWSUM. So, in effect, CALL LOWSUM(A * A,B) is equivalent to the pair of statements

```
TEMP = A*A
B    = AMIN1(TEMP,B,TEMP+B)
```

The manner in which expressions are handled as arguments is known as "call-by-value," whereas variables and arrays as arguments are handled on a "call-by-name" basis.

If a variable or array name is used in a subprogram or main program, can it be used in some other subprogram? The answer is an unqualified yes. The same variable or array name may be used in a main program and in all the subprograms, but the values associated with the name in the main program and in the subprograms are completely independent. Compare the following two programs.

```
  INTEGER FUN                                      INTEGER FUN
  READ 1, INDEX                                    READ 1,INDEX
1 FORMAT(I6)                           Main      1 FORMAT(I6)
  KASE = FUN(INDEX+1)                  program     KASE = FUN(INDEX+1)
  PRINT 1,INDEX,KASE                               PRINT 1,INDEX,KASE
  STOP                                             STOP
  END                                              END
- - - - - - - - - - - - - - - - - - - - - - - - - - - - - - - - - - - - - - -
  INTEGER FUNCTION FUN(INDEX)                      INTEGER FUNCTION FUN(KASE)
  KK = MINO(INDEX,10)                              INDEX = MINO(KASE,10)
  FUN= MAXO(0,KK/2+1,3*INDEX)                      KA5E = MAXO(0,INDEX/2+1,3*KASE)
  FUN= FUN +2*INDEX/5 - KK                         FUN = KA5E+2*KASE/5 - INDEX
  RETURN                                           RETURN
  END                                              END
```

These programs are equivalent. Even though the program on the right may be easier to interpret for the programmer, they both do exactly the same thing. Any systematic substitution of names for variables, arrays, and dummy arguments within any subprogram does not affect the executable program.

There is an implication in this discussion and in the notation that arguments of a subprogram are in some sense "physically" given to the subprogram. An examination of the implementation of most languages shows that the value of an argument is not moved to the subprogram. Rather the subprogram is given the location of the argument to use in finding its value. This process is particularly useful in the case of a large array. If the array were actually passed to the subprogram, then there would have to be space in the subprogram to write all the values, even though they are already written somewhere else. So the subprogram is simply told where the arguments are located in the computer's memory. This implementation causes some effects in computer programs that would not be anticipated from a casual analysis of the situation (such as changing the values of constants).

The memory requirements for the main program (excluding the compiled code) are determined by counting the number of variables and array elements that have been declared. The same rule holds for subprograms, except that the dummy arguments are not counted. An example makes this clear.

Main program:

```
REAL A,B(100),C(50)
....
CALL SUB(A,B,C)
....
END
```

Memory requirements: 151 words
A, B(1), . . . , B(100), C(1), . . . , C(50)

Subprogram:

```
SUBROUTINE SUB(X,Y,Z)
REAL Y(100),Z(50),Q(100),IA
....
END
```

Memory requirements: 101 words
IA, Q(1), . . . , Q(100)

Y(100),Z(50): Storage for these variables allocated by the main program

The memory requirements for the dummy arguments X, Y, and Z are satisfied by the memory words set aside for the variables IA and arrays B and C, respectively.

5–2.2 Common Variables

Internal communication can be performed by using the appropriate lists of arguments. If a subprogram has many arguments, and it is referenced many times by other subprograms, then it is very easy to make a mistake in writing the subprogram reference. The arguments may sometimes be written in the wrong order, or the wrong number of arguments may be specified. Partly to alleviate this difficulty, another means of communication between subprograms is provided.

This second approach, which is very convenient, is to imitate on a larger scale what is done in "small" programs (that is, programs without formally identified parts). Recall that for small programs the values of all the variables are available everywhere. This really means that somewhere there is a list of all the variables and their current values, as shown in Figure 5–6.

Name	*Value*	*Name*	*Value*
X	7.02	ZAP	−382.641908
Y	−983.62	LOGIK	5
ID	17	KONTRL	3
ANTS	4902	BISECT	8.31756

FIGURE 5–6. A sample list of variables and their values in a small program.

If each part of a program is constructed independently, then each part has an associated list of variable names and their values. The second approach to communicating the values of variables is to set up a special list of variables which can be "read" by every part of the program. Variables whose values are to be recorded in this special list are designated global or common variables. The other variables are called local variables as their values are available only locally, that is, in one part of the program. This arrangement appears in schematic form in Figure 5–7.

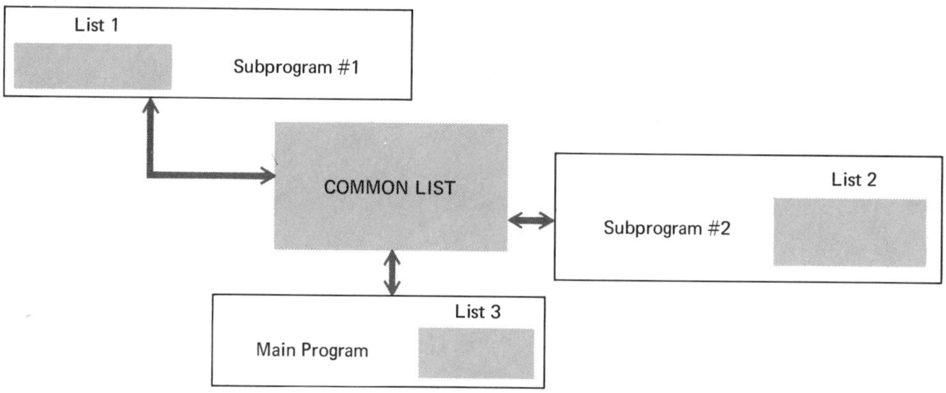

FIGURE 5–7. The configuration of the lists of variables in a program with three parts. The local variables are listed internally in each part (List 1, List 2, List 3). The global or* COMMON *variables are listed externally and each part has access to this list.

This approach is implemented in Fortran by means of the COMMON statement. Variables and arrays that are declared to be COMMON are placed in the list available to all parts of the program. The following examples show how the argument list of a subroutine can be eliminated by using the appropriate COMMON statement.

```
      INTEGER A(100)                                   INTEGER A(100)
      N = 10                                           COMMON A,N
      CALL ZERO(A,N)              Main program         N = 10
       ....                                            CALL ZERO
       ....                                             ....
      END                                              END
  ----------------------------------------------------------------------
      SUBROUTINE ZERO(ARRAY,SIZE)                      SUBROUTINE ZERO
      INTEGER SIZE,ARRAY(100)                          INTEGER SIZE,ARRAY(100)
      DO 10 I = 1,SIZE                                 COMMON ARRAY,SIZE
   10 ARRAY(I) = 0                Subprogram           DO 10 I = 1,SIZE
      RETURN                                        10 ARRAY(I) = 0
      END                                              RETURN
                                                       END
```

The two COMMON statements each define 101 variables to have values accessible and modifiable by both the main program and the subprogram. Any reference to A(I) is at the same time a reference to ARRAY(I) by virtue of their position in the COMMON statements; a similar remark applies to N and SIZE.

COMMON

The general form is the word COMMON followed by a list of variable or array names. The position of a variable in this list determines where it goes and how it is associated with COMMON variables of other parts of the program. If several COMMON statements appear in one subprogram, they are treated just as though one COMMON statement appeared with the names listed in the order they appear on the several statements.

EXAMPLES

```
COMMON A,BB,XBAR,LIST1              COMMON A(10),B
COMMON I,X,ARRAY,ILOW               COMMON DD(5,5,5),X(25,25)
```

The names used in the COMMON statement have no significance except within the subprogram in which the statement appears. The relative position of a variable appearing in a COMMON statement dictates with which variable it will be associated in other subprograms having a COMMON statement. The relative position is determined in terms of the number of "words" involved. Each variable is associated with one word (a machine word), and each array involving n elements, or components, is associated with n consecutive words. All the COMMON statements appearing in a single program need not involve the same number of words. Consider

```
(i)                      (ii)                   (iii)

REAL A,B,C(2,2)          REAL X(4),Y,Z          REAL C,F,G,H
COMMON A,B,C             COMMON Y,Z,X           COMMON C,F,G,H
```

We have the following correspondences set up, as far as communication of values is concerned:

Word position in COMMON list	1	2	3	4	5	6
Program #1—	A	B	C(1,1)	C(2,1)	C(1,2)	C(2,2)
Program #2—	Y	Z	X(1)	X(2)	X(3)	X(4)
Program #3—	C	F	G	H		

The COMMON lists in (i) and (ii) each refer to six words. That of (iii) refers to four words.

A COMMON list in a subprogram must not contain the name of a dummy argument; it can contain only the names of variables and arrays. An array can be dimensioned by use of a COMMON statement. The following three sets of statements are equivalent:

```
DIMENSION I(2),B(3,3)    REAL I(2),B(3,3),JX,KAT    REAL I,JX,KAT
REAL I,JX,KAT            COMMON I,B,KAT             COMMON I(2),B(3,3),KAT
COMMON I.B.KAT
```

It is very important that variables and arrays in COMMON be properly typed as being INTEGER or REAL in all the appropriate subprograms. It normally makes very little sense and very bad arithmetic to assign a real value to a word in COMMON in some subprogram and have another subprogram manipulate the same COMMON variable as an integer.

A COMMON statement may have several continuation cards, or there may be several COMMON statements in the same subprogram. When the latter occurs, it is very important that the several COMMON statements be placed in the right order. Consider the following equivalent ways in which COMMON can be handled:

(i) (ii) (iii)

```
                           5|6|7
COMMON A,B,X(8),H           | |COMMON A,B                 COMMON A
                            |*|       X(2) ,H             COMMON B
                                                          COMMON X(2),H
```

We summarize here by saying that COMMON is a very useful feature of Fortran, but one must pay attention to a number of rules and regulations. Each of the rules listed above is a limitation on the usefulness of COMMON and yet another limitation is illustrated later in Example 5–2. Nevertheless, the mastery of using COMMON is essential for people who want to write Fortran programs on a continuing basis.

In Fortran we can also specify intermediate lists of variables. Thus there might be a global or COMMON list, available to all parts of the algorithm and then several other lists, each available to a specific collection of the parts of the algorithm. For example, the first intermediate list might be available to parts 2, 7, and 13; the second list might be available to parts 1, 3, 5, 7, and 10; and the third to parts 1, 4, 5, 7, and 11. Such lists are of value in the construction of complex programs. This arrangement is illustrated in Figure 5–8.

Consider a main program that uses all the following variables:

```
A,B,DD,R,S,T,U,X(20),Y(20)
```

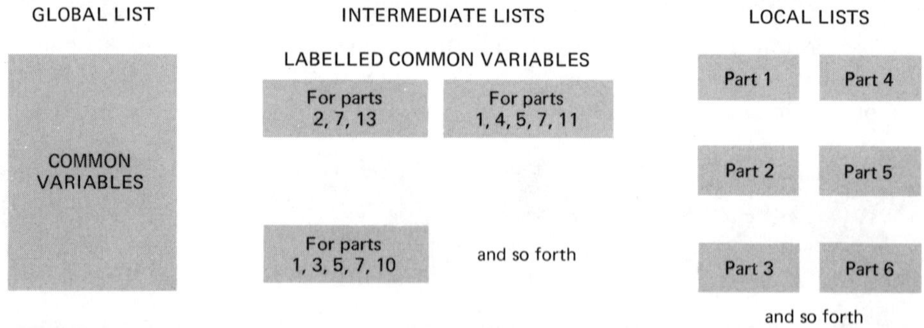

FIGURE 5–8. Schematic diagram of the various lists of variables that might be present in a complicated program with many parts.

Suppose there are three subprograms SUB1, SUB2, and SUB3 where SUB3 also uses all these variables, but SUB1 only uses A, B, and X(20) while SUB2 uses only R, S, T, U, Y(20). We can define two labeled blocks of common variables BLOK1 and BLOK2 as follows:

```
COMMON/BLOK1/A,B,DD,X(20)/BLOK2/R,S,T,U,Y(20)
```

or, using two statements for better readability,

```
COMMON/ BLOK1 / A,B,DD,X(20)
COMMON/ BLOK2 / R,S,T,U,Y(20)
```

Then the main program and SUB2 have both blocks while SUB1 has only BLOK1 and SUB2 has only BLOK2. Of course, SUB1 and SUB2 would use one of the short statements defining BLOK1 and BLOK2 above.

The names of the COMMON blocks may be chosen just as other names in Fortran. They, of course, must be distinct from subprogram names. An important rule is that all blocks labeled with the same name must have the same length (measured in number of words of memory). The ordinary COMMON is called "blank" COMMON.

Common Errors

1. Confusion about the order of the variables in the COMMON list. One should keypunch one COMMON card, then duplicate it to obtain the others.
2. Use of a variable both in COMMON and as an argument.
3. The use of an index out of bounds for an array in COMMON can cause very subtle and difficult-to-locate errors.

Things You Can Do

1. Change the name of variables through COMMON. This is usually a bad practice that leads to confusion.
2. Dimension arrays as you place them in the COMMON list.
3. Use a shorter COMMON list in a subprogram where you do not need some of the variables at the end of the list.

Problems

5–2.1 Write a program in which a subprogram has an array as a dummy argument, but omit the DIMENSION statement. See what happens if the dummy array only appears on the right-hand side in some assignment statement.

5–2.2 Write a function called ROOT that calculates the real square root of its one real argument. Let ROOT also place in COMMON the square of its value and the error, computed from $\sqrt{x^2} - x$. Write a main program that uses ROOT and prints these values.

5–2.3 Write a function subprogram which takes a list of numbers (one-dimensional array) and computes the largest and smallest value in the list and the average value. The inputs are (1) the array name, XX; (2) the length of the list to be processed, NXX. The outputs are (1) the largest value, XXMAX; (2) the smallest value, XXMIN; (3) the average value, AVER (as the value of the function subprogram). The first line of the program is given; complete it. Allow XX to be up to 1000 in length.

```
      FUNCTION AVER(XX,NXX,XXMAX,XXMIN)
```

5–2.4 Statements 21 through 35 of the following program carry out a calculation that is to be separated out and placed into a subprogram. Rewrite these statements into a FUNCTION subprogram so that they may be replaced in the main program by the statement

AVER = AVERG(VALU)

The values of the variables NVALU and FLAG are to be communicated through COMMON. Write the FUNCTION subprogram AVERG and the modified main program.

```
      REAL VALU(200)
      READ 10, NVALU
      READ 20, (VALU(J), J=1,NVALU)
   10 FORMAT(I5)
   20 FORMAT( 10F8.3 )
   21 FLAG = 0
      SUM = VALU(1)
      DO 30 J = 2,NVALU
   30 IF( VALU(J) .GT. 1.0 )  FLAG = 1.0
   35 AVER = SUM/FLOAT(NVALU)
C               IF FLAG = 1.0 PRINT ERROR MESSAGE HERE
      IF( FLAG .GE. 1.0 )  PRINT 40
   40 FORMAT( 10X,18HBAD VALUES LOCATED, ////)
      PRINT 50, NVALU, AVER
   50 FORMAT( 5X,I3,22H VALUES HAVE AVERAGE = ,F12.5)
      STOP
      END
```

5—3 Data Statements and Hollerith Variables

5–3.1 Data Initialization

So far we have seen two ways to assign values to a variable: either using an assignment statement or reading in a value. Note that every variable in a Fortran program has a value, whether or not it has been assigned by the program. If the value is not assigned or read in, then its value is determined by one of two possibilities:

1. It has a value "left over" from the last program which was located in the computer memory. Such values tend to be garbage.
2. It has a value which is assigned to *all* words in memory by the system between the finish of the last program and the start of the current program. The most common value assigned this way is zero.

The choice of these two possibilities is made locally.

It is also possible to initialize (or preset) the values of variables in Fortran by using a DATA statement. These values are assigned before the first time these variables are used. These values are used until they are changed by an assignment statement or by reading in new values. The first part of the example on the left may be replaced by the data initialization statement in the example on the right.

```
      REAL X(5)
      A = 1.5
      B = -3.0
      DO 10 J = 1,5
   10 X(J) = J+1
```

```
      REAL X(5)
      DATA A,B,X/1.5,-3.,2.,3.,4.,5.,6./
```

One sees from this example that the DATA statement can result in a shorter, more compact program. Later on in this section other advantages are illustrated.

There may be several data initialization statements in a program. They can be combined, if desired, into a single such statement as illustrated below. Assume the program has the declaration REAL X(5),Y and INTEGER P,Q(2). The following three DATA statements are equivalent.

```
DATA X,Y/1.,2.,3.,4.,5.,0./
DATA P,Q(1),Q(2)/-1,-2,-3/
```

```
DATA X,Y,P,Q/1.,2.,3.,4.,5.,0.,-1,-2,-3/
```

```
DATA X,Y/1.,2.,3.,4.,5.,0./,P,Q /-1,-2,-3/
```

The constant list may be abbreviated when several consecutive constants are identical. If j consecutive constants are identical, they may all be replaced by one such constant preceded by j*. This replication or repeat convention is

DATA Statement

The general form is

DATA variable list/constant list/

where the variable list is associated with the constant list by the order in which they are written. The constant values are assigned to the variables before the program is executed. One may place several pairs of variable and constant lists in one DATA statement by separating them by commas. The variables may be real or integer, elements of an array or entire arrays. The DATA statement is a declaration statement and appears at the beginning of the program.

EXAMPLES

```
DATA X1,X2,X3        / 14.12,16.8,-107.2/        DATA I,LO/1,-1000/
DATA X(1),X(2),X(3)/ 14.12,16.8,-107.2/        DATA K,XX/11,1.11/
DATA X               / 14.12,16.8,-107.2/        DATA I(4),X/3,8.8/
DATA A,R,I/12.1,13.1,6/,KAT,HAT/-1,14.04/,LAST1 / 999 /
```

similar to that in FORMAT statements except that the asterisk (star) * is used. Its use is illustrated by the following examples:

```
  DATA X,Y,Z,A,B,C,D /1.0,1.0,1.0,-1.0,-1.0,-1.0,-1.0/
  DATA X,Y,Z,A,B,C,D / 3*1.,4*(-1.)/

  REAL ARRAY(100)                        REAL ARRAY(100)
  DO 5 J=1,100                           DATA ARRAY /100*1.0/
5 ARRAY(J) = 1.0
```

Data initialization statements can also be used in subprograms, provided that no dummy arguments appear in the data statement. A name appearing in a COMMON statement may not appear in a data initialization statement.

EXAMPLE 5–2

A SUBROUTINE FOR NUMBERING PAGES, AND SO ON

Imagine that one has a program that is producing pages of a report or similar document. As the program runs it keeps track of the number of lines and words on each page it produces. It is desired to write a subroutine which does the following things:

1. Keeps a running total of the number of lines
2. Keeps a running total of the number of words
3. Prints the page number in the form "PAGE 12" in the lower right-hand corner
4. Advances the paper to a new page.

A subroutine NUPAGE is given which does these things.

```
      SUBROUTINE NUPAGE
      INTEGER WORDS,TOTALL,TOTALW,PAGE
C         ALL INPUT-OUTPUT IS VIA COMMON
      COMMON LINES,WORDS,NLINE,NWORD
      DATA PAGE,TOTALL,TOTALW/ 3*0 /         Initialize the counters
      PAGE = PAGE + 1                         to be zero
C         ASSUME 55 LINES TO WRITE ON
      LEFT = 55-LINES
      IF( LEFT) 90,10,5
    5 DO 8 J=1,LEFT                           Skip lines down to the
    8 PRINT 9                                 bottom of the page
    9 FORMAT( 1H )
   10 PRINT 12,PAGE
   12 FORMAT(70X,4HPAGE,I5 /1H1)
   20 TOTALL = TOTALL + LINES
      TOTALW = TOTALW + WORDS
      NLINE = TOTALL                          Put the line and word
      NWORD = TOTALW                          counts into COMMON
          RETURN
   90 PRINT 95,PAGE
   95 FORMAT(52X10( 1H*),22HTOO MANY LINES ON PAGE I5/1H1)
          GO TO 20
      END
```

There are several points of interest in this subroutine. Note that the variables PAGE, TOTALL, and TOTALW *cannot* be initialized with the ordinary assignment statements.

```
PAGE = 0
TOTALL = 0
TOTALW = 0
```

This would cause their value to be reset every time NUPAGE is called and would destroy the accumulated value. If one does not use a DATA statement, then the main program would have to make a preliminary call on NUPAGE to set these values. For example, one could call NUPAGE with LINES $= -100$ and then insert the following code at the start:

```
      IF( LINES .NE. -100 )   GO TO 2
      PAGE = 0           Code to initialize the
      TOTALL = 0         counters when NUPAGE is
      TOTALW = 0         called with NLINES = -100
          RETURN
    2 CONTINUE
```

Not only does this make the subroutine more complicated, less efficient, and harder to understand, but it also clutters up the main program with a "nonsense" call on NUPAGE. Finally, standard Fortran allows subprogram variables (such as PAGE) to lose their values between calls on the subprogram *unless* the variable appears in a COMMON or DATA statement.

Note the apparently useless statements which assign NLINE and NWORD the values of TOTALL and TOTALW. This is required because these totals are to be communicated back to the main program through COMMON. Some, but not all, Fortran systems allow a variable to appear in both a COMMON and a DATA statement. To be sure, we have introduced two new variables simply to avoid this situation. The situation would be the same if the communication was via arguments rather than COMMON.

This subroutine does the user the courtesy of checking for excessive values of lines and warning him if he has generated more than the assumed 55 lines. Actually, there is also necessity as well as courtesy involved here. If exactly 55 lines were generated, then LEFT would be zero, but the DO loop 8 would still be executed once. This would PRINT 9 and result in the page number being on the 57th line rather than the 56th line where it should be.

Common Errors

1. Different number of the variables and the values to be assigned to them.
2. Omission of the comma following a slash when more than one list is initialized in a DATA statement.
3. Inclusion of COMMON variables or dummy arguments in a DATA statement.
4. Placement of the DATA statement in the main program when it is to preset variables in a subprogram (or vice versa).
5. Use of a DATA statement for an array with more than one dimension.

Things You Can Do

1. Initialize entire arrays or lists in a compact manner.
2. (In some systems) Initialize part of an array using an implied DO loop, such as DATA (A(K), K = 5,8)/6.2, 7.3, 8.4/.
3. Mix real and integer variables and values, such as DATA X,J/12, 3.0/.
4. (In some systems) Initialize a single array element such as DATA X(1), X(8)/1., 999./.

5–3.2 A Format

There are many times when one wishes to process some nonnumeric information such as names, titles, and English words or symbols. The A format allows one to do this as follows:

```
  REAL TITLE(60)
  READ 5, TITLE
5 FORMAT(60A1)
  PRINT 6,TITLE
6 FORMAT(1H1,5X,60A1)
```

This piece of code reads whatever is in the first 60 columns of a card and prints it out at the top of a new page, shifted to the right slightly. A card input and resulting output for this code is shown below.

Card with title on it

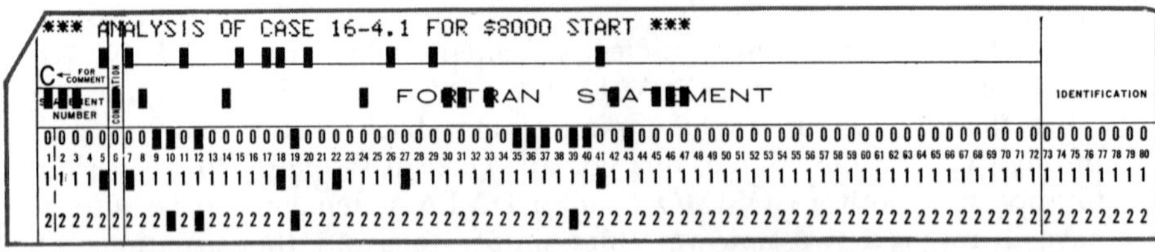

Resulting output – at the top of a new page

```
Column  6|
         |*** ANALYSIS OF CASE 16-4.1 FOR $8000 START ***
```

A Format

The general form is an integer constant followed by the letter A, followed by a second integer constant as in nAw. The constant w is the number of characters (symbols, digits, and letters) per variable and n is the number of variables specified. Each Fortran system has a definite (and small) limit on the value of w. The usual range is from 4 to 10 with 6 as the most common.

EXAMPLES

```
FORMAT(A4,A6,A1)              FORMAT(1H1,3A2,F10.2,A4)
FORMAT(3A4,6X,I5,A4)          FORMAT(6H NAME ,4A6)
```

The A format is very useful even if only used to read various messages and strings of characters and then print them out in the appropriate places. In addition, there are ways to actually process information read in under the A format. This ability is explained in the next section and an understanding of Hollerith variables is required to fully understand what happens when the A format is used.

5–3.3 Hollerith Constants and Variables

The variables processed by the A format are handled in exactly the same way as messages in a FORMAT statement. In each case the characters are encoded numerically and then placed in the words of the computer. The encoding is entirely unrelated to numeric values. The codes used internally vary with the Fortran system, but one rarely needs to know the actual code in order to process Hollerith information. A possible coding scheme is partially shown in Figure 5–9. For concreteness we assume here that the Fortran system has 6 characters per word. If one places fewer characters in a variable (word), the rest is filled out with blanks. Typical character strings, encodings, and appearances

Character	Numeric code	Character	Numeric code	Character	Numeric code
A	21	Y	70	9	11
B	22	Z	71	blank	60
C	23	0	00	=	13
D	24	1	01	,	73

FIGURE 5–9. Part of a coding scheme for Fortran characters. Note that a 2-digit number (base 8) is used for each character.

of the words are shown in Figure 5–10. There is a choice as to whether one pads the word with blanks on the left or on the right. The choice can directly affect things as will be illustrated later.

Character string	Code	Corresponding word in memory					
BAD	222124	22	21	24	60	60	60
ZAB9	71212211	71	21	22	11	60	60
1099	01001111	01	00	11	11	60	60
A = B + 8	211360222010	21	13	60	22	20	10

FIGURE 5–10. Typical encoding of Hollerith variables in the computer memory.

When an A format is used, the characters on the card are translated into Hollerith variables and stored internally in a code such as that illustrated in Figure 5–9. Needless to say, only garbage results from an attempt to add, subtract, and so on, Hollerith variables.

What happens if we use an A10 when a computer word can contain only, say, a maximum of six characters? In general, if a single machine word holds g characters and Aw is specified, then the effect differs depending on whether we are reading or printing:

reading	$w \leq g$:	read w characters, insert g − w trailing blanks
	$w > g$:	read only the right-most g characters
printing	$w \leq g$:	print left-most w characters
	$w > g$:	print w − g blanks followed by g characters

Consider a system that stores up to six characters per machine word (that is, g = 6). The effect of the computer word length is illustrated by the example program, input and output below.

```
   READ 1,X,Y
 1 FORMAT(A1,A8)
   PRINT 2,X,Y,X,Y
 2 FORMAT(2X,A1,2X,A8,2(2XA2))
```

CARD READ WITH FORMAT 1

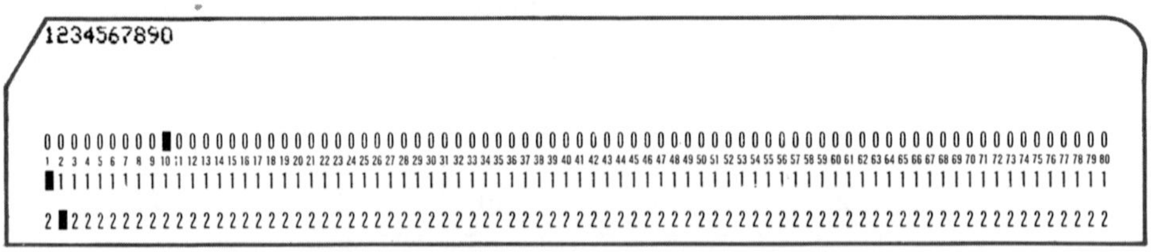

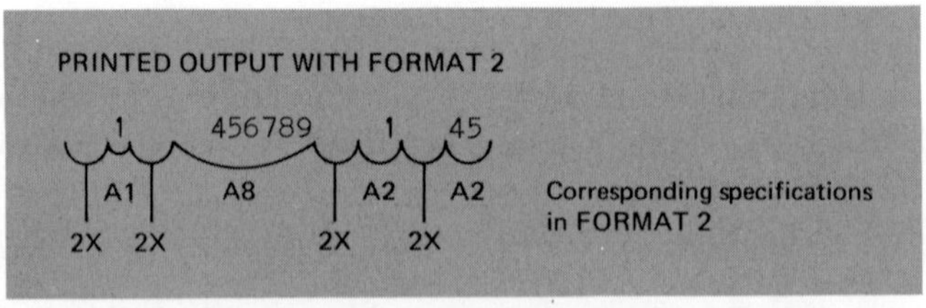

An array may be assigned Hollerith constant values in the same way as it is assigned other values. Thus,

```
      REAL STRING(80),FOURS(20)
      READ 5, STRING,FOURS
    5 FORMAT(80A1/20A4)
```

reads two cards, with the 80 elements of STRING each containing the character from each of the 80 columns of the card, while the elements of FOURS each contain four characters.

The main processing that is done on Hollerith variables involves comparisons for equality. Thus one is normally testing: Is this character an E?, is this character a +?, is this word BLUE?, and so on. In order to do this, one must have some variables of known value to test against. Suppose we were to read cards whose first four columns contain all blanks, ****, ++++, or the word HELP. In order to test which of these occurs we need four Hollerith variables, say BLANK, STAR4, PLUS4, and HELP. A few Fortran systems allow one to write simply

```
      BLANK = 4H
      STAR4 = 4H****
      PLUS4 = 4H++++
      HELP  = 4HHELP
```

Many do not allow the direct assignment of Hollerith variables and require one to use a DATA statement

```
      DATA BLANK,STAR4,PLUS4,HELP/4H    ,4H****,4H++++,4HHELP/
```

or, require one to read in the variable's values with an A format

```
   READ 10,BLANK,STAR4,PLUS4,HELP
10 FORMAT(4A4)
```

Card with the Hollerith constants on it

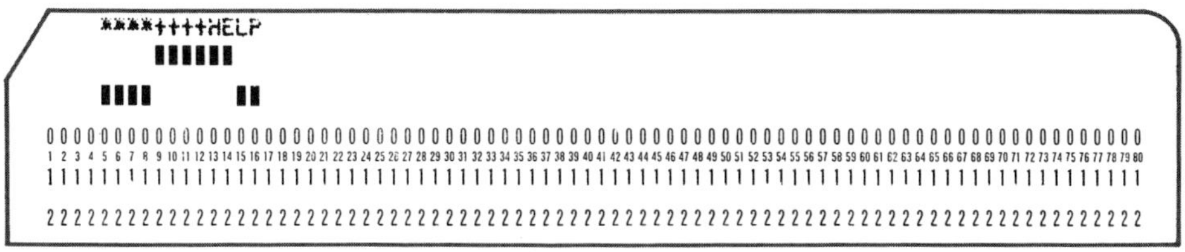

Suppose that one of these methods is used to assign these values. One can then read a card and test for the contents of the first four columns as follows:

```
  READ 8, CLUE,(DATA(J),J=1,5)
8 FORMAT(A4,5F10.4)
  IF(CLUE .EQ. BLANK )  STOP
  IF(CLUE .EQ. STAR4 )  GO TO 20
  IF(CLUE .EQ. PLUS4 )  GO TO 50
  IF(CLUE .EQ. HELP  )  GO TO 300
```

A common source of error is indicated by the following two pieces of programs:

```
  DATA CAT/3HCAT/                       DATA DOG/3HDOG/
  READ 5,KEY                            READ 5,MUTT
5 FORMAT(A3)                          5 FORMAT(A3)
  IF( KEY.EQ.CAT) GO TO 50              WORD = MUTT
  STOP                                  IF(WORD.EQ.DOG) GO TO 50
                                        STOP
```

CARD INPUT

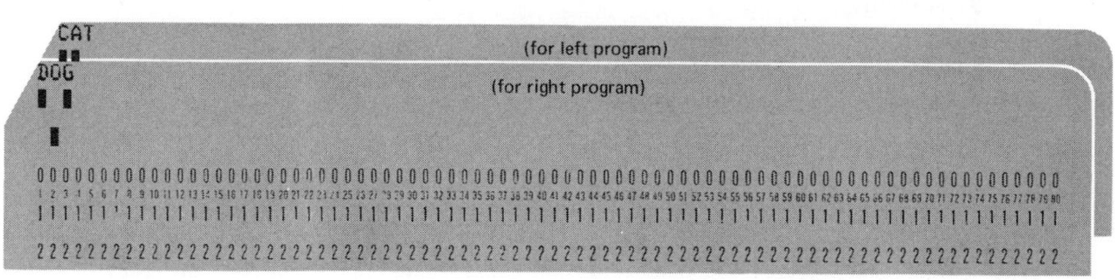

Both of these programs stop rather than transferring to 50. The one on the left stops because of the mixed mode in the logical IF. To see whether KEY is equal to CAT, the computer evaluates KEY-CAT and tests to see if the result is zero. Since this is mixed mode (KEY is integer, CAT is real) arithmetic, the Fortran system either detects this during compilation and issues a diagnostic (it might terminate the compilation also) or it converts one of the variables to the other type. If it changes KEY to a real (the most reasonable thing to do), then the internal content of KEY is rewritten. Thus even though it started out being the same as CAT, it does not end up that way and the equality test fails.

A similar rewriting must occur in the program on the right at the statement WORD = MUTT. Now there is no hope of a diagnostic warning of this danger either. The lesson of these two examples is: *Make all Hollerith variables in a program the same type* (either all integer or all real).

The following piece illustrates a situation where the way the Fortran system packs in blocks becomes crucial.

```
      DATA DOLLAR /1H$ /
      READ 10,WORD
   10 FORMAT(A4)
```

Possible Card Input

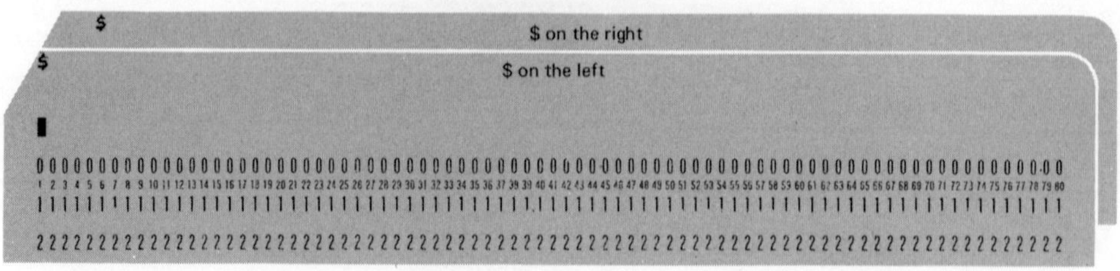

The Hollerith variable DOLLAR has its dollar sign on the left or on the right with the rest blanks. There are four possibilities for WORD as follows:

$bbbb   b$bbb   bb$bb   bbbb$

The particular situation depends on how the blanks are filled in. Unless one knows this, one cannot be sure of testing correctly for the dollar sign. Of course, the best thing to do is to read WORD in with an A1 format or define DOLLAR with an A4 format. Then there is no uncertainty.

To illustrate the use of Hollerith data, suppose that we have input data punched as shown.

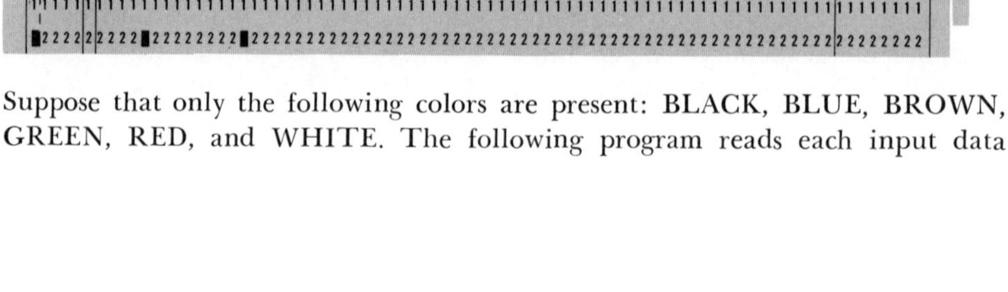

Suppose that only the following colors are present: BLACK, BLUE, BROWN, GREEN, RED, and WHITE. The following program reads each input data card, and when it reads a card with the name field consisting of four zeros, it prints how many people have hair of each of the above colors.

```
      INTEGER COLOR,COL(6),COUNT(6),NAME(2)
      DATA COL/3HBLA,3HBRO,3HGRE,3HRED,3HWHI,3HBLU/,
     *     LAST,COUNT/ 5H0000 ,6*0 /
    1 READ 2,NAME,COLOR
    2 FORMAT(2A5,9X,A3)
      DO 3 J=1,6
    3 IF( COLOR .EQ. COL(J)) COUNT(J)=COUNT(J)+1
      IF( COLOR .EQ. COL(6) ) PRINT 4,NAME
    4 FORMAT(5X2A5,14H HAS BLUE HAIR )
      IF( NAME(1) .NE. LAST )  GO TO 1
      PRINT 5, (COL(J),COUNT(J),J=1,6)
    5 FORMAT(1H110X,11HCOLOR COUNT // 6(11X,A3,2X,I3/))
      STOP
      END
```

It is important to notice that arithmetic or logical IF statements may involve variables whose values are Hollerith constants, as long as the variables are all of the same type (that is, all real or all integer).

Common Errors

1. Using both real and integer variables as Hollerith variables and then testing for equality.
2. Using arithmetic for digits which are Hollerith variables (that is, read in with an A format).
3. Trying to place too many characters in one machine word. The maximum number allowed varies from system to system.

Things You Can Do

1. Present Hollerith variables in DATA statements.
2. Use Hollerith variables as arguments to functions or subroutines.

Problems

5–3.1 Write a program which misuses formats and variable types as follows:
(a) Print a Hollerith variable in I10 and F20.10 formats.
(b) Print an integer, say 1230456, in A6 and E15.6 formats.
(c) Print a real, say 17.403, in A6 and I10 formats.

5–3.2 A deck of cards has the following information (repeated up to 8 times) on each card:

course name and number:	2 letters and 3 digits	8 columns
credit hours:	2 digits	
grade:	1 letter	

Write a program which reads a deck of these cards and prints each card back out with an additional number, the grade point average. The grade point average is based on 4 points per credit hour of A, 3 points for B, 2 points for C, 1 point for D, and nothing for F. Note that there may be from 1 to 8 courses with hours and grade on each card.

5–3.3 Write a program which reads a card that has a date on it (and nothing else) as follows:

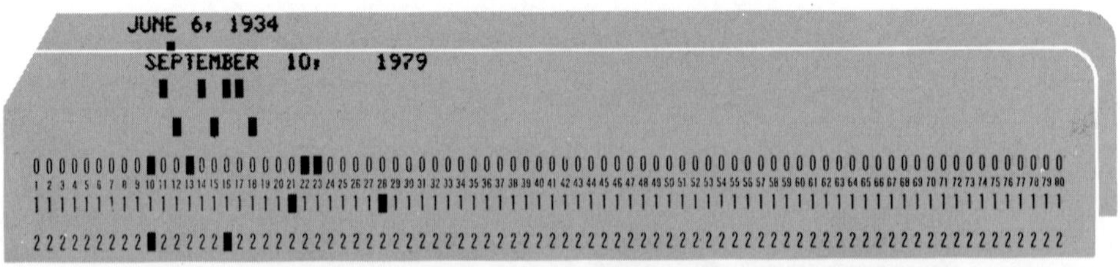

There are no blanks in the middle of words (that is, SEPT EM BER is forbidden) or the numbers (that is, 1 0, 19 3 4 is forbidden). However, you do *not* know where the words or numbers start.

The program is to analyze this card and print it back out as follows:

```
1979, DAY 10, MONTH SEPTEMBER
1934, DAY  6, MONTH JUNE
```

[*Hint:* Read the card in an 80A1 format, search along the card until a nonblank character is found, then search until another blank is found. The characters inbetween spell the month (if you started on the left). Use the same strategy to find the day and year.]

5–3.4 *(Number conversion)* Consider a card that has 1 digit (0 through 9) punched in an unknown column. Write a program that reads such a card and prints the digit out along with its square. Note that you must read the card in an A format, locate the digit, and find its value as an integer before you can square it.

5–3.5 Write a program similar to that of Problem 5–3.4 except that a 4-digit integer appears on the card.

(a) Assume that there are no blanks between the digits.

(b) Allow any number of blanks to be placed between the digits.

5–3.6 Write a program similar to Problem 5–3.5 except that a real number of the form XXXX.XXXX appears on the card. [*Hint:* Find the decimal point, take it out, and convert the string of digits to an integer variable. Then multiply by the appropriate power of 10 to create a real variable with the correct value.]

5–3.7 Consider cards with students' names and ID numbers punched at random positions as follows:

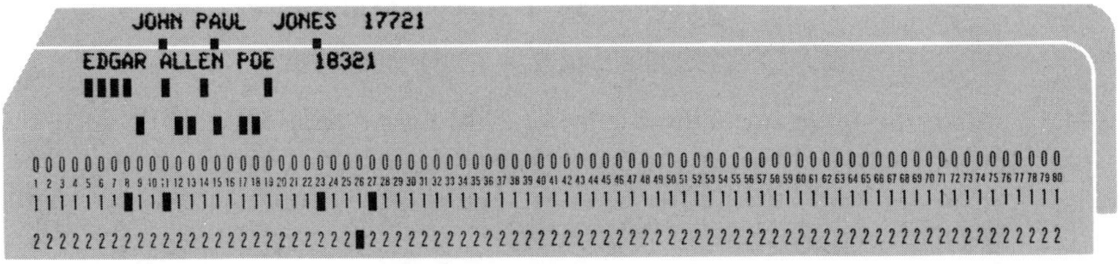

Write a program that reads these cards and prints the names back out in the following edited form:

```
18321 POE, EDGAR A.
17721 JONES, JOHN P.
```

Assume that everyone has a middle name and that there are no blanks in the names or ID numbers. Generate 10 cards of sample data and run them to show that your program works.

5–3.8 Consider N + 1 cards as follows: The first card has the value of N punched in an I5 format (columns 1 to 5). The next N cards have any text consisting of Fortran characters. Write a program that reads these cards and marks a frequency count of all the characters that appear. Print out the last N cards, then the relative frequencies (in a nice table) of the characters that appear. The relative frequency is the number of times a character appears divided by the total number of characters. As data to be processed, use this problem's statement. It happens to contain most Fortran characters such as +, −, *, (,), =, $.

5–4 General Problems

5–4.1 (a) Write a program to compute the number of days between any two dates punched on a card in the following way:

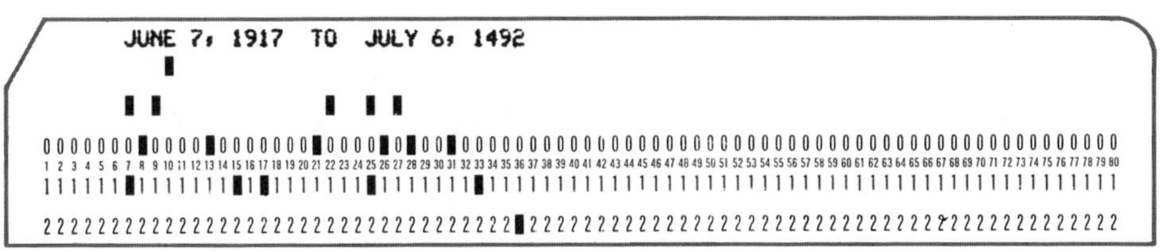

Take into account that 1900, and so on, are not leap years.

(b) Modify the program to take into account the change to the Gregorian calendar that occurred in the 1500s.

5–4.2 Modify the program for Problem 4–1.15 (addition of two integers) to add two reals. Show that your program works for the following two additions:

$$222.333123456 + .0000111144452$$

$$77889902.54321 + 67.314592687525$$

5–4.3 Make the program of Problem 5–4.2 into a subroutine and use it as the basic component of a program that adds an arbitrary set of real numbers. Assume that the numbers are punched one number per card with the decimal point placed arbitrarily.

5–4.4 Write a program that uses the Monte Carlo technique described below to approximate π. Consider the unit square ((0,0), (0,1), (1,0), (1,1)) in the plane and a circle of radius 1 with its center at (0,0). If we generate points randomly in the unit square and count how many lie within the quarter circle, we get an approximation of the area of the quarter circle from the ratio

$$r = \frac{\text{Number of points within quarter circle}}{\text{Number of points generated in square}}.$$

According to Monte Carlo theory, $r \approx \pi/4$ or the area of the quarter circle. Therefore, to get an approximation of π, we use a random number generator to generate 1000 points that lie within the unit square. As we generate the points, we count the number that lie within the quarter circle and form an approximation of π with the formula

$$\pi \approx \left(\frac{\text{Number of points inside the quarter circle}}{1000}\right) * 4.$$

Write out 10 approximations of π (using 10 different sets of random numbers) and their average. What happens if 10,000 or 20,000 points are used instead of 1000?

You must locate and use a random number generator.

5–4.5 Rewrite the program below without the use of any DATA or DO statements and without using any arrays. The new program must do the same thing as the given program.

```
      DIMENSION XVAL(50),MSSAGE(2)
      DATA ENDVAL/ 9999. /, MSSAGE/6HMAXIMU,6HM NO.= /
      I = 0
   10 I = I+1
      READ 25,XVAL(I)
   25 FORMAT( F8.0 )
      IF( XVAL(I) .LT. ENDVAL )  GO TO 10
      N = I-1
      BIG = XVAL(1)
      DO 300 J = 2,N
  300 BIG = AMAX1(BIG,XVAL(J))
      PRINT 30, MSSAGE, BIG
   30 FORMAT(1H1,2A6,E15.7)
      STOP
      END
```

5–4.6 A right triangle has five basic parts as labeled in the diagram. These parts are the angles A and B, the corresponding sides SA and SB, and the hypotenuse HY. There is a large number of relationships between these parts and four of these relationships are listed in the diagram.

The right triangle is uniquely determined by any pair of these parts except A and B. In the latter case its shape (but not its size) is determined. The problem of solving right triangles is more precisely stated as follows:

Given any two parts of a right triangle
determine the remaining three.

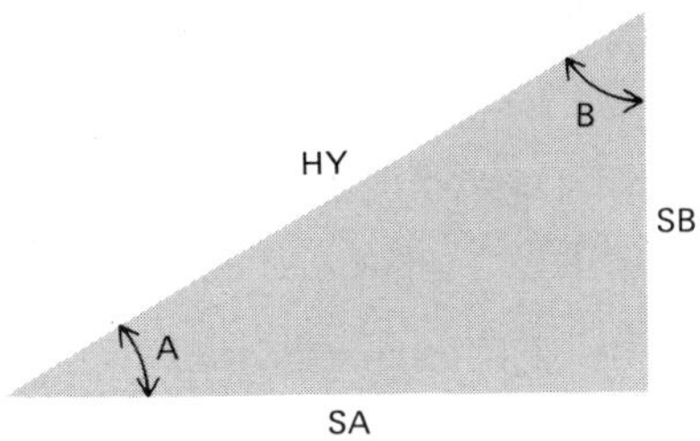

$HY^2 = SA^2 + SB^2$
Tan A = SB/SA
Tan B = SA/SB
Cos A = SA/HY

There are 10 possible pairs of these parts, so a program for this problem must accept 10 different inputs, distinguish between them, and take appropriate action. The program is considerably simplified by noting that four pairs of input parts are the same except for naming. They correspond as follows:

SA, HY → SB, HY
SA, A → SB, B
SA, B → SB, A
HY, A → HY, B

When input pairs on the left column are identified, we can interchange SB with SA, B with A, and use the same procedure as that for the corresponding right input pairs.

(a) Set up a code for these parts of a triangle and specify a format on a card for giving any two parts. Write a program that reads this card, computes all five parts of the triangle, and prints them out with an appropriate message. See Problem 3–2.8 for a flowchart of a simplified version of this program.

(b) Modify the input so that it is of the form

HY = 16.285, SA = 12.412,

and so on. The program must read the card and decide which values are given. (In the next chapter a feature, NAMELIST, of Fortran is described which makes this form of input very easy.)

(c) Modify the output so that an actual triangle is printed out which is the same shape as the triangle found, but scaled to fill most of a page. [*Hint:* Set up an array, say 50 by 50, full of blanks. Then put some character, say X or M, into the array to blacken a (nearly) triangular region of the required shape.]

5–4.7 Which of the following Fortran statements are legal?

```
A.  DO 13 AX = 1,K+1,2
B.  PRINT 16,A,XA,I,(J,QQ(J),J=1,I)
C.  IF( X.LE.(Z+2.) .AND. .GT.(Z-4.))  GO TO 77
D.  XXX = 16.*(BQ -3.(XXX+Y*BQ))
E.  FORMAT( 5H1 ANS,6X,3(I4,4E14.2/)//A4,4A1)
F.  INTEGER XX,BX3,KLOD(N)
G.  CALL GLUBER(XX,A-3.*XX,17.123,BBC)
```

5–4.8 Which of the following statements about Fortran are correct?

(a) A separate FORMAT statement is required for each READ or PRINT statement.
(b) A STOP statement is required in each program.
(c) An END statement is required in each program.
(d) All arrays must be declared in each subprogram where they are used.
(e) One must have one's own code for computing the maximum value of K numbers when K is read in from data cards.
(f) At least one RETURN statement is required in each subprogram.
(g) Different counters (control variables) are required for each DO loop in a nested set of DO loops.
(h) The same names for the variables must be used in COMMON statements of different subprograms.
(i) No subroutine CALL or READ or PRINT statements can follow a logical IF.

5–4.9 Write a program to read and add fractions punched on a card as follows:

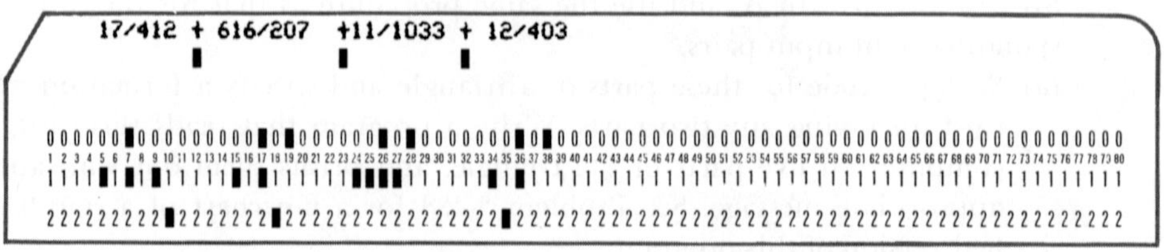

You must read the card in an A format and locate the +'s and /'s, then convert the digit strings to real numbers and carry out the arithmetic. The output should reproduce the input followed by an equal sign and the answer. Assume that all of the digits strings are shorter than 10 digits.

[*Hint:* A subprogram similar to the programs of Problems 5–3.4, 5–3.5 is useful.]

5–4.10 (Fortran statement shortener)

(a) You are to write a program which reads in an ordinary Fortran program deck (columns 1 to 72) and which converts it to another equivalent Fortran program that has NON-blank characters only in columns 1 to 50. You do this as follows:

Step 1: Check to see if there is anything NON-blank in columns 51 to 72. If there isn't, print the card back out and go on to the next card.

Step 2: If there are some NON-blank characters, print out the original card for columns 1 to 50, then create a continuation card with the entire contents of columns 51 to 72 (moved over left enough) and print it out as a legal Fortran continuation card.

(b) Give two different kinds of statements or situations where this program might produce illegal Fortran code. Give a brief explanation.

5–4.11 You have several lists of real numbers on cards separated by a card with the word NULIST in columns 1 to 6. The situation is illustrated below.

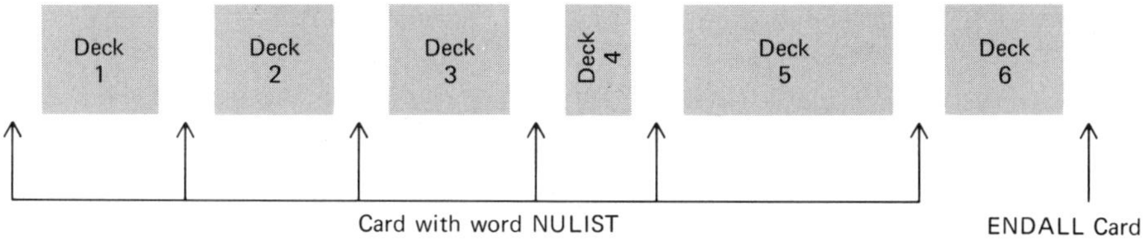

The last card in the deck has the word ENDALL in columns 1 to 6. Each number is in columns 1 to 10 and there are no more than 100 numbers in any one list.

Write a subprogram that computes the average and standard deviation of the numbers as in Problem 4–2.5. Use this subprogram in a program to process this deck of cards and to print a line for each list of the form

LIST 3 CONTAINS 74 NUMBERS WITH
AVERAGE xxxx.xxxx AND S.D. xxxx.xxxx

5–4.12 Consider a deck similar to that of Problem 5–4.11 except that the lists contain words in columns 1 to 10. Write a subprogram that makes a character frequency count for such a list. Incorporate this subprogram into a program to process this deck of cards and to print a page containing the frequency count results for each list.

5–4.13 The following Fortran programs have errors in them. Locate each error and write a new program which corrects the errors. The new statements can be anything reasonably close to the given statements. They must, of course, be correct Fortran. Do not try to understand what the whole program does. Note that no credit is given for such drastic modifications as replacing the whole program by a single STOP statement.

```
C  THIS PROGRAM HAS ABOUT 14 ERRORS IN IT
      REAL MINDIF,A(4),Q(NQ),J
      TERM(X) = (A(1)+A(2)*J/(A(3)*SQRT(A(4)))/(J**3+1.)
      INTEGER COUNT
      COUNT = 0.
      READ 5,A(4),TOL,NQ,(Q(K),K=1,NQ)
    5 FORMAT( 5F10.5/I6,5F8.2 )
      0. = QBAR
      DO 10 L = 1,NQ-1
   10 QBAR = A(L)/*COS(Q(L)/3.7) + QBAR
      PRINT 6,TOL,QBAR
    6 FORMAT( 1H1,5X 9HTOL,QBAR= 2E4.15)
      TOP = 0.
      BOT = 0.
      DO 20 L= 1,1000
      J=L
      TOP = TOP + TERMX(J)
      BOT = BOT + 4.1J/(QBAR*A(2)**2*J)
      MINDIF = ABS(TOP-BOT)
      IF  MINDIF .LT. TOL*.1   GO TO 10
  100 CONTINUE
      STOP
      END
  250 PRINT 251,L,TOP,BOT
  251 FORMAT(5X,9HGOT IT OK,F3.0,14HTERMS,TOP,BOT= F10.8)
      STOP
      END
```

```
C  THIS PROGRAM HAS ABOUT 12 ERRORS IN IT
      REAL IJK,BBAR,XQ
      B(I) = A*(J-1.) + ABS(I+2.*XQ-4.*+6.*A)/BBAR
      INTEGER QX,PBAR,KLM
  500 FORMAT(10XF8.3,I6,F8.3/2I2)
  400 PRINT 500,A,IJK,XQ,QX,KLM
      BBAR = .5(FLOAT(QX)/A-1.)
      PBAR = QX+2.*KLM
      TOL  + .001
      0.=ANS
      PRINT 500,A,XQ,BBAR,PBAR,QX
      DO 180 KK = 1,PBAR
      AK = KK
  170 OANS = ANS
      ANS = ANS + B(KK)/AK**2.
      IF( 1OANS-ANS1.LT. TOL )  GO TO 100
   80 CONTINUE
      KK = 1000
      IF(ANS.LT.800.)GOTO170
  100 ANS = .5*(ANS+OANS)
      PRINT 600,KK,ANS
  600 FORMAT(I8,F6.10)
      END
      GO TO 400
```

```
C  THIS PROGRAM HAS ABOUT 12 ERRORS IN IT
      REAL ERR(101),A(20)
      READ 600,POWER,ACCUR,K
  600 FORMAT( I6,5X,F10.5)
      SCALE = 12.12/SQRT(6*13)
      LSCALE=  LOG(SCALE)
      A(2) = 3.01
      A(3) = 4
      PRINT 610,K
  601 FORMAT(1H1,10X,3HK IS,I12)
      DO 20 J = 4,K+1
      XLFT = 12.12/SQRT(3*J)/SCALE
   15 ERR(J) = FUNK(XLFT) - GUNK(XLFT)
      GUNK AND FUNK ARE OK TO USE
      THEY ARE SUBPROGRAMS NOT SHOWN HERE
   20 XNOT(J) = ERR(J)/XLFT
      IF( XNOT(K+1) = 0. )  GO TO 15
      IF( ERR(4) .LT. 0. )  1.0 = ERR(4)
      PRINT 602, (ERR(J),XNOT(J),J=4,K)
  602 FORMAR(////12F  5.10 )
      STOP
      END
```

5–4.14 *(The Personnel File Problem: The little black book)* Consider a list of people along with information about their ability, likes, dislikes, experience, and other personal qualities. Assume that from time to time you have to choose a person from this list for a particular task, assignment, and so on.

(a) Each choice requires a varying combination of the personal qualities in the list. Devise a measure of goodness of choice for a particular assignment. [*Hint:* Rank the personal qualities of each person on some scale (say 1 to 5 or 1 to 10) and then specify a set of weights that describes what each assignment requires.]

(b) *Specific Case.* You have a little black book that contains the names, addresses, and telephone numbers of your friends. For each one, you have the following information:

Characteristics	*Likes*
1. Appearance	1. Classical music
2. Compatibility	2. Dancing
3. Conversational	3. Movies—T.V.
4. Financial	4. Parties
5. Moral	5. Sports
6. Scholastic	6. World Affairs

You need dates for (a) the football homecoming game and dance, (b) the Phlat Phrat Braul, (c) a relaxing evening. Whom do you call first (or say yes to first) from your little black book?

Make up a little black book for 12 people and specify a set of weights for each of these dates. Write a Fortran program which processes this information and selects the best candidate from your book. The output should be of the form

THE CHOICE FOR DATE 1 IS – – –
THE CHOICE FOR DATE 2 IS – – –
THE CHOICE FOR DATE 3 IS – – –

5–4.15 Consider a program that makes a rough bar graph of a table of values. An example table is the distribution of grades on a test, for example,

Grade	*Number*	*Grade*	*Number*	*Grade*	*Number*
0–10	1	41–50	11	71–80	36
11–20	2	51–60	21	81–90	17
21–30	1	61–70	40	91–100	6
31–40	6				

A bar graph of these data is as shown below.

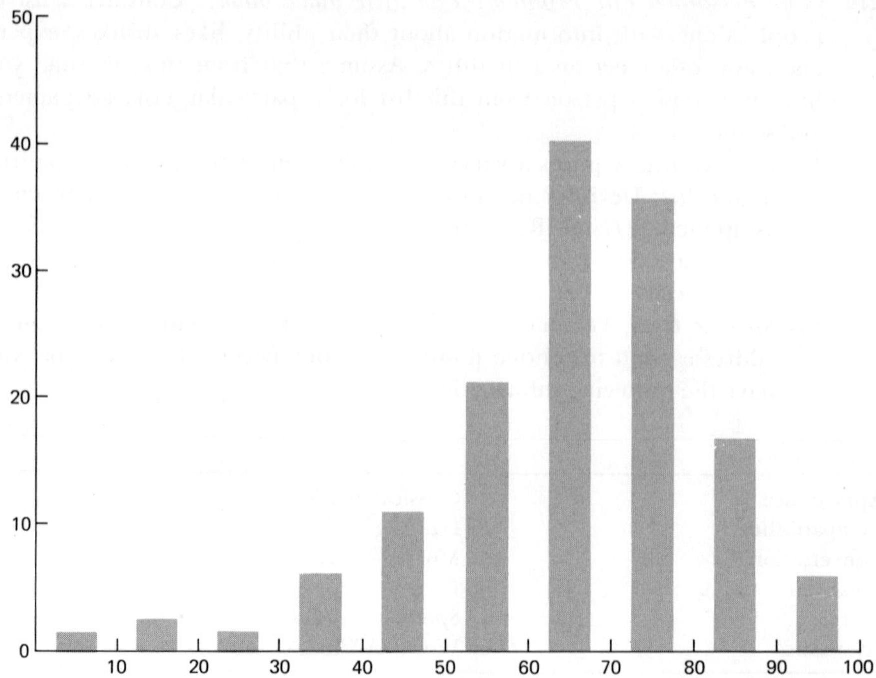

(a) Write a program that accepts a table with 10 entries ranging from 0 to 50 and produces a bar graph on a separate sheet of printed output. [*Hint:* Create an array (two-dimensional, 50 rows and 100 columns) of Hollerith variables. Then.

1. Set them all equal to blanks
2. Put 1's in the left column and minus signs in the bottom row to form the boundaries of the graph
3. Put some letter (say M) in the appropriate rows as high as the bar graph is to go
4. Print this out in an A1 format.]

You must also print out the numbers on the left side and along the bottom.

(b) Write a program that accepts a table with 10 entries in any range and scales the values to fit into the bar graph of part A. You must also put the appropriate values on the left side.

(c) Further generalize the program of part (b) so that the number of entries can be from 5 up to 25. The program must place the bars appropriately across the page.

5–4.16 Write a program that makes a rough graph of a curve given by a formula. The graph should have the vertical and horizontal lines drawn and labeled. Furthermore, place a title (read in perhaps) below the graph.

See Problem 5–4.15 for a detailed hint on how to do programs like this. A sample formula to use is

$$2 + 25 * \text{IFIX}(\text{COS}(X/8.) + 1.))$$

where X ranges from 1 to 100.

5–4.17 Write a program which converts from Roman numerals to arabic numerals. Have the program read the Roman numerals from a card (starting in column 1) and print the Roman numeral and corresponding arabic numerals out on a line.

A set of sample input data (from easy to hard) is given

II, XX, C, VII, MCL, MDCCLXXVI, IV, XLIX, MCMXLIV

5–4.18 Consider pairs of cards punched with digits in all columns. Write a program that reads two such cards and counts the number of matches in the columns. (If both cards have a 7 in column 23, that is a match.)

5–4.19 Modify the program in Problem 5–4.18 to process cards with ordinary English text on them.

5–4.20 Some languages (such as Basic, APL, or PL/1) allow so-called "array operators." If A, B, and C are arrays, then A = 0 causes all elements of A set to zero and A = B + C causes A(I,J) to be set to B(I,J) + C(I,J) for each meaningful I and J. Locate programs in the text or problems where one could take advantage of such operators.

6

Fortran
ADVANCED FEATURES

This chapter presents a variety of features of Fortran that are considered advanced for two reasons. First, several of them are really useful only in special situations that normally arise in complex or sophisticated programs. Thus many students in a first course have a difficult time in appreciating the value of some of these features. Second, many of these features are not at all standardized and there are wide variations between the implementations. Because of this the details of some features are not fully described and one must obtain a reference manual for the particular Fortran system one is to use. In fact, many Fortran systems omit some of the features described in this chapter. Those features which are especially variable are so noted in the text.

6—1 Input-Output Features

This section contains a discussion of five somewhat dissimilar topics related to input and output. Two of these, NAMELIST and *variable formats,* are features that may be extremely useful and are hard to duplicate with Fortran features described so far. Two others, other formats and groupings, are very similar to already described facilities and provide considerable convenience at times. Finally, there is a brief discussion of input-output for devices other than the standard printed output and card input.

6–1.1 Namelist

Namelist input-output is not a standard Fortran feature. However it is available on many systems, and it is worth examining to see a very different way of performing input and output.

The reading and writing we have been doing is called *formatted input-output*. Each input record (card image) has to be described accurately by a FORMAT statement; similarly for each output record (line image). Formatted input-output gives the programmer complete control; however, the slightest discrepancy between the formats and the information being processed can lead to meaningless results.

Namelist input-output is format free (or "free format"). The programmer prepares namelist input on punched cards according to a few simple rules, and he obtains namelist output just by asking for it; programmer-supplied formats are not required.

Suppose you wish to read in values for two variables X and Y, then print X, Y, and a result K. By using namelist, it can be done as follows:

```
NAMELIST /A/ X,Y,K
READ(5,A)
K = X+Y
WRITE(6,A)
STOP
END
```

The card read by this program is

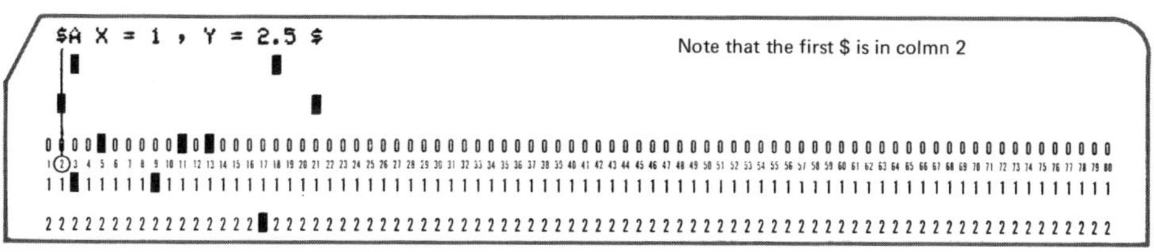

The output from this program is

```
$A
 X = .1000000E+01
 Y = .2500000E+01
 K =            3
$
```

The statement NAMELIST/A/X,Y,K defines an *input-output list* called A, whose elements are X, Y, and K. This is a declaration statement for the list A. In the absence of any other declarations, X and Y are real variables and K is an integer variable. The statement READ(5,A) initiates a search on unit 5 for a record (or card) that starts with the name A preceded by the name-list control character $ which *must appear in column* 2. (The control character depends on the system, and the ampersand & is often used instead of the dollar sign. Refer to Section 1–5.5 for a discussion of unit numbers for READ and WRITE statements if they are not familiar.) After such a record is found, all the names that appear before the next $ must belong to the A input-output list. In this case, the names X and Y are found; since they belong to the list A, the specified values are assigned, after appropriate conversion. The READ is finished when the second $ is reached.

The WRITE(6,A) causes all of the items on the list A to be written in some fixed format defined by the system. The name of the list and the names of all the items are printed also.

NAMELIST

The general form of the NAMELIST statement is

$$\text{NAMELIST}/n_1/\text{list }\#1/n_2/\text{list }\#2/\ldots/n_m/\text{list }\#m$$

Each of n_1, n_2, . . . is a name of the input-output list which immediately follows. These names follow the usual Fortran rules, but they may only be used in READ or WRITE statements. The lists may contain only the names of specific variables or arrays. The same variable may appear in several lists.

EXAMPLES

```
NAMELIST /IN/K,Y,Z,K /OUT/X,Y,K,BQ

REAL D(20),W(50)
NAMELIST /DATA/ D,KBAR,ZAP,W(1)
NAMELIST /PRNT8/D(1),D(2),W(50),EXIT,MUD
```

Some systems require that the NAMELIST statement appear after any other declaration statements that involve variables in the lists. Some systems allow Hollerith variables in NAMELIST statements and some do not allow any subscripted variables at all, for example, D(1). No system allows a variable subscript to appear, for example, D(K).

Data for namelist input are prepared realizing that a namelist READ processes a variable number of items, all of which belong to the specified list. The items associated with a single READ are marked off by an initial and terminal $. The initial $ (which in most systems *must* be punched in column 2) is immediately followed by the name of the list. For each variable to be read, its name is punched, followed by an equal sign, and a value or a list of values. In the case of a single variable, say X, we could have

$$X = 1 \qquad \text{or} \qquad X = 1.0$$

In the case of an array W, dimensioned W(4), we could have W = 1,3,3,7.5, or W = 1,2 * 3,7.5,. If only the name of the array is given, then all the elements of the array must be given a value. If a constant subscript is used, then one or more values may be assigned. For W, we could have W(1) = 1, which would not change the values of W(2), W(3), or W(4). Similarly, W(2) = −2,3.5 does not change W(1) or W(4), but assigns the values W(2) = −2, W(3) = 3.5.

There are a variety of rules about blanks in the input for NAMELIST. Some of these are quite a nuisance and unexpected. For example, all four specifications on the following card are considered erroneous by some systems.

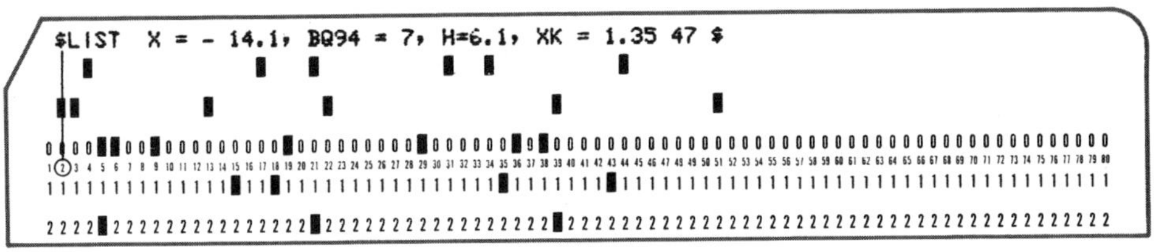

The first one has a blank between the minus sign and the number, the second has a blank in the middle of the variable name, the third does not have blanks on both sides of the equal sign, and the last one has a blank in the middle of the number. Some systems require that *every* name in the list appear in the input data.

If an input list does not fit on one card, then several cards can be used, provided that the last character on each card is a comma or the terminal dollar sign. Column 1 should not be used (leave it blank). For example, for NAMELIST/INPUT/BETA,X, the following three groups are equivalent:

```
 $INPUT BETA = 1,X = 2$      $INPUT X = 2,         $INPUT  BETA = 1,
                             BETA = 1 $                X = 2 ,
                                                     $ENDINPUT
```

Complex constants (discussed in the next section) may be read by punching them with parentheses, as in Q = (1.5, − 7.2). The values punched for real or integer variables may be real, integer, or double-precision constants. The namelist input READ performs the appropriate conversions.

Namelist output is obtained as shown in the preceding example. The entire list is written, each item appearing in the same order as given in the list, according to a format defined by the system.

Namelist output is very useful in debugging a program, in that intermediate results may be printed along with their symbolic names, without expending any effort in preparing correct FORMAT statements.

Common Errors	*Things You Can Do*
1. The use of column 1 of the input card. It is ignored with NAMELIST. The $ must be in column 2 of the first card.	1. A variable name can appear in several NAMELIST statements.
2. The appearance of blanks in either the names or the constants of the namelist card input.	2. One can usually use as few of the namelist variables on an input as one wants.
3. The separation of a minus sign from the constant by one or more blanks.	3. One can have alternate names for the input of the same variable (for example, NUDATE and ND) by placing both names in NAMELIST and then placing both names in an EQUIVALENCE statement; for example, EQUIVALENCE (NUDATE,ND).
4. The separation of a value assignment statement into two parts by the end of a card. Each card must end with a comma, a $, or a $END.	4. Some systems allow Hollerith variable assignments; for example, WORDS = "LIGHT" WORDS = 5HLIGHT

6–1.2 Other Formats—G, P, L, D, and T

There are five more format codes described in this section. The first four of these are standard codes for variables and the fifth, T for tab, is a nonstandard feature for controlling the spacing on a line of output.

G Format

The G (for general) format is of the form

nGw.d

where G is the code letter, w is the field width, d is the number of significant digits to be written, and n is a repetition factor. This format prints "ordinary sized" real numbers in an F format and very large or small numbers in an E format. Most systems allow integer variables to be processed by the G format and the d part is ignored.

EXAMPLES

```
FORMAT( I3,4G16.5,2F10.2/12X,7G11.4)
```

The effect of the G format is best explained by a set of examples as given in Table 6–1.

TABLE 6–1
Examples of the use of the G format

Variable Value	*Printed Output with Format*		
	G11.5	*G13.7*	*G9.3*
−8765.4321	−8765.4	−8765.432	−.876E + 04
−876.54321	−876.54	−876.5432	−876.
−87.6543210	−87.654	−87.65432	−87.6
.042424242	.42424E − 01	.4242424E − 01	.424E − 01
15;555.444	15555.	15555.44	.155E + 05
1,100,100,100,000.	.11001E + 13	.1100100E + 13	.110E + 13

This table illustrates the rules regarding the G format Gw.d which are

1. Numbers less than .1 are printed in E format, Ew.d
2. Numbers greater than or equal to 10^d are printed in E format Ew.d.
3. Numbers between .1 and 10^d are printed with d significant digits justified to the right of the field width.

Some systems allow logical variables (discussed in the next section) to be processed by the G format.

There is a provision in Fortran for scaling the value of a variable during input or output. This is done with the P format.

P Format

The code nP before an ordinary F format causes division by 10^n on input and multiplication by 10^n on output. The code nP before an ordinary E format causes a right shift of n places of the decimal point (but no change in value) in the output.

EXAMPLES

```
FORMAT( 2PF6.2,-4P3F9.4,I8,E14.3)
FORMAT( 3PE16.3, -2PF12.5)
```

The first example format contains specifications for 6 variables. If used on input, it would divide the first value read by 100 and multiply the next three values by 10000. If the second example format is used on output, then the first three numbers have 3 digits printed on the left of the decimal point (for a total of 6 significant digits) and the next number is divided by 100 (multiplied by 10^{-2}) and printed in the F12.5 format. These rules are illustrated for output in Table 6–2.

TABLE 6–2
Examples of the effects of the scale factor on printed output. Note that the effect of the scale factor applied to the E format is not standard

Format Used	*Printed Values for Two Variables*	
F11.4	66.8844	−12.3456
2PF11.4	6688.4422	−1234.5678
−2PF11.4	.6688	−.1234
E15.4	.6688E + 02	−.1234E + 02
2PE15.4	66.8844E + 00	−12.3456E + 00
−2PE15.4	error	error

A facility similar to the tab on a typewriter is available in those systems with a T format.

T Format

The general form is Tn and its effect is to move the column for the next READ or WRITE specification to n + 1. Thus it skips past the *n*th column. Note this is different from skipping *n* columns which is accomplished by the format nX.

EXAMPLES

```
FORMAT(I6,T24,2F10.6,T60,F12.4)
FORMAT(3I8,T40,F10.6,T60,F12.4)
```

The F12.4 field starts in column 61 in both of these example formats. This format is frequently very convenient in preparing tabular output.

Three new types of variables are introduced in the next section (Section 6–2) and two of these have an associated format.

L Format

The general form is nLw for n logical variables with field width w. Logical variables can take on only the values "true" and "false" and these are represented by T and F for input-output purposes. The G format may be used for logical variables in many systems.

EXAMPLES

```
FORMAT(5X,3L5,F12.3,L12)
```

Double precision variables have twice as many significant digits as ordinary real variables in Fortran and thus may require more room for input-output than is allowed with the usual E and F formats.

D Format

The general form is nDw.d for n double precision values of d digits in a field of width w. This format code is exactly like the E format except that it is for double precision variables.

EXAMPLES

```
FORMAT(5X,E12.5,D22.14,3D18.10)
```

6–1.3 Groupings in Formats

Recall that when several consecutive identical field specifications occur in a format, an abbreviated notation may be used; for example, FORMAT(I2,I2, A3,A3) and FORMAT(2I2,2A3) are equivalent. Another kind of abbreviated notation called a *grouping* may be used. A grouping involves introducing a level of parenthesization with a FORMAT. If a pair of parentheses is preceded by an integer *n*, then the items within the parentheses are to be used *n* times. If *n* is omitted, the grouping is used once. For instance, the following formats are equivalent:

```
FORMAT(2X,I2,1X,I2,1X,I2,1X,F5.0)
FORMAT(2X,3(I2,1X),F5.0)
```

The grouping (I2,1X) is to be used three times. Groupings may be used with Hollerith variables, and thus,

```
FORMAT(2X100(1H*)/50(1X1H+))
```

creates a line of asterisks followed by a line of pluses separated by blanks.

There is a second type of grouping associated with restarting a FORMAT when the variable list is longer than the list of format specifications. Recall that the rule up to this point has been to start reading the format at its beginning. One may have the format restarted at some intermediate point by introducing a pair of parentheses *(without* an integer in front) at the point where the format is to be restarted. This is illustrated by the following example:

```
                          PRINT 8,(K(J),J=1,21)
8 FORMAT(I12/3I4)     8 FORMAT(I12/3(3I4/))    8 FORMAT(I12/(3I4))
```

Assume that the value of K(J) is J and the three sets of printed output are then as follows:

```
           1             1             1
  2   3    4     2   3   4     2   3   4
           5     5   6   7     5   6   7
  6   7    8     8   9  10     8   9  10
           9            11    11  12  13
 10  11   12    12  13  14    14  15  16
          13    15  16  17    17  18  19
 14  15   16    18  19  20    20  21
          17            21
 18  19   20
          21
```

The output on the left is generated by restarting the format after every four values. The middle output uses a definite grouping with three repetitions in order to have one line with one number on it followed by three lines each with three numbers. The output on the right uses the "free" parenthesis to mark the restart position just after the slash and the initial I12 specification is used only once no matter how many values are printed.

This grouping convention is particularly useful for printing out a heading according to one format and then (with the same PRINT statement) the body of information with another format. This is illustrated by a table of investment returns as follows:

```
Column   5|6|7
            PRINT 20,(IRATE(K),K=1,5),(L,(RETURN(K,L),K=1,5),L=1,50)
         20 FORMAT(10X18HINVESTMENT RETURNS/7H YEARS ,2X,
           *        5(I2,4H PER,2X)/(I4,3X,5F8.2))
```

Repeated format used for all the table entries

The first few lines of output from this PRINT statement and associated format are given below.

```
          INVESTMENT RETURNS
 YEARS    3 PER    4 PER    5 PER    6 PER    7 PER
   1       1.03     1.04     1.05     1.06     1.07
   2       1.06     1.08     1.10     1.12     1.14
   3       1.09     1.12     1.16     1.19     1.23
   4       1.13     1.17     1.22     1.26     1.31
```

Although all Fortran systems have groupings implemented in some form, there are variations between systems. Thus one must experiment with a number of formats in order to know just how groupings are handled. This is especially true of the "free" grouping used to specify the reuse of only part of a format.

6–1.4 Variable Formats

FORMAT statements can be specified by writing them in the usual way, or in two additional ways, either by placing the format field descriptors in a data initialization statement or by reading them in using an A format. In either case, the READ/WRITE format reference must be the name of an array to which the format field descriptors have been assigned as Hollerith variables. We can rewrite the statements in example (i) in two other ways, shown in examples (ii) and (iii).

(i)

```
  READ(5,1) X
1 FORMAT(I3)
```

Ordinary

(ii)

```
  REAL FM(1)
  DATA FM/4H(I3)/
  READ(5,FM) X
```

Same format specified in a data statement

(iii)

```
  REAL Q(1)
  READ(5,2) Q
2 FORMAT(A4)
  READ(5,Q) X
```

Same format can be read from card input

Whenever a variable format is used (for example, FM or Q) the symbolic names *must* be array names. The values assigned to the symbolic names *must* be Hollerith constants.

Some systems do not allow messages (or Hollerith fields) in variable formats and most systems make it difficult to include them. The problem seems to be due to the way blanks are handled (inserted or deleted) in variable formats and one should be prepared for experimentation.

One of the primary applications of variable formats is a data processing where one wants to write programs to handle data in an unknown format. If one puts the format of the data as the first item (say a separate card) of the data, then the following piece of code solves this problem:

```
  INTEGER FORM(13),DATA(1000)
  READ 8, FORM                          } Read FORMAT
8 FORMAT(13A6)
  READ(5,FORM) (DATA(K),K=1,1000)       } Then read the data
```

One may use the fact that a variable format is simply a Hollerith array in order to change formats during execution of a program. It is not uncommon to want to have a FORMAT(JI4) where J is a variable to be set (say equal to 4 or 8, depending on the circumstances). This is not allowed, but the same result is achieved by the following piece of code:

```
      INTEGER FMT(2),CON(3)
      DATA CON /2H(4,2H(6,2H(8 /, I4/ 3HI4) /
C        PROCESSING HERE DETERMINES J-VALUE
      FMT(2) = I4
      FMT(1) = CON(J)
      WRITE(6,FMT) (KLOD(L),L=1,LMAX)
```

6–1.5 Tape Units and Other Input-Output Devices

This text has assumed so far that all input is via punched cards and all output is printed and that these units (or devices) are the "standard" ones. Most larger computer systems have many input-output devices and these are usually available to programs written in Fortran. There are two phases to the use of other devices, one external and one internal to the Fortran program. The external phase is where one obtains access to the nonstandard devices such as other tape units, paper tapes, disk files, and so forth. The commands to do this first phase are generally part of the operating system and one obtains information about them from the local computing center.

The end result of the first phase is that one has access to several units in addition to the standard ones. If the reader is not familiar with the standard unit numbers, he should read Section 1–5.5 at this point. Each of these units is identified by a number; for example, as listed below:

UNIT 2:	magnetic tape to be filled with output
UNIT 3:	magnetic tape of input data
UNIT 5:	standard input unit (from card reader)
UNIT 6:	standard output unit (line printer)
UNIT 7:	punched card output unit
UNIT 8:	magnetic disk file for temporary storage (a *scratch file*).

Whenever one wants to read or write on these units, one uses the appropriate unit number; for example, READ(3,107), WRITE(2,240).

The reading and writing on these units is controlled by FORMAT statements just as for the standard units. The physical characteristics of the devices may place various restrictions or allow various relaxations on the formats used. Thus one cannot punch over 80 characters in one card even though one can print 130 characters on one line. The basic unit or segment of information in this context is called a *record*. Thus, one card image is a record; one printer line image is a record. The nature of magnetic tapes allows one to have hundreds of characters in one record.

The punched card output unit is very common and most Fortran systems have it as standard output device referred to by the command PUNCH. Thus, in the above situation, PUNCH 330, X, Y, Z and WRITE(7,330), X, Y, Z would be identical. All of the format specifications for printing apply to punching except those peculiar to paged output (such as a request for a new page).

A program may produce results that are not to be printed but are to be processed by subsequent programs. Some programs may write intermediate results for processing by the same program such as on the "scratch file" unit 8 mentioned above. In such cases, it is convenient to write *"unformatted"* records. The representation of the records is not specified by the programmer, nor is he concerned with the representation. These records may be placed on magnetic tape or on other devices such as magnetic disk files. Consider the following example:

```
C  WRITE INTERMEDIATE RESULTS ON SCRATCH UNIT 8
      REWIND 8
C  WRITE ARRAYS A,B AND C
      WRITE(8) A,B,C
      ....
C  WRITE ARRAY X
      WRITE(8) X
C  POSITION SCRATCH FILE IN FRONT OF LAST RECORD WRITTEN
      BACKSPACE 8
      ....
      READ(8) X
      ....
C  POSITION SCRATCH FILE AT ITS BEGINNING
      REWIND 8
      READ(8) A,B,C
      ....
```

The REWIND 8 causes the unit 8 to be positioned at its initial point. The WRITE(8) A,B,C writes the values of the arrays A, B, and C on unit 8. This record is then the first on unit 8. The WRITE(8)X writes a second record on unit 8, corresponding to the values of X. The BACKSPACE 8 positions the unit 8 in front of the last record written, so that the READ(8)X returns to X the values it had at the time of the WRITE(8)X. The REWIND 8 positions the unit at its initial point. The READ(8) A,B,C then reads in the first record on unit 8. Note that a BACKSPACE 8 could be used instead of the REWIND 8, since only one record is involved here. A BACKSPACE has no effect if the unit is already at its initial point.

These statements used in unformatted reading and writing are summarized in the table:

Statement	*Action*
READ (u) list	Reads one record and assigns values to items in "list."
WRITE (u) list	Writes one record using values of items in "list."
REWIND u	Positions unit at initial point.
BACKSPACE u	Positions unit in front of last record.
ENDFILE u	Writes an end-of-file record.

Unit u is specified by an integer constant or an integer variable. It may be a "scratch" or "utility" or some other device normally accessible from a program.

An end-of-file record (often abbreviated as EOF) is used to mark the end of information written on a device. If one attempts to read an EOF record, the program is terminated. This is what happens when one tries to read more data than one has provided at the standard input unit. Most Fortran systems have some means of testing for an EOF record before reading it and stopping execution.

6–2 Double-Precision, Logical, and Complex Variables

In this section we introduce three other variable types in addition to integer, real, and Hollerith. No attempt is made here to give the mathematical background for these variables or to describe applications.

6–2.1 Double Precision

Some problems require that arithmetic be done with as many significant digits as possible. When such increased accuracy is required, it may be profitable to use *double-precision* variables.

Ordinary real variables are *single-precision* numbers. In some systems, double-precision numbers have exactly double the precision of real numbers. In any system, a double-precision number must carry more significant digits than an ordinary real number.

In order for a variable to have double-precision type, it must be declared explicitly in a DOUBLE PRECISION statement, as in

```
DOUBLE PRECISION A,N,X(20)
```

In terms of storage requirements in machine words, each double-precision variable or array element requires two machine words; thus, the above declaration accounts for $2 \times (1 + 1 + 20)$, or 44 words.

Insofar as the construction of arithmetic expressions is concerned, double-precision variables are treated just as real variables, and they may be used along with real variables in the same expression.

To obtain the full benefit of double-precision arithmetic, the appropriate subprograms should be used. That is, if X is a double-precision variable, then SIN(X) produces a single-precision result, using only the most significant part of X (the single-precision part) in the computation.

There is a set of mathematical functions that expects double-precision arguments and that produces double-precision results. Among them are DEXP, DLOG, DLOG10, DSIN, DCOS, and DSQRT. Similarly, there are standard functions such as DABS, which produces the absolute value (in double precision) of its double-precision argument.

Double-precision constants are indicated by using the letter D in front of the exponent, instead of the E for ordinary real constants; for example, + 1.23456789D − 1 and .5D3. Some systems assume that a constant that has too many digits for it to be a single-precision constant is a double-precision constant, in which case the D can be omitted if there is no exponent. Note that constants such as the real constant .1 and the double-precision constant .1D0 might not be equal on some systems, depending on the internal representation.

Reading and writing of double-precision variables is done using the field descriptor D, used in the same way as the E is used for real variables. See the preceding Section 6–1.2 for further details.

Double-precision variables may be placed in COMMON. Some systems require that each double-precision variable be an even number of words away from the beginning of the COMMON list. Thus if A and B are double-precision variables, COMMON X,A,B might not be acceptable. Note that in counting words, each double-precision variable is counted twice.

6–2.2 Logical

Logical variables may only be true or false (for example, the X in X = A.GT.B). All such variables must be declared in a LOGICAL statement, as in LOGICAL X. Logical functions can be created and used in logical expressions, as in

```
      LOGICAL X,XOR,Y,LL
      READ 1,X,Y
    1 FORMAT(3L6)
      LL = XOR(X,Y)
      PRINT 1,X,Y,LL
      STOP
      END
      LOGICAL FUNCTION XOR(A,B)
      LOGICAL A,B
      XOR = (A .AND. .NOT. B).OR.(B .AND. .NOT. A)
      RETURN
      END
```

The logical function XOR computes the "exclusive or" of its two logical arguments. Note that the field descriptor L, described in Section 6–1.2, appears in the above program. In reading with an Ln format, n characters are examined from left to right; the value "true" is assigned if the first nonblank character is a T, and the value "false" if it is an F.

Logical constants may appear in a program. There are only two of them, namely, .TRUE. and .FALSE. Note that periods are placed both before and after the words.

6–2.3 Complex

In standard mathematical notation, complex numbers are an ordered pair of numbers (a,b) usually denoted by the expression $a + ib$ where i represents the square root of -1.

Complex variables may be used in Fortran and the usual complex arithmetic is performed. The declaration uses the word COMPLEX. Thus,

```
COMPLEX A,B(2),D(3,4)
```

declares that A is a complex variable, that B and C are complex arrays with the indicated dimensions. A complex variable or any element of a complex array is stored as an ordered pair of real numbers. They are treated in the same way as double-precision variables insofar as COMMON is concerned (that is, each complex element counts as two words).

A complex constant has the form (a,b) where a and b are real constants. Thus, to assign the complex values $-i$ and $2.5 + i6.1$ to X and Y, we can use either example (i) or example (ii) below.

(i)

```
COMPLEX X,Y
X = ( 0.,-1.1)
Y = (2.5,6.18)
```

(ii)

```
COMPLEX X,Y
DATA X,Y/(C.,-1.1),(2.5,6.18)/
```

If a complex variable is combined with a real or double-precision variable, the result is complex. Only a complex variable may be assigned a complex value. Thus, if R is a real variable and S a complex variable, both statements R = S and S = R are invalid. However, a complex variable may have either or both of its real and imaginary values changed by using the appropriate standard functions.

The standard functions REAL, AIMAG give the real and imaginary parts of a complex variable. The function CMPLX is used to generate a complex variable given two real numbers, as in S = CMPLX(R1,R2) when R1 and R2 are real variables [whereas S = (R1,R2) has no meaning].

No special format is associated with reading or writing complex values. For each complex value, two real number field specifications must be used. The following program shows how complex numbers are used:

```
   COMPLEX A,B,C,POLY
10 READ 1,A,B,C          } Read coefficients (2 numbers read per
 1 FORMAT( 6F8.2)        }            complex coefficient)
   DO 2 K = 1,10
   X = FLOAT(K)
   POLY = A + X*(B + X*C)
 2 PRINT 3, X,POLY
 3 FORMAT(6H POLY(,F4.0,2H)=,2F8.2)
      GO TO 10
   END
```

This program reads in three complex coefficients A, B, and C of a complex-valued polynomial A + B * X + C * X ** 2. Note that six real numbers are specified in FORMAT 1. In the expression A * X * (B + X * C), A, B, and C are complex and X is real. Therefore, the result is complex.

6–3 External

We have used a variety of variables as arguments to subprograms and have been able to pass the values of constants, variables (REAL, INTEGER, Hollerith, DOUBLE-PRECISION, LOGICAL, and COMPLEX), arrays, array elements, and arithmetic expressions. In some situations it is extremely convenient and natural to be able to pass the name of one subprogram to another. The name of a subprogram is a new type of variable and thus a declaration must be made so that the Fortran compiler does not use the name as an ordinary variable. The declaration statement used is EXTERNAL and its use is illustrated below.

```
C          THIS PROGRAM ANALYSES 3 DIFFERENT MODELS
      EXTERNAL MODEL1,MODEL2,MODEL3
      READ 5,DATA
       ....
      CALL ANAL(MODEL1,DATA,JUNK,RESULT)
       ....
      CALL ANAL(MODEL2,DATA,JUNK,RESULT)
       ....
      CALL ANAL(MODEL3,DATA,JUNK,RESULT)
       ....
      END
      SUBROUTINE ANAL(MOD,DATA,INPUT,ANSWER)
C          THIS SUBPROGRAM DOES AN ANALYSIS OF THE
C          MODEL SPECIFIED BY THE SUBPROGRAM MOD
      VALU1 = MOD(0,DATA,INPUT)
       ....
      VALU8 = MOD(3.1,DATA-6.2*XX,IN9-K)
       ....
      RETURN
      END
      FUNCTION MODEL1(TIME,XYZ,KONTRL)
C          THIS FUNCTION IS A MODEL BASED ON THE
C          CONSTANT POPULATION AND NO WAR ASSUMPTIONS
       ....
      END
      FUNCTION MODEL2(TIME,POPP,KONTRL)
C          THIS FUNCTION IS A MODEL BASED ON THE
C          EXPANDING POPULATION AND NO WAR ASSUMPTIONS
       ....
      END
      FUNCTION MODEL3(TIME,PEOPL,LEVEL)
C          THIS FUNCTION IS A MODEL BASED ON THE
C          EXPANDING POPULATION AND LIMITED WAR ASSUMPTIONS
       ....
      END
```

This organization of the program makes it nicely *modular* and gives a great deal of flexibility. One can make changes in the analysis subprogram ANAL without worrying about how the model subprograms behave. One can change the models without affecting the main program or the analysis subprogram and one can add a new model by simply adding a few lines to the main program and supplying the model as another FUNCTION subprogram.

Both FUNCTION subprogram names and SUBROUTINE subprogram names can be passed as arguments by use of the EXTERNAL statement.

6–4 Equivalence

It is sometimes convenient to have different names referring to the same item. For instance, suppose four numbers have to be read to compute a result. This can be done in two ways:

```
READ 10,A,B,C,D                    REAL Y(4)
X = A+B/C+D                        READ 10,Y
                                   X = Y(1)+Y(2)/Y(3)+Y(4)
```

The READ list is longer on the left, but the formula is easier to follow. By using an EQUIVALENCE statement we can refer to the elements of the array Y by the usual names Y(1), . . ., Y(4) or by using the names A, B, C, or D. The resulting program is then

```
REAL Y(4)
EQUIVALENCE (Y(1),A),(Y(2),B),(Y(3),C),(Y(4),D)
READ 10, Y
X = A+B/C+D
```

The saving is marginal in this simple case, but if Y has 50 elements, a considerable convenience is obtained by this technique.

Besides the convenience that it provides, the EQUIVALENCE statement allows several different arrays or variables to share the same storage, thus cutting down on storage requirements.

An EQUIVALENCE statement describes one or more "equivalence groups," where such a group relates several arrays or single variables to each other. The general form is

$$\text{EQUIVALENCE } (k_1), (k_2), \ldots, (k_n)$$

where each k_i is an equivalence group. Such a group is a list of the form a_1, a_2, . . ., a_m. Each a_i is the name of either a single variable or an array element. In the above example there are four equivalence groups, Y(1), A, and so on. Within any group, the order is of no significance. Furthermore, the order of the groups themselves is not significant. The subscripts that appear in an equivalence group must be integer constants, and the names that appear may not be dummy arguments.

Items that appear in a COMMON statement may also appear in an EQUIVALENCE, but no two may appear in the same equivalence group. Consider the case

```
COMMON A,B,C
EQUIVALENCE (A,X,C)
```

By virtue of the COMMON statement, A, B, and C must be allocated three consecutive storage locations. The EQUIVALENCE requires that A, X, and C share the same location. Since A and C are distinct locations, they certainly cannot share the same location.

In most cases the names that appear in the same equivalence group are of the same type. However, the same item may be referred to in a variety of ways as shown below.

```
INTEGER IB(20)
REAL A(2),B(20)
COMPLEX C
EQUIVALENCE (A,C),(B(1),IB(1))
```

The complex variable C has its real part REAL(C) and imaginary part AIMAG(C) named A(1) and A(2), respectively. One can place either real values in the array B or integer values in the array IB and, in effect, obtain an array that contains a mixture of real and integer numbers. There are a few situations where this is extremely convenient and where it results in considerable savings of memory space. These situations occur in fairly complex applications that have integer, real, and Hollerith variables distributed in a list in a non-uniform way. The "MORON simulator" mentioned (but not described) later in Section 8–1.3 uses this ability to good advantage.

6–5 Assigned GO TO

In addition to the unconditional GO TO and the computed GO TO of the form "GO TO (label 1, label 2, . . ., label n), i" where i is an integer variable taking on values between 1 and n, there is a third form of the GO TO called the assigned GO TO. It is of the form

GO TO i, (label 1, label 2, . . ., label n)

where i is an integer variable that is set using the ASSIGN statement of the form

ASSIGN label TO i

[the label must be one from the set of labels (label 1, . . ., label n)].

The operation of the assigned GO TO is illustrated by comparing it with a similar use of the computed GO TO:

```
K = 1                                    ASSIGN 21 TO K
 ....                                     ....
GO TO(21,13,5),K                         GO TO K,(21,13,5)
```

The assigned GO TO eliminates the need to order the labels correctly as in the computed GO TO. It can be useful in situations where a computed GO TO would be clumsy. For instance, GO TO (1,22,22,5,4,4,4,18,21,21),L where L takes on values from 1 to 10 can be replaced by GO TO M,(1,4,5,22,18,21) where M is set using the appropriate "ASSIGN label TO M" label being one of 1, 4, 5, 22, 18, or 21.

6–6 Miscellaneous Features

The eight or so features discussed in this section are all of infrequent use, although most of them can be very convenient in the right situation. Furthermore, they tend to be highly nonstandard (and frequently absent) so that the descriptions given are only general in nature. If one wants to use one of these features, then one should obtain details specific to the Fortran system one is using.

6–6.1 ENTRY—Multiple Entries to a Subprogram

It sometimes happens that one has two subprograms that are almost, but not quite, identical. The ENTRY statement allows one to "enter" a subprogram at two or more points. Two typical variations are shown below.

```
      SUBROUTINE ANAL(T,Q,X)                     SUBROUTINE ANAL(T,Q,X)
      REAL T(20),D(50),X(5)                      REAL T(20),D(50),X(5)
C       SETUP COMPUTATIONS               C          SETUP COMPUTATIONS
          GO TO 100                                 GO TO 100
      ENTRY ANAL2(TIME,Q)                        ENTRY ANAL2
C       DIFFERENT SETUP                  C          DIFFERENT SETUP
  100 CONTINUE                               100 CONTINUE
            MAIN COMPUTATION             C
```

Both cases have different preliminary computations for the main entry ANAL and the second entry ANAL2 that precede the "main" computation. The program on the left has a completely independent argument list for ANAL2 while the one on the right has the same argument list for both ANAL and ANAL2. A particular system, of course, has only one of these (or other) possibilities.

6–6.2 BLOCK DATA—Data Initialization of Common Variables

Some systems do not allow variables in COMMON to also be in DATA statements. Some systems with this restriction provide a special type of subprogram, the BLOCK DATA subprogram, to initialize COMMON variables. The BLOCK DATA subprogram usually *must* be the *first* program processed by the Fortran compiler. The form is as follows:

```
      BLOCK DATA
      INTEGER AND, REAL, DECLAR,ATIONS, ETC
      COMMON LISTS, GO, HERE
C     DATA GO NEXT TO INITIALIZE THE VARIABLES IN COMMON
C     NO EXECUTABLE STATEMENTS ARE ALLOWED
      END
```

6–6.3 Nonstandard Returns

Execution in a subprogram is normally terminated by a RETURN statement. This is the "standard" return which gives control back to the calling program at the next statement (after a CALL to a subroutine) or in the expression evaluation (after use of a FUNCTION subprogram). The nonstandard return facility allows one to have several points of return from a SUBROUTINE. Nonstandard returns are not available for functions. A typical situation is as follows:

```
                               CALL PROG(X,Y,KK,200,999)
Normal return here ——    27    KPROG = KK+J
                               ....
RETURN 1 to here ——     200    DO 210 L = 1,KK
                               ....
RETURN 2 to here ——     999    PRINT 998,TROUB,HELP,X,KK
                               STOP
                               END
                               SUBROUTINE PROG(A,B,K,*,*)
                               ....
                               RETURN
                               ....
                               RETURN 1 —— Take 1st non-standard return (label 200)
                               ....
                               RETURN 2 —— Take 2nd non-standard return (label 999)
                               END
```

The normal return after the CALL PROG leads to statement 27. The other two returns lead to statement 200 (RETURN 1) or statement 999 (RETURN 2). Thus the labels are included in the argument list at the CALL statement and the subprogram has asterisks at the places where labels for nonstandard returns are to appear. Some systems would have RETURN 4 and RETURN 5 in place of RETURN 1 and RETURN 2 as the *'s are in the 4th and 5th positions of the argument list.

6–6.4 Adjustable Dimensions

When arrays are passed as arguments to a subprogram one would not expect any storage to be set aside for the array in the subprogram as that has already been done. Nevertheless, the array must be dimensioned in the subprogram and the question arises as to whether the dimension specified must agree in the two programs. In a few Fortran systems the answer is an unqualified "Yes." In most Fortran systems there is some latitude allowed and sometimes a facility to specify the dimensions in a subprogram at execution time. A simple example of this facility is shown below.

```
SUBROUTINE BLITZ(A,B,N,M)
REAL A(N),B(N,M)
```

Note that this is allowed (if at all) *only* in subprograms where the variable dimensions are for arguments.

The case of one-dimensional arrays is particularly simple since one only needs to know the location of the first element in order to find the address of the other elements. Some Fortran systems take this into account and then one can use a length of 1 for all one-dimensional arrays that are arguments to subprograms. The program segment above might then be

```
  SUBROUTINE BLITZ(A,B,N,M)
  REAL A(1),B(N,M)
  DO 5 K = 1,N
5 A(K) = B(K,1)
```

This apparently contradictory piece of code performs correctly in such Fortran systems. The situation is not so easy for two- or three-dimensional arrays and one *must* specify the dimensions in these cases.

If one does not want to make the dimensions agree exactly in all the programs, and this can be very inconvenient, then one must consult the reference manual for exact details on the rules pertaining to arrays passed as arguments. In some cases it is useful to have a two-dimensional array in the calling program treated as a one-dimensional array in the subprogram. A programmer who wishes to do this must, of course, be very familiar with the exact techniques used to handle arrays in his Fortran system.

6–6.5 PAUSE

The operating systems of the late 1950s and early 1960s were such that a programmer occasionally wanted the computer operator to do something special for him in the middle of his program. The program would print a request for the operator and then pause while the operator responded. After the operator had met the request the program was continued by pushing the "run" button on the console. The Fortran command used to halt execution for a while is the PAUSE command. Many Fortran systems ignore the PAUSE command.

6–6.6 Overflow, Underflow, and DVCHK

There are several ways a program can generate numbers that are too big (*overflow*) or too small (*underflow*). Most Fortran systems print some kind of diagnostic message when this occurs and proceed with the computation. The numbers generated are usually garbage when overflow or underflow occurs. Many Fortran systems have some means to test for the occurrence of overflow or underflow. The mechanisms vary from system to system; two typical examples are shown below.

```
                                  Reset
                                  overflow
CALL OVERFL(JUNK) ─────────────── switch ──────── IF FLOATING OVERFLOW 10,10
A = B*D**N + D*B**(M-K)                         10 A = B*D**N + D*B**(M-K)
CALL OVERFL(ITEST)                                 IF FLOATING OVERFLOW 400,11
IF( ITEST.EQ.1 ) GO TO 400                      11 CONTINUE
```

Fortran systems with this facility have an overflow indicator that is turned on whenever overflow occurs. When this indicator is tested by the Fortran program, the indicator is turned off. Thus the first statement of the two programs above merely serves to turn the indicator off in case overflow has occurred earlier in the execution. The value of A is then calculated and the overflow indicator is tested again. The program on the left uses a standard system subroutine OVERFL for the test. If the argument ITEST is 1, then the overflow indicator is on. Different systems are different schemes to return the results of the test and OVERFL is often used to test for underflow. The program on the right has the test in the form of a special IF statement. If the indicator is on, then a transfer is made to the first label while a transfer is made to the second label if the indicator is off.

A slightly different type of nonsense arithmetic occurs when one attempts to divide by zero. Some Fortran systems ignore this and set the result equal to zero; others print diagnostics and stop and still others have special numbers for the result of division by zero. Many of the systems allow one to check for the occurrence of division by zero with the use of a standard system subroutine DVCHK or by a special IF statement, IF QUOTIENT OVERFLOW label 1, label 2.

One must check the reference manual for the exact details of these features for any particular Fortran system.

6–6.7 CALL EXIT

Some systems allow this statement to replace the STOP statements. There might be optional arguments to the subroutine EXIT which request additional information, and so on.

6–6.8 Memory Dumps—DUMP and PDUMP

One is occasionally unfortunate enough to encounter a program that one cannot debug even after much effort and analysis by expert programmers. One aid in such situations is to examine the contents of all or part of memory at various points during or after the execution of the program. The contents of the memory are usually encoded in some unintelligible way, so that considerable effort is often required to decipher a memory dump. Despite the trouble involved, some errors are so obscure that they are detected only after a detailed examination of such dumps. This is particularly the case if the error is due to the Fortran compiler or the operating system rather than due to the programmer. Many Fortran systems provide standard subroutines to obtain memory dumps. They are often named DUMP and/or PDUMP and they have several arguments to specify the areas of memory to be dumped and the format of the output. The schemes for these requests vary from system to system and one must consult reference manuals to find out how to interpret the dumps. This usually requires that one have some familiarity with the machine or assembly language used by the Fortran system.

7

Historical Survey of Computing

7—1 Ancient History

The history of computing might properly start with man's efforts to develop the concept of numbers and counting. These efforts took place over a period of many centuries and resulted in a wide variety of systems for numbers and symbols for writing them down. As counting and numbers were firmly established, men realized the need to perform calculations. Even the ancient Greeks and Egyptians were concerned about taking square roots, finding the value of π, and simple trigonometry problems. Nevertheless, the simple operations of addition and multiplication could be carried out only by the leading scholars of the day. This was partially due to the number systems used. Consider what a Roman was faced with when he wished to add 197 and 244, or multiply 38 by 1539:

```
   CXLVII        MDXXXIX
 + CCXLIV      * XXXVIII
 = ———?———     = ———?———
```

It is no wonder that few Romans did anything with numbers besides counting.

The Arabic number system provided the key to efficient algorithms for the basic arithmetic operations and Arab mathematicians perfected suitable methods for addition, multiplication, and division. Recall that the word algorithm is derived from the name of one of these Arab mathematicians of the ninth century.

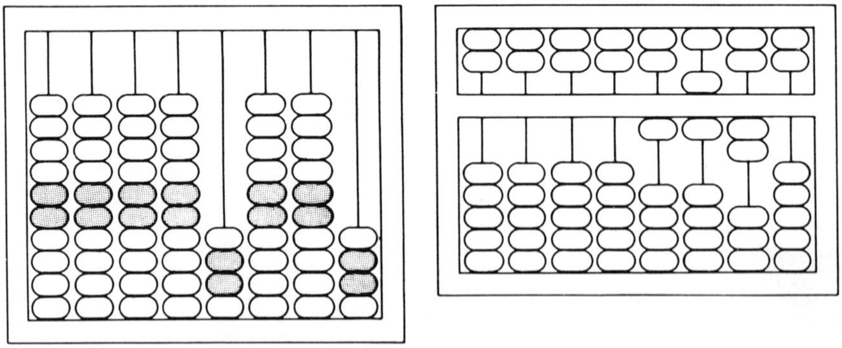

FIGURE 7–1. A typical modern abacus.

The first mechanical aid to computation was the abacus (see Figure 7–1), used over 2500 years ago by the Chinese. Variations of it were widespread throughout the ancient world and it is not known where it originated. The abacus is remarkably effective and a skilled user can compete quite successfully with a modern desk calculator. Despite its effectiveness, the abacus was not widely adopted outside the Orient and computations elsewhere were made by either using pebbles or by the familiar paper and pencil methods. Indeed, one can consider that a good portion of one's training in the elementary schools is aimed at creating a "built-in" calculator in the children's minds. Multiplication and addition tables were used even in Roman times.

A significant aid to paper and pencil calculations was developed by the Scottish mathematician John Napier. His tables of logarithms were first published in 1614 and they allow one to replace a multiplication or division by a single addition or subtraction. His tables and later variations were widely adopted in scientific circles as an aid to computation. They form the mathematical basis for the slide rule (see Figure 7–2), which is an analog computer that is (or at least once was) the trademark of the engineer.

The world's first mechanical adding machine was constructed in 1642 by an 18-year-old French genius, Blaise Pascal. The machine used a scheme similar to the system of wheels and gears on an automobile speedometer. It was made for Pascal's father, an accountant who did extensive calculations in order to find taxes due. Pascal went on to do pioneering work in many areas of mathematics and statistics as well as in philosophy and literature.

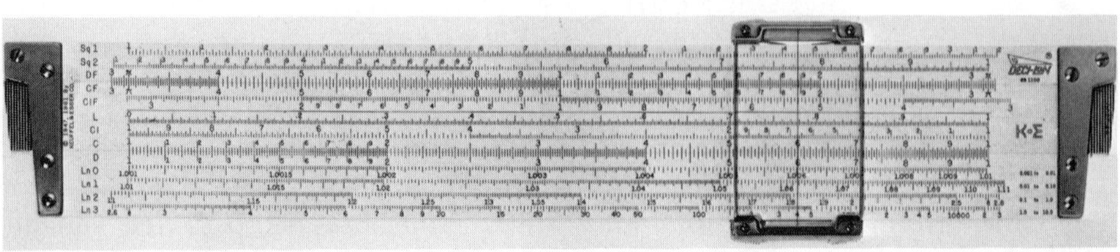

FIGURE 7–2. A slide rule is an analog computer which allows one to perform calculations involving multiplication, division, exponents, trigonometric quantities, and so on, with great rapidity. The accuracy is limited to one's ability to read the scales.

Another young genius, Gottfried von Leibniz, took the next step and constructed a mechanical device that could do addition, multiplication, division, and extract square roots. The machine was built in about 1670 before Leibniz was 25 years old. Like Pascal, Leibniz went on to do pioneering mathematical work, including (along with Isaac Newton) the original development of the calculus.

These machines established the principles involved, but mechanical calculators, the forerunners of modern desk calculators, were not widely used in business and scientific applications until well into the 1800s.

Mechanical problems also plagued the first attempt at a more ambitious calculating machine. Charles Babbage received funds to develop his "difference engine" from the British government in 1822. It was to be able to calculate the various powers, x^2, x^3, x^4, . . . of a given number x. He constructed one such machine and while in the process of perfecting it, he conceived the idea of an "analytical engine." This machine was to be a general purpose calculator which could be "programmed" to evaluate a wide range of arithmetic and algebraic formulas. Babbage spent many years on these machines, but the level of machine technology at that time simply could not provide reliable operation. The papers and drawings that he left show that his design was logically correct.

The analytical engine's design included provisions to "store" up to 1000 fifty-digit numbers. The "mill" or "central processor" would perform additions or subtractions of such numbers at the rate of 1 per second and would multiply two such numbers in 1 minute. Other components included a typewriter-like device to print results and a mechanism to read or punch holes in cardboard cards. Babbage probably got the idea to use punched cards from their use in automatic looms (or weaving machines). Punched holes in a metal drum to control looms were introduced in 1741 and Joseph Jacquar modified the system to use punched cards in 1790.

7–2 Middle History

By the end of the 1800s printing desk calculators and similar machines were introduced into business applications. The impetus for the next step in computing, or more exactly, in data processing, was the U. S. Census. It took almost 9 years to process the information obtained in the 1880 census and it was clear that it would take over 10 years for the next one if something were not done. Herman Hollerith, a statistician and inventor, joined the Census Bureau in the mid-1880s and he developed a new system to record and process the census data. The heart of this system was a punched card. The original data were punched into the card (with a hand punch) and tabulating machines were built to process the cards. For example, a card sorter was developed which could sort cards into one of 12 groups at the rate of 300 cards per minute. After much experiment the system was perfected and the data of the 1890 census were processed in less than 3 years.

The original card that Hollerith designed had 45 columns, round holes, and was the size of a dollar bill. The dollar bill has changed size since then, not the card. The current card format of 80 columns and rectangular holes was introduced by IBM in 1928.

Two of the modern computer companies originated from these census bureau efforts. Hollerith formed the Tabulating Machine Company around 1900 and in 1912 it merged with some other companies to form what later became International Business Machines. When Hollerith left the Census Bureau a new development effort took place under the direction of James Powers. He, in turn, left the Census Bureau in 1911 to form the Powers Accounting Machine Co. which became part of the Remington Rand Corp.

Punched card or unit record equipment was widely adopted for business data processing in the 1930s. This equipment included machines to punch cards, to print on them, to print their information on paper, to sort them and to perform short, simple arithmetic calculations. As this technology was being assimilated by business and industry, the seeds of the next technology were germinating.

On the theoretical side was the work of A. M. Turing. He developed abstract models of computation and the machines that could perform them, and his work prepared the ground for automata theory. He was mainly interested in what things it is possible to calculate and what things it is not possible to calculate. These questions still form one of the cornerstones of automata theory.

On the practical side were efforts to build general purpose calculating machines, much as Babbage had envisaged them. The basic component was changed from wheels and gears to electromagnetic relays. Such relays were widely used in telephone switching and the Bell Telephone Laboratories built (at least) two such computers from 1938 to 1943. The first of these was a special-purpose computer, but the second was general purpose, although built to perform ballistics computations. They included many of the features (or direct ancestors of them) of modern computers.

The best known computer of this era was the Mark I. The ideas of building a general purpose computer had been suggested by several people around 1930 and in 1937 Howard Aiken of Harvard University became interested in the possibility. The construction of the Mark I was supported by IBM (out of their advertising budget) and much of it done in their plants. It was finished in 1944. Many people consider the Mark I to be the first realization of Babbage's concept of an analytical engine. The Mark I was more than a prototype model; it spent many years in productive computations on mathematical and scientific problems.

7—3 Modern History

There are two places where one can draw the line to start the modern era. One of these is the introduction of the electronic devices and the other is the introduction of the internally stored program.

A calculator using electronic devices (vacuum tubes) was started in about 1940, well before the Mark I was completed. The construction took place at the

Moore School of Electrical Engineering of the University of Pennsylvania and was under the direction of John Mauchly and Presper Eckert. This calculator was called the ENIAC, an acronym for Electronic Numerical Integrator and Calculator. The ENIAC, finished in 1946, was a huge machine with over 18,000 vacuum tubes and 1500 relays. It was able to perform an addition in 1/5000 of a second. This rate is dwarfed by later computers, but it is already high enough to make one wonder when one would want so much speed in addition.

The ENIAC and earlier calculators were externally programmed. That is, the instructions about the operations to be performed were external to the machine and fed, one at a time, to the machine via some device such as a punched card reader or paper tape reader. It was a formidable task to write a program for early computers (whether internally or externally progammed). It required complete familiarity with the details of the machine's operation, considerable ingenuity, and a great deal of patience. After reviewing a programming manual for such a computer, one contemporary wrote:

> As it is, coding appears to be an almost insurmountable barrier between the machine and the mere mathematician with a problem to solve.

Even as the ENIAC was being finished, the advantages of the internally programmed calculator were realized. Indeed, it is the internally stored program that distinguishes a computer from a calculator. Thus, the instructions for a computer are stored electronically (or magnetically) inside the machine and they can be interpreted and executed (and modified if need be) at electronic speeds. The chief proponent and developer of the stored program concept was John von Neumann. He was perhaps the most eminent mathematician in the United States and he became convinced that with computers he could solve many important problems in applied mathematics that were otherwise unsolvable.

Von Neumann joined the ENIAC group along with H. H. Goldstine and they directed the construction of the EDVAC (Electronic Discrete Variable Automatic Computer) for the U. S. Army Ordnance Department at the Aberdeen Proving Grounds. The EDVAC project was started in 1946, but delays occurred that postponed the completion of the computer until 1952. The first computer EDSAC went into operation in May 1949, at the Mathematical Laboratory at Cambridge University, England. The development of EDSAC (for Electronic Delayed Storage Automatic Computer) was directed by M. V. Wilkes.

Eckert and Mauchly left the EDVAC project soon after it started (this was one reason for the delay in EDVAC) to form a company to produce another computer, the UNIVAC. The UNIVAC (for Universal Automatic Computer) was the first designed for business rather than scientific applications and the first one was sold to the Census Bureau in 1951.

Although IBM was heavily involved in the business machine field and had sponsored the Mark I, they did not enter the computer field until 1953. They delivered the first IBM 701 (Defense Calculator) which was, for that time, a large scale scientific computer. It had a 2048-word high-speed memory on a cathode-ray tube (TV screen) backed up by both magnetic tapes and a magnetic drum. In the same year they announced the IBM 650 computer, a smaller machine for either scientific or business applications. The IBM 650 is discussed in more detail in the next section where it is taken as a model for the first generation of computers, the simple computers. Earlier in 1949 the CPC (Card Programmed Calculator) was introduced by IBM for business applications. It was not a computer, however, as it did not have an internally stored program.

The first "super-computer," the NORC, was delivered to the U. S. Naval Weapons Laboratory in 1955. A computer is classified as "super" if it is significantly bigger, faster, and more powerful than its contemporaries. They provide a great deal of excitement in the computing community even if sometimes their overall impact is slight. The NORC could perform an addition of two real numbers in 15 microseconds (or 1/67000 of a second) which is an improvement of a factor of about 13 over the addition time of the ENIAC. The actual increase in power is much greater because the ENIAC could only add integers and could not do 5000 integer additions in 1 second even though it could do one addition in 1/5000 of a second. The reason for this is that the ENIAC could not receive instructions at a rate comparable to its calculating speed because it was externally programmed. On the other hand, the NORC could perform 67000 additions in 1 second. At the time the NORC was built most computers required from 3 to 10 times as much time for a multiplication as for an addition. The NORC's multiplication time was only twice its addition time. Furthermore, the NORC executed what is called "3-address code," a form of machine language which, on the average, results in faster operation than the more common "1-address code" form of machine language. The simple machine language described in the next chapter is "1-address code." Only one NORC was built.

The period 1956–1958 saw three significant developments in computing. One of these, on the technological level, was the introduction of magnetic core memories. These memories were larger, had faster access time, and were more reliable than the previous technology. They were also cheaper, although still very expensive.

The second development in this period was in a new direction, the introduction of higher level languages. The first Fortran was issued in 1957 for the IBM 704, the successor of the IBM 701. That version of Fortran was rather crude compared to the Fortran IV described in this book. It is interesting to note that some of the strange rules of Fortran (for example, those for the legal indexes of arrays) are a direct consequence of certain features of the IBM 704. These features are no longer found on most computers, but historical precedence has great momentum—and considerable logic—behind it.

The computing community has had several painful lessons in the cost of adopting new approaches that are incompatible with preceding ones. Sometimes, of course, this incompatibility is unavoidable or even advantageous. But changes in languages seem to be particularly subject to the creation of confusion and headaches. One might make the analogy with natural languages like English or French. Every one of them has a whole array of illogical and unreasonable features (for example, irregular verbs, strange spellings, irregular formation of plurals, and so on). These features make the languages much more difficult to learn and it is doubtful that they add much, if anything, to the usefulness of the language. Attempts to remedy these defects in natural languages have met little success, or even sympathy. Fortunately, the computing community is more receptive to change and many of the disagreeable features of the original Fortran have disappeared in later versions.

The computing community soon recognized the value of higher level languages and that one of the problems with them was machine dependence. Thus a program written in early Fortran was likely to run only on an IBM 704 and on no other computer. This would, of course, make the program useless when another, probably better, computer was installed. As a result an international effort was organized to define a language for computing that did not depend on any particular computer. The resulting language is Algol (for algorithmic language) and its first definition was given in 1958. A modified version of 1960 has been widely adopted, especially outside the United States.

The third development of this period is perhaps the most significant of the three even though higher level languages have had a tremendous influence on computing. This development was the widespread appreciation of the necessity of a "system" for operating a computer. Many systems were developed, most of which were of the "batch-processing" nature. This organization of a computer system is discussed in some detail in Chapter 9. This area of computer science is still under intensive research and development and it has emerged as one of the central, most fruitful, and most challenging.

The second generation of computers started with the introduction of transistorized computers. This technological advance permitted smaller, cheaper, faster, and more reliable electronic circuits. The first of these, the IBM 7090 was delivered late in 1959 and was shortly followed by the CDC 1604, the Philco 2000, and the second "super-computer," the Remington Rand Univac LARC. The addition time for the IBM 7090 was about $4\frac{1}{2}$ microseconds (or 1/220,000 of a second) compared to 24 microseconds for its vacuum tube twin, the IBM 709. The third "super-computer," the IBM Stretch, was delivered a year later to the Atomic Energy Commission. This super-computer did not meet its design specifications by a fair margin and only seven of them were built.

The third generation of computers was announced in 1964 by IBM in its 360 line of computers. It is not clear what distinguishes a third generation computer from a second generation one. The technological advance of integrated circuits is one possibility, another is the provision of facilities for time-sharing, multiprogramming, or other new concepts in computer systems. In any case, almost all computers introduced after 1965 are declared by their manufacturers to be third generation computers. Since 1965 a number of computers have been introduced which are advertised as fourth generation. It is even less clear what distinguishes third and fourth generation computers from one another besides the advertising. This does not mean that technological advances or computer system advances did not continue to be made, for they did. It is just that one cannot single out one of them that is so much more important than the others that it marks a new generation.

The next "super-computer," the CDC 6600, was delivered by the Control

Data Corporation to the Atomic Energy Commission in 1965. This computer executes about 3,000,000 instructions per second, an advance of a factor of almost 200 over that of the first super-computer, the NORC, introduced only 10 years earlier. More super-computers were being built in 1970. These include the CDC 7600 and Star by the Control Data Corporation, the IBM 360 Model 195 by International Business Machines, and the ILIAC IV by the University of Illinois. The internal design of these computers is such that they can execute up to 5, 10, or even 100 million instructions per second. This is to be accomplished through very high-speed circuitry and extensive use of parallelism, or simultaneous computations. The ILIAC IV carries this the farthest in that it is to have many (possibly 256?) independent, but synchronized and coordinated calculating units.

7—4 The Size and Scope of Computing Activities

The historical development given above is centered around scientific and technological themes. In this section we consider some of the other aspects of the development of calculating powers and computers. The ancient developments of Pascal, Leibniz, Babbage, and others, had negligible impact outside a very narrow line of scientific development.

The middle history period (1900–1940) saw two separate types of development. The first of these was the perfection of the ancient ideas and their widespread dissemination throughout the scientific and business world. By the 1930s the ideas of Pascal and Leibniz had led to commonplace tools of society; a wait of about 300 years. The pace of technological development had quickened dramatically and some ideas conceived at the beginning of the middle history period (such as punched card data processing) were perfected and in widespread use; a wait of only 40 years. Even so, it was only at the end of this period that serious efforts were made to perfect the last ancient history idea, the analytical engine of Babbage. It is probably fair to say that the idea could not have been perfected and reduced to practice much earlier because this had to wait for technological developments in other areas. Thus, at the end of this period, most of the ancient ideas had become integral parts of society, especially in scientific and business circles.

The other type of development in the middle period was to lay the groundwork for the modern period. This activity parallels that of the ancient period. A number of important ideas on the mathematical nature and practice of computation were conceived. Equally important were technological developments in other areas (such as electronics) that would make it possible to build the first computers.

The modern period began with the completion of the ideas of the ancients: the general purpose, flexible calculator. It also began with one of the key concepts of computing, the concept of the internally stored program. At this point in time one can visualize two streams of development. One of these was a huge, amorphous activity, business data processing. It was based on the work in the ancient and middle periods, but had little awareness of its historical background. The other stream was a tiny rivulet, a few isolated groups of scientists interested in tools to solve very complicated scientific problems. The two streams were hardly aware of each other's presence and only a few people sensed that they would someday merge.

The Association for Computing Machinery was formed in 1947 and had 246 members. Its primary orientation was mathematics and science and the general public was unaware of computers except for a few Sunday supplement stories about "giant brains." The impact of computers even in the scientific community was still small and restricted to a few areas. The explosive growth was not far away though.

By 1951 the UNIVAC was on the market and the Census Bureau immediately acquired one for its huge data processing activity. The General Electric Company acquired one for its business data processing and the business application of computers was started. The computing community had grown and over 900 people attended the first joint computer conference in 1951. This conference was organized by several societies whose memberships were primarily electrical engineers or "pure" scientists. The activities at the conference were almost exclusively oriented toward science and engineering.

It was only a few years until the computer became an indispensable part of a number of scientific areas, for example, aerodynamics, atomic energy, hydrodynamics, vehicle dynamics, and so on. Computers were cracking many of the tough problems in these areas and were opening up many new vistas for research and development. In the background was the steady introduction of computers into business applications. This event was not very exciting because little innovation was present. One merely did the same accounting and payroll operations using a computer to replace the punched card equipment in earlier use. The size and scope of the computing effort had grown and many segments of the general public became aware of them. Their image, both inside and outside the computing community, was still that of an esoteric scientific research tool.

In the early 1960s the expansion of the use of computers had exceeded even the most optimistic predictions of a few years earlier. The manufacturing of computers had established itself as one of the major industries in the United States. In 1961 some 30 large companies began to make their quarterly reports on Social Security taxes by magnetic tapes rather than typewritten. The typewritten reports eliminated this way were over 1000 pages long for most of these companies. The demand for people trained and knowledgeable in computing was very high and a few universities instituted graduate programs in Computer Science. Up to this time all of the professionals in computing (which by then numbered in the tens of thousands) had been trained in some other discipline and later switched to computing.

In the midst of this explosive growth arose an awareness of the changing nature of computing. The stereotyped notions current then were one of two types (or perhaps a mixture of them). The first of these was as an esoteric scientific tool that would do millions of calculations to solve a problem at the frontiers of science. It was hard for the general public to evaluate the significance of these problems, but they took it on faith that at least some of them were worthwhile (some of them were). The second stereotype was that of computing the payroll for General Motors and spewing out 500,000 checks every week or so. A simple count of the number (or value) of the computers in use showed that the scientific use of computers had fallen way behind their business use. Even more significant than the awareness of the shift of emphasis was the awareness that the stereotype business application was out of date. Computers were no longer solely being used to do the old things faster. They were being used to do things that were not being done before and it became clear that they were going to revolutionize many aspects of business operations. Many exciting and some successful innovative ventures were undertaken in business applications and this trend has continued since then.

This change in the nature of computing was a significant shift in its mainstream away from science and engineering. On the other hand, it represents a significant shift of the mainstream of business management and operation toward science—or at least the use of the scientific method. Thus, many of the novel applications forced businessmen to formulate mathematical models of their operations and to analyze them in a rational, objective manner. Not only was business seen to be a major area of application for computers, but many other areas were also included. These range from agriculture to literature to psychology to music to library science, and so on. It seemed almost as if there was a contest to find the most implausible area in which to apply computers.

Computers were firmly established as an integral part of society in the United States by 1965. There were over 35,000 computers in the United States and the general public had become familiar with the punched card as an ingredient of everyday life. Computer science had a firm foothold in the universities, over 1100 computers were in use at universities by 1966. By 1965 there were several universities which offered a complete program of Bachelor's, Master's, and Ph.D. degrees in Computer Science. The value of the computers delivered in the United States in 1967 was almost $6 billion. By comparison, the value of automobiles delivered in that year was about $25 billion. The Association for Computing Machinery had almost 20,000 members in 1967, and in just a few years it was to adopt 100,000 as its membership goal.

By 1970 the expansion of the computing field had again exceeded predictions made only a few years earlier and its growth continued unabated. By then over 200 universities offered degree programs in Computer Science and predictions were made at some universities that it would be the largest single department on the compus in only five more years. There were perhaps 60,000 computers installed then of an almost limitless variety. They ranged in cost from only a few thousand dollars to the neighborhood of $15 million. Their influence was felt in every corner of society. Typical of the diverse applications were the arrangement of dating, the exploration of the moon, the war on poverty, chess playing, the credit card society, stock market speculation, swinging national elections, and many others. They were viewed with a combination of fear, awe, distrust, and reverence by the general public who did not understand them and many attributed almost magic, or demonic, powers to them. Prophets had erred on the conservative side so often that now utterly fantastic forecasts were being made and only a few were able to judge which of these were nonsense and which were reasonable. It was clear to all that man had developed an enormously powerful tool to remold his world and his society. And, as with his other tools, he had to assume the responsibility to use it wisely and rationally.

8

Computer Languages

8—1 The Simple Computers and Their Language

8–1.1 Problem: How to Exploit Speed

The basic feature of computers is that they can execute certain simple operations extremely fast. In order to appreciate computer organization, we must appreciate just how fast "extremely fast" is. A rather "ordinary" computer can add 1 million numbers together in 1 second. The really fast computers can do much better than this. This is very impressive even though we would rarely want to add such long lists of numbers. But these computers can do other things (for example, multiplications, numerical comparisons, direct and conditional transfers) at comparable speeds. Thus we find it easy to visualize that rather complicated programs can be executed in a few thousandths of a second.

R. W. Hamming has taken another viewpoint in order to emphasize the speed of computers. This is to consider how fast various things can be done by modern technology compared with older ways of doing them. In fact, we can estimate the improvement in various areas of modern technology. We see from Table 8–1 that the increase in two areas, explosive power and computational speed, is startling. These two technological changes are of such magnitude that they are reshaping our society. If there had been the same increase in transportation speed in the last 100 years as there has been in computational speed, then we could travel from Los Angeles to Paris in 1/500 second. Or we could travel from the earth to the moon in 1/10 second or to the sun in 6½ minutes. This is faster than the speed of light.

TABLE 8–1
Comparison of technological increases

Area	Ancient Times	1870	1950	1970	Factor of Increase in: 2000 Years	100 Years	20 Years
Transportation	40 mi/day	200 mi/day	6000 mi/day	35,000 mi/day	900	175	6
Work to make a book	10 man-years	10 man-hours	1 man-hour	½ man-hour	175,000	20	2
Life expectancy (U.S.)	22 years	45 years	66 years	67 years	3.05	1.48	1.07
Massive building	Great Wall of China	Suez Canal	Fort Peck Dam	Aswan Dam	Nil	Nil	Nil
Average formal education (U.S.)	None	1 year	10 years	12 years	—	12	1.2
Explosive power	½ lb of TNT	½ ton of TNT	1,000,000 tons of TNT	100,000,000 tons of TNT	$2 * 10^{11}$	$1 * 10^{8}$	100
Energy per person*	½ unit	1.6 units	10 units	15 units	30	9	1.5
Computation speed**	.005	.005	40	10,000,000	$2 * 10^{9}$	$2 * 10^{9}$	250,000

* The unit for energy is a 1-horsepower motor working 8 hours a day.
** The unit for computation is multiplications per second of two 8-digit numbers.

It is important to note that great changes in magnitude can, and do, change the basic nature of a situation. This is illustrated by considering gifts of money. If we receive 10¢, it has no effect whatsoever. If we receive a thousand times as much, $100, it is nice, but it does not change our financial situation. If we receive a thousand times this amount, $100,000, the situation begins to change. It certainly improves our financial position, but it does not relieve us entirely of financial worries. The entire sum can easily be spent on a new car, a new wardrobe, a new home, and a nice long vacation. Then we are back worrying about money again. If we receive a thousand times more than this, $100,000,000, then the basic nature of our financial situation is changed. It is no longer possible to spend all of our money on personal expenses. The cost of a suit or a meal becomes meaningless.

The change in magnitude in computation speed (and explosive power) is greater than that of the preceding example. This change has already greatly altered our view of what can be done with this computation speed. Many believe that we have only begun to exploit this change in the basic nature of computation.

The goal of the organization of a computer is to effectively and efficiently harness this computational speed. To see that computational speed by itself is of little value, consider the merit of having a desk calculator or adding machine that works instantaneously; that is, the result appears the instant the "add" or "multiply" button is touched. Although some time is spent waiting for ordinary machines to compute, most of the time is spent in punching the buttons, recording the answers, and figuring out what to do next. Thus an instantaneous desk calculator is not much more valuable than an ordinary one.

We conclude from this example that we must do at least two things in order to benefit from extremely fast computing speeds. First, we must arrange things so that the computing machine (or arithmetic unit) can find the numbers it uses very rapidly and can record the answers it finds very rapidly. It simply cannot wait for someone to enter these numbers manually or write them down manually. Likewise, it must have its instructions as to what is to be done in a form that it can interpret very rapidly. If it waits for someone to push buttons, then the advantage of the fast computing speed is lost.

The first series of computers were designed, built, and used with these two facts in mind. These are the "simple computers."

8–1.2 The Simple Computers

The first efforts to exploit the speed of computers resulted in computers with three principal features. They are a central processor, a memory, and a machine language. The *central processor* is primarily the "fast calculator" part of the computer. The *memory* is a place where the computer can read and write numbers or instructions. It corresponds to the sheets of paper used by people at a desk calculator, and is the input-output device for the central processor. The *machine language* is the language in which the instructions are presented to the computer. Thus instead of pushing a button to initiate a multiplication, we write the instruction "multiply." Instead of manually entering a number from a sheet of paper on a keyboard, we write "take the number written at such and such a place in memory and put it in the arithmetic unit." Since the computer must be able to respond to the instructions in machine language, it has another part, the *control unit.* Its function is to interpret the instructions, execute them, and generally control the whole process. This unit is usually part of the central processor, but it makes the operation of the simple computers easier to visualize if we think of it as distinct.

One of the most widely used early computers, the IBM 650, is shown in Figure 8–1. The organization of its components is shown in schematic form in Figure 8–2. The basic steps in computing the solution of a problem on this type of computer are:

1. Prepare the instructions.
2. Put the instructions and data into memory.
3. Push the START button.
4. Compute the solution.
5. Get the results out of memory.

In the case of the IBM 650, the instructions and data are written on paper and punched into cards on a keypunch machine (see Figure 8–3). These cards are

FIGURE 8–1. ***The IBM 650 was the most widely used computer of the 1950s. A card reader and punch is on the right, the computer is in the units to the left and to the rear. (Courtesy IBM Corp.)***

brought to the card reader and punch (the piece of equipment on the right in Figure 8–1) and placed in the hopper (at the left end). This machine then reads in the cards placed in the hopper. Once all the cards are in, the computer is started at the location of the first instruction. This is done by using the console. The operator then waits until the computer stops; he can tell this by watching the lights on the console. When the computation is finished, the results are

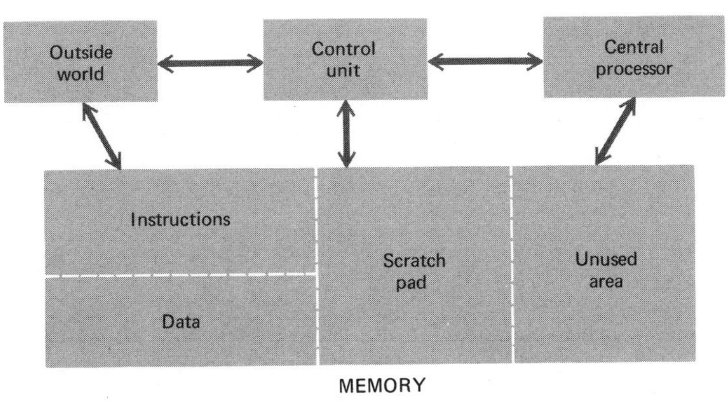

FIGURE 8–2. The organization of a simple computer for the solution of a typical problem.

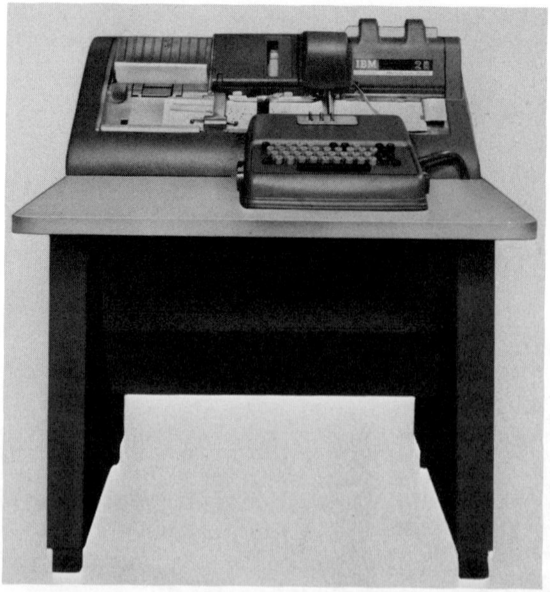

FIGURE 8–3. The IBM 026 printing card punch is the most common keypunch machine. (Courtesy IBM Corp.)

punched into cards by the computer. The hopper in the center of the card reader and punch contains blank cards, and the cards appear in the recess at the right end of the punch as they are punched.

The instructions must be complete for this process to work. In other words, the control unit reads them one at a time, causes the central processor to execute them, and stops when told. Thus an algorithm has to be in the language of the particular computer.

Recall that the goal of the simple computer organization is to remove the person from the execution of the computation. The central processor operates extremely fast, and if the control unit and memory are comparably fast, then the whole program is executed extremely fast. In other words the speed of the calculating machine (central processor) has been exploited.

It is worthwhile to discuss what we mean by "fast" for a memory. There are two distinct places in using a memory where time is involved. The first is in finding the number to retrieve, and the second is in actually retrieving it. One may visualize the memory as a long list where the words are stored. For a typical simple computer the list contains 1000 to 4000 words. The computer keeps track of things in this list by its location in the list. This location is called the *address* of a word. Thus, the 1687th word on the list has the address 1687.

Some memories are built so that no searching is required in finding the 1687th word (in memory). We can visualize this as being accomplished by a switch that we set to the desired address. When the control unit wants the 1687th word, it is switched to location 1687 on the list and retrieves it. Such memories are commonly made from networks of magnetic cores, but advances in technology may replace this construction by others. This fast-access memory is the *main memory*. When the main memory is constructed from magnetic cores, it is commonly referred to as core memory and we speak of things being "in core." A memory that requires no searching time is called a random-access memory. This terminology apparently comes from the fact that words can be retrieved from memory in any desired (for example, random) sequence at the same speed. Some current computers have more than one level (or speed) of random-access memory.

The most common memory without random access is magnetic tape. The words are stored sequentially from the beginning to the end of the tape. Whenever a particular word is desired, the magnetic tape is moved until that word comes to the reading head. These tapes are usually quite long, and it may take 2 or 3 minutes to go from one end of a tape to the other. This searching time is so long that magnetic tapes are not used for the main memory of computers. They are, however, commonly used in other roles in computer systems (see Chapter 9).

Another example of this kind of memory is the drum memory. Here words are stored as magnetized spots on a drum. There might be 20 bands around the drum, each of which contains 100 words (see Figure 8–4). When the control

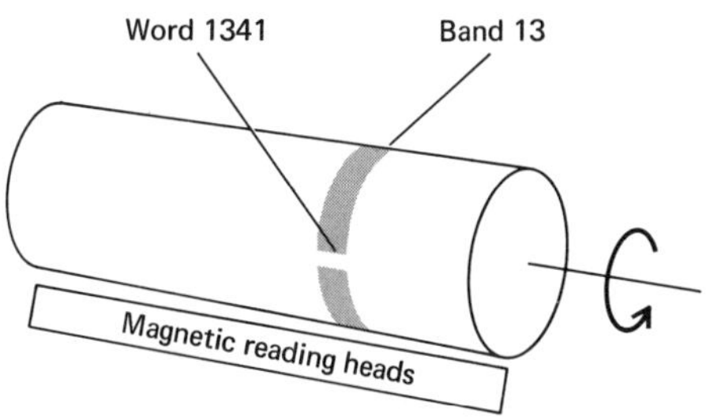

FIGURE 8–4. Schematic drawing of a drum memory.

unit wants the 1341st word, it asks for the 13th reading head to read it. However, this magnetic reader can read only the word directly opposite it. If the 41st word of the band is not available, we must wait for it to come around. Even though the drum may be rotating at 10,000 revolutions per minute, this waiting time can substantially slow down the overall speed of the computer. Other memories that are of this type are those that use paper tapes or magnetic disks. Any memory that requires the movement of a physical object is going to be slow compared to the electronic speeds possible in central processors. The main memory for the IBM 650 is a drum that contains 2000 words.

8–1.3 The MORON

The internal operation and the control unit of a simple computer can be visualized in terms of the "little moron" shown in Figure 8–5. The little moron inside the computer can read simple instructions written on slips of paper. These slips are kept in storage slots that correspond to the main memory. Both instructions and data may be written on these slips. The Moron is told to start at some particular address (storage slot), and he reads the slips in the slots one at a time. He goes through the slots in order unless he is told to do otherwise.

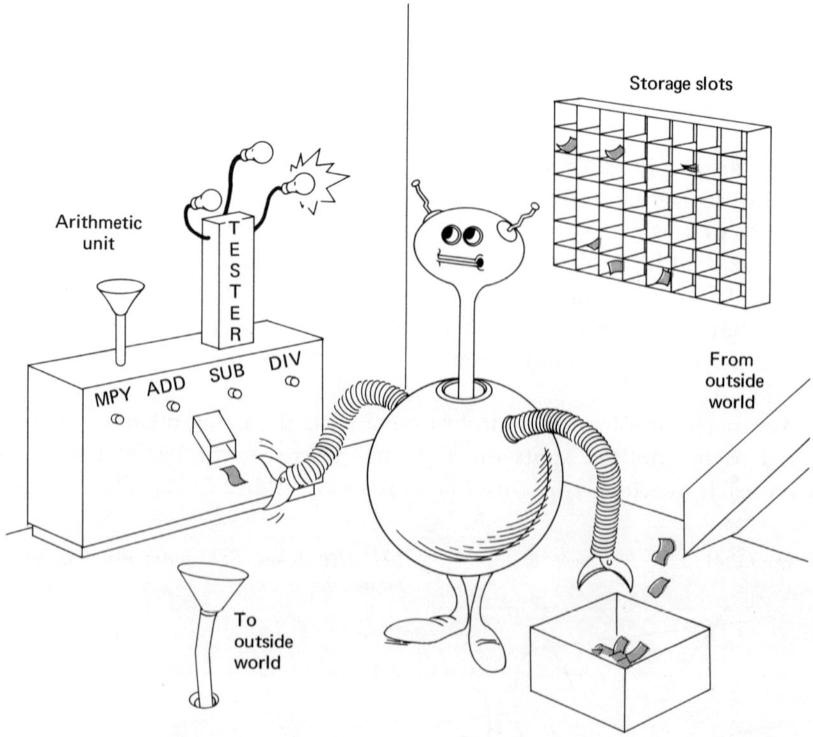

FIGURE 8–5. Schematic illustration of the role of the control unit in a simple computer. The moron follows instructions in the Moron machine language.

Whenever the Moron takes a slip out of a slot, he leaves a copy of the slip in the slot. Whenever he puts a slip into a slot, he throws away the slip already in the slot.

The Moron does not know what numbers are, but he can put slips (with numbers on them) into the arithmetic unit (central processor) as instructed. This unit then writes the result on a new slip which the Moron can, if so instructed, place in a storage slot. The Moron can also look at, and respond to, the lights on the "tester" portion of the arithmetic unit. This is how he can tell if a number is positive, zero, or negative even though he cannot read numbers directly.

The instructions that the Moron can understand form the machine language for this simple computer. The actions and instructions for a simple calculation are given in the next example.

EXAMPLE 8–1

THE COMPUTATION OF $2 * A + 3 * B$ BY THE MORON

The initial contents of the storage slots (pertinent to this computation) are given below.

Address	*Machine Language*	*Meaning and Remarks*
330	056000761	Put the number A into the arithmetic unit
331	104000765	Multiply by 2
332	020000763	Store the result
333	056000762	Put the number B into the arithmetic unit
334	104000766	Multiply by 3
335	231000763	Add contents of TEMP = 2 * A
336	020000764	Store the result
...	...	
761	000012006	The number A
762	000201021	The number B
763	000000000	Temporary storage
764	000000000	Final result
765	000000002	The number 2
766	000000003	The number 3

The Moron is told to start reading the instructions at address 330. He reads them and executes them, and when he reaches 336, the final result is placed at address 764. The contents of two of the storage slots have changed by the end of the computation as follows:

763	000024012	Contains 2 * A
764	000627075	Contains 2 * A + 3 * B

Note that machine-language instructions (and the corresponding assembly-language instructions) consist of two parts. The first part indicates what operation is to be performed (for example, 0560 means put a number into the arithmetic unit) and the second part indicates on what the operation is to be performed (for example, the contents of address 00761 for the first instruction).

Example 8–1 illustrates only part of what the Moron needs to be able to do. We now describe a very simple machine language that allows the computer to carry out arithmetic calculations.

8–1.4 A Simple Machine Language for the Moron

There are three kinds of instructions in this language; namely, arithmetic, testing and control, and manipulation. For clarity we use an alphanumeric language form rather than the numerical form of actual machine language. All but one of these instructions consist of an operation and an address. The one that means stop has only an operation. The thirteen Moron language instructions are:

Instruction	*Meaning*
ADD, X	Add the contents of address X to that of the arithmetic unit.
SUB, X	Subtract the contents of address X from that of the arithmetic unit.
MPY, X	Multiply the contents of address X by that of the arithmetic unit.
DIV, X	Divide the contents of the arithmetic unit by that of address X.
TRA, X	Read the next instruction from address X.
TZE, X	If the content of the arithmetic unit is zero, then read the next instruction from address X; otherwise continue to the next instruction.
TPL, X	If the content of the arithmetic unit is positive, then read the next instruction from address X; otherwise continue to the next instruction.
TMI, X	If the content of the arithmetic unit is negative (minus), then read the next instruction from address X; otherwise continue to the next instruction.
STP	Stop.
SRI, X	Start reading instructions at address X.
CLA, X	Place the contents of address X into the arithmetic unit.
STO, X	Store the contents of the arithmetic unit into address X.
OUT, X	Put the contents of address X into the output device.

A program for the Moron is written on slips of paper (or punched into cards) and these are given to the Moron along with a location (slot number) to place them, for example,

```
location address, (instruction, operation address)
             12,  (  CLA,           106           )
             13,  (  MPY,           707           )
             14,  (  STO,           106           )
```

The Moron goes through the locations in order unless instructed to do otherwise by a transfer instruction. Thus, if the Moron gets to location 12, it will place the contents of location 106 into the arithmetic unit. It then multiplies that number by the contents of location 707 and, at the instruction in 14, places the resulting number back into location 106.

Data are given to the Moron in the form

```
location address,    number
            106,     12
            707,      6
```

Thus, these data along with the above three instructions would result in 6 * 12 = 72 being placed in location 106.

An entire algorithm (program) for the computation of 2* A + 3 * B is as follows for A = 12,006 and B = 201,021:

```
330,(CLA,761)        337,(OUT,764)
331,(MPY,765)        338,(STP)
332,(STO,763)        761,000012006
333,(CLA,762)        762,000201021
```

```
334,(MPY,766)        765,000000002
335,(ADD,763)        766,000000003
336,(STO,764)        SRI,330
```

It is interesting to compare these instructions with those required in Fortran given below.

```
      INTEGER A,B,X
      READ 5,A,B
    5 FORMAT(2I9)
      X = 2*A + 3*B
      PRINT 6,X
      STOP
      END
```

Note that Fortran requires more statements, and more complicated ones, for the input-output and for "setting up" the computation. Thus, for this short computation, the Moron's machine language requires only about twice as many statements as Fortran. However, the ratio is much higher for more complicated computations. There are usually 5 to 10 times as many machine-language instructions as there are Fortran instructions for a computation.

The Moron language is described in more detail in the section at the end of this chapter, and a "simulator" may be obtained to run actual Moron programs on a computer.

8–1.5 The Weaknesses of the Simple Computers

Computer organization of this basic type appeared in the early 1950s and was the only type available until the late 1950s. Such computers are still manufactured and are quite effective for a large number of applications. However, in the late 1950s it became clear that this manner of doing things could not effectively exploit the speed possible in the central processor for the following reasons:

1. It takes too long to prepare the instructions (that is, to correctly write the program in machine language).
2. It takes too long to put the instructions and data into memory.
3. It takes too long to push the start button.
4. It takes too long to get the results out of memory.

Thus, every step in the solution of a problem became much too long compared to the time to took the computer to actually solve it once everything was set to go. Two changes in the use and organization of computers appeared almost simultaneously in order to alleviate these difficulties. One of these, discussed next, was the introduction of higher-level languages. The aim is to increase substantially the efficiency in preparing the instructions for the computer. The other, discussed in Chapter 9, was the introduction of operating systems, input-output buffering, and batch processing. The aim here is to increase substantially the efficiency of input-output and of pushing the start button.

It is noteworthy that these two changes are not really changes in the hardware of the computers, but in how the hardware is used. The IBM 650 has been used both as a simple computer and as part of a system including higher-level languages. This does not mean that the hardware did not change, for there were continual increases in the size, speed, efficiency, and versatility of the computers. Nevertheless the new hardware was still based on the same concept as that used in building the simple computers. At this point appeared the *computer system.* A computer system consists of a physical computing machine and auxiliary devices along with a system for using them. The "system" part of the computer system is embodied in a large number of programs. This collection of programs is called the *software* of the computer system. Originally, the system part was almost nonexistent. Now the system is recognized to be as important as the physical devices for computing. Furthermore, the effort put into developing the systems for a new computer is now larger than the effort put into developing the hardware of one.

Problems

You are to make up the slips of paper (programs) to get the Moron in the simple computer to solve the following problems. The slips are to be prepared for the Moron, in the Moron machine language. *Remember:* The Moron does not do anything without explicit written instructions.

8–1.1 Take the numbers 1382, 7, and 1403 and compute

$$X = 1382 + 7 * 1403.$$

8–1.2 Find which of the numbers in slots 92, 63, 112, and 981 is the largest.

8–1.3 Find the largest of the numbers 112, 63, 92, and 981.

8–1.4 Find the sum of the numbers in slots 1, 2, 3, 4, 7, and 9.

8–1.5 Compute the number

$$(17 - 81/403) * 6.$$

8–1.6 Find the middle number of the numbers in slots 7, 4, 6, 9, 11.

8–1.7 Find the average of 7, 4, 6, 9, and 11.

8–1.8 Take the number 13,971 and find the power of 10 by which it must be divided in order to get the result between 1 and 10. That is, compute P so that

$$1 \leq \frac{13{,}971}{10^P} < 10.$$

8–1.9 Discover whether or not

$$\frac{1}{2} + \frac{1}{3} + \frac{1}{5} = \frac{2}{15} + \frac{4}{5}.$$

8–1.10 For the above problems you wrote several kinds of instructions, and some were used more often than others. How many different kinds of instructions are needed for Problems 8–1.1, 8–1.2, 8–1.6, and 8–1.9?

8—2 Higher-Level Languages and the Translation Problem

8–2.1 The Hierarchy of Languages

We first recall the drawbacks of using natural language (English) for programs. They are:

1. It is often cumbersome (too long).
2. It is ambiguous.
3. It does not reveal the basic structure of algorithms.

Each of these points is serious, and they have led to a variety of other languages for programs. Another drawback particularly pertinent and just as basic as the preceding is

4. Machines do not now understand English.

It seems to be extremely difficult to construct a machine to recognize and respond to a natural language like English.

We think of language as a means of communication and we can consider several languages. We do not study languages in any detail here, but rather consider, in an intuitive way, the following levels of languages:

1. Natural language and jargon
2. Flowchart language
3. Natural programming languages
4. Algorithmic programming languages
5. Machine and assembly languages.

The basic difference between these languages is the power or level of the elementary instructions allowed and the flexibility of the construction of statements. At the top (natural language) we can literally say anything and the construction of statements (sentences) is very free and allows great complexity. At the bottom (machine language) the instructions are extremely limited in power and the statements are short and cryptic.

Natural Language and Jargon This is our ordinary language and it has the four drawbacks listed above. Recall that "jargon" means the technical language of a science, profession, or special group. The jargon that we have used is that of mathematics. This includes not only special words (and special technical meanings for ordinary words) but also special symbols (for example, +, >, ∫, *, and so on) that are an essential part of the language.

It is difficult to say which of the first three drawbacks of natural language is the most serious. The first and third are certainly related, and it is undesirable not to be able to express a simple and natural concept in a simple and natural way. This inability occurs when natural language is used for programs.

By definition, an algorithm must be unambiguous, so it is clearly dangerous to use an ambiguous language for algorithms. We should not underestimate the ambiguity problem in the natural spoken languages. Consider the following:

EXAMPLE 8–2

TIME FLIES LIKE AN ARROW

This statement has, at least, the following interpretations:

1. The common metaphor meaning that time is passing quickly.
2. Certain insects (time flies) desire an arrow.
3. Use the same mechanism to time the flight of flies that was used to time the flight of arrows.
4. The magazine (*Time*) flies like an arrow when thrown.
5. Time goes in a straight manner.

So this sentence, standing alone, is ambiguous. Compare it with the similar statement "Fruit flies like an apple."

Even though natural language is inherently ambiguous, it can be used (and has been used) for unambiguous communication between people. A sentence such as the preceding assumes one particular meaning from the *context* in which it is used. It is easy to note that the mechanism that resolves ambiguity is that of "meaning in context." It is very difficult to understand how this mechanism works, a fact that leads to great difficulty in such an area as mechanical language translation (for example, English to Russian).

Flowchart Language The primary use of flowchart language is to show the logical structure of an algorithm in a form easily recognized by a person. Thus, this language is very appropriate for "thinking" about programs and for communicating with other persons. However, it is not so appropriate for machine communication as the machines are not able to "see" the structure of a program from a flowchart.

There have been efforts to make a formal language for flowcharts with precise definitions, meanings, and symbols. The formalization is not presented here because we use the language mainly for discussions of the rough outline of programs, where formal precision is less important. However, computer systems are now under development which recognize programs given in flowchart form. There is some evidence and belief that it is the "most natural" language for algorithms.

Natural Programming Languages We are just now beginning to see the emergence of natural programming languages. They are all oriented to computer usage, and so the term programming has been adopted. They are also called *problem-oriented languages.* Their basic aim is to use familiar words and phrases from natural language (or jargon) to express programs. In order to accomplish this, the meaning of the words and phrases is restricted, more stringent rules are placed on the formation of statements, and a much smaller vocabulary is used.

Their second aim is to allow more powerful and versatile instructions than algorithmic languages allow.

There is, as yet, no widely established example of such a language. Typical statements allowed by such languages are as follows:

1. Set A = solution of X * cos(X) − 3.2 = LOG(X + 1.).
2. Solve for roots R1, R2 of polynomial

$$3X^2 - 7X + 2.$$

3. Set A = weight of components 3, 5, 8.

Such languages are not likely to allow a great variety of alternative statements of the same thing. Thus the following restatements of item 2 might not be allowed:

2a. Find the zeros R1, R2 of

$$3X^2 - 7X + 2.$$

2b. Compute R1, R2 so that

$$3(\mathrm{R1})^2 - 7(\mathrm{R1}) + 2 = 0 \quad \text{and} \quad 3(\mathrm{R2})^2 - 7(\mathrm{R2}) + 2 = 0.$$

2c. Solve the polynomial

$$3X^2 - 7X + 2$$

for its roots and call them R1 and R2.

The objectives in a natural programming language are:

1. To be unambiguous (this is essential)
2. To be reasonably concise
3. To use familiar terminology with the familiar meaning
4. To eliminate unnecessary, artificial, or redundant statements and instructions
5. To include more powerful instructions.

It is primarily objectives 2, 4, and 5 that distinguish these languages from the next lower class, the algorithmic languages. As more and more languages are developed, the dividing line between these two classes will be more difficult to distinguish.

Algorithmic Programming Languages This class of languages is, in a certain sense, defined by the example of Fortran. An examination of this language shows that it is essentially restricted to arithmetic and use of a few elementary mathematical functions (trigonometric, logarithmic, exponentials).

Furthermore, the requirements on the structure of statements are very restrictive, and a considerable amount of artificial and unnecessary punctuation is required. Finally, the execution by computers of programs in Fortran requires detailed instructions to the computer about certain aspects of the problem, the data entering the problem, and relationships between various parts of the program.

In theory there is no problem in the mathematical-scientific area that can be solved on a computer using a natural programming language that cannot be solved using Fortran. The real motivation for developing the natural programming languages is to reduce significantly the human effort in obtaining the solutions. This is achieved by reducing the time and difficulty of both instructing the computer and learning how to instruct the computer.

Machine and Assembly Languages It is a fact that the elementary instructions that a computer can perform are very limited. They simply do not recognize statements such as

$$Z = X + Y, \qquad Z = \frac{3X}{7}, \qquad Z = \frac{(3X + Y)}{4}.$$

Before a computer can carry out such operations, they must be broken into smaller steps which involve not only the details of arithmetic but also the internal manipulation of the numbers involved. Thus, the third of the statements might take 8 to 10 separate machine operations. The words in the language recognized by the machine consist of groups of digits, for example:

PART A

Address	*Contents*	*Address*	*Contents*
04371	410000004373	04424	007400400000
04372	002000004560	04425	100001004430
04373	053500102161	04426	004602000323
04374	050000001424	04427	000000002214
04375	040000002222	04430	060100002266
04376	060100001424	04431	007400400000
04377	050000001001	04432	100001004435
04400	030200000000	04433	004602000324
04401	060100002266	04434	000000002215
04402	050000000000	04435	060100002267
04403	030200001000	04436	050000002236
04404	013100000000	04437	056000002267
04405	026000002266	04440	076300000000
04406	040200002221	04441	013100000000
04407	010000004411	04442	026000002266
04410	012000004413	04443	040200002221
04411	050000002222	04444	010000004450
04412	060100100000	04445	412000004450

This is a typical machine language. Closely associated with machine languages are the assembly languages which contain statements such as:

PART B

	TNZ	202A	206A	LAC	KNTRT,1
201A	TRA	254A	2316J	CLA	**
202A	LAC	I,1	207A	STO	ROOTS-1,1
	CLA	KNTRT		CLA	ITER2
	ADD	C.3	208A	STO	ORDER-1,1
	STO	KNTRT	209A	STZ	IORD-1,1
203A	CLA	B		CLA	NF
2304J	FSB	**		ADD	C.18
	STO	N.		STO	NF
2306J	CLA	**	210A	NULL	
	FSB	A	211A	TSX	**,4
	XCA			TXI	* + 3,,1
	FMP	N.		PZE	211,,LK.DR
	SUB	C.2		PZE	XP
	TZE	* + 2		STO	N.
	TPL	206A	212A	TSX	**,4
204A	CLA	C.3		TXI	* + 3,,1
205A	STO	INTRT-1,1		PZE	212,,LK.DR

Computer instructions in machine language and assembly language are almost in one-to-one correspondence, but assembly language is much easier to read and write.

It is hard to appreciate the difficulties in the use of machine languages without actually using one. Such a language has a fair number of instructions, but each of them has a very limited scope. Thus programs in machine language are much longer, perhaps by a factor of 5 or 10, than programs in an algorithmic programming language. See Section 8–1.3 or Section 8–4 for simple example programs. For example, it takes 14 instructions in the Moron language to compute $X = 2 * A + 3 * B$. Furthermore, the user cannot refer to A, B, and X, but rather must know their addresses in memory. This means that the user must set up his own list of variables and corresponding addresses in the computer memory.

In a nutshell, the user has to know just how the machine shuffles individual words or even bits of words. Every time a word or number is manipulated, detailed instructions must be given for each tiny step in the manipulation.

Machine language and assembly language have several disadvantages. First, it takes a long time just to write down a program. Second, it takes much longer to get the bugs out of the algorithm. There are so many statements, each of which must be exactly right, that errors are inevitable and they are hard to locate. Third, one cannot understand what a program does (in any general sense) by reading it in machine language. This further contributes to difficulty in debugging programs. Fourth, a really complex program may be so long in machine language that it is almost impossible for one person to absorb and appreciate it all. Finally, it requires considerable study to learn how to use machine language. At least several months of steady study and practice are required for the average person to become reasonably fluent in the use of machine language.

Another disadvantage of a different type is that machine language is machine-dependent. This means that every time a different computer is used, a different machine language is required. The history of computing shows that computers are changed frequently, and thus the effort required to keep up with the machine languages is very significant.

There is one very important thing to note here. One cannot just decide to define a new and better language and then go ahead and use it. Machine language has one property that makes it essential; it is the only language that the machine understands. Thus the introduction of a new language requires that it can be translated into the appropriate machine language. Furthermore, it must be possible to do this translation automatically from some specific set of rules. *That is, there must be a program (in machine language) to translate the higher-level language into machine language.* If this translation has to be done by people, then there is little gain in using a higher-level language. In fact, programming in machine language can be interpreted as translating the expression of algorithms from a combination of flowchart language and natural English into machine language.

The secret of success, then, is to arrange to have the computer do the language translation with another program written in machine language. With this translation program the machine can take a program in a higher-level language, translate it into its own language, then read this program, and execute it.

The programs that do this translation are called *compilers.* They read through the higher-level program (one or several times) and systematically build up a program in machine language. Another approach, usually referred to as *interpretive,* is to translate each statement of a higher-level language into machine language more or less independently of the other statements. Each statement is then executed right after it is translated into machine language.

One can make an analogy of the relationship between interpreters and compilers, with the relationship between the interpretation of a conversation and the translation of a poem. A person who translates a conversation merely translates each sentence or two as it is spoken. It is up to the listener to grasp the overall meaning of the conversation. A person who translates a poem is required to do much more than translate each verse accurately. He must also include in translation the overall sense, spirit, and elegance of the poem. In other words, he translates the poem as a whole rather than as a sequence of independent verses.

We can now see where the catch lies with natural programming languages. As the language gets more sophisticated, includes a larger vocabulary, and becomes less rigidly structured, the problem of translation into machine language increases rapidly. However, since the value of human effort is increasing and the cost of computing is decreasing, it is reasonable to expect that many of the users of computers in the 1970s will use natural programming languages designed for the specific problem area at hand. Just as machine and assembly languages are presently used primarily by programming professionals, we can expect in time that algorithmic languages will be used almost exclusively by professionals in programming and algorithm construction.

8–2.2 Some Translation Examples

It is beyond the scope of this book to describe the language translation process in detail. However, we do give a few examples of translations from Fortran into Moron. These examples illustrate the relative complexity of the two languages and give some appreciation of how translation programs (compilers) work. The first step in the translation process is to find all of the variables in the Fortran program and assign a word of the computer's memory to record their values. At the end of this stage each variable in the Fortran program has an address and the Moron program uses this address. The Moron program, of course, is not aware of the variable's name. This initial step is part of the *storage allocation* process that the compiler performs.

EXAMPLE 8–3

A SIMPLE ASSIGNMENT, X = A

The statement X = A in a Fortran program is replaced by two Moron statements (assumed to be in locations 100 and 101) as follows:

```
100,(CLA,1)    FETCH A
101,(STO,2)    PUT IT IN X
```

The word allocated for A is at address 1 and that for X is at address 2.

The translation of X = 2 * A + 3 * B into Moron is shown in the original discussion of Moron. A significant point in the resulting Moron program is that a temporary variable has to be used to store the intermediate result 2 * A. The compiler must, of course, recognize that temporary variables are required in the translation process. We do not explain here how this is done, but the next example shows the translation of a Fortran statement that requires two temporary variables.

EXAMPLE 8–4

ASSIGNMENT OF AN EXPRESSION, X = 2. * A − B/C + E * (F + 1.)

We first lay out the storage of the variables in this statement (starting at location 1)

```
1, 603.21      VALUE OF A
2, −14.58      VALUE OF B
3, 999.666     VALUE OF C
4, 1.0004      VALUE OF E
5, −.9876      VALUE OF F
6, 2.          CONSTANT 2.
7, 1.          CONSTANT 1.
8, 0.0         VALUE OF X
```

The required Moron program begins at location 100. Before the calculation begins, the value of X is not determined by this assignment statement. The two temporary variables required are in locations 98 and 99.

```
 98, 0.          TEMP 1
 99, 0.          TEMP 2
100, (CLA,6)
101, (MPY,1)
102, (STO,98)    2. * A
103, (CLA,2)
104, (DIV,3)
105, (STO,99)    B/C
106, (CLA,7)
107, (ADD,5)
108, (MPY,4)     E * (F + 1.)
109, (SUB,99)    - B/C + E * (F + 1.)
110, (ADD,98)    2. * A - B/C + E * (F + 1.)
111, (STO,8)
```

We see that one rather simple Fortran statement requires 12 Moron instructions and two other words assigned as temporary variables.

EXAMPLE 8–5

AN ARITHMETIC IF, IF(X ** 2. − 3.) 18,20,60

This Fortran statement involves labels as well as variables and the compiler must associate Moron addresses with each of the Fortran labels. Let us assume that the following associations have been made:

Fortran Statement	*Moron Code Starts at*
18	137
20	156
60	408

We also assume that the following variable assignments have been made:

```
1, 1.5892     VALUE OF X
2, 3.0        CONSTANT 3.
```

We do not use the constant 2. because we replace X ** 2. by X * X. Note that we could not translate X ** 2.3 into Moron directly because there is no exponentiation in Moron! The resulting code is assumed to start at 100 and is as follows:

```
100, (CLA,1)
101, (MPY,1)
102, (SUB,2)      X * X - 3.
103, (TMI,137)
104, (TZE,156)
105, (TPL,408)
```

EXAMPLE 8–6

A DO STATEMENT, DO 22 K = 1, KMAX, KK

The Fortran DO statement is more complicated in that it has a second part, the statement label at the end of the DO loop. As before, the first step is to have addresses for the variables involved.

```
1, 0      VALUE OF K
2, 82     VALUE OF KMAX
3, 4      VALUE OF KK
4, 1      CONSTANT 1
```

The computations inside the DO loop take 80 Moron instructions and the resulting Moron program appears as follows:

```
100, (CLA,4)
101, (STO,1)        INITIALIZE K
102, (CLA,38)       START OF LOOP
   . . .               . . .
181, (STO,66)       END OF LOOP
182, (CLA,1)
183, (ADD,3)        K + KK
184, (STO,1)
185, (SUB,2)        K + KK – KMAX
186, (TMI,102)      TEST
187, (CLA,71)       AFTER DO LOOP
```

We see clearly from this translation the fact that the testing for the Fortran DO loop is at the end of the loop and thus the loop is executed once no matter what the initial, terminal, and increment values of the variables are. Note also that this translation would result in an infinite loop for the statement DO 20 K = K1,K2,K3 if K1 = 8, K2 = 4, and K3 = –5. A more sophisticated translation would not have this property.

Problems

8–2.1 Translate the following Fortran statements into Moron:

```
A.    X = A*(B+(C-D)/(E+7.3)*6.1)
B.    IF( 7.12*X - 3.25*Y/X) 20,30,40
C.    BAG = 6.2*(17.3*18.24/6.03+14.012/(1.+X))
D.    A = 4.83 - 8.43*X*(X+7.2*X(4.04+X/17.1))
E.          DO 20 KLAD = 7,52
            ....
       20 X = 14.1
```

8–2.2 Describe a general procedure to translate a computed GO TO in Fortran into Moron. Illustrate the result for the statement

```
GO TO(25,15,45,25), JUMP
```

8–2.3 Translate the following Fortran program into Moron and verify your translation by running both programs.

```
      A= 10
      B = 6
      C = -7.21
      D = 14.04
      SQ = A+B+C+D
      QS = A*B + C*D
      PRINT 600,A,B,C,D,SQ,QS
  600 FORMAT( E18.7 )
      STOP
      END
```

8–2.4 Translate the following program into Moron and verify your translation by running both programs.

```
      KOUNT = 0
      SUM   = 0
      HIGH  = -1
    2 READ 5, GRADE
    5 FORMAT(F6.0)
      IF( GRADE + 99. )   10,50,10
   10 KOUNT = KOUNT + 1
      SUM = SUM + GRADE
         GO TO 2
   50 AVER = SUM/FLOAT(KOUNT)
      PRINT 52, KOUNT,AVER
   52 FORMAT(11H AVERAGE OF ,I4, 10H GRADES IS F7.2)
      STOP
      END
```

8–2.5 Translate the following program into Moron and verify your translation by running both programs.

```
      REAL X(50),Y(50)
      READ 5,(X(I),I=1,8),(Y(I),I=1,8)
    5 FORMAT( F10.2 )
      BAG = 0.
      DO 25 J= 1,8
   25 BAG = BAG + (X(J)+2.)/(Y(J)-2.)
      GAB = (X(1)+Y(1))/BAG
      PRINT 30,GAB
   30 FORMAT( F12.6 )
      STOP
      END
```

8–2.6 Translate the following Fortran program into Moron and verify your translation by running both programs.

```
      REAL X(50)
      XSUM = 0.
      DO 10 J = 1,40
      FJ = J
      X(J) = 1317.*FJ - 74.2*FJ**2 + FJ**3
   10 XSUM = XSUM + X(J)
      PRINT 20, XSUM
   20 FORMAT( E18.7 )
      XMAX = -1000.
      DO 30 J =1,40
      IF( X(J).LT. XMAX )  GO TO 30
      XMAX = X(J)
      JMAX = J
   30 PRINT 20, X(J)
      PRINT 40, XMAX,JMAX
   40 FORMAT( E18.7,I10 )
      STOP
      END
```

8–2.7 *(Blank removal in Fortran)* The blanks in Fortran are not significant ercept in Hollerith fields, and thus one of the first actions of a Fortran compiler is to remove the blanks from the cards. Write a program to do this stage of compilation. Thus it is to read in a card in A1 format, one character per variable, then remove all blanks in columns 7 through 72 and end up with all the nonblank characters pushed to the left (maintaining their correct order). Run your program with 6 sample cards and appropriate output to show that it works. In particular, print out the entire card before and after the blanks are removed.

8–2.8 *(Word recognizer)* Assume that you have cards with one of the following three words punched starting in column 7: FORMAT, HELP, and UGH. Write a Fortran program which reads these cards and identifies which word is punched. A line of output is to be printed as follows:

```
THE WORD FORMAT WAS FOUND
THE WORD HELP WAS FOUND
THE WORD UGH WAS FOUND
THE WORD WAS NOT RECOGNIZED
```

The fourth line of output is for cards which do not contain one of these three words. Run your program with a number of cards (at least 10) to show that it works.

[*Hint:* Read the cards in one character at a time in an A format. Then compare the unknown word on the card with each of the known spellings of FORMAT, HELP, and UGH. You might put these spellings in arrays of Hollerith variables using a DATA statement.]

8–2.9 You are to write a Fortran program which reads in a deck of cards as data which is also a Fortran program. Your program examines each card and is to decide which kind of Fortran statement is on the card. To simplify things, you need only consider the following types of statements:

```
ASSIGNMENT              X = A+B ,   ARAY(7,K) = K+1- NMAX
LOGICAL IF              IF(L.LT.10) Y=Z , IF(X-1..GT.5.2) GOTO 8
READ                    READ 55,X,Q,DIDDLE
PRINT                   PRINT 666, P,Q,R,STUV
      (ASSUME NO ARRAYS IN READ OR PRINT STATEMENTS)
FORMAT                  FORMAT(6X,I8,2E9.1////)
      (ASSUME NO HOLLERITH FIELDS IN FORMATS)
GO TO                   GO TO 1632
DO                      DO 10 J=1,10 ,   DO 8 KKKK= JJQ,9,LXYZ
STOP                    STOP
END                     END
DECLARATION             REAL I,KL        INTEGER XX,PLOT
      (ASSUME ONLY REAL OR INTEGER DECLARATIONS)
```

Your program is to assume that no other statements are to be found, but if one is accidentally read in anyway, classify it as UNKNOWN. Assume one statement per card, that is, no continuation cards. The output is to appear as follows:

```
    TYPE                FORTRAN  STATEMENT
  DECLARATION           REAL IA,DILL(12)
  ASSIGNMENT         17 X = 1.0
  GO TO                    GO  TO  404
  LOGICAL IF        909 IF(KK+JJ-1 .EQ. 16*IJX)     STOP
  UNKNOWN               DATA BLANK,EQUAL,COMMA/1H ,1H=,1H, /
```

[*Note:* Your program is to work correctly for those kinds or types of Fortran statements specified above. Do not worry what it does with others or with nonsense statements. Thus if it happens to call the last example statement above an assignment statement (because of the = in it) that is all right.]

[*Hint:* Your first task is to develop a set of tests to distinguish between these 10 different kinds of Fortran statements. Check first on the presence, location, and relationship of some special characters = , ( ). Once a preliminary classification is made this way, then check the key words DO, IF, FORMAT, ...]

You must read the Fortran statements in an A format, one character per variable. You must check the contents of a card, character by character, with your tests. [*Suggestion:* Get all of the blanks removed before you start testing (see Problem 8–2.7).]

After the preliminary classification is made, then you check the key words by doing a character by character comparison with known spellings (see Problem 8–2.8).

8–2.10 *(Interpretative Arithmetic)* You are to write a program to read a data card which specifies some sequence of arithmetic operations and then to execute them for data values given on later cards. In particular, the program is to evaluate a polynomial of 2 variables, X and Y, for the X and Y values given on later cards. Typical input is

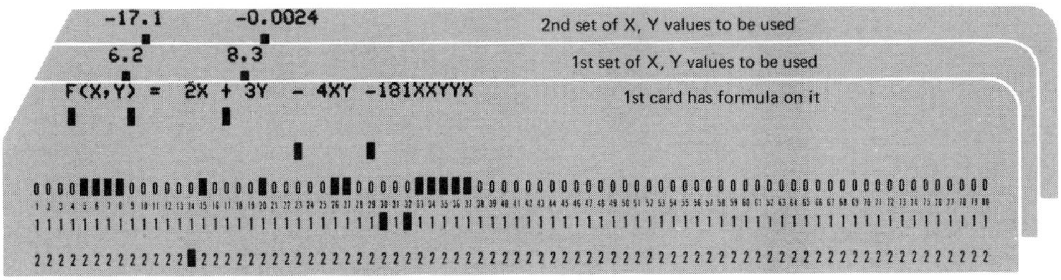

The program is to read card 1 and set up to evaluate F(X,Y) using the pairs of numbers on the following cards (however many these might be). All blanks are to be ignored on the first card and you need only consider integer constants in the formula for F(X,Y). The formula may have blanks in it (see Problem 8–2.7).

More specific requirements are as follows:

(a) All coefficients are integers (+ or −).
(b) Only the variables "X" and "Y" occur. Combinations and repetitions of these letters indicate powers and cross-products. *Example:* "−3XXXYY" means $(-3X^3Y^2)$.
(c) No more than nine X's or Y's appear in any one term.
(d) No parentheses are present.
(e) The data for X and Y are real. Hence, all arithmetic should be done in floating-point.
(f) Ignore *all* blanks in the F(X,Y) formula card. Only one card is to be used for the function statement.

8–3 Higher-Level Languages—A Brief Survey

This section presents a very brief discussion of six important higher-level languages. The objective is to give the reader an idea of the nature and use of these languages. A thorough description or a real understanding is, of course, not possible in the few paragraphs devoted to each of these languages.

8–3.1 Algol

This language was designed by an international committee and a preliminary description appeared in 1958. The design objectives were fourfold: The language should be as close as possible to mathematics, it could be used for publishing algorithms, it could be used for writing programs, and it was to be completely standardized and precisely defined. Algol has had a number of versions, and major additions were made in 1968. The Algol 60 version is widely used throughout the world, especially outside the United States.

```
1. for I: = 0 step L − 1 until K − J do
        begin C[I]: = I ↑ 2 + 1; D4D[I − K]: = L × I − 1.2 end;
2. if SLOPE (X) = 0 or STEP < .000001 then go to OUT else STEP: = STEP/2;
3. OUT: OUTPUT(61,'/, 30B, 'THE ANS', 2(−Z.6D₁₀2Z)',X,STEP);
4. begin real DIST; integer I,J; real array C,D4D[−10:50]
```

FIGURE 8–6. Some example statements in Algol.

There has been considerable emotional controversy over the relative merits of Fortran and Algol and each has several distinct advantages over the other. Algol lacks a number of the artificial restrictions that occur in Fortran and generally has more flexible provisions for program control. On the other hand, it is more verbose for programming than Fortran; its input-output facilities are highly nonstandard and frequently cumbersome; and Algol language translators are generally inferior to those for Fortran, partly due to the nature of the language. PL/1 (discussed later) is partly an attempt to combine the good points of these two languages into a single language.

Despite the above controversy, Algol and Fortran appear quite similar when viewed in the broad spectrum of languages, and most programs in one of them can be easily rewritten in the other. Two major differences are that Algol *procedures* (subprograms) are internal rather than external to the main program and that Algol allows the recursive use of procedures. A number of Algol statements are shown in Figure 8–6. The first item in Figure 8–6 is an iteration loop containing two assignment statements for array elements. The range or scope of the **for** statement is specified by the words **begin** and **end** which are used in Algol as a form of parentheses. Note that a semicolon separates statements and the end of a line or card has no significance. The second item is an **if-then-else** with a natural structure. One can place arbitrarily long pieces of program after the **then** or **else** including more **if-then-else** statements. The second and third items show that statement labels are ordinary names and are distinguished by a trailing colon. The output statement combines the functions of the Fortran PRINT and FORMAT. Some Algol systems have input-output similar to Fortran. The last item in Figure 8–6 is a declaration (except for the **begin** which indicates the start of a block of the program) and all variables must be declared in Algol. The indices in arrays may take on negative values and the range indicated for D4D carries back to the array C.

Figure 8–7 gives a complete Algol program for computing the location of the minimum of the function whose slope (derivative) is given by SLOPE.

8–3.2 APL

APL is an acronym for "A Programming Language" first published in 1962 by K. E. Iverson and it is also referred to as "Iverson's language." The scope of APL applications is extremely broad and includes scientific problems, business data processing, operating systems, and language translators. It is also

```
begin real X,X1,STEP;
      real procedure SLOPE (X) ;
            value X; real X;
            SLOPE: = EXP(X + SIN(X)) × (1 + COS(X)) + 2 × X/(1 + X ↑ 2);
      X: = 6; STEP: = 1;
SIGN: if SLOPE (X) < 0 then X1: = X − STEP
                  else XI: = X + STEP;
      if SLOPE (X) = 0 or STEP < 1₁₀ − 6 then go to OUT;
      if SLOPE (X) × SLOPE (X1) < 0 then STEP: = STEP/10;
      X: = X1; go to SIGN;
OUT: OUTPUT(61,'↑,16S, − 5Z.8D','LOWEST POINT IS',X);
end
```

FIGURE 8–7. A sample Algol program.

used to give a formal description of the functioning of the hardware of a computer, and this is perhaps the only compact and precise way to provide such a description.

The power (and to some, the weakness) of APL comes from its large set of operators, many more than in other languages. This results in a large number of special symbols, for example,

⌊ ⌈ ∧ ∨ ⊤ ⊥ ⊕ \ ↓ ↑ // ← →

which in turn results in a language that is unintelligible to the uninitiated. However, it is these symbols along with a variety of other notational innovations which give this language its power and wide scope of applications.

As hinted above, there is considerable controversy about the value and future of this language. Two extreme camps have formed, one which regards APL as useless and the other which regards it as the replacement for all existing programming languages. The middle ground is occupied by people who recognize its power and potential but who also recognize its practical limitations and disadvantages. No doubt it will have a major influence on further developments in languages and it will probably also evolve in time. The theme is presented elsewhere in this book that computer languages will evolve toward natural language, and perhaps an evolution will occur in APL that will retain its power and yet modify its highly artificial appearance.

A number of sample statements in APL are shown in Figure 8–8. The first item is an assignment statement followed by a direct transfer to statement labeled 25. The second statement is a conditional transfer, the values of x and b are compared. If x = b, then a transfer is made to 10; if x < b, a transfer is made to 20, otherwise the next statement is executed. The third statement uses the standard APL functions ϵ and ν and the array *y* has all components set to zero. The fourth statement uses the "ceiling" operator ⌈ and the "reduction" operator / to set y equal to the largest element in the one-dimensional array (vector) *x*. The fifth statement is a "masking" operation and, without explaining how, the result is $z = (x_1,x_2,x_3,x_4,y_5,y_6)$. The final statement involves the "base

1. $x \leftarrow a + b \times 3; \rightarrow (25)$
2. $x{:}b; (=, <) \rightarrow (10,20)$
3. $y \leftarrow \epsilon\,(\nu y)$
4. $y \leftarrow \lceil / x$
5. $z \leftarrow /\, x;\ \omega^2(6); y /$
6. $d \leftarrow 10(n)\mathsf{T}j$ $\qquad 10 \perp d = 10^{n}|j$

FIGURE 8–8. Some sample statements in APL.

10 representation" operator T and if n = 5, j = 31789, then d = (3,1,7,8,9). The identity at the right expresses two other relations between d and j in terms of the "base 10 value" operator ⊥ and the "modulus" operator |. If n = 4, j = 87654321, then d = (4,3,2,1).

Two short APL programs are shown in Figure 8–9 and we see that their structure is somewhat graphical in nature. Thus, in a computer implementation, statement 3 on the left would be $d{:}x_j;\ (>) \rightarrow (5)$ and statement 9 on the right would be $x_j \leftarrow x_{j-1}; \rightarrow (4)$.

8–3.3 Basic

The Basic language was originally developed as a teaching language for computing. This took place at Dartmouth College in 1965 under the direction of John Kemeny and Thomas Kurtz and was supported by the National Science Foundation as part of its effort to improve science education. The name is an acronym for "Beginner's All-purpose Symbolic Instruction Code."

The original goal meant that Basic must be simple, must be easy to learn, and must provide preparation for using more powerful languages (for example, Algol, Fortran, PL/1). This simplicity made Basic unsuitable for many applications and thus a variety of "improvements" and features have been added at various places. These additions have been successful and Basic is now widely available for commercial use as well as for education.

Basic is oriented to mass direct-access use (usually with a teletype), and

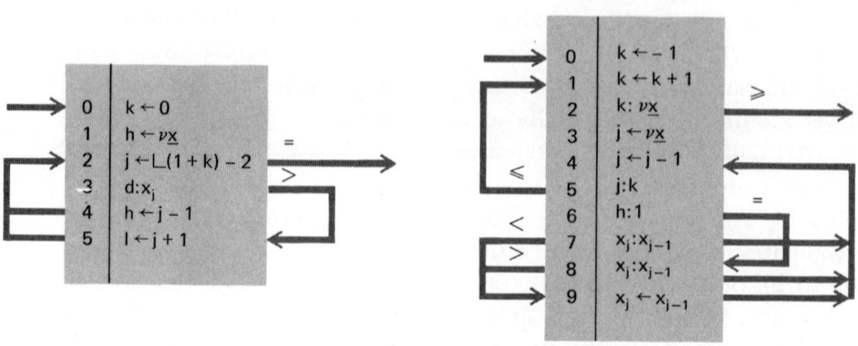

(a) (b)

FIGURE 8–9. Two sample APL programs: (a) locates the position of the data d *in the array* x *by a binary search; (b) uses the bubble sort to order the array* x *(high to low if* h = *1, low to high otherwise).*

```
10  LET A = (C2 + (I-1)*A)/K4

20  REM          NOW PRINT

30  PRINT  K4, A, A/C2H, "FIRST VALUES"

40  IF C(K4) < = 10 THEN 80

50  FOR J = 0.8 TO 2.0 STEP K4/10

58  NEXT J

60  GOSUB 805
```

FIGURE 8–10. Some sample statements in Basic.

thus the language must be easy to translate as well as to learn. Every Basic statement is of the form (label) (keyword) (rest of statement), and the 15 keywords identify the statement type. Furthermore, the complexity of the statements is low and the program structure is simplified. A sample of statements is shown in Figure 8–10. As indicated in Figure 8–10, every statement in Basic must have a label (statement number) and these specify the order for execution. Statement 10 is an assignment, and we note that all arithmetic is real and that symbolic names are a single letter with a digit as an optional second character. Statement 20 is a comment and 30 is a print. Note that the print uses a standard format and allows expressions and messages in the print list. The IF is similar to the logical IF of Fortran but only a direct transfer is possible. Statement 50 shows the start of an iteration loop and it is terminated by statement 58. The final statement is a transfer to a subprogram which starts at statement 805. When a RETURN is encountered in the subprogram, control is returned to the next statement after the GOSUB. There are no arguments and all variables are global (in COMMON). A simple Basic language program is shown in Figure 8–11.

8–3.4 Cobol

The development of Cobol started in 1959 with the U. S. Government and several computer manufacturers. The name Cobol comes from "common business oriented language" and indicates the objective of developing a language particularly adapted to business data processing. A set of specifications was issued in 1961 for Cobol which contains its basic elements and upon which later versions are based.

Cobol is quite different from Fortran both in appearance and structure. Business data processing typically requires very little arithmetic and a large amount of reading and writing files and moving data and information around. Furthermore, a real attempt was made to have Cobol self-documenting. The hope was that almost anyone, even a nonprogramming supervisor or manager, could read a Cobol program and follow the data processing. Even though Cobol is much more readable than most languages, this ideal of self-documentation was not really achieved.

```
  1 REM   RETURN ON $100/MO. INVESTMENTS
  2 REM   P = ARRAY OF INTEREST
  3 REM   S = ARRAY OF SUMS ACCUMULATED SO FAR
  4 REM       FOR EACH OF THE 4 VALUES OF P
 10 PRINT ≠ ≠,≠RETURN ON $100/MO. INVESTMENTS≠
 20 PRINT ≠YEARS≠,≠AT PERCENT RATES OF≠
 30 PRINT ≠ ≠, 4, 8,12,16
 40 READ P(1),P(2),P(3),P(4)
 50 FOR K=1 TO 4
 60 LET S(K) = 1200
 70 NEXT K
 80 REM            MAIN LOOP STARTS
100 FOR Y = 1 TO 25
110 FOR K = 1 TO 4
120 LET S(K) = S(K)*(1.+P(K))
130 NEXT K
140 PRINT Y,S(1),S(2),S(3),S(4)
150 FOR K = 1 TO 4
160 LET S(K) = S(K) + 1200
170 NEXT K
180 NEXT Y
200 DATA .04,.08,.12,.16
300 END
```

FIGURE 8–11. A Basic program to print a table of investment returns. Note that the data for the* READ *are part of the program.

Cobol statements are called sentences and many of them do appear as ordinary English sentences. The names of variables can be quite long (up to 30 characters), and in many situations one can add "noise" words which make the sentences closer to English. Data processing requires extensive input-output and thus Cobol has a very extensive set of input-output instructions and features. These features add to the complexity of the language but in a considerably different way than in Fortran. Even though the appearances are quite different, Cobol does have statements corresponding to the assignment, GO TO, logical IF, READ, PRINT, and so on. The variables in Cobol can either be numerical or alphanumeric (messages) and various statements are needed to declare which variables are of which type. A number of example Cobol statements are shown in Figure 8–12 and an almost complete program is shown in Figure 8–13.

```
1. ADD TOTAL_PRICE TO BILL_SO_FAR GIVING AMOUNT_DUE

2. MULTIPLY WEEKS_PAY BY TAXRATE GIVING TAX_DEDUCT

3. MOVE AMOUNT_DUE TO ACCOUNTS_RECEIVABLE

4. IF WEEKS_SALES IS GREATER THAN QUOTA GOTO OVER_QUOTA

5. PART_NAME, PICTURE IS XXXXXXXX

6. DISPLAY "ORDER ENTERED FOR", PART_NAME, " ON " , DATE
```

FIGURE 8–12. Some example Cobol statements.

```
PROCEDURE DIVISION
GETTING_STARTED. OPEN INPUT SALES_FILE, OUTPUT SUMMARY_REPORT.
    READ SALES FILE RECORD. MOVE ZERO TO TOTAL_ALL_SALESMEN.
NEXT_SALESMAN. MOVE SALESMAN IN SALES_ITEM TO MAN_NUMBER. MOVE
    AMOUNT TO SALESMAN_AMOUNT.
FILE_PROCESSING. READ SALES_FILE RECORD: AT END GO TO FINISH.
    IF SALESMAN NOT EQUAL TO MAN_NUMBER GO TO SALESMAN_TOTAL.
    ADD AMOUNT TO SALESMAN_AMOUNT. GO TO FILE_PROCESSING.
SALESMAN_TOTAL. MOVE SPACES TO SUMREP. MOVE MAN_NUMBER TO
    SALESMAN IN SUMREP. MOVE SALES AMOUNT TO AMOUNT IN SUMREP.
    ADD SALES_AMOUNT TO TOTAL_ALL_SALESMEN. WRITE SUMREP.
    GO TO NEXT_SALESMAN.
FINISH. MOVE SPACES TO SUMREP. MOVE 'EVERYBODY' TO SALESMAN IN SUMREP.
    MOVE TOTAL_ALL_SALESMEN TO AMOUNT IN SUMREP. WRITE SUMREP.
    CLOSE SALES_FILE, SUMMARY_REPORT. STOP RUN.
```

FIGURE 8–13. A sample Cobol program which reads the files names* SALES_FILE *and writes the file* SUMMARY REPORT. *Each record (item) in* SALES_FILE *consists of a salesman's name and a sales amount. Each record (item) of* SUMMARY REPORT *consists of a salesman's name and his total sales. The last record in* SUMMARY REPORT *has the total sales for all salesmen.

The first two statements in Figure 8–12 are simple arithmetic assignment statements, the third one simply moves a variable from one file to another. The fourth statement is the logical IF and the GO TO OVER_QUOTA is the usual GO TO except that labels in Cobol are names and not necessarily numbers. The fifth statement declares that PART_NAME is a variable with 8 alphanumeric characters (for example, AXLEROD1 or BOLT_5.5). The final statement prints a line on the standard output unit (usually a printer).

8–3.5 PL/1

The initial development of PL/1 started in late 1963 in a committee of IBM representatives. The language definition went through many versions and a fairly firm definition appeared in 1966. PL/1 is sometimes called "programming language one," but it was not intended that PL/1 be an acronym of anything.

The objectives in the development of PL/1 were broad and varied. One might summarize them by saying that PL/1 was to be suitable for use by a great variety of users and to be better adopted to the hardware and computer system concepts that appeared in the 1960s. It is specifically designed to be suitable as a replacement for Cobol in business data processing, a replacement for Fortran in scientific computing, and as a partial replacement for machine language and assembly language in systems programming.

The attempt to cover such a range of applications has resulted in a large and complicated language. The problems with obtaining compact and efficient language translators are still not completely resolved. The language is of such complexity that it is not reasonable for a novice in computing to attempt to learn the full language and only professionals in computer science are likely

```
1. BEST_EST = .5*(OLD_EST + (DATANEW + DATA 445)/2);

2. PUT LIST ' MY ANSWER = ', 17.2* GUESS1 + FUDGE_FACTOR;

3. GO TO CASE4;

4. DECLARE X FLOAT(8), BB FIXED(6,2),DATE PICTURE AAAXXX99;

5. IF K > 100 THEN GO TO ENDPROGRAM;ELSE K = K+2; GO TO B;

6. DO CONTROL = 1 TO 50, 60 TO 100 BY 10;
```

FIGURE 8–14. Six examples of PL/1 statements.

to make use of the full range of facilities offered in PL/1. This situation was realized early and the designers expected that various subsets of PL/1 would be selected for various application areas. Thus, one subset would be learned and used by people in business data processing, another subset similar to Fortran would be used in scientific applications, and an elementary subset would be learned by students in introductory courses. It was hoped by the originators of PL/1 that this new language would eventually replace a large number of languages including such major ones as Algol, Basic, Cobol, Fortran, and Jovial.

The final fate of PL/1 is not yet determined, but it has already had a major impact on computing and it is certain to assume a position as one of the most important programming languages.

The facilities in PL/1 include everything mentioned or hinted at in the previous section on Cobol as well as almost everything in Fortran, and there are many other things in addition. Most statements in Fortran have direct counterparts in PL/1 and a Fortran program is easily translated into PL/1. Translation from PL/1 to Fortran is sometimes awkward or very difficult. A variety of example PL/1 statements are shown in Figure 8–14. The first statement in Figure 8–14 is an assignment statement, the second prints a message and a calculated value, and the third is the usual GO TO. The fourth statement declares that X is a decimal (floating) number with 8 significant digits, BB is of fixed size of 6 digits, two following the decimal point (for example, dollars and cents), and the appearance of DATE is given by the PICTURE. DATE could be JAN 5,73 or JUN 17,88. The fifth statement is the simple IF-THEN-ELSE and the last statement is a more general form of the DO statement modeled after the **for** in Algol. The control variable CONTROL goes from 1 to 50 in steps of 1 and then from 60 to 100 in steps of 10.

A complete PL/1 program is shown in Figure 8–15. The first part defines a function SLOPE (x). Then a simple "walking" or "stepping" scheme is used to find where SLOPE is zero. The point where the slope is zero is the lowest point on the curve involved.

8–3.4 Snobol

The work on Snobol started in 1962 at the Bell Telephone Laboratories and is based on an older language, Comit. The language has gone through several versions and extensions and the most recent is called Snobol 4.

The appearance, format, and objectives of Snobol are quite different from the other programming languages discussed here. The aim of Snobol is to provide effective facilities to process messages, character strings, and patterns. Its predecessor, Comit, had no arithmetic capability; one could not even add one plus one. While Snobol 4 does have reasonable arithmetic capabilities, it is not really suited for applications appropriate for Fortran. Although the appearance of Snobol 4 is foreign at first, it is a rather natural language for its application area and a useful subset can be learned easily. The language does have some subtle and sophisticated features which a novice programmer would find meaningless.

```
MIN_FLOAT: PROCEDURE OPTIONS (MAIN);
   DECLARE (X,SLOPE) FLOAT (10);
          SLOPE: PROCEDURE (X);
                 SLOPE = EXP(X + SIN(X))*(1. + COS(X))
                              + 2.*X/(1. + X**2);
                 RETURN (SLOPE);
           END SLOPE;
    X = 6.; STEP = 1.;
  /* MAIN LOOP STARTS HERE */
    LOOP: DO K = 1 TO 999 WHILE SLOPE - = 0. & STEP > .000001;
              IF SLOPE(X) < 0 THEN X1 = X - STEP;
                               ELSE X1 = X + STEP;
              IF SLOPE(X)*SLOPE(X1) < 0. THEN STEP = STEP/2.;
              X = X1
          END LOOP;
    PUT SKIP EDIT (' FOUND LOW POINT ' , X)
                 (A(17), E(17,10));
END MIN_FINDER;
```

***FIGURE 8–15. A sample PL/1 program to find the lowest point on a curve whose slope is given by the formula in the procedure* SLOPE.**

Snobol is not nearly as widely used as Fortran, Cobol, PL/1, or Basic, but it is available at a significant number of computing centers and on the majority of the larger computers. Its area of application is perhaps best defined by some example problems which are easily programmed in Snobol 4.

1. Count the number of times that the letter H is followed by the letter groups EI, AU, or OU in a particular chapter of a book.
2. Count the average number of prepositions per sentence that occur in *War and Peace*.
3. Read information of the type

   07128 JOHN PAUL JONES, AGE 63, JAN. 14,1972, 497,X

   and print it out in the format

   JONES, J.P., NO. = 07128, 1972-14-JAN., 63 = AGE, X***497.
4. Analysis of statements in a programming language (for example, Fortran) in preparation for language translation.

Some sample Snobol statements are given in Figure 8–16.

Statement 1 in Figure 8–16 assigns the variable DIGIT the character string 0123456789. The second statement is the standard READ and INFO takes on the value of the next record (normally a card) at the input unit. The third statement has five parts as follows:

```
DIGIT = '0123456789'

BASIC = INPUT

BASIC ANY(DIGIT) . LABEL LEN(3) . KEYWORD REM . REST

EXECUTE = 'LET' | 'GOT' | 'FOR'

TEST KEYWORD EXECUTE = KEYWORD 'EXECUTABLE' : F(TEST2) S(ANALYSIS)
```

FIGURE 8–16. Five types of statements in Snobol 4.

INFO	name of a character string to examine. (Might be as in problem (d) mentioned above).
ANY(DIGIT) . NUMB	Any leading digits are assigned to the variable NUMB. The period is the assignment operator.
BREAK(",") . NAME	Everything up to the first comma is assigned to NAME.
LEN(1)	One character (the comma) is examined and nothing done with it.
REM . REST	The remainder of INFO is assigned to REST. REM is a Snobol operator.

The fourth group of statements build up a pattern of a valid date. First JAN is defined to be any one of three ways to write January. Then MONTH is defined to be any one of JAN, FEB or DEC. We assume that FEB and DEC are previously defined similarly to JAN and, in a real application, we would have 12 rather than three months. Finally DATE is defined to be the pattern of a MONTH followed by two groups of digits separated by a comma. With a little more effort one can require the first group to have 1 or 2 digits and the second group to have 2 or 4 digits.

The final statement is labeled TEST and the character string REST is examined. If the pattern DATE is found, it is replaced by *DATE*. A transfer is then made to the label ANALYSIS. This transfer is indicated by S(ANALYSIS) which might be read "if the pattern match *succeeds* then go to ANALYSIS". If a pattern match is not found, (the matching *fails*) then a transfer to TEST2 is made.

```
         LETTERS = 'ABCDEFGHIJKLMNOPQRSTUVWXYZ'

         ONE     = LEN(1) . CHAR

         ONECHAR = NOTANY(LETTERS) . TEMP   ONE NULL . TEMP

READ     OUTPUT  = INPUT                          : F(COUNT)

         DATA    = DATA OUTPUT                    : (READ)

COUNT    DATA ONECHAR =                           : F(TABULATE)

         $CHAR   = IDENT(TEMP) $CHAR + 1          : (COUNT)

TABULATE         OUTPUT =

TABLETTERS       LETTERS ONE =                    : F(END)

                 OUTPUT = '     ' $CHAR ' ' CHAR : (TABLETTERS)

END
```

FIGURE 8–17. A sample Snobol 4 program to read some data (text), count the number of times each letter appears, and to print the data with a frequency table for the letters.

If these statements are applied to the line in application D above, the resulting variable values are

NUMB = 07128
NAME = JOHN PAUL JONES
REST = AGE 63,*DATE*,497,X

Snobol 4 has not been explained enough here to understand the details of the program in Figure 8–17, but a few remarks are in order. The third statement defines a pattern which is one character and that character is assigned to TEMP if it is not a letter, otherwise TEMP is the null string and the one character is assigned to CHAR. The next two statements read the data, form it into one string, and print it back out. The next two statements pick one character from DATA, blank it out of DATA and if TEMP is null (that is, if the character is a letter) one is added to the variable whose name is $CHAR. Thus A is the count of the A's, and so forth. If CHAR = X, then $CHAR is the variable whose name is X. This type of operation does not exist in most languages, but is very convenient here. Once the DATA string is gone, the table is printed. Typical output of this program would be:

ABOUT A HUNDRED BILLION HUMAN BEINGS HAVE WALKED THE
PLANET EARTH SINCE THE DAWN OF TIME AND THIRTY
GHOSTS STAND BEHIND EVERY HUMAN NOW ALIVE.

12 A
 4 B
and so forth

8—4 The Moron Language

8–4.1 Introduction

This appendix explains how to use the Moron simulator. This simulator is a Fortran program which reads Moron instructions and carries them out just as the Moron would. This Fortran program may be obtained from the authors or by writing the Computer Science Editor of Holt, Rinehart and Winston, Inc. It is assumed that the reader has read the general description of the Moron in this chapter. The Moron simulator provides for 1000 slots in its memory. This is a very specialized example of simulation. Chapter 14 presents a broad range of examples of the simulation concept.

8–4.2 Instructions

All instructions (and numbers) must appear in the *first 25 columns* of a card. Otherwise, the columns have no special significance. The instruction format is

ADDRESS, (INSTRUCTION, ADDRESS)

The first address is where (slot number) this instruction goes. The second address is that upon which the instruction operates. Both of these addresses must be between 1 and 1000.

The instructions are listed below. For more details see Section 8–1.4.

Arithmetic Instruction

ADD, XXX   SUB, XXX   MPY, XXX   DIV, XXX

Testing and Control Instructions

TRA, XXX   TZE, XXX   TPL, XXX   TMI, XXX   STP

SRI, XXX   (Start Reading Instructions at XXX)

Manipulation Instructions

CLA, XXX   STO, XXX   OUT, XXX

8–4.3 Numbers and Comments

The numbers may be written in fixed or floating point with or without exponent. The exponent has 1 or 2 digits with or without sign. The numbers are in columns 1 to 25 in the form

ADDRESS, NUMBER

Typical examples to place the number twelve at address 101 are

101,12	101, 12.	101, 12.E0	101, 12.0E0
	101, 12E+0	101, 1.2E+1	101, 1.2E+01
	101, .0012E+4	101, 120E−1	101, 1200.00E−02

Comments may be placed to the left of any number or instruction with a separating comma or anyplace beyond column 25.

RETURN HERE, 12, (CLA, 8)   START LOOP

8–4.4 Operational Characteristics

The arithmetic is performed with the same limits as the Fortran system that the simulator uses.

There are a number of diagnostics possible while the Moron is trying to read instructions. This is not true of actual machine languages, but is included to aid students. Any instruction that cannot be interpreted by the Moron is ignored.

There are no diagnostics during execution and the program will run until a STP is encountered or until some illegal condition of the operating system or Fortran is reached (for example, excessive time, excessive overflows or underflows, invalid array addresses).

The Moron cannot generate invalid addresses itself, but it is possible for invalid operations to be obtained. These invalid operations may cause the Fortran simulator to attempt to transfer to nonexistent or invalid addresses.

Address modification if possible simply by adding a number to the corresponding instruction; for example, suppose a program contains

```
8, 12.
10, (STO, 102)
```

The instructions

```
25, (CLA, 10)
26, (ADD, 8)
27, (STO, 10)
```

change the instruction at address 10 to (STO, 114).

8–4.5 Use

The Moron simulator should be placed in the Fortran library. Then a Moron program can be executed by the following:

```
*** ID CARD, ETC. ***
    CALL MORON     }
    STOP           }   Fortran Program
    END            }
*** DATA FOLLOWS CARD ***
    1, 12,3        }
    2, 6.8         }
    3, (CLA, 1)    }
    4, (MPY, 2)    }   Moron Program
      . . .        }
    SRI, 3         }
```

The output of the program is of the form

```
                 MORON PROGRAM

          1, 12.3        )
          2, 6.8         |
          3, (CLA,1)     }      Moron Program
             . . .       |
          SRI, 3         )

    13 CONTAINS 0.12345678 E+1   )
    27 CONTAINS 0.60000000 E+1   |
       . . .                     }   Moron Output
   142 CONTAINS 0.87654321 E-1   )
```

There is an additional column of output on the left which is the contents of the memory slots printed out in ordinary Fortran number format (E format for numbers, I format for instructions).

8–4.6 Example Programs

Four example programs are shown below. The first two are different forms of the same program to compute 6! by multiplying 6·5·4·3·2.

```
        MORON PROGRAM
     2,2
     3,3
     4,4
     5,5
     6,6
     10, (CLA,2)
     11, (MPY,3)
     12, (MPY,4)
     13, (MPY,5)
     14, (MPY,6)
     15, (STO,7)
     16, (OUT,7)
     17, (STP)
       SRI, 10
      7 CONTAINS 0.7200000E 03
```

```
              MORON PROGRAM
          2       , 2.
           3      , 3.0
             4    , 40E−1
              5   , 50E−1
               6  , .006E+3
               10, (CLA,2)
               11, (MPY,3)
COMMENT, 12,(MPY,4)
          IN       , 13,(MPX,5)
        HERE    , 14,(MPY,6)
               15, (STO,7)
               16, (OUT,7)
               17, (STP)
               18, (SRI,10)
                7 CONTAINS 0.71999998E 03
```

The third program computes 30! by setting up a simple iteration loop. One can compute K! by changing the contents of 3 to K. The output is

```
            MORON PROGRAM
               1,1
  COUNT,2,1
       K      ,3,30
            10,(CLA,2)
            11,(ADD,1)
            12,(STO,2)
            13,(MPY,9)
            14,(STO,9)
   LOOP,15,(CLA,2)
   TEST,16,(SUB,3)
   HERE,17,(TMI,10)
            18,(OUT,9)
            19,(STP)
    ANS , 9,1
            SRI,10
                9 CONTAINS 0.26525284E 33
```

The final program generates the arrays X(I) = I and Y(I) = I^2 for I = 1 to 60. These are placed in locations 101 to 160 and 201 to 260 and the computation is made by modifying the addresses in instructions 21 and 23. The program for this is in locations 20 through 35. The second part of the program also uses address modification to add these two arrays and print the results out. This part is in locations 50 to 70. Three variables are in locations 1, 2, and 4 which contain the numbers 1,61 and the counter used. The equivalent Fortran program is

```
      INTEGER X(60),Y(60)
      REAL Z(60)
      DO 10 I = 1,60
      X(I) = I
   10 Y(I) = I*I
      DO 20 I = 1,60
      Z(I) = X(I)+Y(I)
   20 PRINT 600, I,Z(I)
  600 FORMAT( I10,9H CONTAINS, E16.8)
      STOP
      END
```

MORON PROGRAM (Complete Output NOT Given)

```
         1,1                       CHANGE,56,(STO,50)
         2,61                      50    ,57,(CLA,51)
BUILD   ,20,(CLA,4)                51    ,58,(ADD,1)
ARRAYS,21,(STO,101)                52    ,59,(STO,51)
X(I)    ,22,(MPY,4)                53    ,60,(CLA,52)
Y(I)    ,23,(STO,201)                     61,(ADD,1)
         26,(STO,4)                       62,(STO,52)
         24,(CLA,4)                       63,(CLA,53)
         25,(ADD,1)                       64,(ADD,1)
         27,(SUB,2)                ***   , 65,(STO,53)
TEST    ,28,(TZE,50)                      66,(CLA,4)
         29,(CLA,21)                      67,(SUB,1)
MOD     ,30,(ADD,1)                       68,(STO,4)
21      ,31,(STO,21)                      69,(SUB,1)
AND     ,32,(CLA,23)               TEST  ,70,(TPL,50)
23      ,33,(ADD,1)                       71,(STP)
        ,34,(STO,23)                  4,1
         35,(TRA,20)                 SRI,20
ADD     ,50,(CLA,101)                 301 CONTAINS 0.20000000E 01
        ,51,(ADD,201)                 302 CONTAINS 0.59999999E 01
X+Y     ,52,(STO,301)                 303 CONTAINS 0.12000000E 02
        ,53,(OUT,301)                 304 CONTAINS 0.20000000E 02
***     ,54,(CLA,50)                  305 CONTAINS 0.30000000E 02
         55,(ADD,1)                   306 CONTAINS 0.41999999E 02
                                      307 CONTAINS 0.55999999E 02
                                      308 CONTAINS 0.82000000E 02
                                                and so on
```

9

Computer Systems

The introduction of higher-level languages really requires that a "system" be made for operating the computer. However, systems programming would be required even if there were no higher-level languages. The fact is that by 1960 computers had become so fast that the analogy with the "instantaneous" desk calculator became valid again. Recall that we started by saying that an instantaneous desk calculator would not be too valuable because most of the time is spent in entering numbers into the keyboard and copying down the results. The same situation had been reached with computers except now a multiplication or division is replaced by the solution of an entire problem.

This does not mean that all problems were solved so quickly, but a large number of real and interesting problems could be solved in a few seconds. For these problems it took much more time to read in the program, push the start button, and write out the answers than it took to compute the solution. Just as before, a means of doing these things at electronic speeds is required to exploit effectively the computational speed available.

9—1 Systems Programming and the Operating System

The words *systems programming* refer to all of the programs and algorithms required to make the computing system work. This includes the algorithms for language translation, the algorithms for scheduling work on the computer, the programs to "push the start button," the programs to get the programs in and

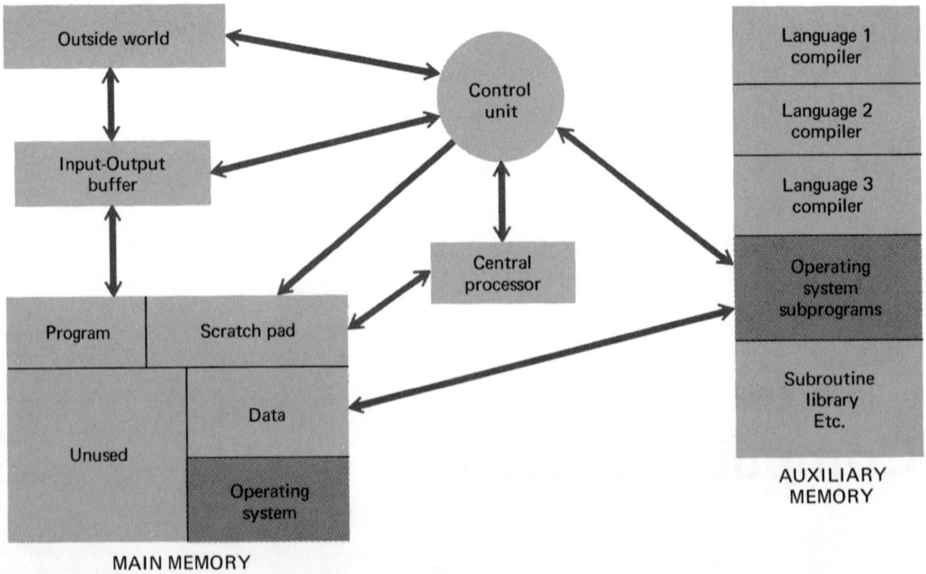

***FIGURE 9–1.** The organization of a typical computer system under the control of an operating system.*

the answers out, and the many other chores that need to be done. The organization of the computer system became more complicated than for the simple computers and is illustrated by the schematic of Figure 9–1.

A general view of such a computer system is shown in Figure 9–2.

9–1.1 Operating System

The programs that oversee the whole operation make up the monitor system, operating system, or executive system. This system has several functions, which include:

1. Coordination of different memory devices
2. Supply of auxiliary programs (for example, compilers, subroutines)
3. Control of the input-output devices
4. Change of representations of information (number formats, and so on) for input-output
5. Allocation of charges for computer usage
6. Scheduling and execution of the programs
7. Communication with the computer operator
8. Overall control of the computer system.

We see that the operating system uses part of the main memory even while a typical program is being executed. However, an operating system is often a very large program that would more than fill the normal main memory by itself. The computer system requires an auxiliary memory to keep most of the operating system's subprograms. They are brought into the main memory by the system when they are needed.

The main memory of a computer system of this type typically varies between 10,000 and 65,000 words. The most common size is 32,000 words. At first glance this seems like ample space, but recall that programs in a rudimentary language like machine language require a very large number of statements. Furthermore, many problems manipulate a large number of variables, both from data and from intermediate calculations. Thus, problems that require most of the main memory are not at all rare.

The typical range of size for compilers is from 12,000 to 50,000 words, and operating systems run from 25,000 to 100,000 words. This means that the 32,000 word memory which originally looked big is actually seen to be fairly small. Thus an *auxiliary memory* is required. There are two differences between the main memory and the auxiliary memory. One is speed; it takes much longer to retrieve something from the auxiliary memory. The other is that the control unit usually cannot directly manipulate words and instructions in auxiliary memory. They must be brought into the main memory first.

We might ask why there are two different kinds of memory since all of that space is required. The answer is that fast memory is one of the most expensive parts of a computer. The things stored in the auxiliary memory are,

FIGURE 9–2. A general view of Control Data 6600 computer system. It was the most powerful computer in the world when it was introduced. (Courtesy Control Data Corp.)

presumably, less frequently used, and thus the slower speed or access time for them does not reduce the efficiency too much. Furthermore, many of the things stored there are large blocks which are brought into the main memory as a whole. This transfer can be accomplished efficiently because searching is required only for the beginning of the block. Once the first word is located, then all the others are right in line to be retrieved without additional searching. This is particularly easy to visualize in the case of magnetic tapes. Typical examples of such blocks are compilers, subroutine libraries, and other pieces of the operating system.

The four principal types of auxiliary memory are magnetic tapes, magnetic disks, magnetic drums, and slow core memories. A group of magnetic-tape units is shown in Figure 9–3. There are two reels, and the tape passes over the reading head as it is spooled from one reel to another. A small magnetic disk pack unit is shown in Figure 9–4. The disks are similar to phonograph records except that the information is recorded by magnetic means rather than by grooves. There are reading heads on arms for each disk. Some disk memories are much larger than the one shown in Figure 9–4. A schematic diagram of a drum is shown in Figure 8–4. A slow core memory is similar to the main memory except it is less expensive, and the time required to retrieve a word is somewhat longer. A slow core memory is usually random access like the main memory.

The *subroutine library* is where the built-in procedures of various languages are kept. When we write cos(x) in some language (say Fortran) a program must be provided by something from someplace to compute cos(x). Note that

***FIGURE 9–3.** A set of magnetic tape units. They function both as part of the auxiliary and as part of the input-output buffer. (Courtesy IBM Corp.)*

FIGURE 9–4. ***A small disk pack unit. These disks are easily exchanged so that this unit may function as part of the input-output buffer as well as part of the auxiliary memory.***

cos(x) is not found from a table of values, but it is computed by an algorithm. It is the combination of the operating system and the compiler which recognizes that this algorithm is needed, locates where it is stored, and brings it to the program when it is needed. The subprogram library may be quite limited or it may contain hundreds of subprograms of various sizes. It depends on the particular computer system and the local installation. This library may contain many subprograms that are not standard procedures in any language. They are useful general-purpose programs placed there for everyone's use.

The operating system controls the input-output devices attached to the main computer. This control is required because the system is the only thing that "knows" what is going on inside the computer. Thus it knows when more data or more programs should be read in and when some answers should be sent out. There is another facet of input-output that the operating system handles: It changes the representation of various kinds of information needed during input-output. Numbers inside the computer are normally in a form such as

100101110001101101101011100

Depending on the particular situation, this number could represent 129,6378, or 21,397,163, or MAXIT. Furthermore, the number 129,6378 might also be written as $.1296378*10^2$. The computer input receives all of these kinds of things, and their representation must be changed to a representation suitable for the computer. This process is more complicated than it appears at first glance, and the algorithms that accomplish it require several thousand statements in machine language.

Since the operating system oversees the computer operation, it knows how long a particular problem runs on the computer. Thus it normally keeps track of the charges for computer usage. This part of the system is usually called the *accounting routine*.

Even though the operating system has overall control of the computer system, it sometimes needs to receive instructions from the operator. Similarly, when something goes wrong, the operating system reports this to the operator. One should keep in mind that the operating system does not really "act" in an independent sense. It is simply a large and complex algorithm for the control of a computer system. The effectiveness of this algorithm depends essentially on the people who constructed it. It is certainly no more resourceful than the people who created the system. In fact, it is probably several orders of magnitude less resourceful than these people. It makes up for this lack of resourcefulness by being very fast and being able to examine exhaustively a very large number of possibilities in a simple-minded way.

It is noteworthy that the operating system is designed to provide services for the computer user. Its job is to do much of the routine record keeping, button pushing, and program manipulation. The role of the operating system is shown in Figure 9–5, where it is visualized as an "executive" in charge of the computer.

9–1.2 The Role of the Operating System

The "executive" inside the computer has many duties and is busy keeping everything coordinated and running.

It examines each job as it passes through. It reads the various things that are to be done and then does them. It returns to the conveyor belt the original job plus any additional output requested by the user or produced by the simple computer. Note that the "executive" does not control the "moron" inside the simple computer, but only supplies work for him.

The executive is similar to the moron in that it does only what is on the written instructions. However, it is much more capable than the moron, and one can ask it to do more complicated things. Not only does it respond to messages from the outside, but it also receives messages sent out of the simple computer. Such messages are sent out, for example, when the moron gets hopelessly confused or when the compilers are inside the simple computer and want something.

9–2 Batch Processing Systems

One manner of operation of the computer system is called *batch processing*. The input buffer is basically a system that collects programs to be run on the computer. It saves them up (in various ways) until it has a "batch" ready. This

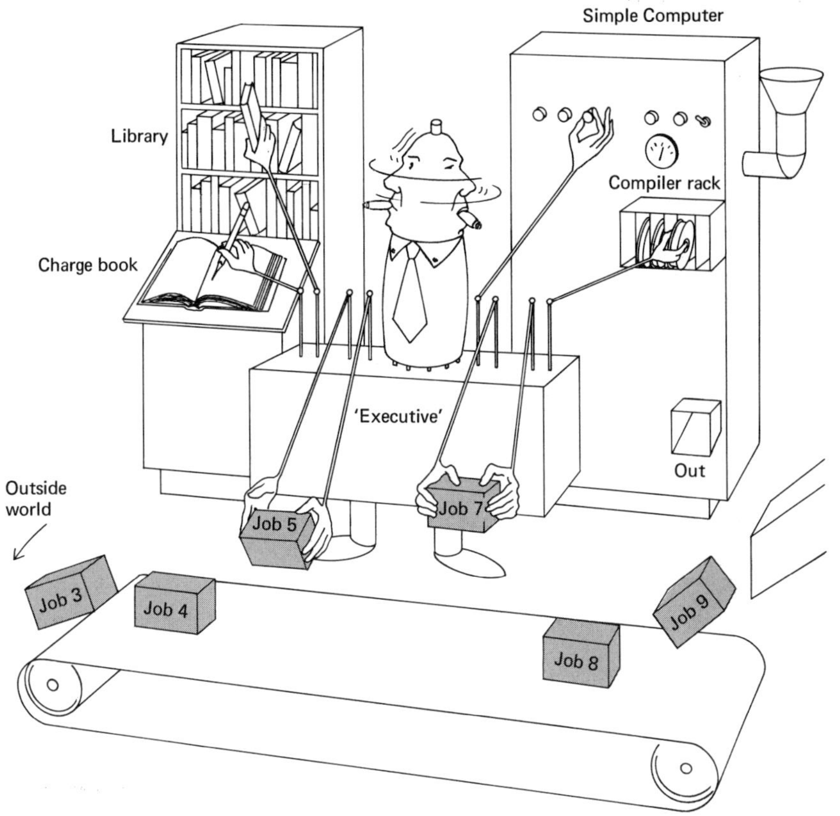

FIGURE 9–5. Schematic illustration of the "executive" of a computer system. He is kept busy running and coordinating the various components of the computer system.

batch is in a form that can be rapidly transmitted to the computer. Once the batch is ready, it is fed into the computer and each program in the batch is run. When the batch is finished, there should be another batch collected, ready to be processed.

The jobs to be run in a particular batch are processed sequentially. They may be visualized as all lined up as in the following schematic diagram:

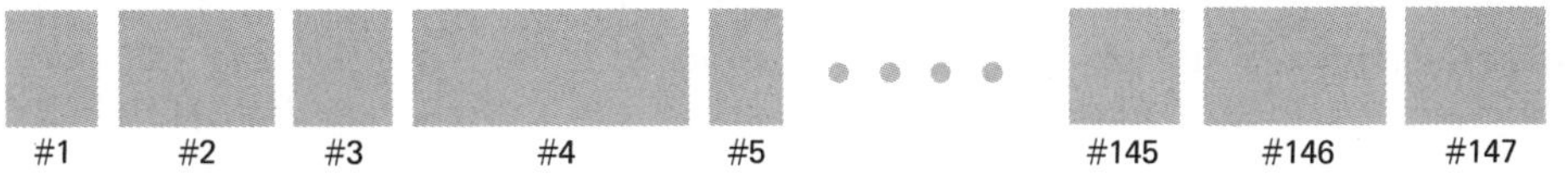

Each of these boxes represents a program to be executed by the computer. In addition to the programs to be executed, there are normally instructions for the operating system. For example, the system is usually told in what language a program is written since most large systems accept several languages. Presumably it could read the first part of the program and discover the language itself, but this does not seem to be very efficient.

The information given to the system includes things such as:

1. The user's name
2. The charge account for the job
3. Nonstandard input devices used
4. Type of output and limits on the amount of each
5. Limit on the execution time
6. Language of the program
7. Nonstandard output devices used.

The system accepts this information and uses it in executing and monitoring the job.

It is instructive to see what a typical system does for a program that is written in a higher-level language. Such a program is often referred to as the *source program* or source deck. The system receives something like this:

```
$    Name John J. Doe
$    Charge to Account 70-4962
$    Output Limits: 30 pages, 100 cards
$    Time Limit: 20 seconds
$    Language = Babel
     Statement 1 in Babel
     Statement 2 in Babel
     ...
     Statement Last in Babel
$    Data for this job follows
*    Data 1
*    Data 2
*    ...
*    Data Last
```

The statements marked by a $ are instructions to the operating system. The statements that are unmarked form a program in the Babel language. The statements marked by an * are data to be used by this program for this particular execution.

As soon as the system sees that a Babel program is coming, it brings the Babel compiler into the main memory. The compiler then begins to read the Babel statements and translates them into machine language. During this compilation, much information is collected about the program in Babel and the equivalent program in machine language. This information includes:

1. The equivalent algorithm in machine language (this algorithm is the *object program* or object deck)
2. The size of the program and its various parts
3. The names and locations of the variables
4. Diagnostics: questionable or unintelligible statements in the Babel program
5. A list of the subprograms needed.

Recall that the compiler may well be larger than the main memory. So this translation process may become very complicated as various parts of the Babel program, the machine-language program, and the compiler are shuffled back and forth between the main memory and the auxiliary memory.

Once the translation is finished, the Babel program (perhaps along with some additional information) is put into the auxiliary memory or sent to an output device. The machine-language program (object program) is brought into the main memory along with the required subprograms from the subroutine library. Then the system has this program executed by the computer. During the execution the program should call for the waiting data. These data may be in an input device, in the auxiliary memory, or already in main memory. When the execution stops, the system sends out any additional output required and sets itself for the next job.

9–2.1 Input-Output Buffer

The problem of getting things into and out of a computer without slowing down the whole process is a difficult one. The basic reason for this is that programs are originally expressed in some nonelectronic form. The manipulation of these physical objects simply cannot be done at speeds comparable with the computing speed available. The input-output buffer is a smaller (presumably cheaper) device that does this physical manipulation for the computer and then presents the problems to the computer at its normal operating speed. In other words, the input-output buffer can communicate with both the outside world and the computer and be efficient in both directions.

The first input-output buffers were in card readers that read the next punched card before the computer requested it. The contents of the card were stored in a small memory before being sent to the main memory of the computer. Present computers still have such special memories (or parts of the main memory reserved for this use). These special memories are also called input-output buffers even though they are only a part of the overall buffering system for input and output.

Although we speak of the input-output buffer as one part of the computer system, it usually consists of a number of different physical devices. A fairly elaborate input-output buffer for a computer system is illustrated in Figure 9–6. From this diagram it is easy to visualize that the input-output facilities for a large computer can be bigger than the computer. Note in Figure 8–1 that the input-output buffer for the IBM 650 consists of a single piece of equipment, a card reader and punch. A number of the pieces seen in Figure 9–2 are parts of the input-output buffer.

Some of the components of the input buffer are shown in Figure 8–3 (keypunch machine), Figure 9–4 (disk pack unit), Figure 9–7 (card reader and punch), and Figure 9–10 (magnetic tape unit). Other card readers and punches are shown in Figures 8–1 and 9–2, and rows of magnetic tapes are shown in Figures 9–2 and 9–3. Note that magnetic tapes and disk packs can be (and are) used either as input-output devices or as auxiliary memory devices.

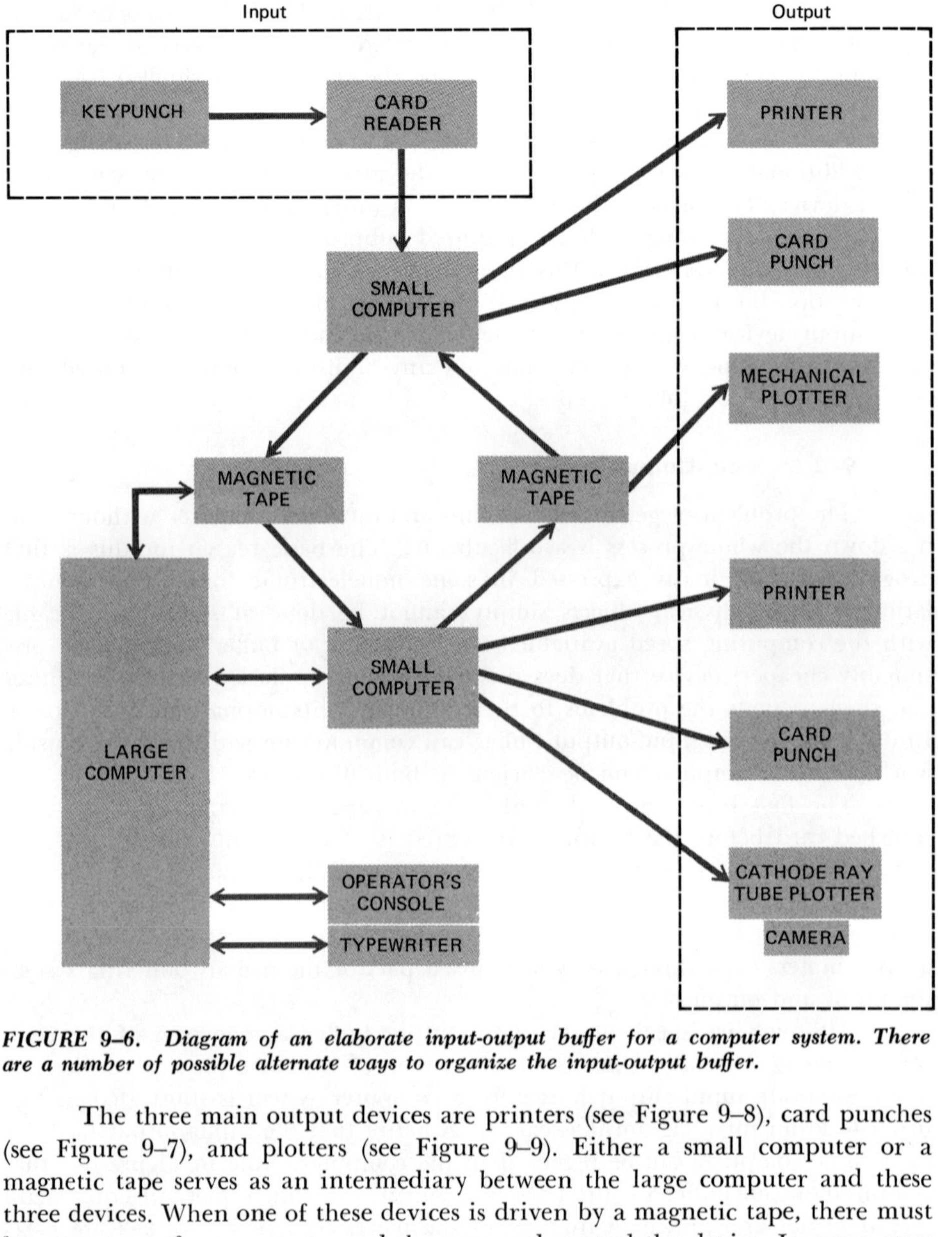

FIGURE 9–6. Diagram of an elaborate input-output buffer for a computer system. There are a number of possible alternate ways to organize the input-output buffer.

The three main output devices are printers (see Figure 9–8), card punches (see Figure 9–7), and plotters (see Figure 9–9). Either a small computer or a magnetic tape serves as an intermediary between the large computer and these three devices. When one of these devices is driven by a magnetic tape, there must be some type of computer to read the tape and control the device. In some cases this computer is an integral part of the output device and is a special-purpose computer (that is, the only thing it does is to read tapes and control the device). A small general-purpose computer is usually used to control printers and card punches. A small computer may operate fast enough to control simultaneously several of these devices. In fact this computer might also be used in the input buffer between card readers and magnetic tapes at the same time it is in the output buffer.

FIGURE 9–8. High speed printers such as this can print from 1000 to 1200 lines per minute. (Courtesy IBM Corp.)

FIGURE 9–7. A card reader and card punch. The cards are read from the stack at the right and punched from the stack at the left. This unit is controlled by a computer. (Courtesy IBM Corp.)

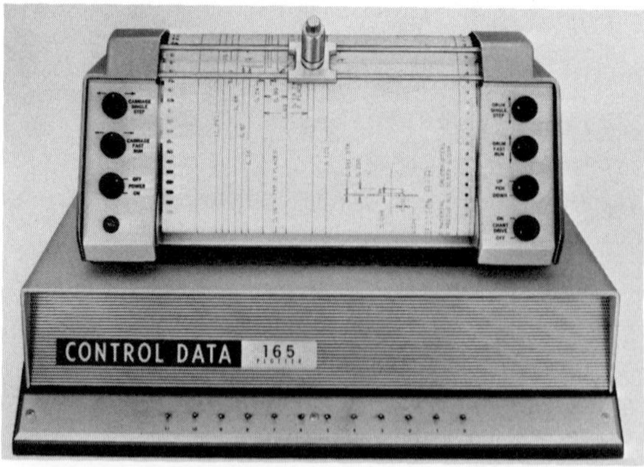

FIGURE 9–9. Front view of a small mechanical plotter. The drawing is done with ink and each letter and line is individually drawn. (Courtesy Control Data Corp.)

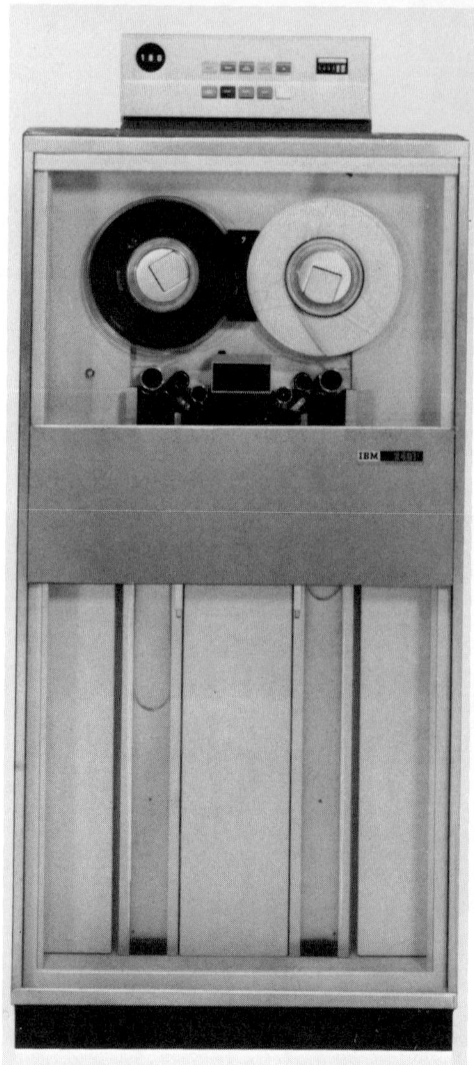

FIGURE 9–10. Front view of a magnetic tape unit showing the reading head in between two reels. The tape can move in both directions, but can be read only while moving forward. (Courtesy IBM Corp.)

Two typical operator's consoles are shown in Figures 9–11 and 9–12. The one in Figure 9–11 appears similar to that of the simple computer in Figure 8–1. The typewriter is the main communication device. This computer may also be directly connected to magnetic tapes, magnetic disks, printers, and card readers and punches. The console in Figure 9–12 is a separate unit, but its functions are basically the same. In the background are a set of magnetic tapes, a mechanical plotter, and other components of the computer system.

In order to see why there are so many devices between the computer and the user, consider Table 9–1. This table contains the range of transmission rates

TABLE 9–1
Transmission rates for various devices

Device	Rate
Coding sheets	10–15 words/minute
Keypunch	5–30 words/minute
Keyboard terminal	5–200 words/minute
Card punch	500–3000 words/minute
Card reader	800–10,000 words/minute
Printer	1,000–25,000 words/minute
Magnetic tape	200,000–1,000,000 words/minute
Magnetic disk	800,000–1,500,000 words/minute
Computer	1,000,000–30,000,000 words/minute
Mechanical plotter	5 minutes per plot
Cathode-ray-tube plotter/camera	5 seconds per plot

***FIGURE 9–11.** The operator's console and typewriter for a medium size computer. Most of the communication is via the typewriter. (Courtesy IBM Corp.)*

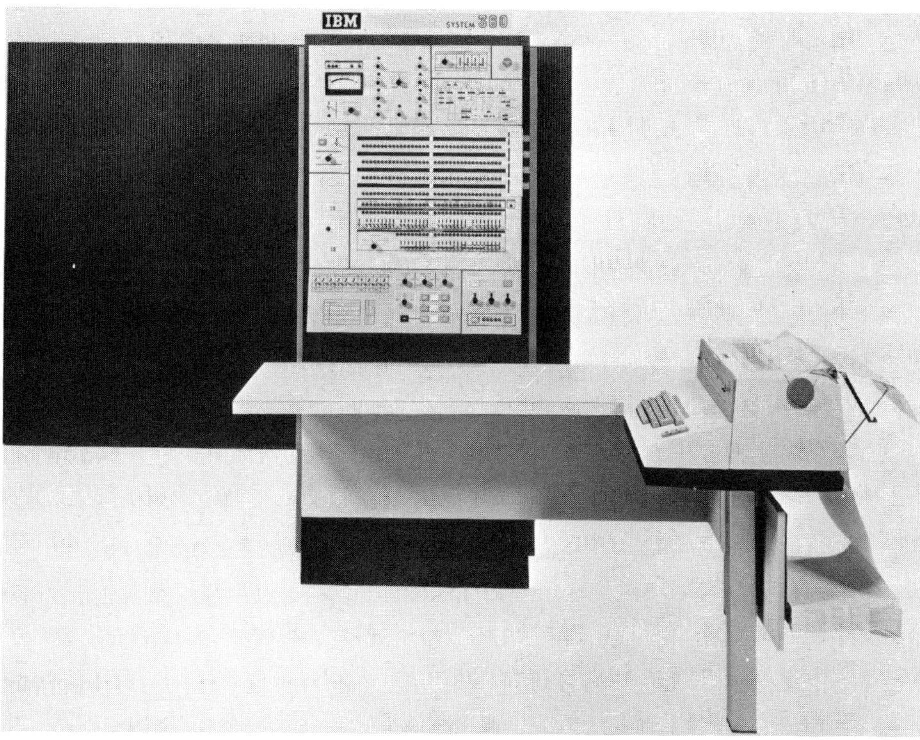

FIGURE 9–12. Operator's Console and general view of a CDC 3800 computer. (Courtesy Control Data Corp.)

for various devices. The words in the computer system are usually all the same size and consist of 32 to 60 binary digits (7 to 15 decimal digits) depending on the computer. The difference between manual and electronic devices is so large that several "layers" of intermediate devices may be present.

The organization of the computer system described in this section results in efficient operation of the computer. The extremely fast central processor is able to run at full speed most of the time without being impeded by the slowness of the outside world. The use of compilers and operating systems introduces a large amount of work for the computer which is only indirectly related to the computation of the solution of a problem. Some of this extra work is simply "overhead" required by a more complex system. Other parts of it (such as compiling) contribute to the efficient use of the computer. Thus, even though there is a considerable reduction in the amount of time spent in computing solutions, the total problem-solving process is much more efficient. This is due to the fact that this computer organization successfully exploits the speed of the central processor.

Despite the efficiency of this organization, there are still two difficulties present. They are:

1. It takes too long to write programs in these higher-level languages.
2. It takes too long in terms of calendar time to solve the problems.

Thus we have increased the efficiency of the computer organization by an order of magnitude, and we still have the original difficulties, namely, input-output and preparation of instructions.

The batch-processing operation of a computer brings into focus an important feature of a computer operation, the *turnaround time*. This is the time that elapses between the time a job is put into the input buffer and the time it is returned to the user in the output buffer. The turnaround time can vary from 10 minutes to several days. It depends on a great variety of factors, but there is one that is crucial. It is the ratio of computing capacity to work load. If this ratio is high (that is, if there is considerable excess-capacity), then very low turnaround times are possible. If the ratio is very close to one (that is, if the computer system is saturated), then very low turnaround times are not possible. In this case the computer is running 24 hours a day, and those jobs run in the middle of the night are almost certain to have been submitted during the day.

To appreciate the importance of calendar time in problem-solving, consider two people with a problem and an algorithm. The first algorithm is short, but it takes 8 runs on the computer to get the program debugged and the problem solved. The second one is longer and it takes 35 runs on the computer to get the program debugged and the problem solved. The 35 runs for the second one includes 8 basic modifications of the algorithm itself.

We consider a computing center with a rather efficient batch-processing system which is operating close to, but not at, full capacity. It takes about 4 days to get the first problem solved. It may take about 1 minute of computer time for these 8 runs. This much computer time may cost from $4 to $10. In many real situations, the user is willing to pay twice or even 10 times this amount if he could get the solution in 4 hours rather than in 4 days. It may be that a project is completely stopped, waiting for the solution of this problem.

It might take as little as 3 or 4 weeks to get the second problem solved. The total amount of computer time may be about 30 or 40 minutes and cost $100 to $300. Again the user may be willing to pay much more if the elapsed time can be substantially reduced. Certainly if 8 basic modifications in the programs are required, it is unreasonable to expect to solve the problem in a few hours. But it is not unreasonable to expect to solve the problem in a few days.

The problem is: How do you organize the computer system in order to accomplish this? Section 9–4 presents some approaches currently under development to solve this particular problem, and more generally, to better exploit the computation speed of computers.

Problems

The following problems require instructions to, or results from, the operating system. The description of the operating system given here is brief, so there is considerable latitude possible in the answers. The main object is to present a reasonable set of instructions, or results, rather than a set correct for an actual system.

9–2.1 You have two jobs, a short one written in Babel, and one long one written in Tranfor. The long one uses a subroutine of J. P. Jones which is in machine language (that is, the Moron can read it directly). The short one only has a little data and printed output, but the long one has a lot of it.

Give a set of instructions for the system in order to get these two jobs run.

9–2.2 You have a program in Algol which does not work and you have no data for it. In order to try to find out what is wrong you want the original program and the translated (or compiled) program in machine language to study. Give a set of instructions for the operating system in order to obtain these things.

9–2.3 You have a friend's program to try out a problem. He says that it will solve the problem in only 30 to 40 minutes instead of the 3 hours your program takes. You are not so sure, but since the charge for computer time comes out of your retirement fund, you want to try it out. So you want to run it a "little while" and see what happens. This program is written in Snowball, and your data are on a special input device called INKwik. Give a set of instructions for the operating system to try out the program this way.

9–2.4 Describe the actions that you think the operating system takes in the following situations:

(a) When it reads the instructions from Problem 9–2.1.
(b) When it reads the instructions from Problem 9–2.2.
(c) When it reads the instructions from Problem 9–2.3.
(d) When a program deck is read-in upside down.
(e) When five cards in the middle of a Babel program turn out to be written in Tranfor.
(f) When a program asks the Moron for a number from storage slot 416,-289,103 and there are only 263,999 slots.

9–3 Natural Programming Languages and Programming in Natural Language

One of the most obvious facts about algorithmic programming languages is that it is easy to make mistakes in writing programs, that is, mistakes in addition to the ones made in algorithm construction because of insufficient analysis or a lack of understanding. These additional mistakes lead directly to an increase in the number of runs through a computer required to solve a problem. It seems reasonable to use languages for programming which are as natural as possible. This means that considerable flexibility is allowed in how a particular statement is written. In certain areas it seems feasible to use natural English for communicating with the computer.

In a nutshell, the objective is to make the computer understand people's language rather than making people understand the computer's language; or even some compromise like an algorithmic programming language. Do not expect the use of these languages to remove all of the difficulties in programming. Even experienced people tend to overlook small (and sometimes large) points in writing programs. This means that several debugging runs can be expected even if the computer does exactly what the programmer has in mind. Furthermore, it takes considerable practice to learn how to "think" in the algorithmic terms required for solving problems with computers.

There is, of course, a price to be paid for the use of natural or nearly natural language. It takes the computer much more effort to translate the program into machine language. From one viewpoint, we might say that the decision on the use of these languages should be based on the efficiency of the translation. In other words, can a computer or a person do it more efficiently? However, it is very difficult to find a measure of efficiency here which is reliable and objective and considers all important factors. It is clear that the cost of computing is going down and the cost of human effort is going up. Thus good efficiency requires that we shift more and more of the work from people onto the computer.

9–4 Direct Access or Conversational Computing

The use of natural, flexible, and easy-to-learn programming languages certainly eases the communication difficulties. Such languages are very desirable with batch processing. However, although the batch-processing operation of a computer system is very efficient from the computer's viewpoint, it might not be so convenient for some users. Thus another organization of the computer system appeared in the middle 1960s.

The principal objective of this organization is to make the input-output system convenient for the user as well as the computer. The input-output buffer is changed so that the user has direct access to the computer. Recall that most users do not generate enough work to use a computer's facilities efficiently. Thus many users are given direct access to the computer simultaneously. The computer is fast enough to work on many problems in a few seconds, and each user gets immediate (it seems) service on his problem.

This is called the *conversational, direct-access, on-line,* or *interactive* mode of operation. The number of users that a particular computer can service depends on its size and speed and the average amount of work requested per user. Smaller and slower computers can efficiently service users whose computation load is not sufficient to justify a large computer. In fact, direct-access operation can be used with only one user connected to a small computer.

Even when many users are directly connected to a single computer, there are two distinct methods of internal operation possible. The first, and simplest, is a modified form of batch processing. The only difference is in the input-output buffer. A typical organization of the computer is given in Figure 9–13.

A simplified description of this type of operation is as follows: The computer is doing batch processing as before. A user is putting in a program at a console. This program is being gathered up by the direct-access input-output buffer. When the program is complete it will be put next in line for batch processing. When the current program is finished, the computer takes the console user's program and runs it. The results are returned to the input-output buffer which, in turn, returns them to the console.

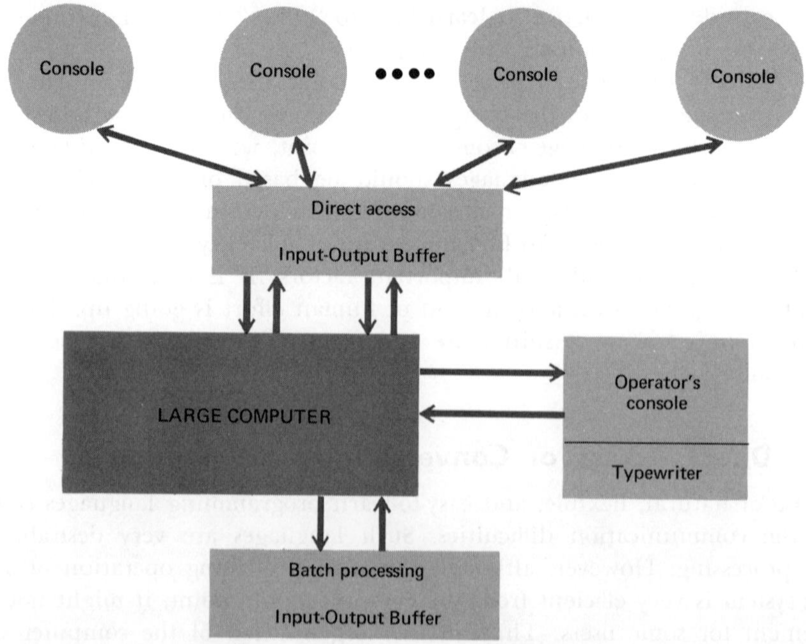

FIGURE 9–13. Schematic diagram of the input-output system for a computer with both batch processing and direct access operation.

One of the keys to the success of this kind of operation is the adequate design of consoles. They range from teletype units (somewhat less versatile than a typewriter), to very elaborate (and expensive) affairs with display (TV) screens, light pens (which allow one to write on TV screens), versatile keyboards, and other devices. Three typical examples are shown in Figure 9–14. A person who uses a keyboard to enter a long program into a computer finds it tedious. This tedium is lessened by having a powerful language so that one can say things in as few statements as possible. It is also lessened in some cases by allowing a combination of direct access and indirect access. Thus a user may submit a problem through the usual batch-processing input and then have it saved inside the computer and run it from the console. In this way he can make minor changes in the program or the data as he sees results. Once he is satisfied with the process, he instructs the computer to give him permanent output (or more extensive output) on the usual batch-processing output devices.

9–5 Time-Sharing Systems

The second, and more complicated, method of internal computer operation is a *time-sharing* mode. This mode of operation is motivated by the following possibility. Suppose there are a hundred users at remote consoles and one of them starts a problem that takes 5 minutes of machine time to finish. Or suppose one of the batch-processing jobs takes this long to run. This means that most of the hundred users are spending much of this 5 minutes waiting. Furthermore, they may have generated enough work that it will take the computer another 5 minutes to get it all cleaned up. Thus, for a period of 10 minutes or so, the users are getting very little done.

It is a trait of human nature that people do not like to sit idle for 10 minutes. Since the purpose of the whole operation is convenient and efficient input-output *for the user*, this situation cannot be allowed to occur often. The solution offered by time sharing is to stop the 5-minute problem after it has run for a very short time and give some computing service to the other users. Then, a little later, the 5-minute problem is run for another short time. These short

(a)

(b)

(c)

FIGURE 9–14. Three consoles for direct access. (a) A simple typewriter design; (b) a keyboard and display scope; (c) an elaborate console. (Courtesy IBM and Control Data Corp.)

periods of time are called *time slices* and may be as short as 0.05 second. This cycle is repeated until the 5-minute problem is finally completed, and it may actually take 10 minutes to an hour to finish the problem. If it is a problem from the batch-processing mode, the time lag is not particularly significant. If it is a problem from a console, then one user must wait much longer in order to allow a hundred others to obtain good service.

The time-sharing mode of operation requires a completely different internal organization of the computer system as well as changes in the physical devices. A possible arrangement is illustrated in Figure 9–15. The organization illustrated is complicated, and yet many essential details have been left out for the sake of simplicity. One of the important points to be made here is that the computer organization is extremely complex for this mode of operation.

In order to help appreciate this organization of the computer, we briefly summarize the function of the main components illustrated in Figure 9–15.

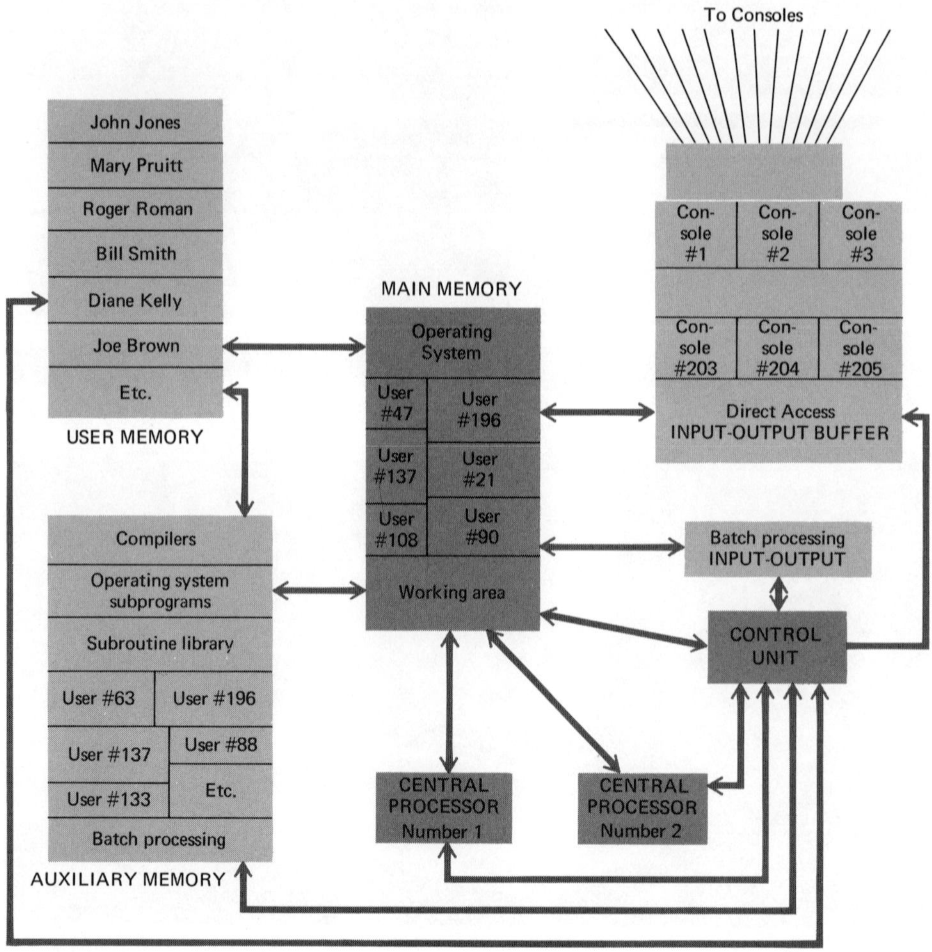

FIGURE 9–15. A possible organization of a time shared, complex computer system.

9–5.1 Direct-Access Input-Output Buffer

The function of this unit is essentially the same as that for the previous mode of operation. Each console has an area assigned in the buffer (at least during operation) and information is received and temporarily held there until some processing is required. This device is, in effect, a special-purpose computer, and it may do some of the very simple processing. For example, it might rewrite each statement received in a more compact form and check to see if it contains illegal characters. When one or more statements are collected and the user wants some computing done, this device sends these statements to the main computer. It then receives the results back from the main computer, puts them in a form suitable for the console, and transmits them to the console.

9–5.2 Batch-Processing Input-Output

This part of the system operates as before and brings the problems to the computer which are submitted for batch processing. Even with 200 consoles, there are times when the main computer would be idle. The jobs submitted for batch processing are run during these idle times and provide a "background" computation load. This load ensures that the computer is being used at all times as well as providing service for those users who want to run a job this way.

9–5.3 Main Memory

This is the main working area of the total memory. The operating system is in part of it, and the remainder is divided among several users. The users are allocated only as much space as they require so as to use this premium memory efficiently. Each job in the main memory is being executed more or less simultaneously; that is, the system is providing each job with small "slices" of time for computation on a rotating basis. With more than one central processor (two are shown in Figure 9–15) there is actual simultaneous execution of instructions. A system with more than one job in the main memory is called a *multiprogramming* system; one with more than one central processor is called a *multiprocessing* system.

9–5.4 Auxiliary Memory

This memory has all of its previous functions plus the storage of problems that have been partially executed. Since the computer is parceling its time out among all the users, it may interrupt a computation in the middle and put it (and all the intermediate results) into the auxiliary memory. It then brings in another problem and works on it for a few moments. Further, only so much of one program is allowed in the main memory at one time, so that larger programs are divided into two parts, one in the main memory and one in the auxiliary memory.

9–5.5 Users' Memory

In addition to the other two memories it is important to have a place where users can save programs for long periods of time (days or even months). This facility is needed, for example, when a user enters a 150-statement program through a console keyboard and has to leave before he finishes running it. Rather than reentering the program the next day, he can have it saved for him in the users' memory. There is room in this memory for each user, and thus it must be very large. A computing center that has a large enough computing load to justify 200 consoles might well need several thousand individual libraries of user programs, which means that this memory must be able to store millions of words. This is an order of magnitude larger than the auxiliary memory, which, in turn, is an order of magnitude larger than the main memory.

9–5.6 Control Unit and Central Processors

The functions of these units are unchanged. The control unit receives instructions from the operating system about the programs and sees that appropriate action is taken. The central processors do the arithmetic, the comparisons, and so forth. They still play the role of the high-speed arithmetic unit originally considered. All of the other parts of the system are to enable us to exploit this tremendous speed.

The time-sharing computer system is so complicated that it is difficult to visualize all that might happen to a particular job as it is processed. It is shuffled many times back and forth between the various devices. During these shufflings it is in various stages of being translated into machine language and then being executed. The normal amount or slice of time allowed a problem when it is in the main memory is 5 to 50 hundredths of a second, so that a job that takes only a second may be transferred many times. A major design problem with this organization is to minimize the "overhead" created by all of this shuffling and manipulation.

There are two new and interesting problems presented by this organization. The first is referred to as *memory protection*. This problem is, essentially, how to keep one user from wiping out another. In the batch-processing mode, the only thing a bad program can affect is itself and the operating system. Since no one else cares if a user ruins his own program and since copies of the operating system are available, little damage can be done. In a time-sharing operation, one user can ruin another's program unless steps are taken to prevent it. The solution is clear; namely, do not allow any operation of a particular user to write anything outside his assigned area. This job could conceivably be given to the operating system, but this solution turns out to be very inefficient for most computers. To do this checking efficiently requires basic changes in electronic devices of the computer.

The second of the problems is the occurrence of duplicate programs in the main memory. Suppose that 10 programs in the main memory all require the logarithm subprogram from the system library. One solution would be to bring

10 copies of it into the main memory and put one copy with each of the 10 programs. Since this wastes space in the main memory, an alternative approach is sometimes used. It is to design the logarithm subprogram so that it can be used simultaneously by all these programs. Such a program is called *re-entrant.* Recall that such a subprogram consists primarily of a set of instructions for computing the logarithm. These instructions can be read by any program. If each of these programs assigns variables and working space for the intermediate results, then each can read the instructions and do the computation in its own area. In this way 10 different programs can be simultaneously computing the logarithms of different numbers using one logarithm subprogram.

If user #93's slice of time is used up while he is in this logarithm subprogram, or any other re-entrant program, then it is possible for the program to start up again in the middle of the computation. Thus all of the intermediate calculations associated with user #93's program are saved. When this program is rescheduled and computations restarted, the program starts reading the instructions in the logarithm subprogram where it left off and uses the intermediate calculations previously made and saved.

There is no doubt that many problems will remain after the above approaches are explored and implemented. The field is changing so fast that one cannot predict with confidence what these problems will be or how they will be attacked. It is clear though that the study and analysis of computer organization is a dynamic process.

10

Sorting and Searching

10–1 Introduction

Information processing is one of the most dynamic segments of computer science and it is based on the ability of computers to reorganize and/or retrieve information. This reorganization and retrieval requires that the original information must be searched in some way. In many applications one takes the information, processes it once for reorganization, and then processes it many, many times to retrieve parts of the information. Thus it is very important that the initial reorganization of the information be such that the retrieval process is quick and efficient. The techniques for reorganizing the information are grouped under the heading of *sorting* and the techniques for retrieving the information are grouped under the heading of *searching*.

The result of a sorting process is to give the information some *structure*. The most familiar structure is the simple, linear ordering or one-dimensional array. For example, the names in the telephone directory are ordered linearly (alphabetized). Think how inconvenient a telephone book would be without this structure. Or consider the frustration of having a telephone book in the order of the telephone numbers rather than the names. Chinese does not have an alphabet, so the telephone books there are ordered by the number of strokes required to print the Chinese characters of a person's name.

There are many information structures much more complex than an ordered array; a few of these are discussed in some detail in Chapter 11. Common examples are two- or three-dimensional arrays of information. For example, a utility company might have its customer information ordered first by district (perhaps containing several counties), then by city, and finally alphabetized. Or a university might have its student information ordered first by school (for example, engineering, business, education, and so on), then by department (for example, economics, industrial management, accounting, and so on), and finally alphabetized. In both cases one has a three-dimensional structure of the information.

Two simple methods of sorting (*bubble sorting* and *radix sorting*) and of searching (*linear search* and *binary search*) are presented in this chapter. There exist many other techniques (often much superior to these) which are standard tools of the professional in information processing.

10—2 Bubble Sorting

The idea behind bubble sorting is quite simple. Assume one has an ordered list and wants to add another item to it. One places the new item at the bottom of the list and lets it rise (like a bubble) to its proper position. As an example, suppose one were alphabetizing names and had the list

Alt
Hull
Mann
Riaz
Ward

and wanted to add the name Lui to this list. The sequence of lists created in the bubble sorting process are:

Alt	Alt	Alt	Alt
Hull	Hull	Hull	Hull
Mann	Mann	Mann	Lui
Riaz	Riaz	Lui	Mann
Ward	Lui	Riaz	Riaz
Lui	Ward	Ward	Ward

We see that at each stage the name Lui is compared with the name just above it. If Lui should go ahead of that name then the two are switched, otherwise Lui is in its proper position and this phase of the bubble sort is finished.

The bubble sort is easy to understand and to program, but it is terribly inefficient for large lists (say those containing more than 40 or 50 elements). Let us estimate just how much effort is likely to be required to order a list of N items using the bubble sort. As a basic unit of effort, we take the comparison and switching of two items. Of course, we do not know exactly how high an item rises in the list, but we expect it to rise about half-way so that if the current list has K items, then about $K/2$ units of effort are required to insert one more item. To completely order a group of N items, we have to insert an item in lists of length $1, 2, 3, \ldots, N-2, N-1$ so that the number of units is about

$$\frac{1}{2}+\frac{2}{2}+\frac{3}{2}+\cdots+\frac{K}{2}+\cdots+\frac{N-2}{2}+\frac{N-1}{2}=\frac{(N-1)(N-2)}{4},$$

where we have used the formula for the sum of the first $N - 1$ integers. If N is large, we may replace this estimate by simply $N^2/4$.

Many lists have several thousand items and then the bubble sort would require several million units of effort to order them. And each unit of effort involves a number (say, 5 to 50 depending on the type of comparison to be made) of actual computer operations. Thus the bubble sort becomes very expensive even with big, fast computers. It is hopeless to use this technique for the really large lists of 100,000 or 1 million items.

While the bubble sort is inefficient, one can do worse. Another simple (and closely related) idea is to use the algorithm for finding the maximum in a group. One finds the maximum of the whole group, removes it, finds the maximum of the remaining group, removes it, and so forth. This technique requires about twice as much effort as the bubble sort.

10–3 Radix Sorting

A much more efficient technique for ordering is *radix sorting*. This technique is explained in detail in Problem 4–2.11 along with an example. The main points are as follows: One has a group of numbers, each with a fixed number K of digits. One wishes to obtain a list ordered from largest to smallest. We visualize 10 pockets of a machine (such electromechanical sorters are common), one for each of the digits 0, 1, 2, . . ., 9. The method proceeds as follows:

1. Examine the right-most digit of each number and place it in the pocket corresponding to this digit.
2. After step 1 is finished for the entire list, create a new list by placing the contents of the 0's pocket on top, then that of the 1's pocket next, and so forth, with the 9's pocket on the bottom.
3. Repeat steps 1 and 2 for the digit immediately to the left of the digit just examined. Do this K times and the final list obtained is ordered.

This technique is implemented in a computer program by using 10 arrays corresponding to the 10 pockets along with one larger array which contains the original set of numbers.

We now estimate the effort involved for this scheme. One basic ingredient is the extraction of a digit and placing the number in the original group of numbers, then this ingredient is performed N times before one proceeds to step 2. In step 2 one must move all of the numbers back to the original array in order to repeat the process. Each of these stages is repeated K (the number of digits) times. Thus, the total effort is $N * K$ units where one unit consists of a digit extraction and examination plus two moves of the number. This unit of effort is about the same as that for the bubble sort.

The use of this method for a set of 5000 numbers of 8 digits requires then $8 * 5000 = 40{,}000$ units of effort. By comparison, we expect the bubble sort method to require about $5000 * 5000/4 = 8{,}000{,}000$ units of effort or 150 times as much.

Note that the absolute minimum amount of effort to order N items is at least N. Clearly one must examine every item at least once and this already amounts to N examinations.

In order to obtain maximum efficiency in sorting one must normally consider any (and all) special properties of the items involved and of the computer system used. For example, the radix sort requires exactly the minimum possible effort in order to sort N 1-digit numbers (if one ever wanted to do that). There are many common situations where radix sorting is not particularly efficient, primarily because the number of digits in an item is large. Note that radix sorting is not restricted to numbers, one can use it for alphabetizing by using 26 instead of 10 pockets.

Most computer centers have one (or several) subroutines for sorting available in their library. These subroutines are normally efficient and easy to use for routine problems.

10–4 Linear and Binary Searching

There is considerable discussion of this topic in Chapter 3 under the heading of table lookup. In that particular case the object is to locate the known table entry (or argument) in order to obtain the corresponding value. It is pointed out that straightforward linear searching (that is, starting at one end of the list and searching item by item toward the other end) is inefficient in ordinary circumstances. The point is made there and is stressed again here that a tailor-made scheme for a particular situation might be very much better (and much different) than a scheme that is normally best in a general, randomly selected situation.

The discussion of binary search in Chapter 3 is in the context of using the arithmetic IF of Fortran and thus is slightly different from the usual binary search. The usual binary search considers a list of N items that are linearly ordered numerically, alphabetically, or in some other way. The idea is as follows:

1. Choose the middle item [the $(N/2)$th one] and see if the desired item comes before or after it.
2. If it comes before this middle item, discard (or ignore) the last half of the list and return to step 1 with the original list replaced with the first half. If it comes after this middle item, return to step 1 with the last half of the list and discard the first half.
3. Repeat steps 1 and 2 until the desired item is located.

In order to estimate the amount of work in binary search we must know how many times we must halve N (the number of items) in order to have just one item left. This number is approximately $\log_2(N)$, a few values of which are listed below.

N	2	4	8	16	64	100	1000	4096	10,000	100,000	1,000,000
$\log_2(N)$	1	2	3	4	5	6.65	9.98	12	13.3	16.6	19.8

Of course one cannot do a fractional number of halvings, but this table gives a good guide as to the number required. Thus, for $N = 100$ we require seven halvings rather than 6.65. The significant point is that the number $\log_2(N)$ grows very slowly with N. Thus, it takes only twice as much effort to locate an item in a list of one million as it does to locate it in a list of one thousand!

There are minor annoyances that occur when the list does not divide exactly in half (which is most of the time). However, a program to take care of all the details is quite simple in Fortran. Let the given list of items be in the array X(K) for K = 1 to NX. We are given the value XLOOK which we wish to find. We introduce two indices NHI and NLO which are the upper and lower indices of the range we search. We assume that the X(I) are numbers so that ordinary Fortran arithmetic can be used for the comparisons. If words ordered alphabetically were involved, then the comparison statements might be more complicated, but the binary search strategy would remain the same.

```
C     NHALF IS ABOUT THE BASE 2 LOGARITHM OF NX PLUS 1
      NHALF = 1.44*ALOG(FLOAT(NX))+2.
      NLO = 1
      NHI = NX
      DO 20 K = 1,NHALF
      MID = (NHI + NLO)/2
      IF( XLOOK .GT. X(MID))    GO TO 10
      NHI = MID
         GO TO 20
   10 NLO = MID+1
   20 CONTINUE
```

This particular code involves the idiosyncrasies of integer arithmetic in Fortran and requires one more halving than is theoretically necessary. When the exit is made from the DO loop we have NHI = NLO equal to the index of XLOOK, that is, XLOOK = X(NHI).

10–5 Computed Index Searching and Hash Coding

Recall from the discussion in Chapter 3 of table lookup that we concluded the best situation is where one can somehow compute the position of the desired item. For example, consider a table of ages from 30 to 100 in steps of 5 years. Given an age of 55 we know that 55 is the sixth entry because

$$6 = \frac{55 - 30}{5} + 1 = \frac{55 - 25}{5}.$$

If the entries in the table are in an array we can pick out the correct item by using the index 6 and without any searching whatsoever. Recall that the computer has the facility to retrieve an indexed item from an array without searching. This fact is mentioned because some features of Fortran seem more efficient but are, in fact, often translated into machine language in a manner to lose this apparent efficiency.

This approach is very efficient and very simple for equally spaced numerical information. The question is how to adapt to other types of linearly ordered information. For concreteness, let us consider the problem of obtaining a person's telephone number from a telephone directory. Specifically we want to divide the directory into 10 parts and to be able to calculate which part should be searched. The searching of each part would be done with perhaps binary or linear searching, but it is crucial that the initial choice of the correct part *not* involve any searching.

One might decide to divide the directory into 10 equal parts and one discovers that the following 9 names come very close to giving an exact division:

BRABO, CROW, FORD, HEIN, LYNCH,
NAZAR, RETT, SLOSS, VENN

However, given a name, say JONES, PAUL S., how does one determine where it falls in this set without searching? The answer is that there is no simple way to do it.

On the other hand, there is an approach that does almost as well and that is based on considering the names to be numbers of a peculiar type. First we associate each of the letters with a number according to its position in the alphabet:

$$A \sim 0, B \sim 1, C \sim 2, \ldots, X \sim 23, Y \sim 24, Z \sim 25.$$

Then we visualize any word as a decimal number to the base 26. For example,

$$\text{BABY} = (1,0,1,24) = \frac{1}{26} + \frac{0}{(26)^2} + \frac{1}{(26)^3} + \frac{24}{(26)^4},$$

$$\text{BED} = (1,4,3) \quad = \frac{1}{26} + \frac{4}{(26)^2} + \frac{3}{(26)^3}.$$

In this way we have a simple association between words and numbers. Recall that letters are represented numerically inside a computer anyway (although not exactly this way) and in fact it is not hard to make this association internally in a computer. This interpretation of words as numbers places each word in some position between zero and 1 and we can directly compute this position. Table 10–1 gives 9 names that are approximately at the positions .1, .2, .3, . . ., .8, .9 and which divide the set of all words into 10 parts. For comparison purposes, they are placed alongside the 9 names that divide the telephone directory into 10 equal parts. We see from Table 10–1 that this calculated index scheme divides the directory into 10 parts which (for a directory of 61,000 names) range in size from 1880 to 11,125. This lack of equal size in the 10 groups formed is caused by the irregular frequency distribution of the names of people. We conclude that while this computed index approach is beneficial, it still needs improvement. Before we illustrate how to improve upon it, we consider in more detail how to use this approach.

TABLE 10–1
Names (and their positions in a directory of 61,000) that divide a telephone book into 10 equal parts (right) and into 10 parts equally spaced in the numerical interpretation of names (left)

Position	*Name*	*Name*	*Position*
5150	BOONE	BRABO	6100
15250	EBAT	CROW	12200
21600	GRUEN	FORD	18300
30375	JIMENEZ	HEIN	24400
33025	MAAS	LYNCH	30500
40250	OPAL	NAZAR	36600
44525	REED	RETT	42700
55650	TUCKER	SLOSS	48800
59120	WIESS	VENN	54900

The essential ingredient of this approach is an array (11 elements in this case) of positions corresponding to the calculated partition names. Let us call this array NDEX(K) for K = 1 to 11 and we have the case of Table 10–1.

NDEX(1) = 0	NDEX(5) = 30375	NDEX(8) = 44525
NDEX(2) = 5150	NDEX(6) = 33025	NDEX(9) = 55650
NDEX(3) = 15250	NDEX(7) = 40250	NDEX(10) = 59120
NDEX(4) = 21600		NDEX(11) = 61000

Given a name we first obtain its numerical value as outlined above. Let us call that number VALUE and then the location of the given name is between NDEX(KV) and NDEX(KV + 1) where

KV = 10. * VALUE

Note that conversion of KV to an integer is in effect.

The division of the telephone directory into 10 parts was chosen here for simplicity of illustration. However, a little reflection shows that (for a directory of 61,000 items) one should have many more parts. By using an array NDEX with 301 elements one can divide the directory into 300 parts and then the average length of the directory segment to be searched is only about 200 names. Note that this reduction from an average of 6100 names to 200 names does not require *any* additional computation. The only price one pays for increasing the number of parts is the memory space devoted to the array NDEX. This memory space is not entirely free of cost, so there is some optimum number of parts which depends on the particular application at hand.

The term *hash-coding* refers to a large variety of schemes to avoid the problem we had above of unequal sizes in the parts of the directory. The *coding* portion of the term is already present in the above scheme; we coded the names in a particular way as numbers. The *hash* portion refers to attempts to break up the original frequencies of the names and to obtain a more or less uniform or random spacing of the names in the coding. One way to do this is to hash (mix up, rearrange) the names before coding. The idea is to break up the relationships that naturally occur in English words. Simple ideas are as follows:

1. Put the 2nd, 4th, 6th letters first, followed by the 5th, 1st, and 3rd, then followed by the rest.
2. Put the 3rd, 4th, and 5th letters in backward order at the beginning, then add their alphabet positions onto the 1st, 2nd, and 3rd letters, place these new letters next and follow with the remaining letters.
3. Add the alphabetical position of the first letter onto that of the second, the resulting letters' position onto that of the third and so forth for six letters. Then put these letters in reverse order and follow them with the remaining letters.

The results of these three schemes are illustrated in Table 10–2. A blank is given the position zero in the alphabet. If the addition of the positions of two letters is over 26 one subtracts multiples of 26 so as to obtain a legitimate position for a letter. These three schemes certainly do rearrange the spellings, but it is not so easy to determine whether they distribute the names in a more uniform manner.

TABLE 10–2
The result of hash coding six names according to three different schemes

Original Word	*Hashing #1*	*Hashing #2*	*Hashing #3*
BOONEN	ONNEBO	NENPTC	MYTFQB
JIMENEZ	IEENJMZ	ENEOWRZ	DYKFSJZ
TUCKER	UKRETC	REKLAN	ZHCROT
SLOSS_	LS_SSO	_SSSEH	FFMTES
CRAMERFORD	RMRECAFORD	REMUWNFORD	FNIVUCFORD
HO_ _ _ _	O_ _ _H_	_ _ _HO_	WWWWWH

None of these three schemes are of the type used in practice where one usually encodes the name as a number first and then hashes that number. The principle is of course the same. A typical scheme used on numbers is to square the number, then move the first 25 percent of the digits to the end of the number. This type of hashing is more efficient to perform because computers are better adapted to arithmetic than to manipulating letters. The development of efficient and effective hash-coding schemes is not a simple matter and involves a variety of subleties that cannot be discussed here. Such schemes are frequently an essential ingredient of an information processing system.

Problems

10–1 The dimensionality of a body of information is naturally associated with its structure. Give examples of information which is naturally one-, two-, or three-dimensional in nature and which would be awkward and unnatural to consider (and to process) with a lower-dimensional or a higher-dimensional structure.

10–2 The family tree of a particular person is neither one-dimensional nor two-dimensional. Explain why this is the case and discuss the structure of this information.
[*Hint:* The word "tree" gives a good clue to the structure.]

10–3 Legislative bodies are usually organized by a system of committees and subcommittees. Each committee and subcommittee has a chairman and several members. A given individual may be on several committees and on several subcommittees of a given committee.
(a) Give a systematic means of identifying members, committees, and subcommittees of the legislative body.
(b) Give a representation of the committee and subcommittee organization of the legislative body. The representation should be constructed so that it is easy to see who is a member and who is chairman of each committee or subcommittee.
(c) Give a representation of the committees and subcommittees to which a particular individual belongs. Include whether or not the individual is chairman.
(d) Describe how to obtain the information for part (c) if only the representation of part (b) is known.
(e) Describe how to obtain the information for part (b) if only the representation of part (c) is known.

10–4 Write a program (or subprogram) which has an array of N numbers as its input and which uses the bubble sort method to arrange them in ascending order.

10–5 Incorporate a counter in the program for Problem 10–4 which measures the number of units of effort (as defined in the text) actually required in the bubble sort. Generate a set of 500 random numbers and order them with this program. Then compare the actual effort required to sort the numbers with the effort predicted in the text.

10–6 *(Double-bubble sorting)* A possible variant of bubble sorting is as follows: One takes a pair of items and determines which follows the other. Then an ordinary bubble sort is made on the second item until the correct position is found for it. The first item must be placed still higher than this point so that an additional "bubbling" is made (from the point where the second item is placed) until the correct position is found.

Write a program which implements the double-bubble sort and run it for a set of test data to verify that your program works.

10–7 (a) Determine the theoretical number of units of effort that the double-bubble sort of Problem 10–6 should require on the average.
(b) Modify the program for the double-bubble sort of Problem 10–6 so as to obtain a count of the units of effort actually required in a sort. Run your program with a set of randomly generated data and compare the actual effort with that predicted by the theory of part (a) of this problem.

10–8 Write a program that implements the radix sort scheme for a set of 8-digit numbers. Generate a set of numbers to order and run it through your program to demonstrate that the program is correct.

10–9 Modify the program for Problem 10–8 so as to sort 8-letter English words alphabetically. The crux of the problem is to be able to ascertain the alphabetical position of the letters that make up the words. The words should be processed as Hollerith arrays of eight letters.

10–10 *(Merge sorting)* A logical extension of the double-bubble sorting of Problem 10–6 is merge sorting (although it is rarely considered from this point of view). For a merge sort one has two ordered lists of equal length. One then compares the first two elements of each list and places the "largest" or "highest" one at the head of the list that is to be created. After this item is removed, one repeats the process with the remaining lists. In this way the two lists are merged together to form one list that is ordered. The process may be started at the "bottom" as well as the "top" in which case it corresponds more closely to the double-bubble sort.

Write a program that implements this sorting method for two equal lists (of up to 1000 elements) of 8 digit numbers. Generate two ordered lists (say of 100 items each) and process them through your program to show that it works correctly.

10–11 Modify the program of Problem 10–10 to measure the effort required to merge two lists. Run the program for a number of suitable lists and produce what you feel are good estimates of the effort required to merge two lists of lengths from 10 to 200 items each.

10–12 Write a program (or subprogram) that implements the binary search method to locate an element of an ordered list of 100 to 1000 numbers. The list and its length N are to be input data. Create an ordered list of 500 numbers and locate several items in the list (including the first and the last) to show that your program works.

10–13 Compare the program written for Problem 10–12 (binary search) with a program that uses linear search. To do this create an ordered list of 500 numbers and select a number (say 25) of random elements to be located. Then have your program count the total number of comparisons needed for each search scheme. How closely do your results compare to the expected number of $6250 = 25 * 500/2$ for linear searching and $25 * (\log_2(500) + 1) = 250$ for binary searching?

10–14 Write a program (or subprogram) that computes the number associated with a 6-letter word according to the scheme outlined in Section 10–5. The crux of the problem is to obtain the alphabetical position (0 to 25) of the letters that make up the word.

10–15 Use the program of Problem 10–14 to implement a computed index plus linear search scheme to locate items in a list of 600 English words with six or more letters. The computed index is to divide the list into 150 parts. One must first obtain a list of 600 suitable words and then order them alphabetically (perhaps using the program of Problem 10–9 or by taking names from an alphabetized list). One then must find the appropriate entries for the array NDEX as discussed in the text. Only after this is done is one ready to complete this assignment.

10–16 Generate a list of 200 numbers from the values of $\sqrt{|X|}$ * SGN(X,1) for X ranging from -1 to 1 in steps of .001. These values range from -1 to $+1$. This set of numbers may be divided into 20 parts by the numbers -1.0, $-.8$, $-.6$, . . ., .6, .8, 1.0. Determine the largest and smallest sets of numbers obtained by this division.

10–17 Take the words in Table 10–1 and use them to divide your local telephone directory (or similar directory) into 10 parts. Do the divisions that result have approximately the same characteristics as described in the text? That is, the names on the right should result in almost equal sets of names while those on the left should have the largest set about 5 times as large as the smallest.

10–18 Write a program which implements the hash-coding of Table 10–2 for
(a) the first scheme
(b) the second scheme
(c) the third scheme.

10–19 Discuss any weaknesses that the schemes of Problem 10–18 appear to have on the surface. That is, weaknesses expected before one experiments with them.

10–20 Obtain a set of 200 names that are typical English names (for example, take every 50th, 100th, 200th, and so on, name from a telephone directory). Apply the hash-coding schemes of Problem 10–18 to this list and then count the number in each of 10 groups that one obtains by applying the techniques of calculated index method of the text (see Problems 10–14 and 10–15). Discuss the effectiveness of these hash-coding schemes in light of these experiments.

10–21 Augment the program of Problem 10–14 to include commas, periods, and hyphens. This extension is especially appropriate for handling short last names. Explain why this is so and what role the comma and period play in this question.

10–22 Write a program that first obtains the numerical interpretation of a 4-letter name (as in Problem 10–14), then squares this number and moves the first 25 percent of the resulting digits to the right end of the number. Apply this process to a set of 200 names (as in Problem 10–20) and evaluate the effectiveness of this hash-coding scheme.

11

Information and Files

11—1 Information

We do not try to define precisely what information "is." We simply feel that it is something abstract that does not have any physical existence. Thus the fact that it snowed three days ago on Prince of Wales Island is a piece of information that does not depend on whether or not it is written down anyplace. And, if it is written down, it does not depend on what language is used.

Whatever information is, we have an intuitive idea that there are big pieces and small pieces of it. An elementary, or smallest, piece of information is called a *bit*. The word bit is a contraction of binary digit. A bit is a piece of information that can be represented by one of the two words "yes" or "no." Equivalently, it is a piece of information that can be represented by one of the two digits 1 or 0. Note that we do not attempt to say what a bit is directly but that we consider only how we can express it, represent it, or test for it. Indeed, a very plausible definition of a bit of information is that it can be represented by a "yes" or a "no."

The fact that it snowed on Prince of Wales Island is a bit of information. We can represent this fact by the single word "yes" or by the single digit 1. The reason that we can do this with a single digit is that we are in a very specific context, that is, someone has posed, either directly or indirectly, the question: "Did it snow on Prince of Wales Island?" Without this context, the information cannot be represented by 0 or 1. Thus we see that a representation consists not only of bits but also of a context of interpretation. In other words, there must be a scheme for encoding and decoding the information into and out of the bits.

The symbols 0 and 1 can be used to represent bits and hence all information. However, we feel more comfortable if we use a larger set of symbols, namely,

0 1 2 3 4 5 6 7 8 9

We can combine these symbols (or characters) into the decimal digits of numbers and represent many bits of information by a relatively short number like 43,697. This number might represent 5 bits of information or it might represent 50,000 bits. It depends on the encoding scheme used.

Consider, for example, a computer that has a special memory of 50,000 words. Imagine that the operating system keeps a list of all the words in this memory that are not assigned. This list consists of 5-digit numbers, the addresses of the unassigned words. When this list contains the single number 43697, there is only one word available. Implicit in this single number is the fact that the other 49,999 words are not available. Furthermore, it is not possible in general to say which words are available with a representation that does not contain 50,000 bits.

One of the important concepts in the study of information is *the difference between a piece of information and a representation of this information.* This difference is seen in everyday life in cooking. Thus the recipe for cooking young wild pigeons with olives can be written in English, or in French, or in Amharic, or in flowchart language. Even though we may have four different pieces of paper with writing, we have only one piece of information. These four writings are thus only different ways to express or represent this one piece of information. In the next examples we consider the more pertinent problem of representing numbers.

EXAMPLE 11–1

MATHEMATICAL REPRESENTATION OF NUMBERS

There are a variety of mathematical ways to represent numbers. Six examples of them are given for the three numbers 121, 1.5, and 1/20.

1. Rational	121	3/2	1/20
2. Decimal	121.0	1.5	0.05
3. Octal	171.0	1.4	0.0314 . . .
4. Binary	1111001.0	1.1	0.000011001100 . . .
5. Floating binary	$.1111001 * 2^7$	$.11 * 2$	$0.110011 \ldots * 2^{-4}$
6. Floating decimal	$.121 * 10^3$	$.15 * 10$	$.5 * 10^{-1}$

These six ways of representing a number are samples of the unlimited number of ways we can represent a particular number. No matter which representation is used, there is only one number, that is, one piece of information, involved.

The average scientist (or computer user) more often considers bodies of information than bits of information. The reason for this is that current computer systems have standard, built-in means of handling the relationships between ordinary representations of numbers and binary numbers and between mathematical and physical representations of numbers. Thus these relationships are "buried" in the computer system.

EXAMPLE 11–2

PHYSICAL REPRESENTATIONS OF NUMBERS

The mathematical representations of numbers are all abstract like the number being represented. So, in order to manipulate numbers mechanically or electronically, we must represent them by mechanical or electronic means. Some of these means are shown in Figure 11–1.

We see then that there are many mathematical and physical representations possible for a particular number. The representation that we would use in a specific situation depends on the requirements of that situation. Thus if the numbers are to be manipulated at extremely high speeds, then the representation must be of such a nature to allow this. If the numbers are to be read by people, then the representation must be at least partially visible.

The popularity of the binary numbers stems from the fact that many electronic representations of numbers are based on an "off" or "on" principle (that is, a "yes" or "no" principle). This physical representation is naturally associated with the mathematical binary representation. People who work closely

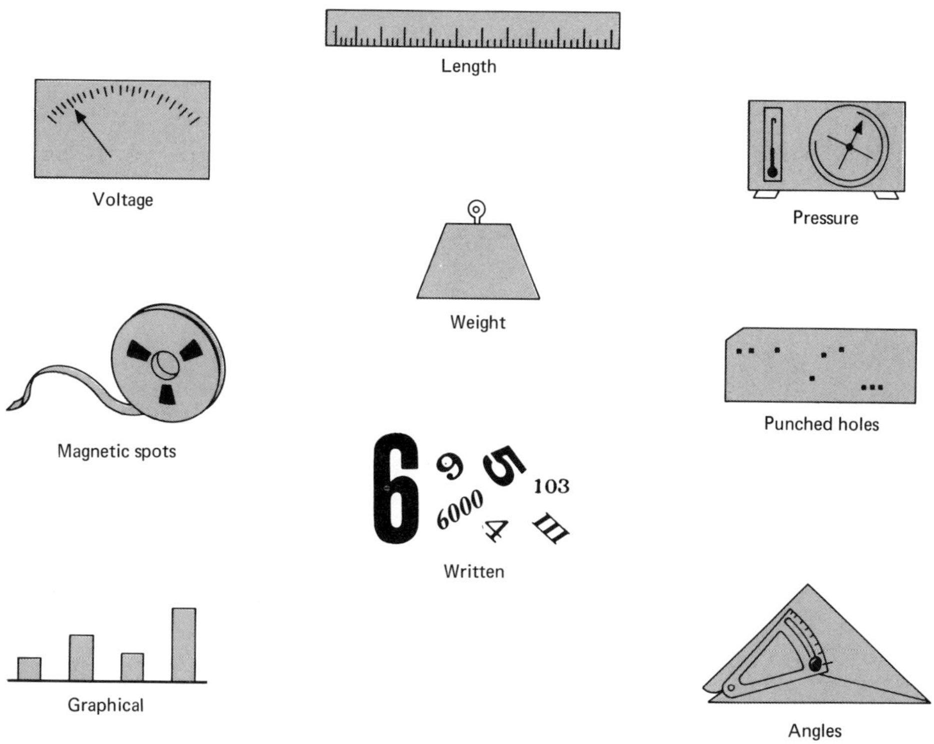

FIGURE 11–1. Some means for the physical representation of numbers.

with such electronic devices (computers, for example) are inevitably brought face to face with binary numbers.

It is difficult to draw an exact line between small pieces of information and bodies of information. We use the rough definition that a body of information is information whose representation requires several numbers and that has some systematic nature or structure.

In most problems there is a certain amount of what we might call "miscellaneous" pieces of information. They are normally easily recognized variables in the problem, and we often give them nice mnemonic names such as Time, Xbar, Kontroll, ID2, and Ndata. These miscellaneous pieces of information are characterized by the fact that they are unrelated or dissimilar in nature. The most common source of bodies of information is from pieces of information that are related to one another in some fashion; that is, the information has some structure or organization.

The great variety of the things that we find in common lists of information is illustrated by the following examples:

1. The names of the students in a class or school
2. The dates of the season's horse races
3. The district warehouses of a company
4. The atomic weights of the elements
5. The required courses for a major in business administration
6. The job vacancies in the state highway department
7. The indices of refraction of various kinds of glass.

Except for 4 and 7 these are just lists of the names of things. The items in lists 4 and 7 are numerical quantities associated with lists of names. Some of these names might be digits, for example, 447-34-0243 instead of Mary Jones, or 6/12/59 instead of June 12, 1959.

We have already stressed the importance of the use of arrays and discussed various techniques to process them. In the next example we see how this type of structure (the one-dimensional array) can be used in the representation of a slightly more complicated structure, graphical information.

EXAMPLE 11–3

GRAPHS AND ONE-DIMENSIONAL ARRAYS

Another source of bodies of information is graphical data. Several examples are seen in Figure 11–2.

The reason for presenting such information in graphical form is to make it easier for people to grasp the information. This information can also be presented in tables, as follows:

Age	0	1	2	3	4	5	6	7	8
Weight	147	316	471	703	964	1197	1321	1412	1488

Month	1	2	3	4	5	6	7	8	9	10	11	12
Ave. Temp.	27	29	34	45	57	69	74	75	65	51	38	31

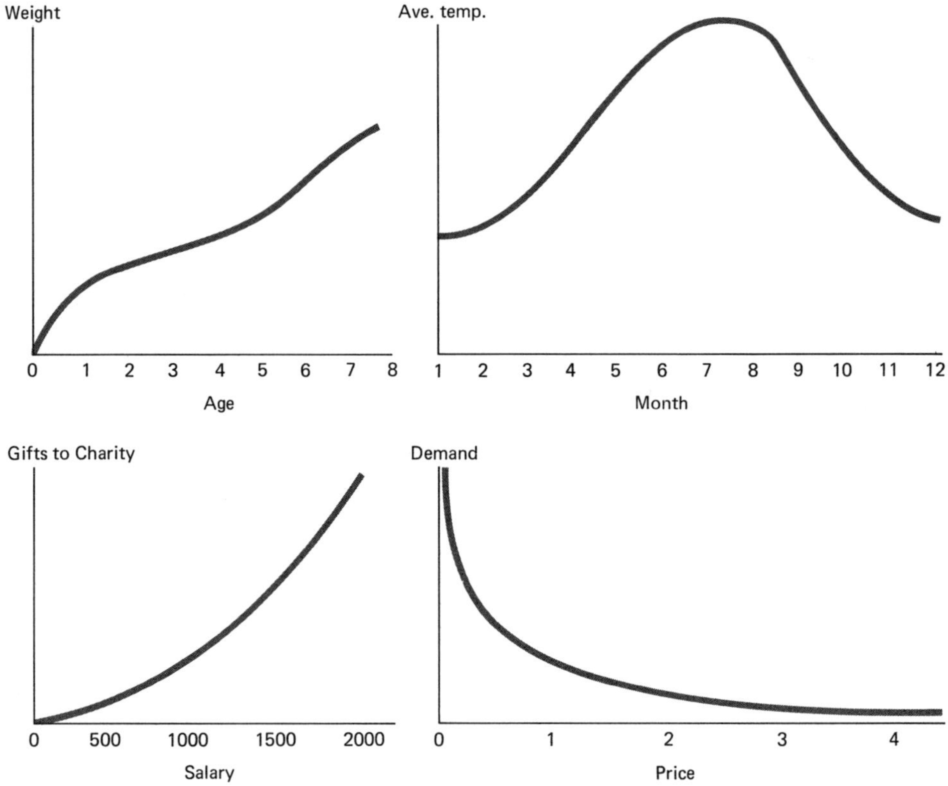

FIGURE 11–2. Four typical bodies of information presented in graphical form.

Salary	0	212	403	597	802	1004	1532	1985
Charity gifts	0	1.7	5.8	21.2	60.5	84.7	108.2	118.6

Price	0	.5	.8	.9	1.0	1.1	1.5	2.0	3.0
Demand	420	195	163	139	105	81	44	35	31

The information in the first two graphs can be represented just as a simple list of numbers. We might call the one-dimensional arrays WT and ATEMP and have

$$\text{WT(AGE) for AGE} = 0 \text{ to } 8$$
$$\text{ATEMP(MO) for MO} = 1 \text{ to } 12$$

Here the indices of the arrays have the mnemonic names AGE and MO.

The information presented in the second two graphs cannot be represented this way because neither of the variables can be made into an index (or counter). We can, however, represent the information using two one-dimensional arrays and a separate counter. For the third graph we call these arrays SAL and CHAR, and the information is represented by the pair of arrays

$$\text{SAL(K) for K} = 1 \text{ to } 8$$
$$\text{CHAR(K) for K} = 1 \text{ to } 8$$

The index K simply counts the number of data points on the graph. Similarly, for the last graph we have the arrays DEMAND and PRICE, and the information is represented by the arrays

$$\text{DEMAND(K) for K} = 1 \text{ to } 9$$
$$\text{PRICE(K) for K} = 1 \text{ to } 9$$

11–2 File Organization for Disk Memory

There is a tremendous variety in the information structures that arise in computer applications. Rather than continue with a survey that touches lightly on many of these, we take one example and study it in some detail. This example is important in many applications and, incidentally, provides an opportunity to study a peripheral device. The example considered is a file of information that is to be kept on a disk memory as it is processed. In this section we consider two topics, first the physical description of the disk memory and second how one retrieves a piece of information from the file.

The physical description given here is considerably simplified as real disks are rather complicated objects. The retrieval process discussed assumes that the file is completely *static*; that is, it has been put on the disk in a form suitable for information retrieval and it just sits as one retrieves information from time to time. There are some important applications that involve static files, but *dynamic files* are much more common. In this case the files are continuously modified (that is, items added, deleted, or rewritten) while being used as a source of information. A few of the problems that arise in the management of dynamic files are briefly mentioned in the next section.

The general relationship of the disk memory to the computer is illustrated in Figure 11–3. The channel and controller are devices (usually complicated and expensive) that control the disk and establish communications with the computer. The *status word* contains the information about the status of the disk. We do not describe these devices in any more detail but rather assume that they allow us to do the things mentioned later on. Note that Fortran does not have any facilities that allow one to communicate with a disk so the programs for such processing are usually not in Fortran. However, some computing centers have extended their Fortran to include file handling capabilities which are, in effect, ways to control the channel and disk controller.

A simple disk unit with only four disks is shown in Figure 11–4. The principal components are the disks (see Figure 11–5), the read-write heads, and the positioner. A side of the disk is divided into a number of tracks and these, in turn, are divided into a number of records. The records are the basic items of information in the file. They might consist of only a few words or many hundreds. The number of records on a track depends, of course, on their size and on the characteristics of the disk unit.

Information on a particular track can be read or written only when the read-write head is directly over (or under, as the case may be) the track. The positioner moves in and out in order to position these heads over the tracks. The

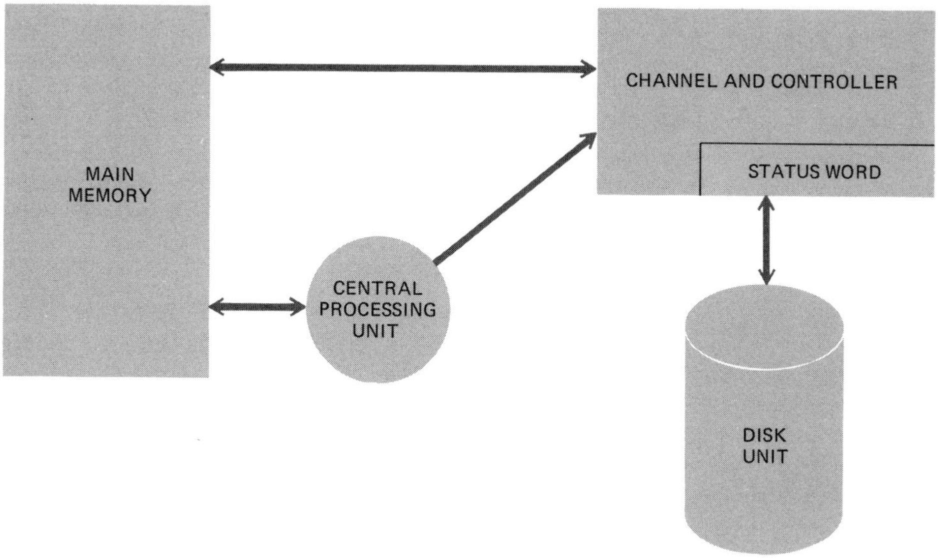

FIGURE 11–3. Schematic diagram of a computer with a peripheral disk memory.

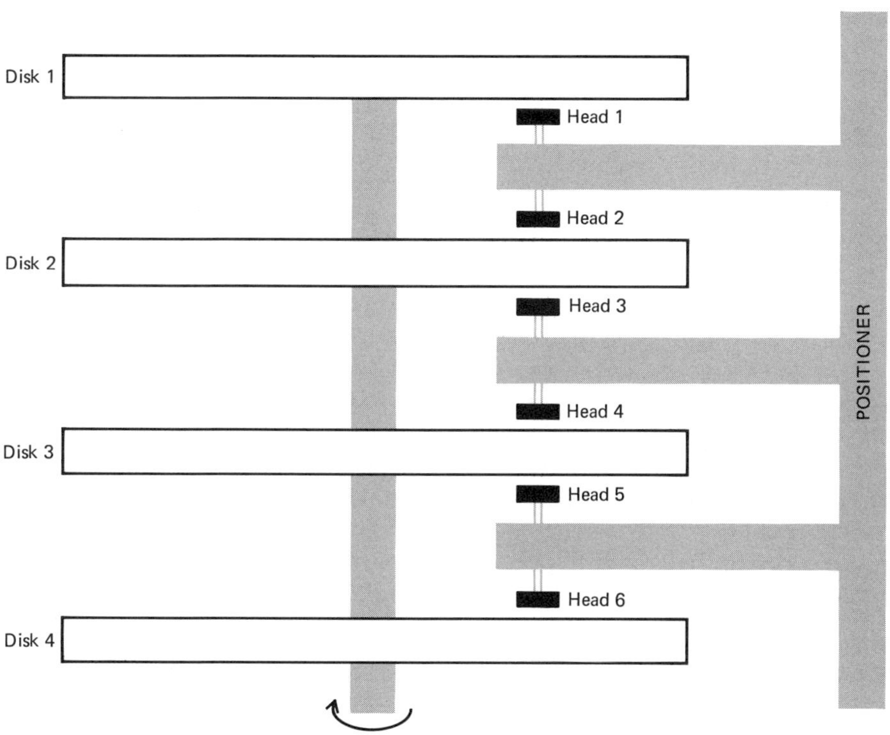

FIGURE 11–4. Schematic diagram of a disk unit with four disks and six read-write heads (side view).

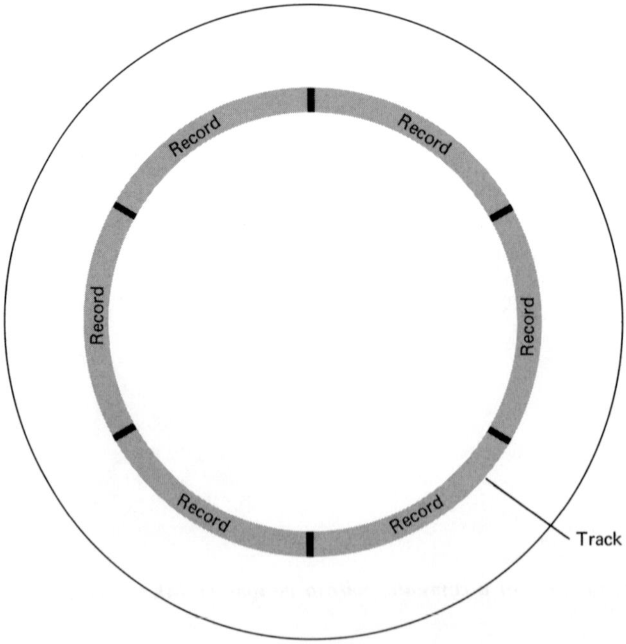

FIGURE 11–5. Top view of a disk showing one track which contains six records.

positioner and the arms that hold the heads form one solid piece of equipment and thus all of the heads move in unison. One can use only one read-write head at a time and the controller has a switch to select a particular head. This switch operates electronically, and thus it is very quick to change from one track on one disk to the corresponding track on another disk. This might require 10 or 100 microseconds while it typically takes more than a thousand times as long (20 to 200 milliseconds) to physically move the head to a neighboring track. This situation gives rise to the concept of a *cylinder* as illustrated in Figure 11–6. The addressing or referencing scheme used for a record of a file is the cylinder, then the head and finally the record. Thus 3-5-4 would be the fourth record with the fifth head (the bottom of disk 3) of cylinder 3 (or on track 3). Note that this addressing scheme gives the file a three-dimensional structure whether or not this is really appropriate for the information involved.

A record on a track consists of three parts as shown in Figure 11–7. There is a great variety in the actual formats used, but one almost always finds these three parts. Frequently the header word is quite long and actually corresponds to several computer words. The *end-of-record* (often referred to as EOR) mark is a special mark that cannot appear either in the header word or in the information. The simplest situation would be for a record to consist of

17 – 6.18257, 8.96342 – EOR

which would be a record (probably the 17th) with two numbers in it. Files usually contain more complicated information, and we consider in more detail a file where the header word is a name and the information consists of many words (the exact nature of this information does not concern us here). Sample records might then appear as

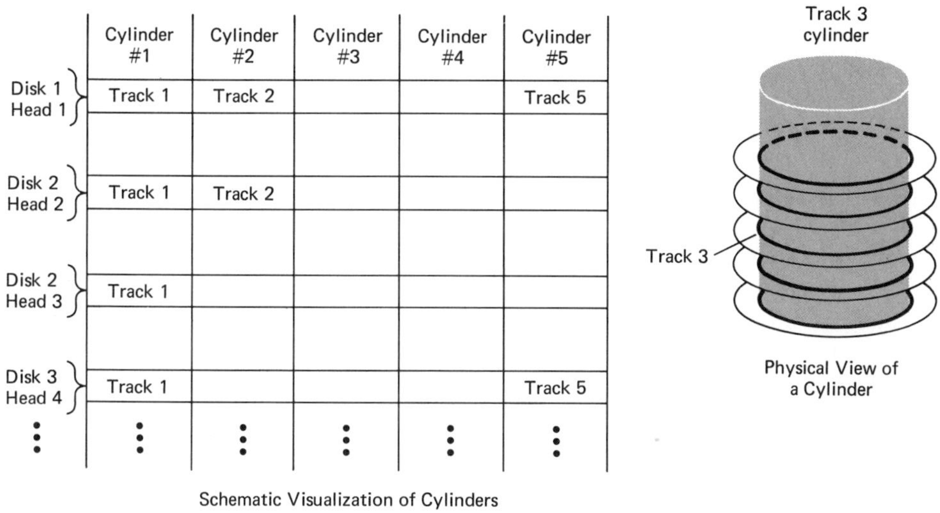

FIGURE 11–6. A physical view and schematic visualization of the cylinder of a disk memory unit gives the file a 3-dimensional structure whether or not this is really appropriate for the information involved.

JONES J Q — (Information on credit rating) — EOR
TRACY W F — (Information on insurance policy) — EOR
DEBOOR C W — (Payroll information) — EOR

We now turn to the first crucial problem in file processing: *How do we retrieve a record of information from this file?* Imagine an on-line credit information system that has just been called by a grocer: J. Q. JONES has presented a check for $182.65 which he wants cashed. Does J. Q. JONES have any record of passing bad checks?

The ideal (and rare) situation is where one knows the exact address of the record requested. Thus one would like to know that the J. Q. JONES record is in cylinder #3, with head #7 (that is, on track 3 of the bottom of disk 4). If this information is known, the computer instructs the channel and controller to move the positioner to cylinder #3, then to switch to read-write head #7. This head then begins to read the information on the track and as soon as the JONES, J Q header word comes around, it transmits the credit information to the computer. Note that one really does not need to have the records on a particular track numbered in any way. The searching along a track is a simple linear search because the head can read only as the disk surface rotates above or beneath it.

However, it is not reasonable to expect one to know the exact address of this record. A second simple alternative is to make a linear search of the entire

FIGURE 11–7. The three basic parts of a record on a disk memory.

file. A fairly realistic disk has 10 disk surfaces, 200 tracks per surface, and requires $\frac{1}{40}$ second to rotate. Thus, to search the 10 tracks in any one cylinder requires about $\frac{1}{4}$ second and since we expect to search half the file, we find that 25 seconds are required for searching and another 10 seconds for moving the positioner. This seemingly short delay is, in fact, intolerable. A successful service of this type must be able to process many information requests simultaneously and a queue of 20 requests leads to over a 10-minute delay in answering the grocer's question.

We conclude then that a more efficient searching technique is essential for such an information system. We outline one of the simpler possibilities which involves two steps. First, the file must be organized before it is placed on the disk. Putting it in some linear order such as an alphabetical one is sufficient. Second, a directory is created which contains the first name in each cylinder. The entries in this directory consist of a list of names such as shown below.

AABLING	. . .	WILLIAMS
AIREY	. . .	WITNOV
AMDOC	. . .	YAMADA

These are the first names on each cylinder. This directory is appropriate for a file with about 200 cylinders. The information retrieval process now takes two steps. First, this directory is searched to find the cylinder that contains the JONES file. This directory is in (or brought into) the computer's main memory and the searching can use any of the techniques discussed in the previous chapter. Once the proper cylinder is located the positioner is moved to this cylinder and then a linear search is made of the tracks in this cylinder until the JONES J Q file is located. This approach reduces the search time of perhaps 30 to 40 seconds mentioned above to a total search time of less than half a second.

A simple, but effective, extension of this approach is to have two levels of directories. The first level is as above and is used to locate the correct cylinder. Then a second directory is kept on the first track of cylinder and this subdirectory is used to locate the correct head to use in order to read the desired record. The reason for keeping this subdirectory on the disk is to conserve space in the computer's main memory. The effectiveness of this extension depends on the number of tracks in a cylinder and in common situations it reduces the search time by a factor of perhaps 3 to 8.

11–3 Updating, Pointers, and Linked Files

The discussion of file organization in the preceding section considers one of the simplest possible cases (that of static files) and then only a few of the more obvious search strategies are presented. Much more common are *dynamic files* where one is required to have provisions for three kinds of modifications in the file:

changing of a record
addition of a new record
deletion of an old record

The performance of these modifications is called *updating* the file.

In many instances, it is as easy to change a record as to locate it. Once it is located, one merely writes the new information where the old information is. However, it may well be that there is more new information than there is old information and then one does not have enough room. This situation is very similar to that of adding a new record which we discuss in more detail below.

One approach to the deletion of a record is just to ignore the situation. Even though it is never to be used again, one can just let the record sit in the file. That might be the cheapest thing to do and it certainly is the simplest. If the information is such that it has to be destroyed, one can locate the record and replace the contents with blanks or something similar. It is one thing to ignore or get rid of the record, it is quite another to reclaim the space that the old record used in the disk memory. This question is considered again after we briefly discuss the most difficult of the three updating operations, that of additions to the file.

Imagine that one has a file with many thousands of records, all in alphabetical order. Further, suppose that the information retrieval scheme uses a directory as discussed earlier. Now consider what must be done in order to add one record, say for John S. Braddock. If the file is placed in the disk memory in the natural, one record right after another, way, then one is faced with an extensive amount of work. In order to obtain space for the new record, one must move *all* of the records after the name Braddock. This, in turn, makes the directory incorrect for *all* of the cylinders after Braddock, so the directory must be updated also. The net result is that this natural way to keep the file in the disk is unacceptable if frequent additions are to be made to the file.

Many methods have been used to overcome this problem and we consider one of these here. The first idea is to leave some extra room on each track for new records. Suppose a track has room for 12 records, then one might put only 9 records on a track to start and leave the remainder for additions. The price one pays for this tactic is the requirement of extra memory (in this case 33⅓ percent more). Furthermore, it might (and probably will) break down long before one has added 33⅓ percent more records. The new records might come in bunches as when Mr. Braddock, his two brothers, three sons, and seven nephews move into town. A good hash-coding technique rather than straight alphabetizing can materially help in making the new records appear uniformly in the file, but even then a few tracks become full long before the entire memory space is used.

A possible solution to this problem is to designate one of the tracks in the cylinder as an *overflow track*. Then when one track is full, the new record is placed on the overflow track. The situation is illustrated in Figure 11–8. In the beginning the overflow track is empty and the other four tracks are partially filled (shaded area). After considerable processing and additions, the second and fourth tracks are full and the overflow track is half full. The added records are indicated by hashed regions.

It is feasible to place records on the overflow track without regard to where they came from. However, let us assume that we have an application where it is important to know the exact order of the records in the file. Thus when a new record is placed in a file, it is inserted in the proper position and the appropriate records in the track are moved to make room for it. The question is: What to do when the track overflows and a record is to be placed in the overflow track?

One solution to this is to have a cylinder directory that contains two items per track, the first name on the track and a *pointer* to the first item that should be on the track, but is, instead, on the overflow track. This directory might appear as follows:

(Gulik,0) (Gutherie,5) (Haber,0) (Hahn,8)

for the situation of Figure 11–8. Thus the first and third tracks have not overflowed, and the second track has an overflow record that is number 5 on the overflow track and the fourth track has an overflow record that is number 8 on the overflow track. Thus if one is searching for a record that should be on the second track, one knows that one of the overflows from the second track is the fifth record on the overflow track. Suppose we examine that record and it is not the desired one, what do we do next?

One way to add records to the overflow track at random times and still preserve the order is to make *linked files* (or *linked lists*) of the overflow records. To do this we add a pointer to each record in the overflow track which points to the previous record that overflowed from a particular track. If there are four tracks that can overflow onto an overflow track, then these are four linked files on the overflow track. Each record has the form

(Name) (Pointer) (Information) (EOR-mark)

for example,

Guyman 3 (Information) (EOR-mark)

might be the fifth record on the overflow track. Thus if we have searched the second track and not found the record, we go to the fifth record on the overflow track. If this is not it, we then follow the pointer to the third record on the overflow track. That record might appear as

Haas 0 (Information) (EOR-mark)

Its pointer is zero which means that it is the end of the overflows for the second track.

These linked files are chained together by the pointers and are sometimes referred to as *chains*. A more complicated situation is illustrated in Figure 11–9 where all four tracks have overflowed and the links are illustrated for tracks 1 and 4.

If another record overflows from track 1, it is placed in record 15 of the overflow track and its pointer is 12 (where the overflows used to start). The first entry in the cylinder directory is changed to (Gulik,15) and the insertion is complete.

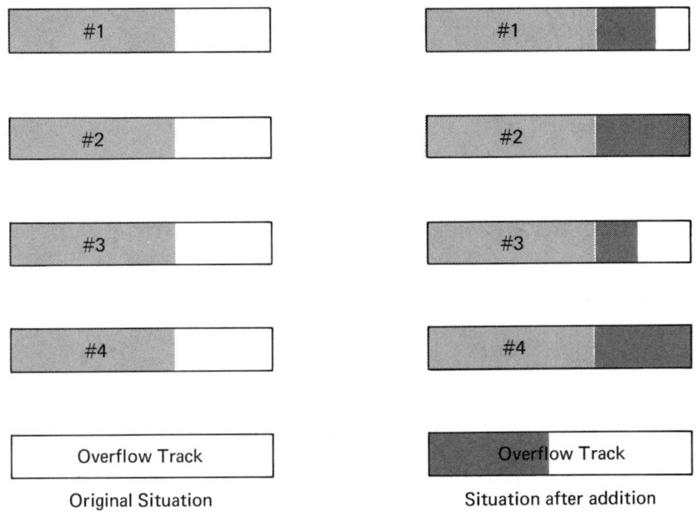

FIGURE 11–8. Schematic diagram of the used space in the five tracks of a cylinder originally (left) and after many additions have been made to the file (right).

Even though we have described a fairly complicated method for managing this file, we have only scratched the surface of the wide variety of possibilities. The design of an efficient file management system is a delicate operation that requires one to weigh many conflicting objectives and to exploit the particular properties of the devices and files involved.

Note that one can delete a record from a file in the overflow track by merely making the pointers skip over it. However, we still have not faced up to the problem of how to recover the space taken up by deleted records. Techniques which reclaim this memory space are often referred to as *garbage collection* methods. The most common approach is to periodically reorganize the file from beginning to end. One might do this weekly, monthly, yearly, and so on, depending on the circumstances. Note that there are two undesirable trends as the overflow portion of the file increases. First, there is the increase of wasted space because of records deleted. Second, there is an increase in the average

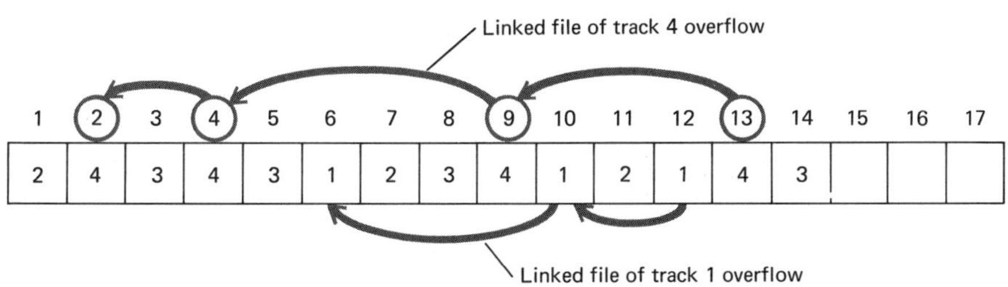

FIGURE 11–9. Schematic of the records in the overflow track. The numbers in the boxes indicate where the record originated and the records from a track are linked together by pointers. The directory shown contains the starting points for the four linked files.

search time because more of the file is in the overflow and it takes longer to follow the links in the overflow lists. In most practical information processing systems one cannot let either one of these trends continue very long.

Problems

11–1 The Morse code is a representation of letters by groups of dots and dashes. Give such a representation for the letters A to Z, the digits 0 to 9, and the punctuation marks "." and ",".

11–2 Give a representation of the letters A to Z using groups of the characters +, −, *.

11–3 Describe a device to measure rainfall so that each inch of rainfall is represented by a length of 1 foot on the device.

11–4 Give a concise and compact representation of the dates in this century (for example, June 12, 1957) using only the letters A to M.

11–5 You are a secret spy on a mission inside Transaxia. You are to report on the strength of the forces at Fort Vat. You must report:
(a) The number of regiments of infantry present.
(b) Whether or not heavy artillery is present.
(c) Whether or not heavy tanks are present.
(d) Whether or not the morale is good.
(e) Whether or not any troops are preparing to leave.
You must report this information back to ACEY with just two numbers, called PQ and ID.

Present a scheme to encode this information into two numbers, PQ and ID. Present in flowchart form an algorithm to decode this two-number message.

11–6 We represent words visually by writing them down. An important feature of this representation is that it is often redundant; that is, we use more letters than are really required to represent the word. The advantage of this is that if one letter is missing or wrong, we can still tell what the word is. For example, we have little difficulty recognizing the "words"

memury, memoty, memorz, memor, Mekory

as misspellings of the word memory.
(a) Give five examples of words that are highly redundant.
(b) Give five examples of words that are not redundant at all.
(c) There is another means that we use to detect and decipher misspelled words in addition to redundancy. What is it?

11–7 Redundant representations of information are sometimes used to guard against errors.
(a) Show how to represent the letters A to Z by triplets of the digits 0, 1, and 2.

(b) Show how we can add a fourth "check-sum" digit, and then determine if there is an error in any one of the four digits. This fourth digit is related in some way to the sum of the first three digits.
(c) Show how this check does not protect us against certain combinations of two errors in these groups of four digits; that is, show how two errors in the digits can compensate for one another.

11–8 Suppose you are to write a program to compute the average value of various lists of numbers. Give the specific instructions that you would prepare for the users of this program about the representation of the data that this program accepts.

11–9 You are presented from time to time with long lists of names in the form

John Paul Jones
Mary Ann Mee
Philip Richard Carpenter

You are to alphabetize these lists and print up new lists with last names first and only initials, for example,

Carpenter P R
Jones J P
Mee M A

Describe how you would represent your original lists in order to make this processing convenient.

11–10 Consider a large amount of information about the students in a college. Assume, in particular, that you know for each student:

name, age, class, major, sex, home town, local mailing address, grade point average, place of work (if any), rank in high school class, social organizations, telephone number, courses taken each term with grades.

Organize this information and represent it in a way that makes it convenient to prepare specialized lists for:
(a) The registrar (who needs information about major, courses, grades, and address),
(b) The dormitory counselors (who need information about major, grades, work, and social items),
(c) The departmental counselors (who need information about courses, grades, and work),
(d) The student directory (which needs information about address, telephone number, and class).

11–11 You are studying the vibrational characteristics of the blooms of tomato plants. Each experiment is time-consuming, but until you have analyzed a large number of experiments, you do not know what the important variables are. So you decide to measure everything that might be important.

These variables are:

1. humidity	6. vibration amplitude
2. vibration frequency	7. time of day
3. plant identification	8. age of bloom
4. amount of pollen that falls	9. date
5. size of bloom	10. temperature

Construct a representation of these data which is a good compromise between being short and compact and being easy to process. That is to say, you are to design a system for encoding this information into a small number of words (or variables) of the computer. Assume that the computer has room for at most 8 decimal digits or 6 alphanumeric characters per word. A system which is easy is to use one word for each of the 10 variables. However, one can pack more than one value into a word if one wants. Thus, dates are easily encoded as 6 digits (June 12, 1959 becomes 061259). Temperatures are between 40 and 120 so that the temperature minus 40 is less than 100 and one can encode the temperature as 2 digits (88 becomes 48, 103 becomes 63). Then one can combine the date code with the temperature code into one number (June 12, 1959 and 103 degrees becomes 06125963).

11–12 You have the following information about a large number of married men:

Annual income	Age
Value of home	Savings
Education level	Value of car
Occupation	State of residence
Army service	Life insurance
Number of children	Job experience

You want to gather statistics about this group of men concerning the following:

1. Financial situation at various educational levels.
2. The relationship between occupation and savings.
3. The amount of life insurance as a function of age for men with the same number of children.
4. Financial situation as a function of age.

You have this information on paper, one sheet per man. You are to have it keypunched and read into a computer for processing to obtain the required statistics.

(a) Describe the representation you would use for this information. Choose the representation so the processing for these statistics is simple and efficient.

(b) Describe how you would represent every item of information that you have keypunched.

(c) Describe what you would have to do, if anything, to get your raw information into the representation you want to use for processing.

11–13 A girl has charged the textbooks at the university book store on a stolen credit card. The books are for the courses History 103, English 113, Zoology 214, and Mathematics 161. It is decided to attempt to identify this girl by checking through the Registrar's records for people enrolled in all four of these courses. Assume that each record in the Registrar's files contains the following items:

Name of student
Class (1 for freshman, 2 for sophomore, and so on)
Sex (1 for male, 0 for female)
Course name and number (up to 8 pairs of the first three letters of the department and the three digits).

(a) Describe (in flowchart form) a method to search the Registrar's files and to locate all the suspects. The method should attempt to be efficient as there are about 27,000 students in this university.

(b) Write a program which will process a file of this nature and carry out the search. You must assign variable names and formats for the information in the file and create a sample student file to process. The program is to print out the name of each suspect; be sure that there are at least two suspects in the sample file.

11–14 A sociological survey included the records of telephone calls made between members of a group of 25 people. The following information was recorded for each member:

1. The number of telephone calls he received from each other member.
2. The number of telephone calls he made to each other member.

   (a) Describe a suitable way to represent this information for use in Fortran programs which will manipulate and analyze these data in various ways.

   (b) Give an algorithm (in flowchart or Fortran) which, when given the variable I and the above data, will return the value of the quotient

$$\frac{\text{total number of calls made by person number I}}{\text{total number of calls received by person number I}}$$

   Be very explicit in your algorithm; define the variables involved and use mathematical formulas and relations and not ordinary English sentences.

11–15 The sports editor for a newspaper must compute and tabulate the batting averages for all the players on the local baseball team and for each day they play a game. This task may be automated as follows: First one creates a master file that has one record for each player with 5 pieces of information:

The player's name
His uniform number
The number of times at bat so far this season
The number of hits so far
The number of runs-batted-in so far
The number of home runs so far

Then after each game one prepares an update list that contains the player's uniform number and the number of times at bat, the number of hits, the number of runs-batted-in, and the number of home runs for the last game. This update list is then processed along with the master file in order to produce a new master file and printed output of the form

NAME	AVERAGE	RBI	HR
RUTH, BABE	.282	64	17
DIMAGGIO, JOE	.296	52	16
GUBER, FLOYD	.202	11	2

The average is the ratio of the hits over the times at bat.

(a) Give a flowchart of the process to use the update file to create a new master file and to simultaneously produce an output file for the printed output.

(b) Write a program that implements the process described in part (a). Create an original master file for 8 ball players and update this file four times. Print the output file after each update of the master file and then print the final master file obtained.

(c) Incorporate a sorting technique so that printed output is arranged from highest batting average to lowest.

(d) Describe a sorting technique and implement it in the computer program which exploits the fact that the order of the players does not change much from game to game.
[*Hint:* Keep the master file in this order as well as the output. Then after the updating of the master file one uses the bubble sort method starting with the top of the list. The normal situation then is that each new player added to the sorted list is at the bottom of the list and no interchanges are made.]

11–16 Consider a disk that has two read-write heads per disk surface on each arm of the positioner instead of one as shown in Figure 11–4. Discuss what effect such a construction has on the search time for a file and on the organization of a file on the disk. In particular, give a physical description of a cylinder for such a disk.

11–17 Consider a disk that has two independent positioners each with one read-write head per disk surface. One strategy for the use of this arrangement is to synchronize the two positioners so that they both are on the same track. Another strategy is to have them on different tracks so that one can either: (a) move one positioner to another track while the other is processing information, or (b) arrange them so as to decrease the distance that a positioner has to move when a new track is to be searched.

Discuss the advantages and disadvantages of these arrangements as compared to one another and as compared to the simpler mechanism described in the text.

11–18 A two-level directory for a disk file consists of one directory with which one can locate the proper cylinder and then another directory (one for each cylinder) with which one can locate the proper head to use.

(a) Assume that all of the directories are in the computer's main memory and that it takes a negligible amount of time to search them. What then is the expected length of time required to locate an item of information on a disk file? Use the timing estimates given in the text for the various operations that occur.

(b) Assume that the first directory is in the computer's main memory, but that the second is on a track of the disk itself. Thus the first level directory is searched, then the appropriate cylinder directory is read from the disk and searched, and finally the correct track is searched for the desired item. What is the expected length of time required to locate an item of information on the disk file with this arrangement?

11–19 The text describes a linked file arrangement for keeping track of records that are placed on the overflow track of a cylinder. One can also imagine that some type of identification is placed in the header word of each record that is put on the overflow track.

(a) Describe an identification scheme of the overflow records that would allow one to tell on which track the record belongs and what its proper position should be.

(b) Describe a method to retrieve all the records from a track (including those that overflow) and to put them in their proper order. Compare the work required for this approach with that required for the linked file approach.

11–20 The problem of overflow during the updating of a disk file is accentuated if the file does not grow evenly. This results in part of the file completely overflowed while much empty disk memory is still available in other parts. Discuss the possibility of applying a hash-coding technique to the organization of a disk file. In particular, discuss:

(a) Specific details for a file of people's names and associated information.

(b) The effect on the search time required using either a simple directory or a two-level directory.

(c) The effect on a linked-file technique for handling records placed on an overflow track.

11–21 A brief description of a drum memory is given in Chapter 8 (see Figure 8–4). Drums are also frequently used as memory for large files and a file must be organized in a manner compatible with the drum.

(a) Describe a file organization scheme and a search technique for the file which uses a directory.

(b) Compare the search technique of part (a) with the analogous one for a disk. Given that the rotation time for a disk and a drum are the same, which memory device provides the fastest access (on the average) to information on the device? Explain the basis for the choice made.

11–22 The physical characteristics of a disk memory play a central role in the way one organizes a file. If a file is kept in the main memory (or in an auxiliary random access memory), then the search is not delayed by a waiting time for physical motion. Nevertheless, a dynamic file with frequent updating causes many problems if the order in the file is not to be lost.

(a) Explain how one can adapt the idea of "spare track space" and of "overflow" tracks to dynamic file processing in a random access memory.

(b) Explain how one can designate a single overflow area for the whole file and then use the linked-file concept to preserve the order of the file in dynamic processing.

12

Mathematics

It has been pointed out earlier that the creation of a mathematical model is one of the essential elements of the problem-solving process. This is particularly true in computer applications where the computer program written is (or at least contains) the mathematical model. It is natural then that mathematical problems arise out of these models even if the problem originated in engineering, economics, or psychology. There is a tremendous variety in the problems that arise and many nonmathematical areas lead to quite difficult mathematical problems. Mathematics contains a tremendous array of methods to attack and solve these problems and one can take courses for several years and still only have an introduction to the methods of applied mathematics.

The advent of the computer has opened up new approaches to solving mathematical problems and in this chapter we examine three typical mathematical problems and the corresponding approaches. Each of these problems is much older than computing, and classical mathematics (primarily the calculus) has a number of completely different methods that can be used to attack them. Neither the modern computational methods (usually called *numerical analysis*) nor the classical methods (usually called *symbolic analysis*) is going to replace the other. They are complementary to one another and some problems are trivial with one approach and impossible with the other—and vice versa.

The three problems considered here are illustrated in Figure 12–1. Each of these problems involves one or two curves or graphs. These curves represent a mathematical specification of the relationship between two quantities. The specification might be a simple formula, for example,

$$\text{COST} = 1.05(\text{X} - 1)^3 + 14.3/(\text{X} + 1)$$

$$\text{Y} = 18.3 * \text{LOG(X)} - \sqrt{\text{X} + 2}$$

or by a 20-page Fortran program. The first problem is to find the area between two curves or between one curve and the x-axis. The second problem is to find the maximum or highest point of a curve, and the third problem is to find where two curves intersect or cross one another.

It is important to realize that a vast array of real problems can be reduced or reformulated as one of these three simple, but abstract, mathematical problems. Thus, a problem solver must analyze his problem well enough to identify the underlying mathematical problem. He can then apply the mathematical methods appropriate for that problem. For example, suppose that one is considering the location of a new regional warehouse somewhere along the one railroad through the region. Suppose that construction costs, land costs, taxes, and so on, are the same throughout the region so that the crucial element in the cost is the cost of shipping from the factory to the warehouse plus the cost of shipping from the warehouse to the various retail outlets in the region. These costs can be expressed mathematically and we want to minimize these costs. But to minimize something is exactly equivalent to maximizing its negative, so we have a problem of the second kind illustrated in Figure 12–1.

EXAMPLE 12–1

THE ESTIMATION OF AREAS

The crucial idea in the estimation of areas (and many other mathematical problems) is to replace the curve by something much simpler. This is illustrated in Figure 12–2 where a quarter circle is replaced by a broken line with six pieces. Now we know how to find the area under a broken line because it is just the sum of the areas of the trapezoids formed as shown in Figure 12–2. The area of a trapezoid with base H and sides A and B is given by the formula area $= H(A + B)/2$. If we break the quarter circle into P pieces, then the base of each trapezoid is $1/P$. We number the trapezoids from left to right, and we find the sides of the Ith trapezoid are given by

$$\text{A} = \sqrt{1 - ((I - 1)/P)^2},$$

$$\text{B} = \sqrt{1 - (I/P)^2},$$

Thus, the area of the Ith trapezoid is

$$(\sqrt{1 - ((I - 1)/P)^2} + \sqrt{1 - (I/P)^2})/2P.$$

This formula for the trapezoid area directly uses the formula

$$Y = \sqrt{1 - X^2}$$

for the quarter circle curve. If some other curve were involved, then this formula would be replaced and the estimate would proceed in the same

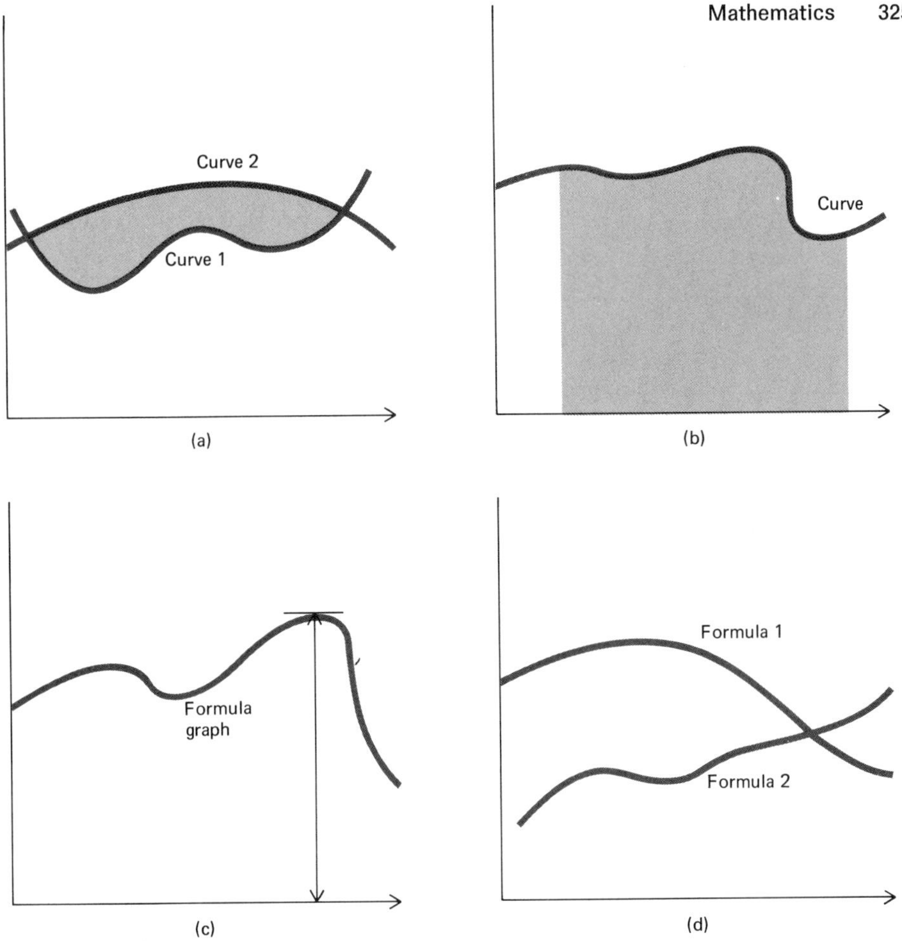

FIGURE 12–1. ***Three mathematical problems: Find the area between two curves (a) or, almost equivalent, find the area between a curve and the x-axis (b). Find the highest point on the curve from a given formula (c). Find where the graphs of two formulas intersect (d).***

manner. A Fortran program is given below which computes the area estimate for any number *P* of pieces used.

```
C         THE CURVES FORMULA IS CURVE(X)
      CURVE(X) = SQRT(1.-X*X)
      INTEGER P
      READ 5,P
    5 FORMAT(I5)
      FP = P
      AREA = 0.
      DO 10 K=1,P
      FK = K
   10 AREA = AREA + CURVE((FK-1.)/FP) + CURVE(FK/FP)
      AREA = AREA/(2.*FP)
      PRINT 15,P,AREA
   15 FORMAT(5X13HESTIMATE WITH,I4,9H PIECES =,F12.6)
      STOP
      END
```

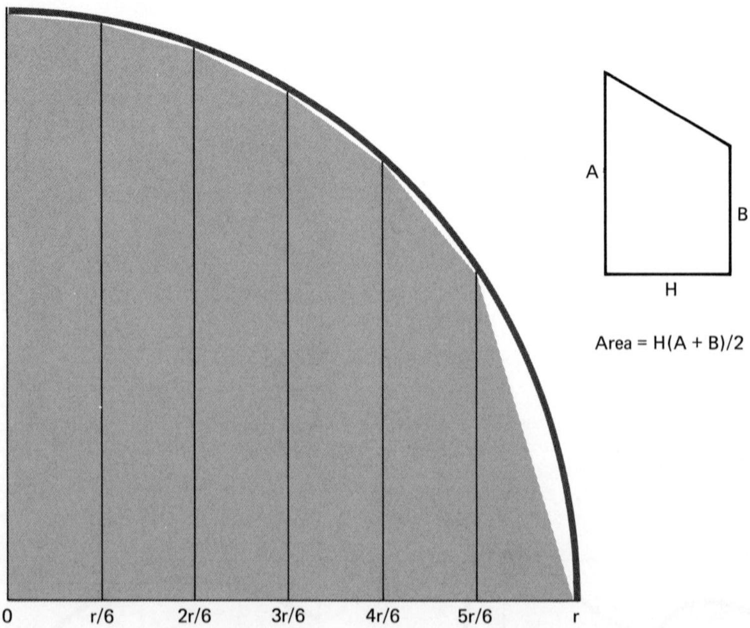

FIGURE 12–2. The estimation of the area of a quarter-circle by breaking it up into trapezoidal pieces.

Crucial questions at this point are: How good is the estimate we obtain? How many pieces should we use? How does one know when enough pieces are used? The answers to these questions are not easy and a thorough discussion of them is much beyond the scope of this book. However, in many situations one can answer these questions using one's knowledge of the particular curve involved and common sense. One particularly useful approach is to make estimates with more and more pieces. As P gets larger the estimates get closer to the true answer and hence to one another. When the differences between the estimates are satisfactorily small, one says the estimates have *converged* and accepts them. This approach is *not* infallible so one must always proceed with caution. If the estimates do not converge, then, of course, something is definitely wrong.

The careful reader may have noticed that the computation in the above program can be made more efficient. That program evaluates the formula CURVE(X) twice at each point except the end points. This double evaluation may be avoided and if we let C(I) denote the value of CURVE(I/P), then the area estimate is given by

$$\text{AREA} = [C(0) + 2 * [C(1) + C(2) + \cdots + C(P-2) + C(P-1)] + C(P)]/(2P)$$

$$= \frac{C(0) + C(P)}{2P} + [C(1) + C(2) + \cdots + C(P-2) + C(P-1)]/P.$$

One may improve the efficiency for smooth curves by replacing the broken line with something smoother. A variety of such schemes exist, and the most common one (*Simpson's rule*) is based on using pieces of parabolas rather than broken lines. See Problem 12–5. This method is much more effective for smooth curves and requires hardly any additional computation.

The methods used for maximizing and for finding the intersection of curves are closely related to one another and we consider only the latter problem here. The related methods for maximizing are given as part of some of the problems at the end of this chapter.

EXAMPLE 12–2

THE ESTIMATION OF ZEROS OF A CURVE

We first note that locating the intersection of two curves is exactly equivalent to locating the zero of a single curve which is the difference between the two original curves. Thus we may restrict our attention to this apparently simpler problem.

The methods most appropriate for this problem belong to the class of *scientific trial-and-error* methods. The basic steps in the scientific trial-and-error method are as follows:

1. Guess at the solution (the location of the zero)
2. Examine the situation and determine a direction to move that (hopefully) improves upon the guess
3. Make a move in that direction
4. Return to step 2.

The "scientific" part of the method is supposed to enter at step 2 where a systematic and scientific analysis is to be made. That analysis might be very simple or very complicated. Two such methods are examined here.

Perhaps the simplest of all the methods is known as the *bisection* or *half-interval* method. The first step is to find two points, one where the curve is above the x-axis (positive) and one where it is below (negative). The process is then continued as illustrated in Figure 12–3. One then examines the curve at the point half-way between these points. The curve at this point is either above or below the x-axis unless one is lucky and has found the solution. The curve here is thus on the opposite side of the x-axis from one of the end points and the zero must lie in between. In this

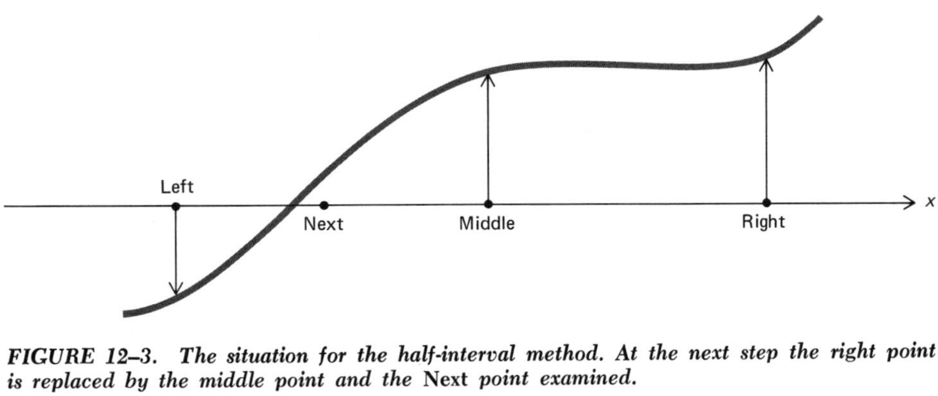

***FIGURE 12–3.** The situation for the half-interval method. At the next step the right point is replaced by the middle point and the* Next *point examined.*

way the interval in which the zero must lie is cut in half or bisected. This process is repeated with the middle point replacing the appropriate end point. At each iteration of this method the uncertainty in the possible location of the zero is halved and one continues it until the uncertainty is satisfactorily small.

The other method we consider is the *secant* method. It is usually much more efficient than the half-interval method, but then it sometimes fails to work at all. Of course, the half-interval method might fail also if one cannot locate appropriate left and right points to start the process. In fact, some curves (for example, $Y = X^2$) have a zero value but never change sign. The basic ingredients of the secant method are illustrated in Figure 12–4. One again makes two guesses at the solution (call them X1 and X2) and then draws a straight line through the two points on the curve determined by X1 and X2. This secant line meets the x-axis (is zero) at some point, say NEXT. This point then replaces the one of X1 or X2 farthest from it and it is the next estimate of the zero.

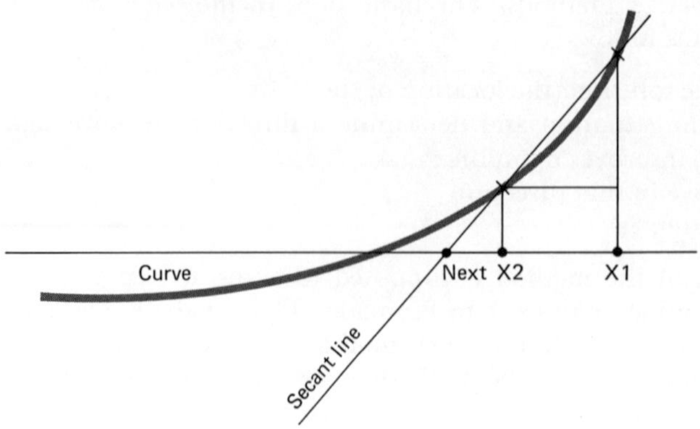

FIGURE 12–4. The situation for the secant method. Once the* Next *point is determined from the secant line, it replaces the point* X1 *and the process is repeated.

One can determine the location of NEXT without drawing by using either geometry or trigonometry. From the geometry of similar triangles we know that

$$\frac{\text{NEXT} - \text{X1}}{\text{X2} - \text{X1}} = \frac{0 - \text{CURVE(X1)}}{\text{CURVE(X2)} - \text{CURVE(X1)}}.$$

If α is the angle between the x-axis and the secant line, then from trigonometry we know that

$$\tan \alpha = \frac{\text{CURVE(X1)}}{\text{X1} - \text{NEXT}} = \frac{\text{CURVE(X2)}}{\text{X2} - \text{NEXT}}.$$

In either case we can solve for the value of NEXT as follows:

$$\text{NEXT} = \text{X1} - \text{CURVE(X1)} \left[\frac{\text{X2} - \text{X1}}{\text{CURVE(X2)} - \text{CURVE(X1)}} \right].$$

This formula may then be used to compute the next point, and the secant method is used iteratively until it either converges or until one is ready to give up.

A program to illustrate the secant method is given below. One initial guess is read in as data along with a tolerance value UNCERT. The program then calculates a second initial point and iterates up to 100 times or up to convergence.

```
C        THE CURVES,FORMULA IS CURVE(X)
      CURVE(X)=EXP(2.9-X)-(1.+ABS(X)**1.4)/(.3+(X-4.)**4 )
      REAL NEXT
      READ 5,X1,UNCERT
    5 FORMAT( 2F10.5)
      X2 = X1 + .5 + .01*ABS(X1)
      C2 = CURVE(X2)
      DO 10 J = 1,100                                    ┐
      C1 = CURVE(X1)                                     │
      NEXT = X1 - C1*(X2-X1)/(C2-C1)                     │ Main
      IF( ABS(NEXT-X1) .LT. UNCERT )   GO TO 30 ── Test for convergence
      X2 = X1                                            │ loop
      C2 = C1                                            │
   10 X1 = NEXT                                          ┘
      PRINT 20,X1,C1                                                      ┐ "No
   20 FORMAT(2X8(1H*),11HDIVERGED TO,E14.5,8H CURVE =,E14.5)             │ convergence"
      STOP                                                                ┘ message
   30 V = CURVE(NEXT)
      PRINT 40, NEXT,V,J
   40 FORMAT( 10X,12HCONVERGED TO,F14.8,8H CURVE =,E14.5/
     *                   I16,12H  ITERATIONS )
      STOP
      END
```

Problems

12–1 (a) Apply the algorithm developed in Example 12–1 to estimate the areas determined by the formulas and values of a and b given below.

(i)	$y(x) = \sin x$	$a = 0,$	$b = \pi/2$
(ii)	$y(x) = e^{x+1}$	$a = -1,$	$b = 1$
(iii)	$y(x) = 1 + x^2 - x^3$	$a = 0,$	$b = 2$
(iv)	$y(x) = \lvert x - .5\rvert$	$a = -1,$	$b = 1$

Use 50 or 100 points in the broken lines to replace the curves. Compare the estimates you obtain with the exact values.

(b) Apply the algorithm to estimate the areas determined by the curves and values of a and b given below. The exact values for these areas are not known.

(i)	$y(x) = \sin x/x$	$a = \pi/2,$	$b = 2\pi$
(ii)	$y(x) = x \log(x^3 + 3)/(1 - \sqrt{\lvert x\rvert})$	$a = 2,$	$b = 5$
(iii)	$y(x) = \cos(x^2 + 1)\sin^2(x + 2)\tan(x^3 - 4)$	$a = 0,$	$b = \pi/4$
(iv)	$y(x) = (x^2 \sin(x))/\log((x^2 + 1) + \sqrt{\lvert x\rvert})$	$a = -1,$	$b = +1$

(v)
$$y(x) = \begin{cases} 1 + \sqrt{1 - (x+1)^2} & -2 \leq x \leq -1 \\ 2e^{x+1}/(x+2) & -1 \leq x \leq 0 \\ 2e^{1-x}/(2-x) & 0 \leq x \leq 1 \\ 1 + \sqrt{1 - (x-1)^2} & 1 \leq x \leq 2 \end{cases} \qquad a = -2, \quad b = +2$$

12–2 Extend the methods used in Problem 12–1 to estimate the following areas:

(a)

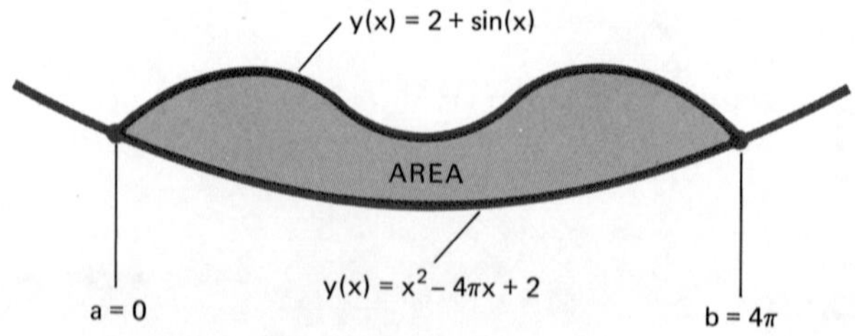

(b)

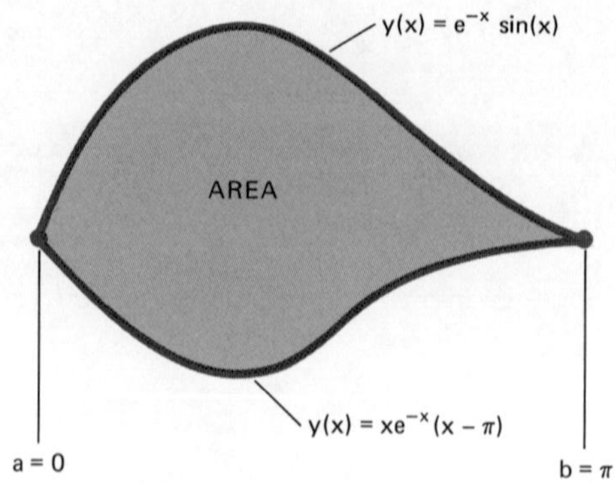

(c)

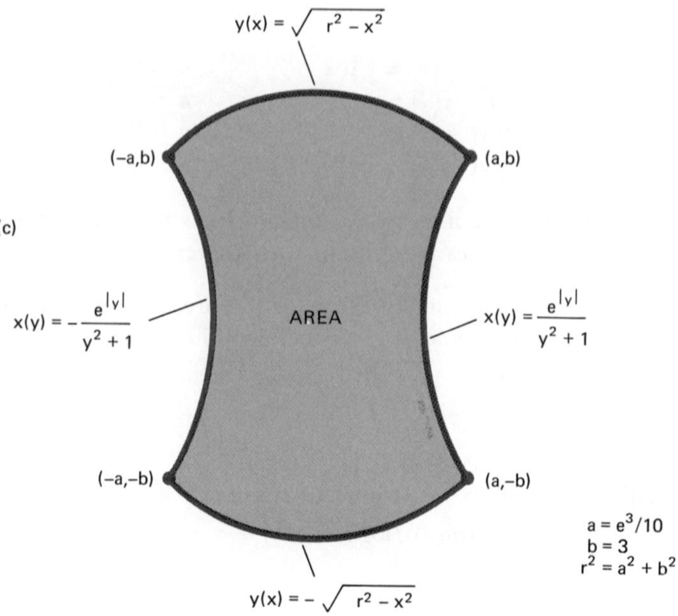

12–3 *(Monte Carlo integration)* Consider the following diagram:

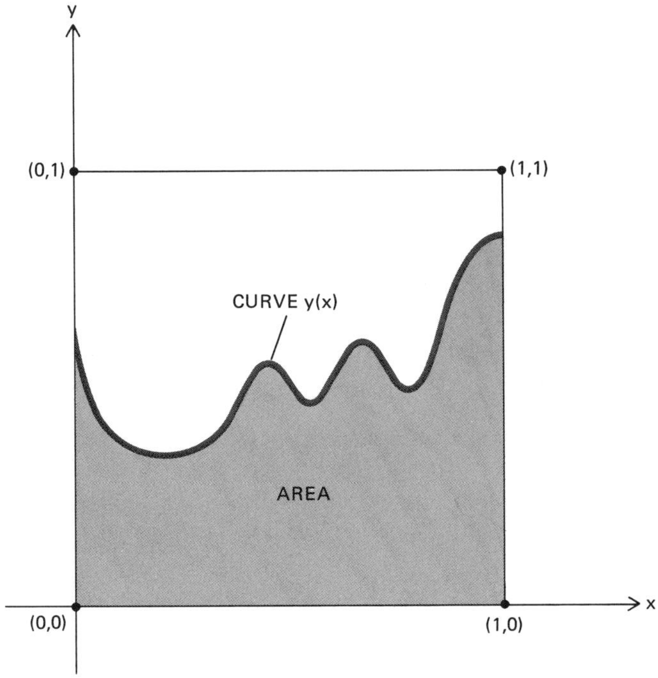

If we choose a point at random in the square, the probability that it lies in the shaded region is just the area of the shaded region. Thus, if we choose 100 points at random in the square and 69 of them are in the shaded region, we could expect that region to have approximately 69 percent of the area of the square. If we choose 1000 points at random and 678 of them are in the shaded region, we would then estimate the area to be about 0.68. This approach to estimating area is known as Monte Carlo integration.

(a) Show how we can obtain a random point (x,y) in the above square if we can compute random numbers between 0 and 1. How do we know if the random point (x,y) lies in the shaded region?

(b) Use a random-number generator and estimate the areas given in Problem 12–1. Show your estimates based on 50, 100, 150, 200, 300, and 500 random points.

(c) Describe how to use this technique to estimate the areas of Problem 12–2, especially Problem 12–2(c).

(d) A similar, nonrandom, approach is to place points systematically in the square in order to make the estimates. Thus, given two integers K and L, we place (K + 1) * (L + 1) points in the square at

$$X_I = \frac{I}{K}, \qquad I = 0, 1, 2, 3, \ldots, K,$$

$$Y_J = \frac{J}{L}, \qquad J = 0, 1, 2, 3, \ldots, L.$$

Repeat the estimations of part (b) with this approach. Show your estimates based on K = L = 6, K = L = 11, K = L = 13, K = L = 16, and K = L = 21. Compare the accuracy obtained this way with that of part (b) and that obtained in Problem 12–1.

12–4 *(Three computations of the value of π)* The ancients knew (or at least believed) that the area of a circle is proportional to the square of the radius of the circle. This constant of proportionality was given the name π. The value of 3 was widely used even though the more accurate value of $256/81 = 3.1605$ was used by the Egyptians before 1700 B.C. This was obtained empirically.

The greatest scientist and mathematician of antiquity, Archimedes, found a way to calculate the value of π as accurately as is desired. He proceeded as illustrated below.

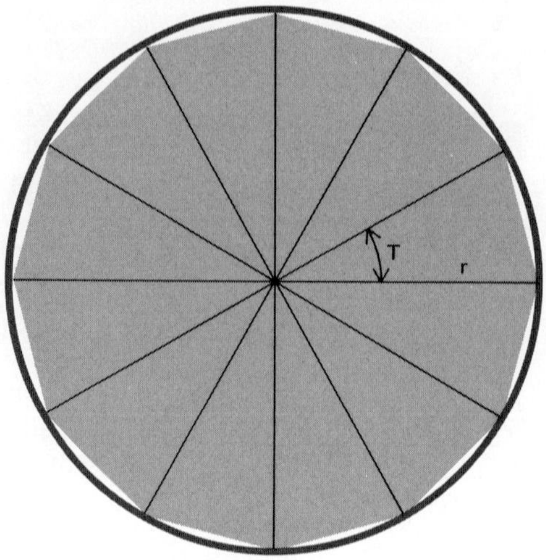

We inscribe a regular polygon with many sides inside the circle. We then calculate the area of this polygon. This calculation can be made in terms of calculating the area of triangles, which is a solved problem. We then inscribe the circle inside another regular polygon and calculate its area in a similar manner. The first area is smaller than that of the circle and the second area is larger. Archimedes carried out this calculation for polygons with 96 sides and obtained the following estimates:

$$3.1409\ldots = 3\frac{1137}{8069} < \pi < 3\frac{1335}{9347} = 3.1428\ldots.$$

We may proceed similarly and note that the area of one of the small inscribed triangles is given by

$$\text{Area} = \sin(T/2) * \cos(T/2) = \frac{\sin(T)}{2},$$

where T is the angle at the apex of the triangle.

A second method that may be used to estimate π is based on the infinite series

$$\pi = 4(1 - \frac{1}{3} + \frac{1}{5} - \frac{1}{7} + \frac{1}{9} - \cdots) = 4 \sum_{I=0}^{\infty} \frac{(-1)^I}{2I+1}.$$

A third method is to proceed similarly to Archimedes except that the area of a quarter circle is estimated using the method of Example 12–1.

(a) Write three Fortran programs to estimate the value of π using each of these three methods.

(b) Each of these programs will encounter some difficulty, and one is not able to find the value of π as accurately as one would hope. Explain and discuss the nature of the difficulties with each of these three methods.

12–5 *(Simpson's rule)* A more accurate area estimation scheme for smooth curves is obtained by replacing the straight lines of the trapezoidal rule (Figure 12–2) with parabolas. The situation is sketched below.

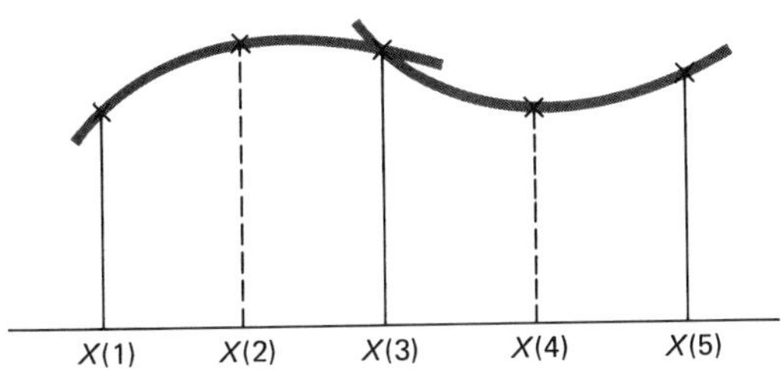

One picks sets of three points off the curve and then finds the parabola that passes through these points (there is exactly one). One then uses the formula for the area under a parabola to obtain an estimate of the area under the curve. The algebra required to carry this out is rather tedious, but the end result is a very simple formula for the estimation. If we let $C(I)$ be the values on the curve and break the interval into P pieces [so that $X(I+1) - X(I) = 1/P$], we find that

$$\text{Area from } X(1) \text{ to } X(3) \sim [C(1) + 4C(2) + C(3)]/(3P),$$

$$\text{Area from } X(3) \text{ to } X(5) \sim [C(3) + 4C(4) + C(5)]/(3P),$$

$$\cdots$$

These area estimates may be added together to obtain the formula for Simpson's rule (for $P + 1$ points on the curve)

$$\text{Area} \sim [C(1) + 4C(2) + 2C(3) + 4C(5) + 2C(6) + \cdots + 2C(P-1) + 4C(P) + C(P+1)] * \frac{1}{(3P)}.$$

This formula assumes that the total length under the area is 1 and the factor $1/(3P)$ must be changed to $L/(3P)$ if the length is L.

Write a program to obtain Simpson's rule estimates of areas and apply it to the areas of Problem 12–1(a). Compare the accuracy obtained with 50 or 100 points by Simpson's rule with that obtained using trapezoids.

12–6 Apply the half-interval method to locate a zero of each of the curves specified.

(a) $y = \cos(x) - \sqrt{|x|}$
(b) $y = \ln(10 + \sqrt{|x|}) - 3x^3$
(c) $y = 1 - (8x^3 - 12x^2)\ln(10.5 - x) - 6x$
(d) $y = \sqrt{\ln(3 - e^x + \sqrt{|x|}/2) + .001}$

12–7 Apply the secant method to locate a zero of each of the curves specified.

(a) Any of the curves of Problem 12–6
(b) $y = (1 - e^{1000(x-.99)})e^{20(x-1)}$
(c) $y = 8(x - .2)^3 - 12x^2 + 10.8x - 2.68$
(d) $y = (1 + \ln(|x| + 1))\cos x - 4\tan(x/2)$
(e) Compare the amount of effort (computing time) for this method and that of Problem 12–6.

12–8 We want to deposit a sum of money in the bank which will grow to $10,000 in 11 years. The bank pays 4 percent interest the first year, 4.5 percent interest the second year, and 5 percent interest thereafter. The interest is computed and added to the principal annually.

(a) Formulate this problem in such a way that the sum X to be deposited is the value such that a particular curve $y = f(X)$ is zero at X. Determine the sum X.
(b) Suppose the bank makes a special offer to attract large accounts. The offer is to pay an extra .01 percent interest for each $1000 in the account (with a limit of .2 percent extra interest). Determine the sum to be deposited in this situation.
(c) Take the sums found in parts (a) and (b) and determine the constant rate of interest needed for them to grow to $10,000 in 11 years.

12–9 We have a $21,000 mortgage on a house at 6.5 percent annual interest. The mortgage is to last 27 years. The interest on the balance of the mortgage is computed each month, and we must pay this interest plus an amount to reduce the balance.

(a) Determine a constant payment on the mortgage which pays it off in exactly 27 years. Formulate this problem in such a way that the sum X to be paid is the value such that a particular curve $y = f(X)$ is zero at X. What is the total amount of interest paid?
(b) Suppose we expect substantial inflation to take place. Determine the amount paid on the mortgage in terms of today's dollars if the value of a dollar decreases 4 percent each year. Assume that the decrease takes place all at one time at the end of the year. How much is the last payment in terms of today's dollars?

12–10 Consider a married man with two children ages 5 and 10. If he dies, he wishes to leave an estate that provides support for the family as follows:

1. Provide \$500 per month until the oldest is 18
2. Provide \$700 per month for the next 4 years
3. Provide \$400 per month the following year
4. Provide \$600 per month the next 4 years
5. Provide \$150 per month the next 15 years
6. Leave a sum of \$20,000 at this point.

Assume that the estate is invested at 5 percent interest paid annually and that the above sums are withdrawn monthly.

The problem is to determine the size of the estate that must be left in order to provide this support. Formulate this problem in such a way that you require a value of x such that the curve $y = f(x)$ is zero. With this formulation of the problem:

(a) Apply the half-interval method,
(b) Apply the secant method,
(c) Compare the amount of effort (computing time) required by these two methods.

12–11 If a curve is smooth, then the points on a curve where it is highest and lowest have a special property: Either they are at the ends of the curve or the slope (tangent, derivative) of the curve is zero there.
(a) Discuss how one can use this observation to find the maxima and minima of curves by using a method to find the zeros of a curve.
(b) Give an example to show that the slope may be zero without a maximum or minimum and discuss how this would affect one's effort to find the highest point on a complicated curve.
(c) The use of this observation requires one to be able to obtain estimates (at least rough ones) of the slope of a curve at a point. Discuss how this might be done.

12–12 *(Blind man's search for a maxima)* A blind man can determine an "uphill" direction by getting on his knees and feeling around. A method to "climb up" a curve can be modeled from this observation. One takes steps of a certain length "uphill" until one starts down hill. One then turns around and starts back taking smaller steps (say half as long). This may be repeated many times to locate the highest point accurately.
(a) Formulate this method more precisely and write a program that uses it.
(b) Explain the difficulty that arises when this program is applied to the curve given by the formula

$$Y = X(X-1)(X-3)(X-4)(X-5)(X-7)/(1+(X-2)^6).$$

12–13 *(Trisection method for maximization of concave curves)* A curve is concave if its slope continually decreases (often going from positive to negative) as one goes from left to right (as x increases). One may take four equally spaced points to trisect the curve as in the diagram

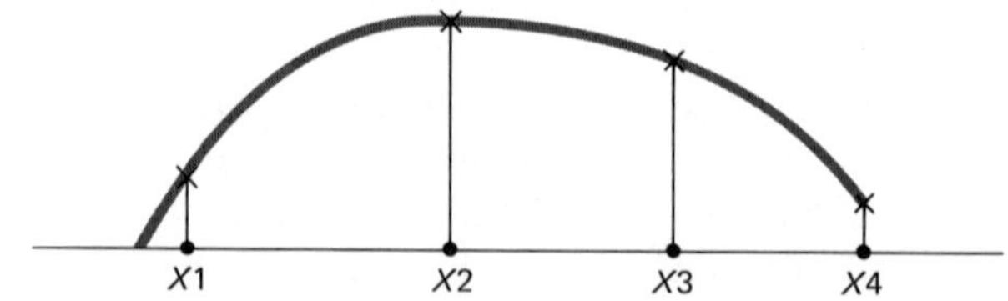

Consider the two middle points. If the one (X2) on the left is highest, then the maxima of the curve is between X1 and X3. If the one (X3) on the right is highest, then the maxima is between X2 and X4.

(a) Explain why the location of the highest point is constrained as stated above.

(b) Write a program that incorporates this method in an iterative manner and apply it to compute the maximum value on the curve

$$Y = X\sqrt{1 - X}$$

for X between 0 and 1.

12–14 Use one of the methods of Problems 12–11, 12–12, and 12–13 to determine the lowest point on the following curves:

(a) $y = e^{x+\sin x} + \ln(1 + x^2)$

(b) $y = (e^{x * \sin\sqrt{1+|x|} * \ln(1+x^2)})\,(1 + x^2)\ln(1 + |x|^3)$

(c) $y = e^{1/|x|} + e^{1/|x-1|} + (x - .3)^2$

(d) $y = 1 + \sqrt{x}\sin(1 - \sqrt{x})\cos(x) \qquad \text{for } 0 \leq x \leq 10$

12–15 Take the method developed in Problem 12–12 and extend it to mathematical surfaces by searching in eight directions for a lower point; that is, evaluate the function defining the surface for all combinations of slightly smaller, slightly larger, and the same values for x and y.

Apply this method to the following surfaces:

(a) $z = (x - y)^2 + (x + y)^2 + \ln(3. + |x - 1|)$

(b) $z = 1 + \sin(xy) * \cos(x - y) + (.5 - x + y)^2$

(c) $z = (x + y)^2 * \ln(1.5 + 5|xy|) + \cos(xy)$

(d) $z = 1 + (x - y)^3\,|x + y|\,\sin(xy) * \sin(x - y)\,e^{xy}$

12–16 Construct an algorithm to estimate the sum of an *infinite series*

$$\sum_{n=1}^{\infty} a_n.$$

Apply the algorithm as implemented by a program to the following infinite series:

(a) $\displaystyle\sum_{n=1}^{\infty} \frac{1}{n^2}$ (d) $\displaystyle\sum_{n=1}^{\infty} \frac{(-1)^n}{n^3 + n^2}$

(b) $\sum_{n=1}^{\infty} \frac{n^2}{3^n + 1}$ (e) $\sum_{n=1}^{\infty} \frac{n^4 \sin(n^2 + 1)}{\log(n^4 + 4)4^n}$

(c) $\sum_{n=1}^{\infty} \frac{1}{n}$ (f) $\sum_{n=1}^{\infty} \frac{\log(1 + \log(1 + n^2))}{(1 + 1/n)^n \sqrt{n^7 + n^9}}$

12–17 *(The estimation of derivatives)* The definition of the derivative of a function $f(x)$ at the point x is

$$f'(x) = \frac{df}{dx} = \lim_{\Delta x \to 0} \frac{f(x + \Delta x) - f(x)}{\Delta x}.$$

The derivative at x is the slope of the curve $y = f(x)$ at the point x.

(a) Interpret the definition of the derivative as a method for estimating slopes based on approximating a curve by a broken line and then using the slope of the broken line.

(b) We can also obtain the derivative by

$$f'(x) = \frac{df}{dx} = \lim_{\Delta x \to 0} \frac{f(x + \Delta x) - f(x - \Delta x)}{2\Delta x}.$$

Explain how this formula can also be interpreted as a method for estimating slopes in the same way as the original definition.

(c) Use each of these two algorithms to estimate the derivatives of the following functions at the specified points. A suitable set of Δx's is also given.

	Function	*Estimate $f'(x)$ At*	*Suitable Δx Values*
(i)	e^x	0, +1, −1	.2, .1, .05, .01, .001, .0001
(ii)	$\sin x$	0.$\pi/4$,$\pi/2$	same
(iii)	x^2	0, 1, 10	1.0, .2, .1, .01, .001, .0001
(iv)	x^{10}	0. 1, 5	same
(v)	$\log x$	1.0, 2.0, 100.0	same
(vi)	$\log x$	.001, .01, .1	.01, .005, .001, .0001, .00005

(d) Compare the estimates (in particular, the best estimates) you obtain with the exact values of the derivatives.

13

Economic Models

13—1 The Construction of Economic Models

Economics and business operations are areas where the construction and use of mathematical models has had (and will continue to have) a large impact. These areas are quite complex and even greatly simplified situations often result in rather complex models. The models are collections of relationships which are primarily equations (for example, the cost of shipping is the number of items shipped times $10.50) and inequalities (for example, the number of items manufactured in a week must be less than 450). There are, of course, frequently other types of relationships such as large tables of data, but the models normally consist of a *large* number of equations and inequalities. By large, we mean several hundred or several thousand. Thus, it might be a major project just to identify and write down all of these relationships, never mind doing anything with them. Except for the most simplified and elementary situations, it is hopeless to solve the resulting problems without the aid of a computer.

We consider three examples of problems in this chapter which illustrate some of the variety of applications and the way one constructs economic models. These examples are, of necessity, from simple situations so that the models are not overly complex. It is important to be aware of the fact that many diverse application areas lead to the same mathematical problems. That is to say, after the model is constructed (and we have a mathematical problem) the techniques for obtaining a solution are the same. The areas of *linear programming* and *nonlinear programming* contain a large body of theory and methods which are particularly important in the solution of problems that arise out of economic models. The use of the word "program" in these two names is of uncertain origin, but it does not refer to computer programming in any way (linear programming is an older discipline than computer programming).

13–2 Production Scheduling and Product Distribution

The problem of economically supplying several places, say warehouses, with material from several sources, say factories, arises in many situations. Some concrete examples are:

1. Stocking warehouses from factory production
2. Filling dealer's orders from warehouse stocks
3. Supplying a pipeline distribution system from oil fields
4. Deploying troops to the front lines from home bases.

In each of these situations the problem is to determine how the distribution is to be made so as to minimize the cost of transportation. Furthermore, there are often constraints on the materials to be supplied or differences in their cost which are to be taken into consideration.

The example we consider is illustrated in Figure 13–1. We might suppose that this example occurs for a company that makes earth movers. It has 3 factories and 5 warehouses that keep supplies for dealers. There are three basic kinds of variables that appear in the model of this situation:

Production Capacity: Let F(I) denote the monthly production capacity of the Ith factory.

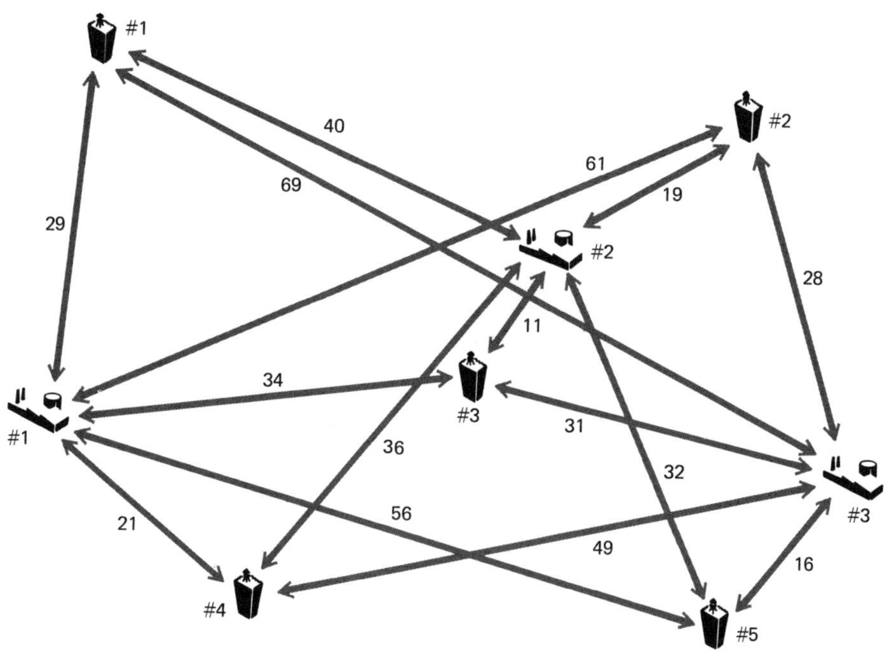

FIGURE 13–1. A typical distribution system with three factories and five warehouses.

Product Demand: Let W(J) denote the monthly demand at the Jth warehouse.

Transportation Costs: The cost of transporting one earth mover from the Ith factory to the Jth warehouse is denoted by T(I,J).

The natural approach to this problem is to supply each warehouse from the factory closest to it. If the production capacity of the factories is sufficient for this, then it is the most economical thing to do. The difficulty arises when the production capacity is insufficient. The following set of values of the variables illustrates this possibility:

$$F(1) = 20 \quad F(2) = 12 \quad F(3) = 8$$
$$W(1) = 8 \quad W(2) = 10 \quad W(3) = 4 \quad W(4) = 5 \quad W(5) = 9$$

Transportation Costs T(I,J)

		I: 1	2	3
	1	29	49	69
	2	61	19	28
J	3	34	11	31
	4	21	36	49
	5	56	32	16

We see that factory 3 is the closest to warehouse 5, but the demand there is more than the production capacity of factory 3.

In order to analyze this problem further, we introduce the

Distribution Array: The number of items shipped from the Ith factory to the Jth warehouse is denoted by S(I,J). These are the variables that are to be determined so as to minimize the costs involved.

These variables must satisfy certain requirements and constraints in order to be candidates for a solution to this problem. They are:

Demand Requirement: The number of items shipped to the Jth warehouse must equal the demand there. This is expressed by the five equations

$$\begin{aligned}
S(1,1) + S(2,1) + S(3,1) &= W(1),\\
S(1,2) + S(2,2) + S(3,2) &= W(2),\\
S(1,3) + S(2,3) + S(3,3) &= W(3),\\
S(1,4) + S(2,4) + S(3,4) &= W(4),\\
S(1,5) + S(2,5) + S(3,5) &= W(5).
\end{aligned}$$

Production Limits: The number of items shipped from the Ith factory must not exceed the production capacity of this factory. This is expressed by the inequalities

$$\begin{aligned}
S(1,1) + S(1,2) + S(1,3) + S(1,4) + S(1,5) &\le F(1),\\
S(2,1) + S(2,2) + S(2,3) + S(2,4) + S(2,5) &\le F(2),\\
S(3,1) + S(3,2) + S(3,3) + S(3,4) + S(3,5) &\le F(3).
\end{aligned}$$

The total transportation cost for any choice of the distribution array is given by

$$\text{COST} = \sum_{I=1}^{3} \sum_{J=1}^{5} S(I,J) * T(I,J).$$

We can now formulate the problem as follows: *Determine the distribution array* S(I,J) *so as to minimize the transportation cost COST subject to the demand requirement and the production limits.* The economic problem has been reduced to a purely mathematical one of determining certain variables (the S(I,J)) which satisfy certain equations (from the demand at the 5 warehouses) and certain inequalities (from the production capacities of the 3 factories) and which minimize a certain quantity (the cost equation). We briefly consider below the use of a "brute force" technique of solving this problem. This kind of technique is *rarely* efficient except for the *tiniest* of problems (which is not the case here).

There are only a limited number of choices for S(I,J) which satisfy the requirements. Thus we can evaluate COST for each of these choices and choose the one that gives the minimum value. This raises the important question of how to generate all the possible candidates for the S(I,J) array. The simplest scheme is to note that

$$0 \leq S(I,J) < \text{minimum } [F(I), W(J)].$$

We could use iteration statements in Fortran to generate values systematically between these limits. We could then check demand requirements and production limits and, if these conditions are satisfied, evaluate COST. In this way we would eventually evaluate all the possible candidates for a solution and locate the one with lowest cost. An obvious improvement on this approach is to force the demand requirements to be met by setting, for J = 1, 2, 3, 4, 5,

$$S(3,J) = W(J) - S(1,J) - S(2,J).$$

If S(3,J) is negative, then the set of values used is not a candidate for a solution.

In order to see how much computation is involved, let us determine how many possibilities there are for the distribution array S(I,J). The ranges of values in the above case are as follows:

$$\begin{array}{lllll}
0 \leq S(1,1) \leq 8 & 0 \leq S(1,2) \leq 10 & 0 \leq S(1,3) \leq 4 & 0 \leq S(1,4) \leq 5 & 0 \leq S(1,5) \leq 9 \\
0 \leq S(2,1) \leq 8 & 0 \leq S(2,2) \leq 10 & 0 \leq S(2,3) \leq 4 & 0 \leq S(2,4) \leq 5 & 0 \leq S(2,5) \leq 9 \\
0 \leq S(3,1) \leq 8 & 0 \leq S(3,2) \leq \ \ 8 & 0 \leq S(3,3) \leq 4 & 0 \leq S(3,4) \leq 5 & 0 \leq S(3,5) \leq 8
\end{array}$$

The total number of combinations that we would examine with the first simple approach is

$$9 * 11 * 5 * 6 * 10 * 9 * 11 * 5 * 6 * 10 * 9 * 9 * 5 * 6 * 9 = 19{,}291{,}308{,}300{,}000$$

or about 19 trillion. This is clearly too many for any actual computation to be made. The improvement of determining S(3,J) from W(J), S(1,J), and S(2,J) decreases this number substantially. The total number of combinations is then

$$9 * 11 * 5 * 6 * 10 * 9 * 11 * 5 * 6 * 10 = 882{,}090{,}000.$$

This improvement is of several orders of magnitude and makes a computation almost possible; for example, it might take about 250 hours on a large computer. Note that we can modify this improvement slightly to determine S(1,J) from W(J), S(2,J), and S(3,J) which reduces the number of combinations to examine to

$$9 * 11 * 5 * 6 * 10 * 9 * 9 * 5 * 6 * 9 = 649{,}539{,}000.$$

The number of combinations to be examined can be further reduced by noting that we must have

$$\begin{aligned} &0 \leq S(3,J) \leq W(J), \\ &0 \leq S(2,J) \leq W(J) - S(3,J), \\ &S(1,J) = W(J) - S(3,J) - S(2,J). \end{aligned}$$

A short calculation shows that this leads to 28,704,375 combinations to be examined. Note that this approach now always gives a candidate that satisfies the demand requirements.

Even though the number of candidates has been drastically reduced, the number is still very large, and the solution of the problem is just barely feasible with this method. This particular type of problem has been extensively analyzed, and much more efficient methods from linear programming are available to solve it.

A program on a typical computer using an efficient method can solve this problem in a few seconds compared to the few hours required for the brute force or *enumeration* approach. The solution of the problem is

$$\begin{array}{lllll} S(1,1) = 8, & S(1,2) = 0, & S(1,3) = 3, & S(1,4) = 5, & S(1,5) = 0 \\ S(2,1) = 0, & S(2,2) = 10, & S(2,3) = 1, & S(2,4) = 0, & S(2,5) = 1 \\ S(3,1) = 0, & S(3,2) = 0, & S(3,3) = 0, & S(3,4) = 0, & S(3,5) = 8 \end{array}$$

and the lowest cost is 800.

The problem in this example is really not very large. The automobile manufacturers have 8 to 25 assembly plants and supply several thousand dealers from these plants.

13—3 Enumeration and the Traveling Salesman Problem

The brute force approach sketched in the previous section is called *enumeration*. This approach is very common (and effective) for small problems, but becomes completely impractical as the complexity of the problem grows.

The basic idea of the enumeration method is to examine all the possible candidates for the solution and select the one that is the solution. There are two essential ingredients in this method. They are:

1. The candidates for the solution must be known, and their number must be small enough so that they may all be examined.
2. There must be some test or criterion to find out which of the candidates is actually the solution.

Once these two ingredients are present, we need only examine all of the candidates systematically to find the solution.

The actual numbers that we consider "small enough" may vary greatly. It depends on the amount of effort required to examine a particular candidate and the amount of effort we want to put into the solution of the problem. Sometimes three or four candidates are too many, and at other times we may be willing to examine millions of them.

There are two distinct kinds of tests that we may use. The first kind can be applied to each candidate independently of the others. For example, we may want the name of a book written by Karl X. Deal. We check each book on the shelf to see if it is written by Karl X. Deal. Once one of his books is located, the search is over.

The second kind of test is "built up" during the examination. It is usually associated with a problem that involves comparisons. These problems want solutions that are "best," "fastest," "cheapest," "maximum," "shortest," "highest," "representative," "average," "middle-sized," and so forth.

We consider another problem which is a widely studied example and which arises in many situations. This problem is known as the *traveling salesman problem* and is formulated as follows:

A traveling salesman must go from one city to another and make stops at several intermediate cities in route. The problem is to find the shortest route for him to take. Similar problems arise in building pipelines, laying communication lines, designing transportation networks, and so forth. The problem is illustrated in Figure 13–2 where 18 cities are shown. Also shown is one possible route from Detroit to New York which passes through the remaining 16 cities.

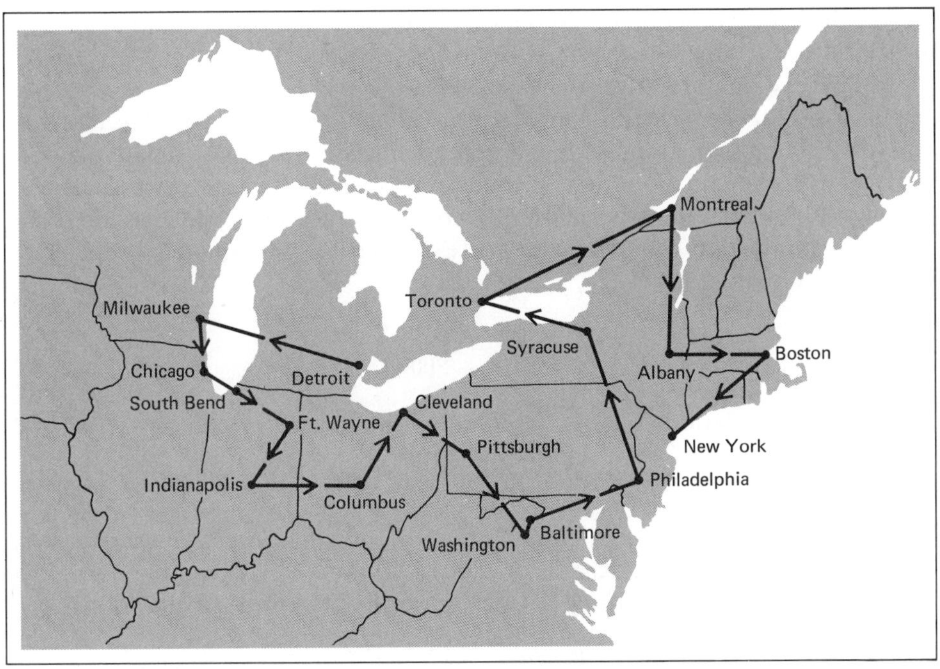

FIGURE 13–2. The cities to be visited by the traveling salesman.

The method of enumeration applied here requires computation of the lengths of all of the possible routes from Detroit to New York. Recall that the number of ways to arrange n items is $n!$. Thus, the number of different routes from Detroit to New York through these 16 cities is 16!. Factorials grow very large very fast. A few approximate values are listed below.

$$\begin{aligned} 4! &= 24; \\ 8! &= 40{,}000; \\ 12! &= 470{,}000{,}000; \\ 16! &= 20{,}900{,}000{,}000{,}000; \\ 20! &= 2{,}400{,}000{,}000{,}000{,}000{,}000. \end{aligned}$$

If the length of a particular route could be computed in one millionth of a second, it would take about 50,000 years to find the shortest route through 20 intermediate cities. In the present case, with 16 cities and a more realistic computation time of one hundredth of a second, it would take about 4000 years to find the shortest route. Thus, this problem is not to be solved by the enumeration method unless there are only a very few cities.

13—4 Models for the Theory of Taxation

The discussion in this section involves a situation where the computations required are simple and can be easily made by hand. The point is to illustrate the use of economic models in studying alternative methods of taxation. In a more realistic situation one would obtain complex models and a computer would be helpful in carrying out the necessary computation.

First we consider the situation when there are no taxes and a certain manufacturer has to price his product, say automatic fly swatters. He has long experience in this area and through careful analysis and experimentation has arrived at two key relationships. These are between consumer's price (call it P) and monthly sales (call it X) and between production rate (which is the same as X) and production costs C. These are expressed by two equations (but given in terms of cents):

$$\begin{aligned} \text{P} &= 190 - .01 * \text{X}, \\ \text{C} &= 70\text{X} + 20000. \end{aligned}$$

From these two relationships he can obtain a formula for profit:

$$\text{PROFIT} = \text{X} * \text{P} - \text{C} = \text{X}(190 - .01 * \text{X}) - (70\text{X} + 20000).$$

The manufacturer can set the price P and, of course, he wants to choose it so as to maximize PROFIT. Recall there is a formula for obtaining the value XMAX of X which maximizes a value V given by a formula of the form

$$V = aX^2 + bX + c.$$

The formula for XMAX is (provided a is negative as in our case)

$$\text{XMAX} = \frac{-b}{2a}.$$

The manufacturer applies this formula to his equation

$$\text{PROFIT} = -.01 * \text{X}^2 + 120\text{X} - 20000$$

and finds

$$\text{XMAX} = \frac{120}{.02} = 6000.$$

In order to obtain a sale of 6000 automatic fly swatters a month the price is set at \$1.30 = 190 − 6000 * .01 cents. The net profit can now be evaluated and it is found to be 340,000 cents or \$3400 per month.

This example shows how one can use a simple economic (or mathematical) model in order to give some guidance to managing a business operation. Suppose now that the government decides that it has to have more money and that about \$550 per month is the right share for the automatic fly swatter segment of the economy. There are a number of possible taxes that might be imposed and some of these are presented in Table 13–1.

TABLE 13–1
Five kinds of taxes that could be imposed on the production and/or sales of automatic fly swatters

Name	*Description*
Excise Tax	A fixed amount of tax per item, paid by the manufacturer directly to the government.
Sales Tax	A fixed percentage of tax on the consumer's purchase price, paid by the consumer to the retailer who gives it to the government.
License Fee	A fixed amount paid periodically (monthly or yearly) by the manufacturer to the government. The amount does not vary with costs, prices, sales, profits, or anything else.
Income Tax	A fixed percentage of tax on the manufacturer's net profit, paid by the manufacturer to the government.

The imposition of each of these taxes changes something in the economic model and results in different prices and profits. We consider five rather than the obvious four possibilities given in Table 13–1. The fifth possibility comes from the two assumptions one can make about the consumer's reaction to the sales tax. He might decide solely on the basis of the price before the tax or he might figure the sales tax in the price and then decide. Both assumptions are considered here.

The equations for the resulting models are given below in Table 13–2. We do not go through all of these, but rather only one, the most complicated one. The reader should examine all the models if he wishes to understand how

TABLE 13–2

The three crucial formulas in the models for each of the five taxes and for no tax. The 7 percent Sales Tax 1 refers to the case where the consumer ignores this tax and the 7 percent Sales Tax 2 is the case where it is considered by the consumer

Tax	*Price Formula*	*Cost Formula*	*Profit Formula*
None	190 – .01*X	70X + 20,000	X(190 – .01*X) – (70X + 20,000)
10¢ Excise	190 – .01*X	80X + 20,000	X(190 – .01*X) – (80X + 20,000)
7% Sales Tax 1	1.07(190 – .01*X)	70X + 20,000	X(190 – .01*X) – (70X + 20,000)
7% Sales Tax 2	190 – .01*X	70X + 20,000	.93X(190 – .01*X) – (70X + 20,000)
$550 License	190 – .01*X	70X + 75,000	X(190 – .01*X) – (70X + 75,000)
16% Income Tax	190 – .01*X	70X + 20,000	.84[X(190 – .01*X) – (70X + 20,000)]

the various taxes interact with the automatic fly swatter business (or any other business). The most complicated case is for a 7 percent sales tax where the consumer takes this added cost into consideration before deciding to buy or not to buy. In this case the price P *includes* the tax and is still given by the formula

$$P = 190 - .01 * X.$$

The manufacturer receives only 93 percent of this money and so the equation for his profit becomes (his costs are not affected)

$$\text{PROFIT} = X(190 - .01 * X) * .93 - (70X + 20000).$$

A little calculation and the formula for maximization lead to the conclusion that

$$\text{XMAX} = \frac{106.7}{.186} = 5750.$$

This value may then be substituted back in the equation for P to find that the retail price is $1.33 = $1.24 plus 9¢ tax. The government's revenues are .09 * 5750 = $518 and the manufacturer's profit is $2850 per month. As one would expect, this tax results in higher costs for the consumer and lower profits for the manufacturer. Note, however, that it has another important effect, it results in lower production by the manufacturer.

Once the models for the relationship between profits and price are formulated, the manufacturer can then determine the proper prices to maximize his profits. This has been done for the cases in Table 13–2 and results are summarized in Table 13–3. One can make a number of observations about the results from these models. One sees that the excise tax is the "worst" in that it raises prices considerably, depresses profits the most, and lowers production the most. Although it is not safe to trust completely the results of a simplified analysis like the one given here, this characteristic of the excise tax is also exhibited by more detailed studies. In the United States one finds that excise taxes are used primarily in areas where the government does not care about these effects. For example, luxury items (jewelry, cars, and so on) and items that are semiobjectionable morally (cigarettes, liquor, and so on) have heavy excise taxes placed upon them. Tariffs placed on imported items are another form of excise tax and then, of course, the objective of the government is to discourage imports.

One would conclude from this analysis that licenses and income taxes are the "best" taxes. Of course, the sales tax that is ignored by the consumer looks attractive to everyone except the consumer. He ends up paying the entire tax without really realizing it. However, a more thorough analysis would show that the consumer cannot pay all of the taxes and still buy all of the things he would have bought if there were no taxes. So some manufacturers' sales must inevitably decrease unless the consumer took the money entirely out of his budget for savings, gifts to charity, or something similar. This situation illustrates the pitfalls of reaching general conclusions on the basis of an oversimplified model of the economic situation.

TABLE 13–3

The effects on prices, sales, profits, and government revenues of six different taxation models

Tax	*Consumer's Price*	*Manufacturer's Profit*	*Government Revenues*	*Monthly Sales*
none	$1.30	$3400	0	6000
10¢ Excise	1.35	2825	550	5500
7% Sales Tax 1	1.39	3400	540	6000
7% Sales Tax 2	1.33	2850	520	5750
$550 License	1.30	2850	550	6000
16% Income Tax	1.30	2850	550	6000

Problems

13–1 You have three warehouses (named W1, W2, and W3) with the following number of cases of bamboo shoots in stock:

W1 has 3 cases, W2 has 5 cases, W3 has 16 cases.

You must supply 4 grocery stores (named S1, S2, S3, and S4) with the following number of cases:

S1 needs 4 cases, S2 needs 3 cases,
S3 needs 5 cases, S4 needs 4 cases.

The cases are delivered by coolies who can carry two cases (they charge the same price for carrying one case as they do for carrying two cases). The cost (in satangs) of a delivery trip by a coolie is given as the entries in the following array:

		FROM W1	W2	W3
TO	S1	3	9	10
	S2	7	12	11
	S3	3	11	8
	S4	9	5	19

(a) Let N(I,J) be the number of cases delivered to the Jth store from the Ith warehouse. Determine the relationships that these variables must satisfy.

(b) Determine how to compute the delivery cost for any particular scheme of supplying the stores with bamboo shoots. Give all of the equations, inequalities, and formulas that make up the model for this situation.

(c) Determine a method of generating all the possible ways to supply these stores with the required number of cases.

(d) Search through all of these possibilities and find the most economical scheme of supplying the stores. Count the number of possibilities that are examined.

13–2 A commercial farm needs a fertilizer that is 12 percent nitrogen, 8 percent phosphorus, and 80 percent filler. It cannot obtain this blend directly, and so it has to make its own from the following available fertilizers with the indicated percentages of nitrogen and phosphorus. The percentage of filler is omitted.

	FERTILIZER					
	#1	#2	#3	#4	#5	#6
Nitrogen, %	20	25	0	4	15	80
Phosphorus, %	12	10	10	4	10	0
Cost per ton	$450	$400	$150	$100	$375	$1000

Assume that no more than three fertilizers are blended to obtain the required fertilizer.

(a) Given any three of these fertilizers, determine the proportions or percentages that are required to give the correct blend. This involves solving three linear equations for the three unknown percentages (name them P1, P2, and P3); that is, for the combination of fertilizers #1, #2, and #3, we have

$$\begin{aligned} P1 + P2 + P3 &= 100, \\ 20(P1/100) + 25(P2/100) &= 12, \\ 12(P1/100) + 10(P2/100) + 10(P3/100) &= 8. \end{aligned}$$

Note that this particular combination cannot be used at all since this system of equations leads to negative percentages which is impossible.

(b) Determine all the possible blends that give the desired fertilizer, and find which gives the lowest cost per ton.

13–3 A home builder plans to build 20 houses in a new subdivision. He has four styles of homes: ranch, split level, colonial, and modern. He has two building crews, one for the foundation and framework and one for finishing the interior. The number of days each crew works on a particular model is given below.

	Ranch	*Split Level*	*Colonial*	*Modern*
First crew	8	10	9	7
Second crew	9	7	11	9
Profit	$2400	$2800	$3000	$2300

The summer building season is 180 days, and the builder wants to build all 20 houses this season.

(a) For any particular selection of styles determine whether all 20 houses can be built this season and, if so, what the builder's profit is.

(b) How many possible ways are there to select the styles and still get all the houses built this season?

(c) What selection of styles gives the builder the most profit?

(d) Suppose the builder decides to build at least two of each style. Does this reduce the profit the builder can make?

13–4 Consider an electric utility company which is to build a new power plant to supply four cities as shown in the diagram.

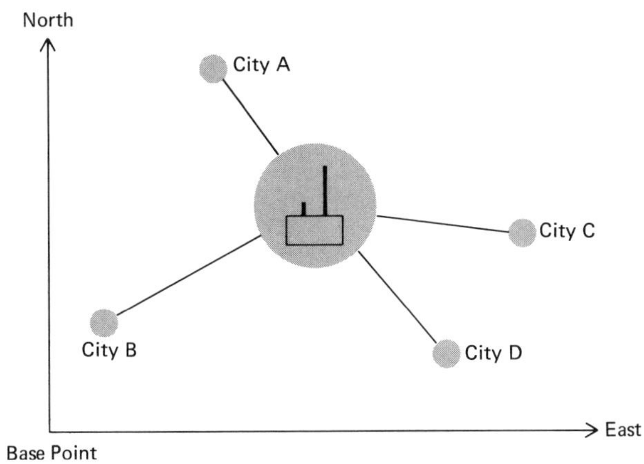

One wishes to locate the plant so as to minimize the total length of the power lines needed. The cities are located relative to the base point as given in the following table:

	City A	*City B*	*City C*	*City D*
Miles east	31	6	73	65
Miles north	49	18	31	15

Introduce appropriate variables and identify relationships between them so as to create a mathematical model of this situation. Give the model explicitly. Note that this problem cannot be solved by enumeration because there are infinitely many places that one can place the power plant.

Recall the Pythagorean Theorem that allows one to compute the length of the hypotenuse of a right triangle. (Hypotenuse squared = sum of the squares of the sides.) Thus the distance from City A to City B is

$$\sqrt{(31-6)^2+(49-18)^2}=\sqrt{1586}=39.8 \text{ miles.}$$

13–5 Consider Problem 13–4 and the diagram given. The diagram suggests that the power lines connecting the cities and the new power plant be laid out in a certain way. That arrangement is likely to be incorporated in the model constructed. However, there is another possibility that might be much better, namely, not to have separate lines from the power plant to each city, but rather to have lines that go from the power plant to one city and then to another.

(a) Use this new arrangement of the power lines in a new model for this situation. Find a location for the power plant that minimizes the length of the power lines.

(b) There is an assumption about power lines which is implicit in this second model and which, if it is not valid, would invalidate the results obtained. What is the assumption?

13–6 There are difficulties with the equation that the manufacturer of automatic fly swatters uses to relate the price P with the sales X. It becomes completely unreasonable for some situations. (For example, a price of 200¢ leads to −1000 in sales!)

(a) An equation of the form

$$P=\frac{1{,}690{,}000}{X}-7000$$

might be more appropriate. Note that if the price is 130¢, then the sales are 6000 and a change of 1¢ in the price results in a change of 100 in sales. Discuss the advantages that this equation has over the original one as far as realistic behavior is concerned for very high or very low sales.

(b) Incorporate this new equation into the economic model for the effect of four kinds of taxes that the government might impose.

(c) Write a computer program that incorporates this new model and determine the resulting prices, profits, and sales. Note that one cannot apply a simple formula in order to determine the best prices so that a technique of numerical analysis must be used. Such techniques are discussed in Chapter 12, especially in Problems 12–11 and 12–12.

13–7 Consideration of simple tax models like those of Section 13–4 leads one to experiment with various possibilities. The ideal is to find a tax that results in lower prices, higher profits, and increased production! Such taxes seem to be difficult to devise, but the results of a tax are not always obvious. Consider a negative excise tax of 20¢ (that is, a direct subsidy of 20¢ per swatter manufactured) combined with an income tax of 30 percent. Construct the model that incorporates these two taxes and determine the resulting price, profit, sales, and government income. You should find that the price is decreased (but not by 20¢), sales are increased, profits decrease a small amount, and the government receives a small sum.

13–8 *(Airline routing problem)* The problem is to determine a route between two cities that has the smallest number of intermediate stops. If an intermediate city is specified in addition to the origin and destination, then the route must pass through this city and still have as small a number of intermediate stops as possible. A specific airline network is shown in the diagram below along with the abbreviations for the cities involved.

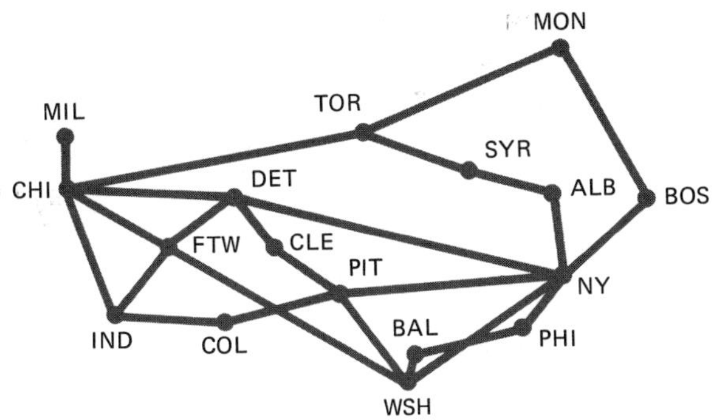

ALB–ALBANY	COL–COLUMBUS	NY–NEW YORK
BAL–BALTIMORE	DET–DETROIT	PHI–PHILADELPHIA
BOS–BOSTON	FTW–FORT WAYNE	PIT–PITTSBURGH
CHI–CHICAGO	MIL–MILWAUKEE	SYR–SYRACUSE
CLE–CLEVELAND	MON–MONTREAL	TOR–TORONTO
		WSH–WASHINGTON

(a) *(Mathematical model)* In order to solve this problem, one must obtain a representation or model of the airline network. Then one must have a representation of a route in the network. Construct a model that contains the information about this problem and formulate the problem that is to be solved.

[*Hint:* A convenient way to represent a network is to use a two-dimensional array with one row for each node (city). Each row contains the city (first) and then all other cities that are *directly* connected to it. A route is just a list or one-dimensional array of cities with the origin first and the destination last.]

(b) *(Method of solution)* One possible way to solve this problem is outlined as follows: A two-dimensional array of routes is created. The first row is the origin, the second row is the first intermediate stop, the third row is the second intermediate stop, and so forth. The columns are routes that are being created. When one finds a row that contains the destination, one has generated a route. The final array generated to find a route from Milwaukee to Pittsburgh is as follows:

MIL	MIL	MIL	MIL	MIL	MIL	MIL	MIL
CHI	CHI	CHI	CHI	CHI	CHI	CHI	CHI
IND	IND	DET	DET	WSH	WSH	TOR	TOR
FTW	COL	CLE	NY	BAL	PIT	MON	SYR

The sixth column contains the desired route to Pittsburgh. Formulate this method of solution in detailed, precise terms by a flowchart.

[*Hint:* One must be careful not to neglect any cities, not to wipe out routes in creating and enlarging the array of routes, and not to turn backward toward the origin. Thus, one would not want to find the route MIL-CHI-IND-CHI.]

(c) Extend the method of part (b) to handle a route with one designated intermediate stop (for example, Milwaukee to New York via Fort Wayne).

(d) *(Computer program)* Write a computer program that implements the method of part (b) [or part (c)]. The input to the program is of the form

Request:	MIL TO DET	for part (b)
	MIL TO DET VIA PIT	for part (c)

The output is to be of the form

ROUTE IS MIL-CHI-DET
ROUTE IS MIL-CHI-WSH-PIT-CLE-DET

The exact format of the input is to be specified. Run a number of requests that show that the program is correct.

14

Simulation

14—1 The Simulation Concept

One of the more interesting and powerful approaches to using computers in problem-solving is *simulation.* As in other approaches, one must first construct a model of the problem situation. The models in simulation have the additional feature that they may be considered as "working" models. Since they are working models, one sets them in "motion" (via a computer program) and then observes what happens. A simple situation of pursuit (a dog trying to catch up with his master) is considered in detail in the next section, where we see that one writes a computer program that *imitates* (or simulates) the actions the dog takes in order to catch up with his master. One knows the situation when the master calls his dog and then one puts the model into "motion" and observes the path the dog takes in his pursuit of his master.

Let us examine the ingredients of a situation that make the simulation approach applicable. First, one must have a process that is "ongoing" in some sense. It might be a dog chasing his master, an investment growing in a company, a traffic jam building up at a freeway entrance (or at a hot dog stand), and so forth. This requirement eliminates some types of problems such as solving equations, the traveling salesman problem, alphabetizing a list of names, or translating languages. The second ingredient is an understanding (or adequate model) of how the process works at any particular instance. Thus even though we do not know the path the dog will follow (neither does the dog), we assume that we know the action that he takes, that is, how fast he runs and in what direction he chooses to run. Finally, we must know the original situation.

These three things are then combined in a computer program and the one goes through the process step-by-step in order to find out what happens. This step-by-step simulation can introduce some real uncertainties in the case of processes that actually move continuously or smoothly (as the dog runs). These uncertainties are in addition to all those introduced by the rest of the development mathematical model. One never has all of the details of a real situation incorporated in a model, and simulation studies one particularly susceptible to defects in the model.

14—2 The Dog and Master Problem

A dog and his master are walking in a field. As the master is walking along a path he calls his dog and the dog begins to run toward the master. How long does it take the dog to catch his master? The situation is illustrated in Figure 14–1.

When the dog hears his master call we assume that he begins to run directly toward the master. However, the master keeps on walking so the dog has to change his direction to keep pointed toward the master. This results in the dog running in a curved line rather than a straight one.

If the master's path is a straight one, this problem can be solved by a mathematical formula. If his path is curved, the problem becomes much more difficult and normally cannot be solved directly. We approach this problem from the viewpoint of the dog. When he hears the call, he looks at his master and runs a few steps in that direction. Then he notices that his master has moved, so he changes his direction and runs a few more steps. Again he notices that his master has moved, so he changes his direction again. This continues until he finally catches up with his master.

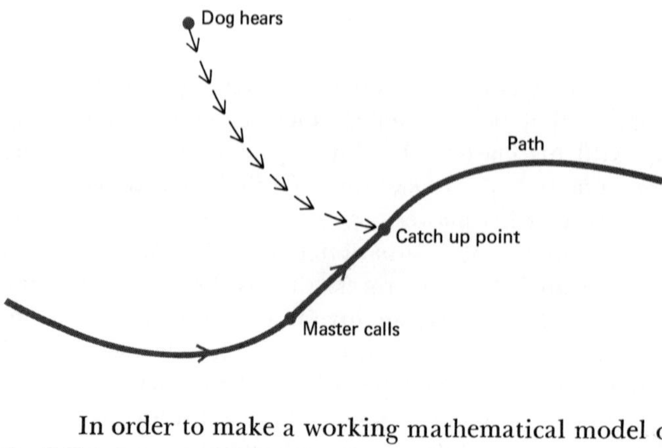

FIGURE 14–1. The situation when the master calls his dog.

In order to make a working mathematical model of this situation we make the following assumptions:

1. The master takes a 3-foot step every second
2. The dog takes six 1-foot steps every second
3. The dog changes direction every time the master takes a step.

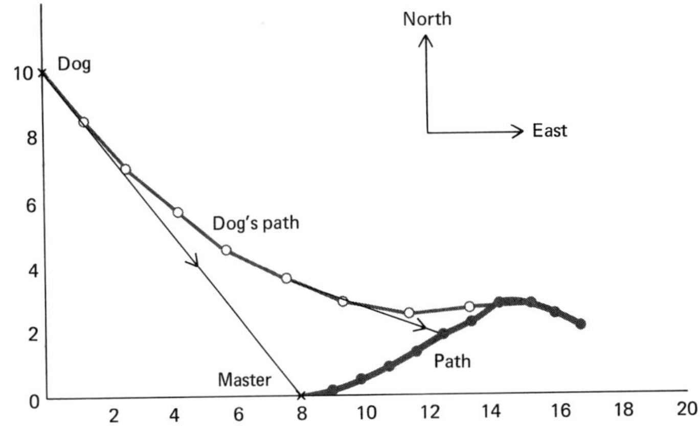

FIGURE 14–2. The path the dog takes to catch up with his master. A rectangular coordinate system (in yards) is introduced into the field.

In order to simplify the situation, we

4. Assume the field is flat
5. Introduce a rectangular coordinate system in the field, scaled in yards as illustrated in Figure 14–2.

We choose the point due south of the dog and due west of the master as the origin of the coordinate system. We measure the distances of the dog and master from this origin to be 10 yards and 8 yards, respectively. We also measure where the steps of the master are along the path. We can now solve this problem with a ruler, and we find that the dog catches the man just as he takes his eighth step.

In order to set this problem up for a computer to solve, we must do more. We represent the path the man takes by two arrays, the north coordinates and the east coordinates of each step. We call these coordinates NMAN(T), EMAN(T). They are presented in the following table. We start measuring time when the

T	0	1	2	3	4	5	6	7	8	9	10
NMAN(T)	0	.2	.5	.9	1.5	1.8	2.3	2.9	2.8	2.5	2.1
EMAN(T)	8.0	9.0	9.9	10.8	11.6	12.5	13.3	14.1	15.1	16.0	16.9

man whistles. Likewise we represent the path of the dog by two similar arrays, NDOG(T) and EDOG(T). We know that

$$\text{NDOG}(0) = 10, \qquad \text{EDOG}(0) = 0,$$

and we must compute NDOG(T), EDOG(T) for T = 1, 2, . . . until the dog catches the man.

Let us consider how we find NDOG(1) and EDOG(1). This can be done using either elementary trigonometry or plane geometry and the same equations are obtained. Using trigonometry, we note that the slope θ of the line from the dog to its master is the same as the slope of the line from the dog to its new position. This angle may be calculated in terms of

$$\text{DIST} = \sqrt{(\text{NDOG}(0) - \text{NMAN}(0))^2 + (\text{EDOG}(0) - \text{EMAN}(0))^2}$$

by the relations

$$\sin\theta = (\text{NMAN}(0) - \text{NDOG}(0))/\text{DIST},$$
$$\cos\theta = (\text{EMAN}(0) - \text{EDOG}(0))/\text{DIST}.$$

In the first second the dog moves east by the amount $2\cos\theta$ and north by the amount $2\sin\theta$ so we have

$$\text{EDOG}(1) = \text{EDOG}(0) + 2(\text{EMAN}(0) - \text{EDOG}(0))/\text{DIST},$$
$$\text{NDOG}(1) = \text{NDOG}(0) + 2(\text{NMAN}(0) - \text{NDOG}(0))/\text{DIST}.$$

This procedure is clearly repetitive in nature; that is, we find NDOG(2), EDOG(2) from NDOG(1), EDOG(1) and NMAN(1), EMAN(1) in exactly the same way.

Now that we have a mechanism working for finding the path the dog follows, all we have to do is check for the point where the dog catches up with the master. We do this by saying that once the distance between the dog and its master is 1 yard or less, then the dog catches the master in the next second.

The flowchart expression of this simulation is a simple iteration loop as shown in Figure 14–3. This approach may be implemented by a Fortran program as given below.

```
      REAL NMAN(51),EMAN(51),NDOG(51),EDOG(51)
      INTEGER T
      READ 5,(NMAN(T),EMAN(T),T=1,11)
      READ 5, NDOG(1),EDOG(1)
    5 FORMAT( 11F6.3 )
      T = 1
   10 DIST =SQRT((NMAN(T)-NDOG(T))**2+(EMAN(T)-EDOG(T))**2)
      EDOG(T+1) = EDOG(T) + 2.*(EMAN(T)-EDOG(T))/DIST
      NDOG(T+1) = NDOG(T) + 2.*(NMAN(T)-NDOG(T))/DIST
      T = T+1
      IF( DIST .GT. 1. )  GO TO 10
      PRINT 15, (K,NDOG(K),EDOG(K),K=1,T)
   15 FORMAT( 1H15X1HT10X4HNDOG10X4HEDOG/(I7,2F14.3))
      STOP
      END
```

The key to this approach is knowledge of the basic process involved in the problem. In this case we know (or assume we know) how the dog would behave at any particular instant. Thus we can predict what happens from instant to instant even though we cannot make one long-term prediction. We formulate the mechanics of this basic process in mathematical terms. This allows us to have a computer go through the instant-to-instant predictions for as many instants as we want.

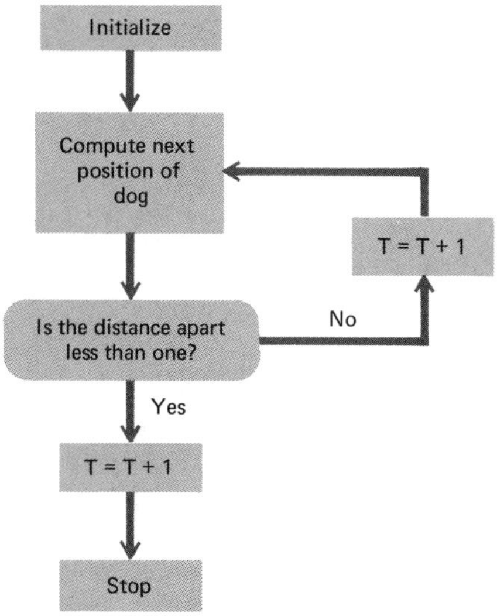

FIGURE 14–3. A flowchart of the logic of the working simulation model for the dog and master problem.

This approach can be used for any pursuit problem where we know the path the pursued takes and the mechanism by which the pursuer directs himself. These problems arise in situations where

1. missiles are chasing planes
2. submarines are chasing ships
3. ships are chasing submarines
4. missiles are chasing missiles
5. hawks are chasing doves
6. coyotes are chasing rabbits.

In many of these situations the pursuer uses a more sophisticated strategy in trying to catch his quarry than the dog uses to catch his master.

The construction of a working mathematical model can be very delicate. Many times people have made models that seemed to be very good, but were, in fact, poor, because when the models were "run" they gave obviously unreasonable results. Thus such models must be tested and double checked thoroughly before we place confidence in them.

14–3 Simulation With Random Events—The Queuing Problem

There are many situations when one does not know exactly when an event occurs, but rather that it occurs at some known *average* rate. A simple situation of this type occurs at a cafeteria every meal time. At first people arrive slowly and go right through, then they arrive more frequently and a line or *queue* begins to form. This queue grows in length and then, when people begin to arrive less frequently, it decreases until finally it disappears. In this section we formulate a model of this process which is appropriate for simulation.

First we must establish the two basic facts about the situation: the time it takes to go through the line and the rate at which people arrive for service. We simplify the cafeteria process and simply assume that it takes 20 seconds to be served. One might interpret this as the actual time required at the slowest point (or bottle neck) of the cafeteria line. Thus the cafeteria can provide service at the rate of 3 meals per minute.

The average rate at which people arrive is a more complicated piece of information as it varies during the serving period. We assume this rate is given graphically as in Figure 14–4. The line should start to form at about 11:45 A.M. and disappear before 2 P.M. A little calculation shows that the cafeteria expects to have about 390 customers in this period and they can serve 405. There is, however, an obvious problem that occurs shortly after noon and the crucial question is: How long does the line get and how long do people have to wait? We wish to simulate this situation in order to estimate these quantities.

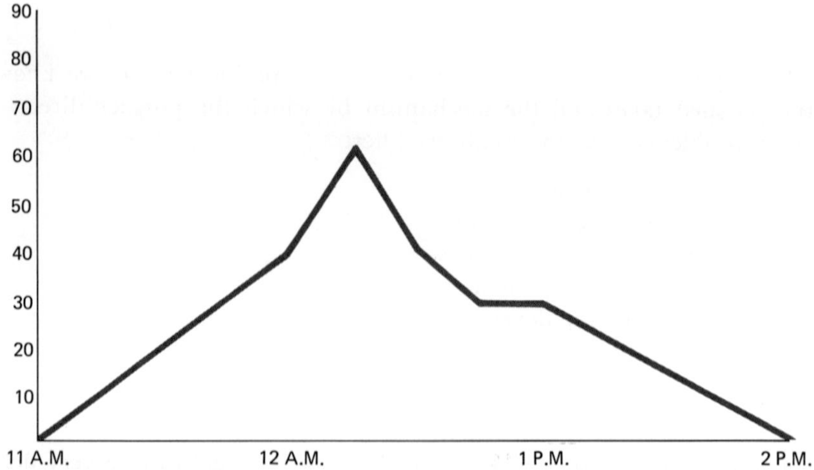

FIGURE 14–4. Average rate at which people arrive at the cafeteria for a lunch period.

We introduce a variable Q which is the number of people in the queue and we wish to determine how this variable behaves during the lunch period. We break the lunch period into 1-minute intervals, and it is easy to see the rate at which people leave the queue, 3 per minute. We might assume that the number of people who join the queue is read directly from Figure 14–4. Indeed, this is a reasonable approach. However, the rates in Figure 14–4 are only averages and in some minutes there might be no additions to the queue. In order to simulate this aspect of the situation we proceed as follows: First, we read a value from the figure, divide by 10 (since those rates are for 10-minute intervals), and call that A (for average). Then we pick a number at random between 0 and 2 * A and add this to Q. In order to do this we assume that we have a random number generator (either from the Fortran library or written by ourselves) called RAND(X). The value of RAND(X) is a random number between 0 and 1. In order to have a random number between 0 and 2 * A we compute

```
ADDQ = IFIX((2.*A+1.)*RAND(X))
```

as the quantity to add to Q. The IFIX is to ensure that one does not have fractions of people and the 2 * A + 1 is used instead of 2 * A because of this rounding (otherwise, we would never get 2 * A people added).

This simulation is implemented in a Fortran program as follows:

```
C          CAFETERIA LINE SIMULATION
C       Q = QUEUE LENGTH            M = MINUTES AFTER 11 AM
        QMAX =0
        Q = 0
        PRINT 10
     10 FORMAT(27H1    MINUTES     QUEUE LENGTH //)
        DO 100 M = 1,180
        A = ARATE(M)/10.
        ADDQ = IFIX((2.*A+1.)*RAND(X))
        Q = Q + ADDQ - 3.
        Q = AMAX1(0.,Q)
        PRINT 50,M,Q
     50 FORMAT( I9,F13.0)
    100 QMAX = AMAX1(Q,QMAX)
        WAIT = QMAX/3.
        PRINT 150,QMAX,WAIT
    150 FORMAT(/5X12HMAX QUEUE IS,F4.0, 5H LONG/
      *          5X12HWAIT THEN IS,F4.0, 8H MINUTES)
        STOP
        END

        FUNCTION ARATE(M)
        MM = 1+ (M-1)/60
        GO TO( 10,20,30),MM
     10 ARATE = MAX0(2*M/3,4*M/3-40)
           RETURN
     20 ARATE = MAX0( 160-4*M/3, 100-2*M/3,30)
           RETURN
     30 ARATE = 90-M/2
           RETURN
        END
```

Main loop (bracket beside the statements from DO 100 M = 1,180 through 100 QMAX = AMAX1(Q,QMAX))

Number that arrive this minute is "randomized" here (beside A = ARATE(M)/10. and ADDQ = IFIX((2.*A+1.)*RAND(X)))

Function that gives the arrival rate in the quene (beside FUNCTION ARATE)

The program is a rather straightforward iteration loop where Q is modified each minute as M varies from 1 to 180. The function subprogram ARATE is novel in that it uses the built-in function MAX0 to aid in evaluating the formulas for the average rates given in Figure 14–4. This technique can also be used with MIN0 at times and it is not restricted to broken line information.

The queue simulation described so far may be viewed as the basis for constructing much more elaborate simulations. Other features that one might want to add to the model include:

1. Additional service for the queue made available at peak periods. For example, the cafeteria might operate a second line from 11:45 until 12:45 and then the queue is unlikely to ever be of any significant length.
2. Potential customers who leave when the line is too long. Thus, one might expect 10 percent of the people that arrive to leave immediately if there are over 20 people in the queue. This percentage would rise as the length of the queue increases and it is a major factor in the behavior (and simulation) of real queues.
3. Temporary breakdown in the service such as the rail for cafeteria trays breaks off and requires 8 minutes for repair. Or perhaps there are no trays available for a 4-minute period. A temporary stoppage of service can cause the queue to grow very long and, if the preceding factor is present, can cause a significant decrease in the number of customers.
4. The arrival of a large group of people (say 50 people from a bus tour) can cause an instantaneous large growth in the length of the queue. It is then of considerable interest to know how long it takes the queue to return to its "normal" length.

Each of these features can be added to the program that simulates the situation and it requires only a few additional lines of programming.

Queues are present in all types of service situations. Cafeterias, grocery stores, banks, toll booths, and traffic lights are obvious places where queues form. Less obvious but equally interesting situations involving queues include opportunities for promotion in an organization, execution of programs in a time-shared computing system, succession to the throne in England, and so forth.

14—4 Simulation of Inventory Control

We now consider the simulation of a slightly more complicated situation than a simple queue. This is inventory control where we visualize the situation of a warehouse manager for a large corporation. There are two different processes involved: filling orders from retail outlets and sending orders to the manufacturers. The first of these is a somewhat random process as the weekly number of items sent to retailers varies from 20 to 60 with an average of 40 items per week. The second process is completely under the manager's control; he initiates the orders to the manufacturer whenever he so desires. We state a few basic facts about this operation:

1. Items shipped out vary from 20 to 60 per week with an average of 40.
2. It takes 3 weeks to obtain a carload lot of 150 items from the manufacturer.
3. It costs $8 per week for each item in the warehouse.
4. It takes 1 week to obtain a truckload of 25 items from the manufacturer and it costs $10 per item more than ordering by carload lots.
5. Items may be shipped from the manufacturer directly to the retailer by air freight. The delivery time is the same as from the warehouse,

but it costs \$38 more. This action is, however, taken whenever the warehouse cannot supply a retailer from its stock.

The warehouse manager has a great variety of alternatives in operating this warehouse and we simulate one of the more simple-minded of these. The manager ignores the possibility of ordering by truck. He checks the stock every Friday and if it is below 150 items, he orders another carload of 150 items. If he runs out of items before the delivery is made, he then uses air freight to supply the retailer.

Before we consider the details of a simulation, let us see how to obtain a random selection of orders from retailers. If we merely pick a number at random between 20 and 60 we end up with an average of $40 = (20 + 60)/2$ items per week, but this is not completely satisfactory. This scheme makes it equally likely to have orders for 20 or 40 or 60 items and we would expect 40 to be much more frequent. One way to simulate this is to pick two random numbers, each between 10 and 30 and then add them together. The result is still between 20 and 60 with 40 as the average, but now orders near 40 are more likely to occur. Thus a low number (such as 21 or 22) can occur only when *both* the random numbers between 10 and 30 happen to be very close to 10. If RAND(X) is a random number generator for equally likely numbers between 0 and 1, then we obtain an appropriate random value for ORDER (the number of items ordered by retailers) from the formula

$$\text{ORDER} = 20. + \text{IFIX}(20.5 * (\text{RAND}(0) + \text{RAND}(0))).$$

Recall that each of RAND(0) produces a *different* random number.

A Fortran program that implements this simulation is given below.

```
C         INVENTORY SIMULATION
C   ORDER - WEEKLY RETAILERS ORDER TOTAL
C   AMOUNT- NO. OF ITEMS IN WAREHOUSE
C   COST  - COST SO FAR THIS YEAR
C   K     - COUNTER OF WEEKS
C   KCAR  - LAST WEEK THAT A CARLOAD WAS ORDERED
      KCAR = -10
      AMOUNT = 200
      COST   = 0
      PRINT  10
   10 FORMAT(24H1    WAREHOUSE SIMULATION /
     *        6X4HWEEK,3X6HAMOUNT,3X5HORDER,6X4HCOST )
      DO 100 K = 1,52
   20 IF( K .EQ. KCAR+3 )  AMOUNT = AMOUNT + 150.
      COST = COST + AMOUNT*8.
      ORDER = 20 + IFIX(20.5*(RAND(0)+RAND(0)))
      AMOUNT = AMOUNT - ORDER
      IF( AMOUNT .GE. 150.)    GO TO 100
   30 IF( K .GT. KCAR+2 ) KCAR = K+1
   40 IF( AMOUNT .GE. 0.)      GO TO 100
      COST = COST + 38.*ABS(AMOUNT)
      AMOUNT = 0
  100 PRINT 110, K,AMOUNT,ORDER,COST
  110 FORMAT( I10, 2F8.0, F12.2 )
      STOP
      END
```

A key variable in this program is KCAR which records the last time a carload of items was ordered from the manufacturer. Note that an action is taken in 1 week whose effect does not show up until 3 weeks later and KCAR serves as the "memory" for this action. It is thus tested at statement 20 to see if a carload is due and the inventory is checked at statement 30 to see if another carload is needed. The three statements at 40 check to see if some items have to be sent by air freight and the additional cost is included.

This simple simulation allows us to experiment with various strategies of inventory control. For example, waiting until one has less than 150 items before resupplying is risking frequent use of air freight. It might well be much better to resupply when one has less than 175 or 200 or ? items. One can vary this key decision variable in several computer runs and find out which is better.

Perhaps it would be worthwhile to take advantage of the truck delivery. After all, if one has less than 75 items in stock on Friday and no carload lot due for 2 weeks, then one is very likely to run out of items week after next. Twenty-five items delivered by truck might save a considerable amount in this situation. In order to include this strategy in the simulation one can introduce a variable KTRUCK (similar to KCAR) and then insert the following statement between statements 30 and 40:

```
IF( AMOUNT.LE.75. .AND. K.LT.KCAR+2) KTRUCK=K+1
```

The variable KTRUCK would be tested right after KCAR and would also be initialized at something like −10.

Problems

14–1 Six bugs are placed on a floor at point with coordinates X(I),Y(I) for I = 1 to 6. Each bug tries to catch the next one, that is, #1 chases #2, #2 chases #3, . . ., #5 chases #6, and #6 chases #1. They each head directly toward the bug they are chasing and crawl at a speed of 3 inches per minute.

(a) Make a working model of this chase and observe the pattern that the paths of the bugs make.

(b) Assume that four bugs are at the corners of a 1-foot square and that each bug heads toward the one clockwise from him. How far do the bugs travel before they meet?

14–2 Make a more general simulation model of Problem 14–1 where an arbitrary number (less than 50) of bugs are allowed.

14–3 In the ocean we find that sharks eat cod, cod eat herring, and herring eat shrimp. Suppose that we have one of each of these in the water, and they begin to chase their quarry. Suppose further that a shrimp swims 40 feet per minute, a herring 60 feet per minute, a cod 90 feet per minute, and a shark 200 feet per minute. Each fish swims directly toward the one it is chasing. Write a simulation program for this chase which allows for movement in three dimensions and for various initial positions. The simulation should continue until all fish are either eaten or safe. Note that sharks do not eat herring, and so on.

14–4 Develop the model of Problem 14–3 further by having the shrimp swim a crazy pattern in trying to get away from the herring. Assume that every time the shrimp changes direction abruptly, it gains a foot on the herring, but it can change direction at most 15 times in a minute and it averages changing direction 10 times per minute when chased. The exact timing of the changes and the new direction are random and this fact is to be incorporated in the model constructed.

14–5 A pursuit strategy more sophisticated than that used by the dog in this chapter is for the pursuer to lead the pursued by some amount. Suppose we apply this to the situation of a tugboat trying to catch up with a freighter. The tugboat captain knows both the direction the freighter is moving and how far away it is. The freighter travels at 12 miles per hour in a straight line and the tugboat at 16 miles per hour. The tugboat captain steers his boat toward a point which is directly ahead of the freighter by an amount equal to one-quarter of the distance between them.

Write a program which simulates this pursuit strategy. Determine which situations (initial positions) make this strategy the best compared to steering directly toward the freighter and determine the resulting saving in time to catch the freighter if the boats are initially 8 miles apart.

14–6 *(Cops and robbers simulation)* Consider a band of bank robbers who plan to rob a particular bank and then make a run for the border and safety. The main difficulty is the presence of two patrol cars which are constantly stationed between the bank and the border. Furthermore, there is a police helicopter in the air at all times over the city and it will direct the police cars in their pursuit of the robbers. The general layout is shown in the diagram.

The city is laid out in square blocks in all directions from the bank which is 20 blocks from the border. The robbers must choose an escape route and the helicopter must choose a strategy with which to direct the police cars. Of course, neither one knows about the other's plan. Whenever a police car gets within half a block of the bank robbers it can shoot out the tires of their car and capture the robbers.

Write a program which simulates this chase with the following features included:

(a) The robbers travel 10 blocks a minute and the police cars travel 11 blocks a minute.
(b) Whenever the robbers turn a corner they lose 1/10 of a minute while the police cars lose 1/8 of a minute.
(c) Whenever the robbers are traveling toward a police car, the helicopter directs the car toward the street the robbers are on and, if they are on the same street, toward the robbers.

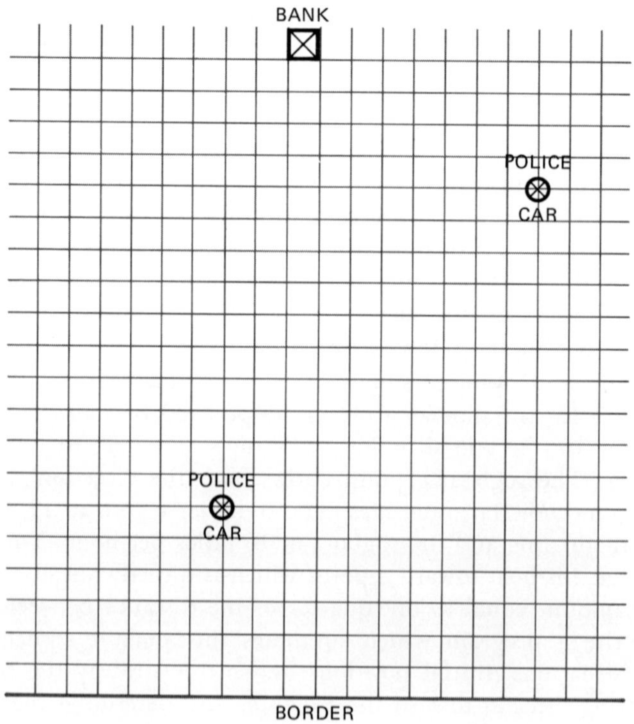

(d) The helicopter does not start the chase by the police until the robbers have gone four blocks.
(e) Whenever the robbers are traveling away from a police car, the helicopter directs the police to travel parallel to the robbers.
(f) The robbers may reverse their direction with a loss of 1/4 of a minute while it takes the police 1/3 of a minute to reverse directions.

The program is to start with a prepared escape route for the robbers and then determine whether or not they reach the border.

[*Hint:* Choose time steps of 1/120 of a minute so that all turns, and so on, can be made at an exact number of time steps.]

14–7 Modify the model for Problem 14–6 so that the two patrol cars are in some random location at the start of the chase. Estimate the chances of the robbers reaching the border (for a particular escape route) by running the simulation program a number of times, say 20.

14–8 The manager of the cafeteria discussed in Section 14–3 observes that 20 percent of his customers take only a snack (soup, sandwich, and drink) for lunch. He decides to open a special snack line from 12:00 to 12:45 for these people. Include this new strategy in the queue simulation and determine its effect on the queue length. Pick (at random) 1 out of 5 people that arrive and place them in the snack line.

On a particularly heavy day there may be 15 percent more customers for the cafeteria than normal. Run the simulations of the cafeteria with and without a snack line for such a day and determine the effect a snack line has on the queue length for such a day.

14–9 *(Random service queue)* A random service queue is one where the next person served is chosen at random from those waiting for service. Consider such a situation where 10 people are in the queue at all times and 1 person joins the queue each minute and 1 person receives service each minute. One would expect to have to wait about 10 minutes in the queue, but it might take more or less time. Estimate the percentages of people whose wait times are in the following ranges: 1 to 5 minutes, 6 to 10 minutes, 11 to 15 minutes, 16 to 20 minutes, and over 20 minutes.

[*Hint:* Write a program to simulate this queue and then run it for several hundred minutes and keep track of how many people fall into each of these ranges of wait times.]

14–10 A more complicated random service queue occurs where the queue is ordered, but the next person served is chosen at random from the five at the head of the queue. Furthermore, once one is in the first five, one is guaranteed service in 10 minutes or less.

Write a program that simulates this queue and use it to estimate the various waiting times (with the ranges of Problem 14–9) that one can expect. Assume that there are always 20 people in the queue. Queues that behave approximately in this way are rather common. Describe a realistic situation where this simulation analysis might be reasonably applicable.

14–11 There are 6 toll booths on a particular expressway. One of them takes only exact change and can handle 10 cars a minute. The others have attendants and handle an average of 4 cars a minute. In the middle of the afternoon, the expressway carries 1000 cars per hour past a given point. There are 3 booths open then, including the exact change booth. At 4 P.M. the traffic begins to increase as given by the following table:

Time	*Cars*	*Time*	*Cars*	*Time*	*Cars*
4:00	1025	5:00	1650	6:00	1800
5:15	1100	5:15	1800	6:15	1500
4:30	1200	5:30	2000	6:30	1200
4:45	1400	5:45	2000	6:45	1050

Assume that the increase is spread evenly over the 15-minute intervals given in the table. A fourth booth is opened at 4:30, and the fifth and sixth at 5:00.

Simulate the situation at the toll booths, and determine how long cars have to wait and how long the lines are at various times during the rush period (a car in line takes up 25 feet).

14–12 Consider the situation of Problem 14–11 and simulate it with the following modification: On Friday the traffic is 10 percent heavier but starts 15 minutes later. How bad does the traffic jam get then? How much would the addition of another booth help? How much would it help to change one of the booths to an exact change booth?

14–13 Suppose you are the only maker of a scarce material. At present you can make up to 1000 pounds per month and sell it for $100 per pound. By using overtime, and so on, you can increase production, but you must also increase the price in order to make your normal profit of $40 per pound. The extra amount you can produce and the corresponding increased price is given by the following table (for example, if you sell from 1500 to 1800 pounds, then you must price it at $150 per pound to make a profit of $40 per pound).

Extra production	200	300	500	800	1500
Increased price	105	110	125	150	200

The demand for this material is predicted to rise 8 percent per year provided that the cost stays at $100 per pound. As the price rises a certain number of buyers are expected to switch to a substitute material and never return to using this material. This percentage is thought to be as follows:

Price	100	105	110	125	150	200
% who switch	0	2	5	10	25	50

Simulate this company's operations over the next 20 years and obtain data on the expected sales and profits for each of these years. Also determine what the sales would be in each of these years if you were able to increase production and still maintain the $100 per pound price.

14–14 Consider the situation of Problem 14–13. You can invest $80,000 and raise by 200 pounds the amount of material that you can produce and sell at $100 per pound (with a $40 per pound profit). Assume this investment is made and simulate the resulting operation for the next 10 years in order to determine the return you make on this investment.

14–15 Consider the situation in Problem 14–13. You can invest some money in your plant and reduce the production cost. There are three alternatives available.

(a) Invest $80,000 and raise by 200 pounds the amount you can produce and sell at $100 per pound. This alternative can be done only one time.

(b) Invest $300,000 and raise by 500 pounds the amount you can produce and sell at $100 per pound.

(c) Invest $600,000 and raise by 1200 pounds the amount you can produce and sell at $100 per pound.

It takes 6 months to carry out alternative (a), 18 months for alternative (b), and 2½ years for alternative (c). If you invest this money, you must pay it back in 10 years at 6 percent interest (that is, you pay one-tenth of the principal each year plus 6 percent of the balance of the loan at the start of the year). Your advisors have presented three plans of action:

(a) Do nothing.
(b) Invest the \$80,000 two years from now, then invest the \$300,000 in about 10 years.
(c) Invest the \$80,000 as soon as possible, then build the new \$600,000 plant in 4 years.

Simulate the company's situation over a period of 20 years under these three plans. Which of the plans do you think is best? Can you find a better plan by experimenting with the model?

14–16 Modify the simulation (in Section 14–4) of the warehouse so that the amount of the orders from retailers is picked at random between 20 and 60 with each number equally likely. Does this apparently minor change make any significant difference in the results of the simulation?

14–17 A more ambitious manager of the warehouse operation of Section 14–4 might check his inventory every day rather than every Friday. Modify the simulation to work on a daily basis and obtain an estimate of the savings that result.

14–18 Further modify the simulation of Problem 14–17 to include the use of truck delivery from the manufacturer. Such orders are placed when the inventory drops below 75 items.

14–19 An increase in rail rates is proposed for the items involved in Section 14–4 and the cost by rail would only be \$3 less than the cost by truck. Would it pay the warehouse manager to switch entirely to truck delivery if he simply orders another truckload whenever his supply drops below 75 items? Simulate this new situation and estimate the differences in the cost of the two modes of operation.

14–20 Consider the warehouse simulation of Section 14–4 and determine a nearly optimum level at which to order a carload of items from the manufacturer.

14–21 Consider a modified operation of the warehouse where truck delivery only is used (see Problem 14–19). Determine a nearly optimum level at which to order a truckload of items from the manufacturer.

14–22 *(Simulation of rabbit breeding)* You have a pasture of 20 acres in which you raise rabbits. As your rabbits multiply, you add additional pens. You can put about 32 pens on an acre of land and each pen holds up to 35 rabbits. You have 6 adult pairs of rabbits, and you intend to let them multiply until your land is used up. If each pair of rabbits over 9 months of age has a litter of 7 every 5 months, how long will it be until your pasture is full of rabbits?

Glossary

The technical vocabulary in computing changes almost as rapidly as other aspects of the field. Nevertheless, an understanding of the jargon and language is essential to understanding this book, and we give a set of definitions relevant at the time of this writing. The American Standards Institute has prepared the "USA Standard Vocabulary for Information Processing" which may be purchased by writing to 10 East 40th Street, New York, New York 10016.

Computing follows the lead of the other sciences and uses many ordinary English words with specialized meanings. Sometimes these meanings are unrelated to the ordinary meaning. Likewise, some ordinary things and concepts are given specialized words when ordinary words would do as well. All of this tends to erect an unfortunate barrier between the layman and the specialist.

The terms defined below are for the most part not discussed in detail in this book. The definitions of terms explained in this book should be located by means of the index.

Absolute address The label or number permanently assigned to a specific memory location.

Absolute error The amount of error in the same units as the variable containing the error (without regard to sign).

Access time The amount of time between the instant of request of information (or access) from a storage device and the instant that information (or access) is completely available.

Accumulator A *register* in which the result of an arithmetic of logic operation is formed.

Adder A register which forms the sum of two numbers.

Address A label, name, or number identifying a location where information is stored.

Address modification The process of changing the address part of a machine instruction during the execution of a program.

ADP Automatic Data Processing.

Algorithm A set of well-defined instructions to carry out a process in a finite number of steps.

Alphanumeric Pertaining to a name or item that may contain both letters or numerals and usually other characters.

Analog computer A computer that operates by creating an analogy, often electrical, between the mathematical problem and a particular physical device. The operation of the physical device is then observed to estimate the solution of the mathematical problem.

Arithmetic unit The unit of a computing system that contains the circuits that perform arithmetic operations.

ASCII American Standard Code for Information Interchange.

Assembler A program that translates assembly language into machine language.

Associative Memory A memory where storage locations are identified by their contents, not by name, position, or address.

Automatic coding The machine-assisted preparation of *machine-language* routines.

Base A number base is a quantity used implicitly in a system to represent numbers by a positional notation; radix.

Base address A given address from which an *absolute address* is derived by combination with a *relative address.*

Baud A rate of information flow of one bit per second.

BCD Binary Coded Decimal.

Binary Coded Decimal A system for representing a set of alphanumeric characters by a fixed number (usually 4) binary digits.

Binary number A number expressed in the binary system using any combination of 0 or 1.

Bit Contraction of binary digit used as a unit of information capacity.

Boolean Algebra A mathematical system formulated by George Boole for the operations of formal logic.

BPI Bits per inch, a measure of the density at which information can be recorded on a device, especially magnetic tapes and disks.

Buffer A storage device used to compensate for a difference in rate of flow of data or time of occurrence of events, when transmitting data from one device to another.

Byte A sequence of adjacent *binary digits* operated upon as a unit and usually shorter than a word.

Calling sequence A specified arrangement of instructions and data necessary to set up and call a given *subroutine.*

Card image A representation of the complete contents of a punched card, usually contained in a storage device or medium.

Central processor The unit of a computing system that includes the circuits controlling the interpretation and execution of *instructions.*

Chad The piece of material formed when punching holes in cards or paper tapes.

Channel A communication path for the transmission of information between two or more points.

Character set A collection of all the character symbols used by a language or system to communicate meaning.

Check digits One or more digits carried within a unit item of information (that is, machine word) which provide information about the other digits in the unit in such a manner that if an error occurs, the check fails, and an indication of error is given.

Clock A device in a computer that generates periodic signals to synchronize its operation.

Closed subprogram A subprogram that may be placed at one location and then called from one or more places by linkages. Compare with OPEN SUBPROGRAM.

Collate To compare and *merge* two or more similarly ordered sets of items into one ordered set.

Compile To prepare a machine-language program from a source program written in another programming language by making use of the overall logic structure of the program, or by generating more than one machine instruction for each symbolic statement, or both, as well as performing the function of assembling.

Console A device which gives a person (either the operator or a user) direct access to a computer.

Core storage Memory made out of magnetic cores.

CPU Central Processing Unit; the same as Central Processor.

Cycle time A basic unit of time for computer operations; most instructions require more than one cycle for execution.

Data base A collection of information, usually large and of a general nature, for an applications area.

Data cell An auxiliary memory device characterized by a very large capacity and relatively slow access time.

Data set A device that converts the signals of a business machine into signals that are suitable for transmission over communication lines.

Decision table A format used to describe and display the logic of a decision-making process in a tabular form of organization.

Declaration statement A part of a computer program that defines the nature of other elements of the program or reserves parts of the hardware for special use.

Default option An assumption made by a system or language translator when no specific choice is given by the user or his program.

Delimiter A symbol or word that indicates a breakpoint or termination point in the grammatical structure of a language.

Diagnostic routine A routine designed to locate a malfunction, either in other routines or in the computer itself.

Display A device, usually a TV screen, that shows either messages or graphical output from a computer.

Down time The time during which a computer is malfunctioning or not operating correctly due to mechanical or electronic failure as opposed to available, idle, or stand-by time during which the computer is functional.

Dump A copy of all or a large part of a computer's memory.

Duplex channel A communications channel that allows simultaneous transmission in both directions.

EBCDIC Extended Binary Coded Decimal Interchange Code, an 8-bit code that provides for 256 different characters.

Echo check The checking of information transmission by the immediate return of information received.

EDP Electronic data processing.

Electrostatic printer An electromechanical device that electrostatically charges specially coated paper, which is then dusted with ink particles to bring out the character impressions.

Eleven punch A punch in the second row of an IBM card.

Emulation A process where one computer is set up to behave exactly like a second kind of computer. Programs written for the second computer can then be run on the first.

END-OF-FILE mark A special symbol placed at the end of files of information.

EOF End-Of-File mark.

Error correction A system that detects and inherently provides correction for errors caused by transmission equipment or facilities.

Facsimile Transmission of pictures, maps, diagrams, and so on, by communications channels. The image is scanned at the transmitter, reconstructed at the receiving station, and duplicated on some form of paper.

Fetch To obtain data or an instruction from a computer's memory.

Field A specified area of a record used for a particular category of data.

File A collection of information that is organized for some purpose.

File management The development and use of specific rules, procedures, and methods for creating the file, updating it, and retrieving information from it.

Fixed point calculation Calculation assuming a fixed or constant location of decimal or binary points in a number.

Flag A character that signals the occurrence of some condition, such as the end of a file.

Flip-flop A circuit or device containing active elements, capable of assuming either one of two stable states at a given time.

Floating point calculation Calculation in which the computer automatically handles the positioning of the decimal point in arithmetic operations.

Graphics Facilities to provide computer output in the form of displays, drawings, and pictures.

Hard copy A recording of computer output in a permanent, human-readable form.

Hardware The mechanical, magnetic, electrical, and electronic devices or components of a computer.

Head A device that reads, writes, or erases information on a storage device.

Header The first part of a message containing all the necessary information for directing the message to its destination(s).

Heuristic program An algorithm that makes decisions on the basis of intuitively plausible, but not guaranteed, criteria which are designed to evaluate the progress made toward the successful completion of a task.

Hexadecimal A number system with base or radix of 16. The digits are 0, 1, 2, 3, 4, 5, 6, 7, 8, 9, A, B, C, D, E, F .

Index register A temporary storage device, usually in the control unit, which is used primarily for modification of the direct address portion of an instruction. Index registers are also used for counting and looping.

Indirect addressing Instructions that contain the address of a memory location which, in turn, contains the address of an item to be processed by the instruction.

Information retrieval The process of recovering specific information from stored data.

Integrated circuits A manufacturing process where electronic circuits are produced as a whole rather than assembled from individual components; for example, wires, resistors, transistors, and so on.

Interface A common boundary between two or more items of equipment.

Interpreter (1) A program that translates and executes each *source language* expression before translating and executing the next one. (2) A device that prints on a punched card the data already punched in the card.

Interrupt To stop a process in such a way that it can be resumed.

I/O Input-Output.

Keyboard entry A device used to record data on some storage medium by depressing keys on a keyboard.

Keywords (1) The most informative words in a title or document. (2) Words in a programming language statement which indicate the type of the statement.

Line printer An electromechanical device that consecutively prints an entire line of output at one time.

Linkage The codes and statements that connect two independent programs or subprograms.

Load To fill the internal storage of a computer with data or programs from auxiliary or external storage.

LSI Large scale integration of electronic circuits.

Macro An instruction in a source language that is equivalent to a specified set of statements either in the same source language or in an object language.

Main memory The primary storage device directly under central processor control.

Map A table that gives the association between program elements and words in memory.

MICR Magnetic Ink Character Recognition.

Microfilm Photographic film with extremely reduced images; may be used for computer output or for large capacity auxiliary memory.

Microprogramming A facility to modify the basic machine instructions for a computer.

Microsecond One millionth of a second.

MIS Management Information Systems.

Mnemonic A word or name which is easy to remember and identify.

Multiplexor A device that simultaneously transmits and receives from several other devices.

Multiprocessing The simultaneous or interleaved execution of two or more programs by a computer system utilizing two or more central processing units.

Multiprogramming The execution of two or more programs simultaneously by one central processing unit, through the overlapping or interleaving of their execution.

Nanosecond One billionth of a second.

Noise Loosely, any disturbance tending to interfere with the normal operation of a device or system, including those attributable to equipment components, manual interference, or natural disturbance.

Nondestructive read A read process that does not erase the data in the source.

Normalize To adjust the representation of a quantity so that the representation lies in a prescribed range.

Object language The language used to express the results of a language translation process.

OCR Optical Character Recognition.

Octal A number system with base or radix of 8.

Off-line processing Operations performed by auxiliary equipment on data prior to their entry into the central processing unit of the computer. Human intervention is usually required between data entry and ultimate processing. Compare with ON-LINE PROCESSING.

On-line processing The processing of data under the complete and absolute control of the central processor, eliminating the need for human intervention.

Open subprogram A subprogram that is to be relocated and inserted into a routine at each point it is used. Compare with CLOSED SUBPROGRAM.

Overflow The generation of a quantity beyond the capacity of a counter or register.

Overlay The technique of repeatedly using the same blocks of internal storage during different stages of a problem. When one program segment is no longer needed in storage, another program segment can replace all or part of it.

Parallel processing The simultaneous execution of two or more sequences of instructions by a computer having multiple arithmetic or logic units.

Peripheral equipment The auxiliary machines not under the direct control of the central computer, such as tape reader, card reader, or typewriter.

Postmortem dump A dump used for debugging purposes that is performed at the end of a machine run.

Problem-oriented language A programming language designed for the convenient expression of a given class of problems.

Procedure-oriented language A programming language designed for the convenient expression of procedures used in the solution of a wide class of problems.

Random access Pertaining to a memory device where the time for access to information is independent of location of the information or status of the device.

Record A collection of related items of data, treated as a unit. Contrast with FILE.

Recursion A set of operations or program statements where one of the operations or statements is specified in terms of the entire set.

Redundant information A message expressed in such a way that the essence of the information occurs in several ways.

Register A special computer unit whose purpose is to receive, hold, and transmit a specified amount of data as directed. See specific types of registers.

Relocate In programming, to move a routine from one portion of storage to another and to adjust the necessary address references so that the routine, in its new location, can be executed.

Report generation A technique for producing complete machine reports from information which describes the input file and the format and content of the output report.

Reproducer A device that will duplicate in a card all or part of the data contained in another card.

Response time The time interval between the initiation of a request of the information system and receipt of an answer.

RPG Report Program Generator language for business reports.

Scratch pad A small, exceptionally fast memory used by a central processor for holding temporary or intermediate results.

Semiconductor An electronic device that behaves like a vacuum tube but is much smaller, much cheaper, faster reacting, and consumes much less power.

Shift To move the admissible marks in a word one or more places to the left or right. In the case of a number, this is equivalent to multiplying or dividing by a power of the radix.

Simulate To represent the functioning of one system by another, for example, to represent one computer by another, to represent a physical system by the execution of a computer program, to represent a biological system by a mathematical model.

Software The programming systems, libraries, and other programming and nonhardware operating aids in a computer system.

Solid state The electronic components that convey or control electrons within solid materials; for example, transistors, germanium diodes, and magnetic cores. Thus, vacuum and gas tubes are not included.

Source language The language that is input to a language translation process.

Special character In a character set, a character that is neither a numeral, a letter, nor a blank; for example, virgule, asterisk, dollar sign, equals sign, comma, period.

Storage allocation The assignment of programs and blocks of data to specific blocks in a computer memory.

Supervisor The part of the operating system that has internal control over all subsystems of the computer system.

Syntax The vocabulary and grammatical rules required for the correct combination and formation of a computer language.

Tape drive A device that moves tape past a read/write head.

Target language Object language.

Teleprocessing A form of information handling in which a data processing system utilizes communication facilities.

TELPAK A service offered by common communication carriers for the leasing of broadband channels between two or more points.

Terminal An input-output device designed to receive or send source data, as part of a data transmission system.

Tracing A program debugging technique that involves printing out the value of a specified variable every time the value changes.

Track The portion of a moving magnetic storage medium, such as a drum, tape, or disk, that is accessible to a given read/write head position.

Transfer rate The speed at which data can be transmitted through a given type of channel.

Truth table A table that describes a logic function by listing all possible combinations of input values and indicating for each such combination the true output values.

Twelve punch A punch in the top row of an IBM card.

Utility programs A set of programs that provides the very basic facilities of a computer system; for example, copying one tape onto another, copying information from memory onto punched cards.

Variable word length The number of characters used for an item of data is exactly equal to its length, whether short or long. Marks are used to indicate the end of a data item.

Word An arbitrary number of binary digits or bytes handled as a unit by the computer for the purposes of operation, transmission, and storage.

Working storage Memory locations used for intermediate results for a computation.

Index

A

Q

R

S